Primary Prevention of Psychopathology
George W. Albee and Justin M. Joffe, General Editors

I. The Issues: An Overview of Primary Prevention, 1977
George W. Albee and Justin M. Joffe, Editors

II. Environmental Influences and Strategies in Primary Prevention,
1978
Donald G. Forgays, Editor

III. Social Competence in Children, 1979
Martha Whalen Kent and Jon E. Rolf, Editors

IV. Competence and Coping during Adulthood, 1980
Lynne A. Bond and James C. Rosen, Editors

Competence and Coping during Adulthood

Competence and Coping during Adulthood

Lynne A. Bond and
James C. Rosen, editors

Published for the Vermont Conference on the
Primary Prevention of Psychopathology
by the University Press of New England,
Hanover, New Hampshire, and
London, England 1980

University Press of New England
Hanover, New Hampshire, and London, England

Brandeis University
Clark University
Dartmouth College
University of New Hampshire
University of Rhode Island
Tufts University
University of Vermont

Contents

Preface by Lynne A. Bond and James C. Rosen   vii

PART I
DEVELOPING MODELS FOR COPING AND
COMPETENCE   1

1. Individual Psychology: An Obstacle to
    Comprehending Adulthood   6
    SEYMOUR B. SARASON

2. The Stress and Coping Paradigm   28
    RICHARD S. LAZARUS

3. A Competency Model Must Replace the Defect
    Model   75
    GEORGE W. ALBEE

4. Promoting Competence and Enhancing Development
    through Life Development Intervention   105
    STEVEN J. DANISH and ANTHONY R. D'AUGELLI

5. A Model for Promoting Competence and Coping
    in Adolescents and Young Adults   130
    DAVID F. RICKS

PART II
LIFE SATISFACTION AND LIFE STRESS
DURING ADULTHOOD   151

6. Quality of Life   156
    JOHN C. FLANAGAN

7. Stresses and Strains in Adolescents and Young
    Adults   178
    GISELA KONOPKA

8. Promoting Positive Health Behaviors in Adults   195
    NATHAN MACCOBY

PART III
THE ROLE OF WORK IN COMPETENCE AND
LIFE SATISFACTION   219

9.   An Overview of Stress and Satisfaction: The
      Contract with Self   224
      HARRY LEVINSON

10.   On the Well-Being of Adult Women   240
      GRACE K. BARUCH and ROSALIND C. BARNETT

11.   Career Success and Life Satisfactions of
      Middle-Aged Managers   258
      DOUGLAS W. BRAY and ANN HOWARD

12.   Promoting Competence and Coping through
      Retirement Planning   288
      RUTH GLICK

PART IV
COPING, COMPETENCE, AND THE FAMILY   305

13.   The Empty Nest: Beginning or Ending?   309
      LILLIAN B. RUBIN

14.   Healthy Family Coping: Transnational
      Perspectives   332
      HENRY P. DAVID

      Name Index   367

      Subject Index   377

Preface

The First Vermont Conference on the Primary Prevention of Psychopathology was held at the University of Vermont in June 1975. It proved to be the first of a continuing series of annual conferences dealing with primary prevention and supported by the Waters Foundation. To meet the growing interest in the area, it was decided to publish the proceedings of each conference and thus facilitate a more general dissemination of current thought on research, theory, and applications in the field of primary prevention.

The First Vermont Conference provided an overview of perspectives and approaches to the subject, while subsequent conferences focused on more specific issues in the field. Thus the Second Vermont Conference, held in June 1976, focused on environmental factors contributing to the development of psychopathology and environmental manipulations that may effectively prevent psychopathology. In his keynote address to the second conference, Emory Cowen suggested that the literature and research on primary prevention falls into two basic categories: (a) analysis and modification of impactful social systems, and (b) promoting competence. Inspired by this conceptualization, the conference planning committee organized the Third Vermont Conference in June 1977 on promoting social competence and coping in children.

The success of the third conference and the growing awareness of the fact that human development does not halt at age twenty-one led to the selection of the topic of competence and coping in adulthood for the fourth Vermont Conference. Increasing numbers of psychologists, sociologists, and mental health workers are recognizing that our conceptualization of the early "formative years" has restricted our examination and hence our understanding of factors influencing development through adulthood. The Fourth Vermont Conference on the Primary Prevention of Psychopathology was therefore devoted to consideration of competence and coping during adulthood.

The speakers included theoreticians, researchers, and practitioners—innovative, creative individuals who are grappling with issues in the area. Their work provides a representative but not exhaustive indication of the major sources of support and stress through adulthood.

As with each of the previous conferences, the Fourth Vermont Conference was organized by a small group of people in the Psychology Department of the University of Vermont with the support and collaboration of James and Faith Waters and the Waters Foundation. The planning activities of the fourth conference were facilitated by the administrative help of Barbara York, conference coordinator. The tremendous success of the fourth conference was a result of the contributions of all these individuals in addition to our speakers and conference participants who helped to create the occasion for a stimulating exchange of ideas.

Burlington, Vermont   *Lynne A. Bond*
January 1980   *James C. Rosen*

I
Developing Models for Coping and Competence

Before serious efforts can be made to enhance coping and competence in adulthood, there must be advances in the models of adult coping and competence upon which interventions are based. In accord with the familiar dual focus of primary prevention, the chapters in Part I point to the interaction between individual characteristics and impactful social environments as setting the stage for adult development. Although different weight may be given to each variable, the role of both in positive adult development, not just in psychopathology, must be evaluated. The authors differ in the changes they recommend in research strategies and helping systems.

Seymour B. Sarason is a professor in the Department of Psychology and a member of the Institute for Social and Policy Studies at Yale University. In his keynote address Sarason called for a redirection in the way psychologists view adulthood. Psychology, he contends, has been preoccupied with the individual. Because it ignores impactful social contexts in which adulthood evolves, individual psychology cannot fully explain adulthood. In this regard, Sarason maintains that new methods of coping and new competencies develop during adulthood as people become aware of the effects of social structures. Individual psychology, with its overemphasis on "know thyself," may be misleading because it reinforces the belief that people are independent of their social web.

Richard Lazarus is a professor of psychology at the University of California, Berkeley. In his chapter he draws upon his productive and imaginative research on stress and coping to expose the pitfalls of traditional approaches to these concepts, and he develops a paradigm that offers the concepts new vigor. He points to the need to replace the static, unidimensional concept of stress with an interactional model and to consider that stress may have benign or positive effects as well as deleterious ones. With regard to coping, Lazarus reminds us that there is little descriptive knowledge of which patterns of coping work for which people under which circumstances. Before efforts to change coping strategies can succeed, more naturalistic research will be necessary. Meanwhile, before attempting interventions, a better understanding is needed of which pathologies are diminished and which are aggravated by changing coping responses.

George W. Albee is a professor of psychology at the University of Vermont. He has been involved in the politics of intervention and prevention in mental health for many years, his most recent role being coordinator of the Task Group on Prevention for the President's Commission on Mental Health. Albee is critical of psychology and related professions for perpetuating an illness or defect model of mental disturbance. Why has the defect model persisted so long? Albee argues that the reasons are to be found in professional advantage, profit, professional status, and ethnocentrism, not in scientific fact. A competence model, as he envisages it, depends upon an egalitarian political and moral philosophy, the prime mover for competent social roles. Mental health professionals can help to enhance adult competence by redirecting their attention to environmental causes of psychopathology and by refraining from "blaming the victim."

Steven J. Danish is professor in charge of Continuing Education/Community Services at the Pennsylvania State University. Anthony R. D'Augelli is associate professor of Human Development at the Pennsylvania State University. Danish and D'Augelli, who have both practiced and taught in the areas of helping skills, the counseling process, and human relations training, and written extensively about them, discuss the basis of their pessimism about the potential effectiveness of primary prevention in today's helping system. They suggest that the prevention movement has overemphasized the absence of pathology as its goal, giving little consideration to the dimensions of health. Their own human developmental model of competence contends that "stressful" life events can be junctures for enhancing adulthood. Where are people learning to enhance their lives? Not from professionals. Rather, the self-help movement today is spurred by natural caregivers in communities and by the dispensing of life skills through the mass media. Danish and D'Augelli advocate a pyramid model of human service delivery that capitalizes on people helping people in their own communities.

David F. Ricks is professor of psychology and head of the Department at the University of Cincinnati. His writing in the area of psychopathology includes two co-edited volumes of proceedings of the Society for Life History Research in Psychopathology. In his chapter in Part I, Ricks develops a model to demonstrate how competence or incompetence results from the period of rapid change known as adolescence. He notes that most observers are not surprised by the so-called identity crisis of adolescence as adolescents are jolted from physical immaturity and psychological dependence at the same time that their parents enter a midlife transition. Many adolescents are disillusioned with the gap between their current competencies and their dreams. Ricks concludes that disturbance in adolescence results from stages of separation, namely protest, despair, and apathy; he consequently calls for a broader view of interventions for adolescents. His ideas should stimulate new thinking about competence-building efforts based on his thoughtful appraisal of current adolescent realities.

1

Individual Psychology: An Obstacle to Comprehending Adulthood

SEYMOUR B. SARASON

One of the most obvious features of our society is that it is not organized for the individual. Over our span of life, each of us encounters obstacles, choice points, and phenomenologically new problems that are stressful and potentially destructive to our hopes. This may be true of any society, past and present, but a case can be made that today the points of conflict between the individual and society are more frequent. Conflict is not really the appropriate word, although it well describes many of the interactions between the individual and organized society. Another concept that would have to be employed is discontinuity: the requirement that the individual enter a new situation, learn new things, depart from an accustomed psychological and/or geographical position. The requirement may be perceived as internal or external but in either case the individual frequently (though not always) experiences a tension or disjunction implying a temporary or sustained break with the person's accustomed pattern of living. The requirement, whether external or internal, may on the surface appear initially to be—and may really be—conflict free. That is to say, it may not be perceived as a requirement at all. For example, if you ask young school children why they go to school, most of them will not say: "I *have* to go to school." "I am *required* to go." Indeed, one of the purposes of socializing young children is to get them to experience going to school as an internal, not an external requirement. It is not until the middle and high school years that you will find students saying that they are required to go to school. By the time they are adolescents and young adults, most of them know that there are two major types of requirements: the explicit and the implicit, and the implicit have more booby traps. The sense of wariness among young adults that I described in a recent book (Sarason, 1977) is in large measure a reaction to the perception that the abstraction called society would like them to meet a long series of requirements about which they have many doubts. The future may make them feel discontinuous with the present, and that may not be desirable. The sense of discontinuity may be in relation to the past or to an imagined future; it may be positively or negatively toned.

Let me use a personal example about a minor discontinuity: me at this conference. George Albee invites me. George cannot require me to attend, but I like and respect him, I have been very impressed with the published proceedings of the previous conferences, and, of course, I am flattered by the invitation. I happen to believe in collegiality and its implication that one has obligations to colleagues to share with them what one thinks one knows—to be helpful if possible. The obligations of collegiality involve but go beyond those of courtesy. So, phenomenologically, I had a choice, but the fact is that I felt I should want to say yes at the same time I also wanted to say no. I wanted to say no because George was calling me months before the conference and how did I know what life would be like at the end of June 1978? By age 59 I had learned that making a commitment to the future on the assumption that life is stable, predictable, and controllable is the ultimate in naiveté. For seven years before George called, my wife and I had been taking care of four dying parents. The requirements to do so were both internal and external and, of course, they conflicted with discharging many other types of internal and external requirements. These requirements determined and colored our existence, and if you like understatements, you can say it was rough. No one likes to feel that planning a life is subject to gross error, because one underestimates or ignores possible future requirements and discontinuities. All of us want to feel that we can control our lives, and we invest a lot of energy nurturing the myth of personal freedom, in the process overlooking how in the present we are hemmed in by requirements, and therefore tending to see the future in similarly unrealistic terms. So, while I was talking to George, I was vaguely aware that if I said yes I would be going against a very strong feeling that I wanted to be free of all requirements, internal or external. "Don't tell me what I can do for you, tell me what you can do for me"—that is one way to describe my view of my world. Two considerations tipped the scales in favor of saying yes. Coming to Burlington would be a break, a way of getting away, however briefly, from an accustomed locale in which I felt bombarded by requirements. Also, my wife might be able to come along, and she needed a break no less than I did. It would be a minivacation, which can be defined as a sought-for, desirable discontinuity. We justify vacations on numerous grounds but surely the need "to get away," "to feel free" from pressures, "to enjoy ourselves" are the most common. When a person says "I want to enjoy myself," that person is saying "I want only to take myself into account, I want to feel that I am doing something for and only for myself, I do not want to have to take the needs of others into account, I want the experience to be the opposite of what I ordinarily experience." I am no scholar of history but it is my impression that the concept of a vacation as a form of personal indulgence and freedom from a web of requirements is relatively new in human history. The advertisers tell us what we want to hear: our daily lives have a prison-like quality and in order to take this daily routine and survive, you need to get away from it. There are places you can go to on Eastern's wings of man through United's friendly skies where you can let American do what it does best: take care of every one of *your* needs.

So I go home and tell Esther about lovely Burlington when June is busting out all over. She tells me what I already knew: she has clinical responsibilities until the very end of June and it may not be possible for her to go. My response is that she should stop being so damned conscientious and start giving priorities to *her* needs, the kind of response that brings smiles to the faces of travel agents and advertisers. It is a short conversation because June is months away and we do not have to make decisions now. Then in February I find myself in the hospital for emergency surgery. That was not a sought-for discontinuity! But it was like a lot of other undesirable discontinuities in that it reminded me that I am not the captain of my fate and the master of my soul except within narrower limits than I like to think. However, there was one unintended consequence of the hospitalization and convalescence: nobody required anything of me and everybody was marvelously indulgent of all my presumed needs. Then

May rolls around on its way to June. How about it, Esther, are you going to go? I shall not bore you with the protracted negotiations between the two of us. I wish only to state the obvious: each was putting requirements on the other in the course of which each of our views about a desirable discontinuity inevitably changed. Esther and I approach going on any trip in very different ways so that what initially appears to be a conflict-free experience always contains elements of conflict. We adjust to each other as much because we feel we have to as because we want to. Neither of us is a free agent. In the meantime I am writing a paper for the conference, furious that I said yes, doubtful that I had anything interesting to say, and feeling quite unfree. Why do I conspire with my world to feel closed in?

If you are a psychologically minded person—and who is not in this age of psychology—my personal account has raised questions in your mind about me as a person. What makes him tick? Why the seemingly dysphoric overtones to what he has recounted? What is his wife like? Why is he so interested in requirements? Are his advancing years getting the better of him? Does he look back with regrets at what he did and did not do? Is he in therapy or should he go into therapy? My purpose in telling you what I did was far more modest and simple than these complicated questions would suggest. I suggest that at different times over the course of our lives we are confronted with requirements and discontinuities, many of which are predictable but for most of which we are unprepared. And by "unprepared" I mean that we simply do not think about them, or if we do think about them, it is with a large dose of wish fulfillment, or it is inevitable that actually experiencing these requirements and discontinuities will be different in very important ways from what we imagined. Let me be concrete by telling you some of our interview findings with college seniors making a career choice, with first and fourth year medical students, first and third year law students, and professionals of varying ages over the life span (Sarason, 1977). In our interview we had a question for seniors who were going into medicine, law, or some graduate school program, and they represented a clear majority of the seniors. The question was: "Have you ever considered a career in business, finance, or industry?" Their answer was universally an emphatic no, and they gave one or all of three reasons: you would be a small cog in a big wheel, it takes a long time to get to the top, and the chances are good that you will become morally corrupt in the process. In other words, if you go into medicine and law, you can retain and even develop your individuality and stay true to your idealism. Put in another way, business, finance, and industry are organized on a scale and in ways that require people to give up something in themselves, to accommodate to external requirements, to become unfree. Is it not astounding that these college seniors have divided the world into two parts, one good, the other evil? How does it happen that they know so little about the part of the world they plan to enter: its increasing scale, its structure and organization, its culture, its requirements, its similarities to the "evil" half of the world? How will they experience the discontinuities they seek? Of course, when we interviewed students actually in medical, law, and graduate schools, the picture changed. Without exception they knew that they were going to be in or around large, bureaucratically organized institutions, small cogs in big wheels, scrambling competitively to get a place in the sun, and sensitive to the obstacles to remaining true to their ideals. With some exceptions they look back nostalgically to their good old days and look forward with wariness to the future. Some say explicitly that they are disillusioned; others say they are now more realistic about the world they are in or will be. No one is unscathed. I do not want to convey the impression that they have become depressives shorn of hope and ambition and dripping with cynicism. What I do wish to convey is that they have been through a series of discontinuous experiences that have left them with a sense of incompleteness and frustration, and with the knowledge that their lives in large measure are and will be determined by forces beyond their control. Most of them by conventional standards have coped well and are competent. By their internal, private standards they have eaten the fruits of worldly knowledge and they are uncertain about how to judge the taste. Turow's (1977) description of life as a first-year law student at Harvard confirms and deepens the thrust of the conclusions we came to from our interviews—namely that medical, law, and graduate students would not justify avoiding a career in business, finance, and industry the way they did as seniors.

Let me tell you also about two other groups we have interviewed but have not written up. One is a handful of seniors headed for a career in the arts or the theater. How remarkably clear they are about the obstacles they will confront, and their small chance for success! They are no less idealistic than others, they are no less hopeful that Lady Luck has a special place in her heart for them, but they also know how the "industry" they seek to enter is organized, the disappointments they must be prepared to expect, and how their capacity for self-denial will be tested. They want to be successful, but they know they may not be, and they will go on from there. Because we have not interviewed people like them at different stages of their careers, we cannot say how they tend to react to obstacles and externally imposed requirements. We can assume, however, that by conventional standards a fair number of people who go into these fields will be failures or marginally successful—they will not make it. But again, by internal standards, the conventional criteria for judging coping and competence may be misleading.

The second group we interviewed consisted of 25 seniors who had majored in the administrative sciences. They *were* headed for careers in business, finance, and industry. Like the small group of arts and theater majors, and unlike the premed, prelaw, and pregraduate school seniors, they seemed to have an appreciation of the characteristics of the organizations in which they planned to work. Here again these students had their ambitions and ideals and knew that their working days would not be without conflicts, frustrations, and moral-testing experiences. But they felt that there would be challenges, and opportunities for creativity. They, too, were wary, but they felt they knew what they were getting into.

There are two other groups I have known well over the years: teachers in training, and experienced teachers seeking credentials to become administrators. I have discussed the training and education of these groups in detail elsewhere (Sarason, 1971); let it suffice for present purposes to say that when they begin the careers, they are remarkably unknowledgeable about the culture, organization, and traditions of a school and a school system. Years ago some colleagues and I (Sarason, Davidson, and Blatt, 1962) wrote a book entitled *The Preparation of Teachers: An Unstudied Problem in Education*. The theme of the book was that the preparation of teachers ill prepared them to understand a classroom, let alone the cultural-structural dynamics of a school and school system. The book went into oblivion rather quickly and our only solace is that what later happened in the sixties confirmed what we had said. That nobody took us seriously should not have surprised us. After all, we were suggesting that the conventional criteria by which coping and competence were being judged were inadequate, and no one knew this better than teachers and school administrators—who, of course, were not about to make the truth public.

Now let me state some similarities between what I have described about these groups (with the exception of the administrative science and theater majors) and what I said about me and the conference.

I was not well prepared for the discontinuities I experienced in connection with taking care of old parents. My world was structured around family and work, and that structure had a future thrust to it, and a content, to which I looked forward. I was aware, of course, that our parents lived elsewhere, they were obviously aging, and that we would have to be prepared for their increasing dependence on us. But that knowledge was hazy, containing a large dose of wish fulfillment. We would handle matters as they came up. What we did not know but could have known was that when old people become sick and dependent, they and you have to deal with a part of our society that has structure and traditions which, if you do not understand them and know how to cope with them, can make life difficult indeed. No less significant is the effect of coping (with doctors, hospitals, nursing homes, home care aides, medicare, social service agencies) on the structure and functioning of your family and work worlds. It is not that you become aware of how these worlds have become interrelated, but rather than you are no longer as free as you were and the future is now suffused with oppressiveness and anxiety. Planning a future becomes a kind of luxury as you find yourself caught in a web of requirements, wondering how long you can or should take it, torn between feelings of anger and compassion, hardly able to control rage against "them": against everybody who expects you to conform to their needs and rules. What I have just related about myself I have heard from several medical, law, and graduate students. They were extreme cases, but I can assure you that a lot of interviewees reported the feeling of being unprepared, of having had their eyes opened to the culture and structure of the setting they were in. Here again I must caution that you not conclude that these students were in a state of shock, unable to cope and to be competent. I am saying only that they have varying degrees of disillusionment and disappointment about how their working world is structured, so that they are less certain than before that they are in control of their lives. And they perceive a sharp break between their past and present lives. For the bulk of them there is a poignant moral dilemma. How can they survive in the structures they are embedded in and not sell out? How will they know when they are being brainwashed? Will they ever really be free to go their own way?

Another story. A Yale student, headed for graduate school in psychology, worked with me for a year, and when we parted for the summer, we agreed to meet in the fall about what schools he should consider. When we met in the fall, he told me his plans had changed and he wanted to go to medical school. He had found a job that summer in a large general hospital, and he was aghast at the impersonal treatment patients received, the small amount of time physicians gave to patients, the view of patients as objects rather than people, and the psychological insensitivity of medical personnel. Larry wanted to become a general practitioner who would really treat his patients the way they deserved and needed to be treated. He was a bright, creative, hard-working young man prepared to devote his life to others. I listened, my heart sank, and I did something I never did before. I tried to dissuade him. I described in detail what medical school was like, its structure, the formal and informal hierarchy of values by which students are judged, the financial indebtedness he would incur (he was not a rich boy) over a seven-year period of training, what this would mean for his love life (he had a girl friend), the costs of setting up and sustaining a practice, and how time will become money and what that means for how much time he could give a patient. I concluded by saying: "To be with patients the way you want to be, to charge them fees they can afford—to treat them without regard for the clock or the number of patients in the waiting room—mean that you will have to be satisfied to live on $30,000 or $40,000 a year. That sounds like a lot to you now, but after years of training and indebtedness, and after marriage and children, is that income likely to be satisfactory?" Larry was not disposed to listen. He applied to medical school and was accepted. I have never heard from him. I hope I was wrong in my forecast. Our interviews suggest that I stand a change of having been correct. Incidentally, lest you think that I am picking on physicians or medical schools, or the culture and structure of American medicine, I should tell you that I was prepared to discuss with Larry what graduate school in psychology would be like, and my speech would have been similar to the one I gave to him.

All that I have so far said leads to a conclusion that is crucial to how one thinks about coping and competence in adulthood. But before stating that conclusion, and as a way of looking at its significances, I will describe what I do in my seminars, all of which are concerned with structural-cultural features of our society. I present the students in the very first meeting with the following task:

There are two kinds of people here: Yale seniors and graduate students from different departments. You have all experienced several years of living in a university. Now this seminar is not about universities but about other kinds of institutions: public schools, mental hospitals, correctional facilities, institutions for the retarded, human services agencies, and the like. Our focus will be on how these institutions have changed over time and how we think they ought to change in the future. But if you want to change these institutions, you have to understand them. I can safely assume that you have little or no knowledge of or experience with these institutions. I can also assume that you feel that you are ignorant with respect to them, that there is nothing in your experience which would permit you to say that even though you may never have set foot in them, you know something about them. I suggest that you do know or could quickly learn some important things about these institutions based on your past experience with the university. To prove this, I want you to take the next half hour and answer these questions:

1. How many schools does Yale (or any other university) consist of? What are the administrative relationships among these schools?

2. Describe the procedures by which a university grants tenure to a faculty member. When does the procedure begin,

who participates when, what information is sought, when, and from whom, when is the decision final, and why are some people granted tenure while others are not?

3. How are departmental chairpersons chosen, what are their responsibilities and formal powers, and how do they relate to higher levels of administration?

4. You have had many dealings with individual faculty members, deans, and other staff. How would you characterize these dealings? Were they helpful, instructive? If not, how do you explain it? Do you feel the university exists for you, the alumni, the faculty?

The exercise serves two major purposes. First, it impresses on the students the fact, surprising to them, that although they have been living in the university for several years, they are amazingly ignorant of its structure, functions, and practices. In their interactions with different people and parts of the university, they form impressions and opinions about the university, but they are unable to place those interactions other than in an individual framework. Their explanations of how they have been influenced by their university experiences are psychological, and they are almost wholly unable to place themselves at some distance and see the hows and whys of organizational structure, dynamics, and functions. And when I say "wholly unable," I mean that in the normal course of living they feel no particular need to describe and understand the characteristics of the large organizational picture in which they are embedded. They are, for example, interested in how Yale selects students and the consequences of that selection process for their lives at Yale. But they are far less interested in how faculty are selected, even though they know how they are being affected by the faculty, whom they see as bewilderingly varied.

The second purpose of the exercise is for me to help them understand better the part of the university which impacts their lives in countless important ways even though they are ordinarily unaware of it. Just as the architecture of a house or building has psychological consequences for its inhabitants, so do the organizational traditions and structure of the university affect the lives of all of its inhabitants. The point I try to impress on the students is that you can *see* people, *you cannot see an organization and its structure*, but if you want to understand a setting, you cannot restrict yourself to seeing it literally. You must have a set of concepts that allow you to go beyond the concrete, the palpable, the percept. So, I ask them, how many of you see the faculty as consisting of individuals each of whom seems to be absorbed in what he or she considers important? How many of you have noticed how rare it is for faculty members to work with one another? The answer to the first question is an emphatic yes; to the second question the answer is that it is rare. How should we go about trying to understand what we see? We discuss many things, among which is a factor I stumbled on one day after 25 years at Yale. That I stumbled on it then is important because it came at a time 10 years ago when I was trying to understand why I experienced my adulthood in the ways I did. My explanations had been primarily, but not exclusively, psychological: I was a certain kind of person, and "they" were different kinds of people; I had certain needs, assets, and vulnerabilities that tended to clash with those of "them." Needless to say, I was responding to them and me as individuals, and whatever clashes had occurred, to put it neutrally, were due to individual differences. Then the clouds parted and some light came through in the form of two questions: Who tries to make it in the university? Whom does the university select? The answer to both questions is rugged individualism. You have a selection process that gives you assertive, ambitious, prima donna types. Why should you wonder that they go their own way and frequently clash? You need more than psychology to understand faculty behavior.

I am of the opinion that adulthood cannot be productively understood in terms of psychology, at least the psychologies that are currently dominant. Paradoxically, they suffer from the defect of their virtue: the attempt to rivet on the development of internal structure and organization. Freud, Piaget, the Gestaltists, and their descendants, focused on the individual psyche, what Murray Levine calls the emphasis on "intrapsychic supremacy." In no way do I wish to derogate their contributions and influences. But it needs to be recognized that their pioneering efforts to conceptualize internal content, structure, and organization were at the expense of doing justice to the fact that we are born into and live out our lives in a variety of contexts possessing structure and organization no less fateful than those of our psyches. (Freud understood this in small measure in terms of family structure and organization.)

When I try to make sense of my adult years, and when I reflect on the many interviews we conducted with people at different points in adulthood, I come to the conclusion that adulthood is that long period of our lives in which we learn that every part of our individual worlds, every experience, reflects two kinds of impact: our impact on an existing external structure and organization, and the impact of that external structure and organization on us. I deliberately do not use the term environment because it is too global and too easily distracts us from the crucial characteristics of structure and organization. Whether we are in an airplane, a classroom, or a faculty meeting, at the dinner table or a conference, or in a new work setting, our experience is not understandable without seeing it in relation to the structure, organization, and traditions of the setting. That may seem obvious to you but my experience and research suggests that we have an amazing capacity to ignore the obvious. We are psychologically minded not structure-organizationally minded.

Adulthood has become increasingly problematic for many people as they find that in all spheres of living they are part of organized, complex structures they can neither understand nor change. It would be more correct to say that their understanding is so personal, so psychological, that they are cut off from ways of thinking and acting that might be more effective. No less important, they cannot entertain the possibility that what they have experienced is generalizable to many other structured settings. So the students in my seminars have difficulty with the idea that if they understood the structure and organization of Yale, and how it has directly and indirectly shaped their lives, they would know a lot about life in seemingly very different settings. This is not to say, of course, that Yale is the same as these other institutions but rather that all of them—by virtue of being complex, structured, hierarchically organized, historical settings in a society like ours—will present similar problems to those who live in these settings. The similarities have little or nothing to do with personalities but far more with the history and traditions of the society in which these settings evolved.

When I compare college freshmen with college seniors; college seniors with first-year law, medical, and graduate students; these first-year students with those finishing professional and graduate schools; and all of these groups with people who have been full-fledged professionals for varying periods of time, I am forced to the conclusion that adulthood is a continuous process during which blinders become removed from the eyes of individuals as they are forced to recognize that far from being free individuals, they are always part of and restricted by a social matrix. They do become more structure-organization minded, but, more often than not, it is with reluctance or bitterness or resignation. Some of them reach the understanding that what they have learned about how our society is structured and organized was new to them but that it has been true of our society for a long time. Many people take it far more personally, as if it were all arranged to defeat them.

Prior to World War II our country was self-consciously and deliberately isolationist. We wanted to involve ourselves as little as possible in the entanglements overseas. We viewed ourselves as self-sufficient as a country could be: protected by two oceans and possessed of boundless resources. We recognized that there were other societies, but their problems were *their* problems and we should not allow ourselves to be affected by what they did. Now we know how shortsighted, self-defeating, and ignorant we were of the forces loose on this earth. We had to be hit over the head to make us recognize that we were part of this world, like it or not. Mostly, we have not liked it, because we are so new at understanding and dealing with how the world is organized, puzzled by our increasing dependence on others, angry at finding ourselves in a web we did not weave, regretful that we were not better prepared for our adulthood as a nation. Analogously, that is the way many people today look on their individual adulthoods. And that is why so many of them seek new life styles or new places in an attempt to escape from their social web. Some of them fail because they still need to believe that they can be independent of social webs—i.e., that one can weave one's own web independent of the webs of all other people. Some succeed in the sense that they do not deny the facts of social living in our society but use their new understanding to strike a better compromise between internal needs and external structures. This new understanding, I have to emphasize, is only in part psychological in the narrow sense. This new understanding is in large part based on new knowledge about external structures.

World War II ushered in the Age of Psychology, some would say the Age of Mental Health. As individuals we were interested in ourselves, and so were myriad professionals eager to tell us how to understand ourselves. I should not use the past tense because this new age is still with us, flourishing and spawning a thriving industry. It is an industry that is providing people with what they feel they need. But it is also an industry that unwittingly colludes with its consumers in believing that the locus of trouble in people is within them. There is, of course, passing recognition that the troubles are somehow related to our social context that confine and frustrate us and seem to become interrelated over time. The problem, as someone once put it, is: how do you stay sane in an insane world? The question implies that there is little point in trying to understand the world, and if you make the effort, you will end up more convinced than ever that the less you have to do with the world, the better. But the world is not insane, and we must be careful to avoid the error of using a psychology of the individual to understand how and why our worlds are structured as they are. Society is not a random collection of entities and forces. It did not take the shape it did for the hell of it. We may not like that shape, but surely we cannot be content with aesthetic judgments, because if we are, we can never glimpse how and why that shape evolved and is still evolving.

Permit me to make one more effort to illustrate the unfortunate consequences of looking at persons, any person, with our customary focus on individuals. As you will see, these consequences are no less unfortunate when we look at an *organization* or setting as we do individuals. Take the film *One Flew over the Cuckoo's Nest* (Douglas and Saul, 1975), whose locale is a mental hospital. We are not concerned here with the artistic quality of the film, but rather with the major themes it conveys. The first is that there is an *interpersonal* struggle between two very dominant and assertive people. A second theme is that the struggle is not only between two people of unequal status and power but that the *personality* of each is lethal to the other. A third theme is that the patient-hero is fated to lose in his battle against *officialdom of the hospital*. There are other more muted or less articulated themes (e.g., the ward patients are "sick" people who need and even want hospitalization; doubt is raised about the therapeutic value of the hospital, but if these patients were to leave, as they do en masse at one point, they would prove they were indeed sick people from whom the community needed protection just as the patients need protection against themselves). It is hard to avoid coming away from the film without feeling that if either of the two protagonists had been different, tragedy would have been avoided. In short, it is a drama of individuals.

We did an informal study. Whenever we met social scientists, we asked them how they reacted to the film. Almost without exception they said they like the picture—i.e., it was a moving and involving, although upsetting, experience. Why was it upsetting? By far the most frequent answer was in terms of people's inhumanity to other people, witting or unwitting. As one put it: "If that nurse had not been stupid, insensitive, and rigid, there would be no point to the film." Or as another said: "It is frightening to see how power can be abused." The next most frequent answer was an expression of puzzlement: granted that the nurse was a hateful creature, how do you deal with such an assortment of crazy people? One person said: "I suppose a hospital like that brings out the worst in everybody." Not one of these social scientists showed the slightest recognition that this mental hospital was part of a state system of mental health services having a central office staffed with professionals who have policy-making and policy-implementing functions, the scope of which is in part a reflection of policies and arrangements arrived at through the political process involving the executive and legislative branches of government; and that all of the foregoing is tied in with and affected by federal policies and grant support, and in the formation of these federal policies mental health professionals play an important but not an exclusive role. But what is the relevance of this to their reactions to the film? There are two ways of answering—one general and one specific. The general answer is that the study of public policy rests on, among other things, the assumption that any particular policy (e.g., on energy) will have consequences for more than one system or sector in society (e.g., public utilities, automobiles), and that the policy always reflects political and economic factors. Put in another way: when an energy policy (federal and state) was developed, it altered the thinking and planning of countless individual agencies, and organizations. Or, when the federal or state governments change their welfare policy, there are consequences not only for the welfare "system" but for many other systems. Indeed, perhaps the most troublesome task in policy reconstruction, analysis, and formulation is to understand effects on interacting systems. But for our purposes one can disregard interacting systems and still make the important if obvious point that a public policy in regard to one system affects all parts of that system, and no one part can be understood in terms only of itself. The mental hospital in the film was part of a system, and one cannot understand that hospital unless one sees it in terms of its embeddedness in that system. The specific part of the answer concerns the last part of the film, when we see McMurphy, the patient-hero, electroshocked into submission and senselessness. All to whom we spoke found themselves shuddering at these scenes. Some thought it brutal, period. Some thought it brutal but were bothered by the question: What do you do with a McMurphy? Some people equated the brutality with conscious sadism, but most people viewed it more as institutionalized stupidity and insensitivity in the service of institutional law and order. *However, if the general answer above has validity, then this part of the film cannot be understood in terms of that hospital alone, and its personnel.* For example, most of the film takes place in a ward, but for all practical purposes a psychiatrist is never there. That, of course, is not happenstance. It is the case in almost every mental hospital. It is beyond my scope to pursue this matter except to say that it cannot be understood apart from the resources available to the state and federal hospital system and the consequences for hospital organization and functioning—e.g., what kinds of people will be hired, to whom responsibility will be given, the kinds of treatment to be employed, the development and maintenance of community placements, criteria for admission and discharge. The state hospital, far from being autonomous, must function in conformity with a system. No one knows this better than hospital employees, professional or otherwise. Just as urban teachers see their problems in large part in terms of "downtown," hospital staff similarly look to "the central office" in the capital, who in turn look to the state executive and legislative branches, who in turn look to "Washington" as insensitive, penurious, and capricious. If you think of the hospital as a person, you can say that just as, in the film, McMurphy was electroshocked into conformity, the hospital feels that in countless ways it is forced to conform to the "system."

To try to understand what a mental hospital is by studying *it* is conceptually nonsensical; it is the kind of nonsense that has the unintended effect of making sure that immorality will flourish.

To comprehend adulthood in our times and in the foreseeable future, we have to look at two factors. The first is that we have become a psychologically minded society. Self-actualization, self-realization, human potential, and self-expression have become household phrases. The psychotherapies in their myriad forms are available to almost everyone. "Know thyself" has, twenty-five hundred years after Socrates, been incorporated in public policy and insurance policies. And in the controversies that have swirled around the field of public education, the only point of agreement is that all children should realize their full potential—i.e., be made aware of and helped to develop their capacities. All of this has become so familiar, so much a part of our way of thinking, that to question any of it on any basis is to run the risk of being considered stupid, obtuse, and obviously in need of deeper, self-knowledge. From a theoretical and technical standpoint, the major questions have become: how can we help everyone get to know themselves better? What is the best and quickest way to do that: by therapies that deal with one's past, or by those which focus on the here and now? And which of several scores of professions should be empowered to help us, teach us, to know ourselves better? But although each of these therapies deals with individuals who have problems, each of them is based on an implicit or explicit conception of how you can prevent problems, and, very briefly but not surprising, that conception centers on individual characteristics and patterns of abilities.

This emphasis on a psychology of the individual, long a characteristic of American psychology but never so clear as in the post World War II period, is matched in its pervasiveness by a feature of western society that for all practical purposes this individual psychology has ignored. I refer to the fact that the organizations in which we live our lives are bigger, more bureaucratic, more interconnected among themselves, less autonomous, more subject to centralized government control, and more vulnerable to international economic dynamics than ever before. I am not making or implying a political judgment. I am saying something all of you sense: when you turn your attention away from yourself and have to look at and deal with the structure of and interconnections among organizations, it is as if you are dealing with wheels within wheels—i.e., everything seems to have become related to everything else. When I say "related," I do not mean that the relationships are understandable in terms of cause and effect or that their functional relationships are the result of rational planning. On the contrary, the reverse is true. All we are confident of is that even while we feel that everything is related to everything else, we also feel that disorganization is increasing. Even while we say that individuals suffer from loneliness, anomie, isolation, and unconnectedness, the external world—the world of societal organizations and structures—is on the road to greater connectedness and interpenetration.

It is beyond the scope of this paper to attempt to explain these two factors that are so characteristic of our times. It is central to my purpose, however, to emphasize that adulthood has become psychologically problematic, in large measure because so many people come to, and live through, adulthood without knowing *how* to understand the nature and thrust of the world of social organization. The two factors have been on a collision course. When young adults go out into the real world, they are not aware that they have already been living in the real world. From the time they enter school as young children to the time they leave college or postgraduate schools as adults, they have been living in complex organizations, but they learn little or nothing about these organizations *qua* organizations. They are taught a lot of things, but not about how their parochial context of learning bears the stamp of larger, interconnected organizational structures. So when they finish schooling and are catapulted into the larger society, many of them are jolted by the experience because they simply do not have schemas by which to accommodate to and assimilate what they are experiencing. Of course they do accommodate and assimilate, but if you are partisan to a Piagetian way of viewing things, you would never conclude that they understand the structure of the social world.

The reverence for Piaget is explainable on three grounds. First, he brilliantly clarified the development of logical thinking in relation to the perceptible world. Second, his contributions fit smoothly into an individual psychology. And third, they were, so to speak, tailor-made for an age that believed in science as the means by which all major societal problems would ultimately be solved. As Piaget's star was reaching its zenith, hundreds of people began to explore ways in which his findings and ideas could be incorporated into education, with the goal, of course, of better preparing people for adulthood—i.e., if you want to prepare more competent people for adulthood, then Piaget had given us a good part of the answer. Not that the aim was to prepare everyone to become logicians or scientists; rather, it was to ensure that they would end up with the schemas by which they would be able more effectively to comprehend and cope with their world. Unfortunately, none of these people was asking what that world was. What aspect of the world were they talking about? The world as anthropologists may see it? As political scientists may see it? As sociologists may see it? As the head of a task force on governmental reorganization may see it?

Our knowledge of the atom would not have gone much beyond that of the Greeks if along the way people had not begun to make the assumption that the atom had structure. What is that structure and how can we get to know it—that was what people began to ask. And how is that structure related to or manifested in other types of structures in the imperceptible world? Can we control, manipulate, exploit these structures? Analogous questions are asked by people throughout their adulthood about their social world. But unlike the atomic scientist, adults ask questions about their social world less out of curiosity and more because they feel forced to in order to remain sane and to survive. Some stop asking questions, however early they may have reached the highest levels of logical thinking. Some—independently of their level of logical or scientific thinking—accommodate to perplexities about their social world by assimilating, childlike, theories that explain everything. Most people, I would guess— and especially because what they know about the larger society comes from television and movies—change their explanations to accord with fads and fashion. Elsewhere (Sarason, 1978) I have discussed the interesting case of the atomic scientists who, at the very moment they were at the apogee of public respect and acclaim because they had learned to control nuclear processes and successfully explode a bomb, experienced a massive disillusionment when their efforts to influence public policy in certain ways were rebuffed. Like so many young adults, these sophisticated scientists were babes in the woods of societal structures, institutions, and traditions. They were eating a new species of the fruit of knowledge, and the taste was not to their liking.

I trust that no one here believes that you can or should try to make the experience of adulthood as unproblematic as possible. Such a goal would reflect the most profound ignorance of what societies have been, are, and will be. It is a goal no less illusory than the belief that the phenomenology of living can be uninformed by the knowledge of our mortality. To the extent that we view and study adulthood in terms of our current psychologies, which are riveted on the individual, we will be wasting time and perhaps causing more harm than good, because we will be reinforcing the mistaken belief that you can know yourself without knowing your society, that you can know your changing self without knowing your changing society.

Just as a parent's relationship to a child begins before the child is born, an adult's conception of adulthood begins long before society's definition of adulthood has been met. And in those early preschool years, those messages children receive, we adults know, contain a lot of myth. (Yes, Virginia, there is a Santa Claus.) I have no strong objections to these myths, and I have no desire to make young children worldly philosophers. But I do object to the belief that as children acquire a formal and informal education, they will have developed an understanding of the real world that will permit them in adulthood to be competent in that world. From my standpoint, competence is more than successfully competing, or utilizing one's capacities effectively, or being able to change adaptively to new circumstances, or deepening one's knowledge of self. The missing ingredient is how well we persist with the effort to deepen our understanding of the fact that we are embedded in and are expressions of a near and distant social world. Without that missing ingredient we are perilously close to defining human and subhuman competence by the same criteria, with the exception, of course, of deepening one's knowledge of self. But that is my point: as soon as you include deepening one's knowledge of one's self, you imply that the validity of such knowledge can be determined independently: yet understanding of how what one does, thinks, and concludes always reflects embeddedness in a near and distant social world. If my personal life is any guide, and my work with people at different points in adulthood encourages me to think that I am not atypical, the missing ingredient forces itself into our thinking as we learn how naive we were about the structure, forces, and underpinnings of our near and distant social worlds. Why was that ingredient missing earlier in our lives? Or, if it was not missing, why was our understanding so wrong?

If we are different from subhumans, it is in our potential to comprehend ourselves in relation to the natural world and the social world. We have done well with respect to the natural world, although it could be argued that our ignorance about the social world permitted the advances of science to transform the social world in ways inimical to human existence or, at the very least, to make comprehending the social world extraordinarily difficult because it has made the interconnectedness of the social world so difficult to experience and comprehend. In any event, the social world will become more interconnected and complex, we will be increasingly affected by it, and, it may be, we will continue to conceptualize and deal with it in narrow psychological terms. If we continue to be enamored with the psychology of the individual, it will be a monument to trivialization. And if, when we talk about the prevention of the disabilities that can occur in adulthood, we restrict ourselves to their prevention in the individual, our efforts are doomed. I am not a Marxist—although I was when I entered adulthood, because I thought it explained to me how society was organized and where it was going, as well as a good deal about myself. Marx and especially the Marxists that have come after him were at best incomplete, wrong, and misguided in their thinking, and at worst witting and unwitting perpetrators of social catastrophe. But I must emphasize: Marx was dealing with a most important problem—the relationship between how people think and the structure and dynamics of the social world. And he was right when he said that the task is not only to understand this relationship but to change it. I am not making a political statement or calling for political action. At this point I would appreciate a little more understanding and less misplaced emphasis.

REFERENCES

Douglas, M., and Saul, Z. Producers of the film *One flew over the cuckoo's nest,* United Artists, 1975.

Sarason, S. *The culture of the school and the problem of change.* Boston: Allyn and Bacon, 1971.

Sarason, S. *Work, aging, and social change: Professionals and the one-life one-career imperative.* New York: Free Press, 1977.

Sarason, S. The nature of problem solving in social action. *American Psychologist,* 1978, *33*, 370–380.

Sarason, S., Davidson, K. S., and Blatt, B. *The preparation of teachers: An unstudied problem in education.* New York: John Wiley, 1962.

Turow, S. *One L.* New York: Putnam, 1977.

2

The Stress and Coping Paradigm

RICHARD S. LAZARUS

If I correctly understand Thomas Kuhn (1970), and others who have commented on his ideas, a scientific paradigm is a set of interrelated assumptions—a metatheory—about certain classes of phenomena, and it contains also a closely linked set of methods or procedures for observing and analyzing these phenomena. My own work since the 1950's on psychological stress and coping illustrates, I believe, the evolution of a paradigm, one that has fewer adherents than I would wish in my more grandiose moments. In this presentation I would like to explore some steps in the evolution of my present position about the dynamics of stress and coping, and while doing so to deal with the consequences of this position for psychiatric science or, as I would prefer to call it, for the scientific study of human functioning.

To speak of an evolution implies that one is asking different questions now than were asked in an earlier period. Not only have my research questions changed, but as each new concept was assimilated into a growing system, I became increasingly radicalized, and other even more profound changes in general outlook occurred. I felt forced to look at things differently, and to prefer a different type of research approach than is characteristic of the field. Let us start with the state of things around

This paper was first presented at a conference organized by Drs. Carl Eisdorfer, Arthur Kleinman, and Donna Cohen, Department of Psychiatry and Behavioral Sciences, University of Washington, Seattle, and was then entitled "The Critical Evaluation of Behavioral Paradigms for Psychiatric Science." The conference was held November 3–6, 1978, at Salishan Lodge, Gleneden Beach, Oregon and will be published as a proceedings by Spectrum. The writing of this paper was supported in part by a research grant from the National Cancer Institute (CA 19362).

1950, when my interest in psychological stress began to crystalize.

STRESS AND COPING, CIRCA 1950

When I first came on the scene, psychologists viewed stress mostly as a disrupter of skilled performance. In clinical psychology and psychiatry, anxiety was conceived of as the major drive source of pathological modes of adaptation. Stress (or anxiety) was thought to generate inherently pathological defensive operations, such as repression, denial, isolation, undoing, intellectualized detachment, projection, and so on, leading to a distortion of reality. Such defenses reduced drive tension (anxiety), and the reductions made them refractory to unlearning or deconditioning. In short, psychopathology was considered, in large measure, to result from intense and/or prolonged stress which, in especially vulnerable persons, was comprised of dysfunctional ways of living and adjusting. Moreover, the origins of such pathogenic stress were commonly considered to be mainly intrapsychic and conflict-laden (endogenous) rather than lying in the environment (exogenous) (see also Roskies and Lazarus, 1979).

The central research questions my associates and I (e.g., Lazarus, Deese, and Osler, 1952) then asked were: "Under what conditions of stress does deterioration of functioning occur?" and "Who are the people most vulnerable to such deterioration?" During the Korean War and World War II, in which under battle conditions men developed diverse emotional disorders and even failed to fire their weapons, such a question was of great practical importance. But even in ordinary life such effects were observed to be common. For example, severe anxiety and blocking of thought and speech commonly occur in school examinations and other kinds of evaluative circumstances. It was obviously important to discover the general rules about how stress impaired human functioning.

Soon, however, we discovered that three kinds of results occurred under stress: (1) no measurable effect, (2) impairment of performance, and (3) facilitation of performance. Try as we might, the key factors making for these differences in result remained highly elusive, despite the generation of theories having limited utility in a narrow range of settings (e.g., Child and Waterhouse, 1953; Easterbrook, 1959; Spence and Spence, 1966; Yerkes and Dodson, 1908). The traditional linear S–R perspective could not be made to work well enough to produce usable rules that would link stress and performance, especially in natural settings. The terms of our original questions therefore had to be changed, and I came to believe that we would never understand the way stress affected performance until we began to treat individual differences as mediators of the reaction to stressful conditions. Our choice of mediators at that time included motivational and emotional traits and their interaction with task demands (Lazarus et al., 1952).

It is also of interest that at this time psychology began to experience two metatheoretical transitions that are still going on today, especially in personality and clinical psychology. The first was a shift away from an exclusively normative research focus toward a greater emphasis on individual differences. This shift was, of course, unsettling for the scientific types who were then dominated by logical positivism and the need to have neat normative rules that applied to everyone.

A manifestation of this shift of emphasis was the New Look movement in perception, which got some of its steam from the European gestalt tradition but blossomed in the 1950's with the expansion of personality and clinical psychology. Traditional perception psychologists were asking: "How is it that we come to see the world as it is, or as an analogue of it, so that we can behave adaptively in it?" This is a normative question, about people or animals in general. What is more, it presumes veridicality, that is, accurate perception, and it occurs in a "cold" (laboratory) context (to paraphrase William James) in which emotion is typically absent because the person had no special stake in what is perceived. The New Look movement asked a different, seemingly alien question, namely, "How is it that given a similar environmental display, individuals perceive it (learn it, remember it, or interpret it) differently?" Such a question puts the emphasis on individual differences, and, as in perceptual defense research, the context is "hot"—emotional— because important motives are engendered (see also Folkman, Schaefer, and Lazarus, 1979).

To this day no one in perception theory has successfully integrated these two seemingly contradictory perspectives, and,

in fact, the same dichotomy may be found in the current research of information-processing psychologists on the one hand
and stress and coping specialists on the other. Information pro-
cessers employ "cold," universalistic machine analogues, and make
the assumption that effective adaptation consists of correctly
(veridically) processing the information in a display. Stress and
coping specialists work in the "hot" context, making the assumption that effective adaptation can make use of nonveridicality
(denial or the maintenance of hope in the face of bleak odds),
and they emphasize the many ways individuals can construe the
same input, depending on their divergent patterns of motivation,
belief systems, and styles of thinking and adapting.

The second shift in psychology was to turn away from drive
and tension-reduction concepts and toward cognitive processes
as central in human adaptation. Whereas thirty years ago the
dominant behavior model emphasized tissue deficit (as in hunger,
thirst, and sex) and secondary or acquired drives (Dollard and
Miller, 1950), we now speak forcefully of the fusion of cognition and motivation (Bolles, 1974) and the "cognitive revolution"
(Dember, 1974). During the years between, cognitive processes
had, at least, been brought in almost reluctantly as a moderator.
For example, in the late 1950's White (1959) was still trying to
shore up the collapsing drive-theory edifice by suggesting new,
cognitive drives like effectance, and Klein (1958) was arguing that
drive could not be defined adequately without reference to
cognitive processes, as in the following comment:

It seems more economical to . . . think of drive as a construct
which refers, on the one hand, to the "relating" process—the
meanings—around which selective behavior and memories are
organized; and in terms of which goal-sets, anticipations and
expectations develop, and, on the other hand, to those processes which accommodate this relational activity to reality.
In this way drive is defined solely in terms of behavior and
thought products . . . (pp. 8–9)

We are now fully into a cognitive emphasis in psychology in
general, even in areas that were once the exclusive property of
motivation and emotion (cf. Folkman et al., 1979, Klinger,
1975; Lazarus, 1966; Lazarus, Averill, & Opton, 1970; Lazarus,
Kanner, & Folkman, 1980). In this dramatic transformation of

thought, the distinguished tradition of William James, Kurt Lewin, Edward Tolman, Fritz Heider, George Kelly, and Henry Murray seems, at last, to have come into full realization.

My own approach to stress and coping is explicitly cognitive-phenomenological. The questions I now ask have changed, as have to some extent the variables and how they are defined and interrelated. For example, whereas in 1950 coping was almost universally viewed as a product of emotion and emotion viewed as a drive, my colleagues and I press the argument that emotions (and stress) are products of cognition, that is, of the way a person appraises or construes his or her relationship with the environment. This does not mean, however, that the relationship goes only one way—that is, from cognition to emotion; rather, once aroused, emotions can also affect cognition. Moreover, motives and modes of thought influence the cognitive appraisal of all adaptational encounters.

Another change in my own thinking has been a de-emphasis of a predominantly structure or trait orientation toward the events intervening between the person and the environment, and an increasing emphasis on a process orientation centering on the person's continuing relationship with the environment. In the early days, our (Lazarus et al., 1952) approach was to study stable motivational differences among persons as a predictor of the outcome. Such a variable was explicitly shown to predict differential effects of stress on performance (Vogel, Raymond, and Lazarus, 1959). Although such trait determinants are still important, my colleagues and I are far more radical today, arguing for flux as much as stability, for change both within the person and between the person and the environment in any given encounter, and over the life course. As we shall see later, such shifts in the way the problems of stress and coping were conceptualized have profound consequences for one's mode of research. To indicate these consequences I shall turn now to the major tenets of the current research and thought of my colleagues and me.

MAJOR TENETS OF STRESS AND COPING THEORY TODAY

There are four such tenets, dealing respectively with (1) the naturalistic emphasis, (2) transaction and process, (3) multiple levels of analysis, and (4) ipsative-normative ways of studying people. Although these tenets actually evolved from a substantive-cognitive theory emphasis, it is best to defer review of that theory for last.

The Naturalistic Emphasis

During the last century psychologists have become so enamored of the laboratory that they have tended to forget and distort what the laboratory can and cannot do. The great recent impact of ethologists like Tinbergen (1951), Lorenz (1953), Eibl-Eibesfeldt (1970) and others has jolted that complacency, as has the gradual recognition of the drabness, irrelevance, lack of coherence, and instability of much of the research emanating from the laboratory, especially in personality and social psychology. We hear frequently about the "crisis" in personality psychology and social psychology as illustrated in recent papers by Carlson (1971; 1975) and others. Even earlier, Klein and Schlesinger (1949) had published an unsettling paper entitled, "Where is the Perceiver in Perceptual Theory?" attesting to the distortions of understanding inherent in the tendency to study part functions of persons rather than integrated, living humans. There are at least five serious limitations in laboratory research on stress and coping that should be noted:

(a) The laboratory cannot provide descriptive data on sources of stress in people in general or in subgroups of persons based on age, sex, type of community, socioeconomic status, subculture, and personality type. After all this time in which stress has been of multidisciplinary interest, we still do not know the stressors ordinary people or special subgroups face, their daily hassles, sources of positive feeling, or their patterns of daily emotional response. In the absence of such basic ecological information, how can we expect to know much about how these stressful encounters and their emotional outcomes are generated (their socio- and psychodynamics), or about their adaptational outcomes as in somatic health, morale, and social functioning? And how can we respond knowledgeably to the implications of a poetic statement by Charles Bukowski (1972) in "Shoelace" that:

It's not the large things that send a man to the madhouse . . .

No, It's the continuing series of small tragedies
that send a man to the madhouse . . .
not the death of his love
but a shoelace that snaps
with no time left . . . (p. 114)

Although I believe it is true that people can be distressed over what seem at the moment to be trivialities, they are not really trivial at all in meaning, for they symbolize things that are very important to a person. The shoelace might break, but a major part of the psychological stress created thereby is the implication that one cannot control one's life, that one is helpless in the face of the most stupid of trivialities, or, even worse, that one's own inadequacies have made the obstacle occur in the first place. This is what brings the powerful, stressful, and pathogenic message that breaks one's morale. In any case, how is one to evaluate such a momentous issue in the traditional style of laboratory stress research? No way.

(b) By the same token, laboratory research cannot create the full range of coping processes, the conglomeration of thoughts and actions that people ordinarily employ in dealing with both the small stresses of living and the major ones, like bereavement. The laboratory permits us to explore single or at best a few such coping processes, and only the few suitable to laboratory analogues at that, leaving obscure the overall patterning of coping processes routinely used in nature.

(c) Adaptational outcomes, such as somatic health/illness, morale, and social functioning, emerge over an extended time period from stressful encounters with which we continually struggle to cope, not in the short periods in which we have the laboratory subject at our disposal. With experimental stressors, we may produce momentary elevations in blood pressure, say, but such research is not capable of creating the health-related effect in which we are most interested, namely, the shift from a momentary rise in blood pressure to the chronic disease of hypertension (Herd, 1977; Lazarus, 1978; Stahl, Grim, Donald, and Neikirk, 1975). To study the mechanisms linking stress to disease or dysfunction requires time and can only be accomplished in the field study or field experiment in which we observe concurrently the ups and downs of an adaptational outcome along with the ongoing, causal psychological and social processes (Lazarus, Cohen, Folkman, Kanner, and Schaefer, 1980; Luborsky, Docherty, and Penick, 1973). Usually we cannot follow the human subject around to observe the daily adaptational encounters as can sometimes be done with animal species (e.g., Schaller, 1964; van Lawick-Goodall, 1971; Washburn and DeVore, 1961). However, we can develop other naturalistically oriented methods. One that my colleagues and I are using is to work regularly with human subjects and over an extended period of time, to reconstruct from memory important recent adaptational encounters. The message has been spreading that more naturalistic research on stress and coping, on adaptational outcomes, and in human psychological research in general, is badly needed (cf. Willems and Raush, 1969).

(d) Perhaps the most obvious limitation of the laboratory is the impossibility, for ethical and practical reasons, of subjecting humans to the kinds and degrees of stress that are encountered in everyday life. The stresses produced in the laboratory are pale shadows of the real thing, and as such, rules derived from them may not be stable or valid in the natural setting.

(e) Last, and most exasperating of all, much of what we take to be precise control over measurement and confounding variables is illusion, particularly when one's concerns are psychodynamic or sociodynamic. Yet this supposed control is presumably the primary virtue of the laboratory. Our *saying* that a given experimental stimulus is the basis of a subject's response does not make it so. Confounded with this stimulus are a host of irrelevant but potent factors, including what the subject thinks is happening, the complex, intrapsychic, adaptational processes, and the changing relationship with the experimenter. Much of what is psychologically important occurs in these other, unintended relationships, and these most commonly are unacknowledged and unmeasured. We must be wary of treating this type of research with veneration, as having some special precision and dependability beyond well designed and thoroughly analyzed naturalistic field studies in which the "ecological validity" is far greater.

Transaction and Process

No one seriously doubts that the way a person thinks, feels, or

acts is a product of the interaction of external situation characteristics and person characteristics. Person characteristics are
forged over a lifetime and nestled in a genetically shaped physical
constitution; a situation contains three important elements to
which persons can attend and react: demands, constraints, and
resources (Klausner, 1971). In stress and adaptation a person with
a given set of beliefs, values, commitments and skills encounters
such a situation. To survive and flourish, countless such encounters must be experienced by a person over a lifetime. When a
person construes an encounter as damaging, threatening or challenging, we speak of psychological stress; when it is evaluated as
positive, a positively toned emotional state usually accompanies
or follows it. Psychological stress (as well as positive experiences)
resides neither in the situation nor in the person, though it depends on both. It arises from the adaptational relationship as it
is appraised by the person. Such a relationship is best termed a
"transaction."

Why emphasize "transaction" rather than "interaction?"
"Interaction" connotes a partitioning of variance, as in "analysis of variance," implying the causal interplay of two sets of
variables, such as a stable property of the person (trait) and a
property of the environment (e.g., a demand, a constraint, or a
resource). "Transaction," on the other hand, contains two special
kinds of meaning. First, a transaction means that not only does
the environment affect the person, as in an S–R sequence, but
also that the person affects the environment; both influence each
other mutually in the course of an encounter. The interaction
goes both ways. The model is no longer a linear, one-way street,
but transactional. Consider, for example, how Altman (1976)
states this for the realm of social psychology:

> Partly because of our adherence to a principle of parsimony,
> and partly because of our view of the experimental model as
> a primary methodological strategy, I believe that social psy-
> chology has come to adopt what can be termed a "linear" or
> "input-output" model of causation in contrast to a "social
> systems" model. That is, we seem to search only for linear
> relationships between variables, i.e., how variations in inde-
> pendent variables cause changes in mediating variables which,
> in turn, produce changes in dependent variables . . . I believe

that we have come to neglect the possibility of multidirectional causation between variables, and that a relationship in which variable A produces changes in variable B does not rule out the possibility that variable B can also be a "cause" of changes in variable A. For example, we typically assume a one-way relationship between environment and behavior, such that environmental factors cause behavioral variations of one type or another. But it is also the case that behavioral variations can produce environmental changes, so that environment or behavior can reasonably be viewed as either causes or effects. (pp. 105-110)

However, there is a crucial, second meaning inherent in the term "transaction" which distinguishes it from "interaction" (see also Pervin, 1968). In interaction, the causal, antecedent variables still retain their separate identities, whereas a transactional concept describing a relationship offers a new level of discourse in which the separate variables are now lost or changed. The point is the same as that made by the gestaltists' slogan that "the whole is different from the sum of the parts." When a cell or a group of cells is organized into an organ or tissue system, the individual identities of the cells and organs are lost or changed in the formation of the new unit. A body organ is not just a collection of cells, as might be found lying together in a petri dish, but an organized system with its own special characteristics. In this sense, a transaction, brought about by the interaction of person and environment variables, is a new entity that expresses some special relationship between the interacting variables to which we give a new name. In physiology the transactional characteristics are those of the "organ," or "organ system"; in sociology they are "social systems in decay," "under strain," "in a state of alienation," "united," "interdependent," or whatever, depending on the concerns of the theorist-observer.

In psychological stress theory as I elaborate it, various kinds of appraisal define the relationship through the subjects' eyes, as it were. It is one of harm/loss, threat, or challenge. The term "threat" expresses a new unit of psychological analysis. It refers to neither the person nor the environment alone, but to both, fused into a special kind of relationship described by the word "threat." Thus "transaction," in addition to implying mutuality of influence—which, incidentally, the term "interaction" could do adequately—implies the fusion of person and environment into a unit, a relationship, a system. Although "system" would be perfectly appropriate as an overarching term, I prefer transaction because system is very general while transaction is clearly concerned with a specific kind of system, namely, a person-environment relationship in an adaptational encounter.

A transactional view of stress and coping has one other important characteristic that should be identified. Rather than focusing exclusively on what is stable in the person-environment relationship, the emphasis is on process or dynamics—that is, on what is actually happening in any given stressful encounter and how what is happening changes. Thus, as I use the word, "process" refers to what happens over time or across encounters. It contains two elements: first, an actual interchange between the person and the environment (or among forces within the person); and second, the flow and transformation of the interchange over time, either as the encounter gets under way, proceeds and ends, or during its transformation across diverse encounters.

The first element—namely, an actual interchange—can be illustrated by a research study on the way surgical patients coped with the threat of surgery and how this affected postsurgical recovery (Cohen and Lazarus, 1973). We were able to dimensionalize patients into those with the trait of avoidance and denial at one extreme, and vigilance at the other, by using a traditional trait measure, the Epstein and Fenz (1967) version of Byrne's scales of repression-sensitization (Byrne, 1961, 1964). In addition, we obtained a process measure based on an interview with the patient the evening before the surgery. In the interview patients were asked to tell what they knew about their illness, the strategy of treatment, and their postsurgical expectations. Some knew a great deal and sought more; others knew little or nothing and seemed to avoid such information. This is a process measure in the first sense noted above because, rather than trying to assess patients' usual coping style (trait), measurement was centered on how they were *actually* coping with the *specific threat* at the moment it was happening. It turned out that the trait measure bore no relationship to either the process measure or the postsurgical outcome. Moreover, the process measure modestly predicted such outcome, with persons coping by avoidance-denial having a shorter hospital stay, fewer minor complications, and less distress than those who coped by vigilance.

The second element in understanding what is meant by "process," a key one in my estimation, is an emphasis on *flux and change*, over time or in diverse encounters. In stressful transactions psychological events are constantly moving and changing. Depending on what happens in the environment and within the person, anger gives way to anxiety or guilt, or it melts or grows stronger with each successive interchange. A stressful episode is not just a momentary, static stimulus in the environment to which the person gives a single response, say, a thought, act, or somatic reaction, as in the analogy of a single still photo; rather, it is a continuous flow of events over time, sometimes a short time as in an argument that quickly ends when one party leaves the room, at other times a long, tortuous, complex, sometimes repetitive process of achieving a new equilibrium in a relationship.

I have always believed that the best model for this notion of a coping process is the grief work in bereavement. The entire process may actually extend over a very long time, sometimes years, and it encompasses many encounters and psychological changes. What happens at the outset when discovery of the loss occurs—the shock, dazed state, confusion, bustle of activity of family and friends taking care of necessary tasks such as the funeral and giving emotional support—changes greatly as time passes. Ultimately the full realization of the loss must occur, then its acceptance, and finally, after perhaps a period of depression and withdrawal, a reinvestment in living and a search for new commitments. These coping tasks are accomplished in multiple encounters, with the children, financial accounts, the car, lawyers, friends, family, people at work, new social contacts, many or most of these encounters engendering many forms of stress and calling for varieties of coping processes.

There is a certain similarity between this emphasis on transaction, process, flux, and change and the dialectical perspective, both in the literature dealing with the life course (e.g., Riegel, 1972, 1975) and in social psychology (e.g., Gergen, 1977). One problem for those who adopt this emphasis is the difficulty of developing research methods suitable to flux and change as opposed to stability. Concepts of both structure and process are essential to scientific understanding but research psychology has overemphasized the former at the expense of the latter, probably because it is easier to tackle structure than process.

It is possible, however, to make the issue of flux and stability empirical. My associates and I have been exploring ways of studying processes such as coping. By repeated study of the same persons across stressful encounters and over time, we are able to assess the degree of stability and flux of given coping patterns, and to examine the settings and types of encounters that influence these patterns. Clinicians do this too, but we can do it systematically with a planned research design. Such research is best generated within a transactional frame of reference, and it depends on developing ways of measuring the processes that occur and change from moment to moment within the same encounter, or across encounters.

Multiple Levels of Analysis

Theory and research on stress, coping, and adaptational outcomes take place at three separate but partly interdependent levels of analysis: social, psychological, and physiological. The most important and potentially pathogenic stressful transactions take place socially—that is, between a person and other persons, if not directly, then in an implied social context. At the individual psychological level (as opposed to the social system level), a mind perceives and evaluates these events with respect to their personal meaning and significance, shaping the emotional reaction as well as the future course of action. The very process of mobilizing to act which is stimulated by such mental processes produces profound effects on the tissues of the body—an interdependence between levels commonly referred to as psychosomatic—and making possible sustained coping as well as creating the "diseases of adaptation."

The distinction between levels of analysis is vitally important because there is also a considerable degree of independence among them. One cannot automatically go from one level to the other in speaking of stress, since the rules that link all three levels are not clear (for other discussions of this, see Lazarus, 1966, 1971; Lazarus and Cohen, 1976; Smelser, 1963). For example, in a nuclear family when the parents are planning an imminent divorce, although such strain (the sociologists' term for stress) will produce psychological stress in one or several of the family members, its quality and degree, and the forms of coping it produces, will vary among the participating persons, as will the somatic effects. For example, the husband may be severely disturbed and depressed while the wife may experience substantial relief and optimism, or vice versa. One of the children may appear to be untouched psychologically while another may be highly disturbed, delinquent, even suicidal. And if both parents undergo major stress, one may develop hypertension even though he or she claims to feel positive, the other an emerging gastric ulcer, or perhaps show no tissue symptoms at all.

The tendency to use events at one level to stand for events at another level—often without recognizing that the levels have been switched—has been a great source of confusion in the stress field, leading a number of social epidemiologists to question the viability and utility of the stress concept (cf. Cassel, 1974; Hinkle, 1973). For example, social strain may be taken as prima facie evidence of stress at the psychological level, or physiological stress measures may be used to index psychological stress despite the fact that the same somatic response could have many nonpsychological causes. However, there is nothing wrong with the stress concept that cannot be fixed by a more precise differentiation of the three levels of analysis at which the concept is used, especially in research that crosses levels of analysis.

Lazarus and Cohen (1976) have made a detailed analysis of this problem, illustrating some of its dimensions with specific research examples. Their first example comes from a study (Pearlin, 1975) of status inequality as a source of stress in marriage. By means of interviews, Pearlin obtained information about the social status of both the husband's and wife's parents (ascribed status), as well as about the importance of status to the respondents, some of the details of their married life, and the amount of marital stress they experienced. In this way he was able to relate a *social system variable*, namely, inequality of ascribed status, to stress reactions via *psychological mediation*.

Pearlin's findings include three points of importance to us here. First, status inequality by itself did not produce stress in the marriage unless the higher-status partner considered status striving important (the psychological mediator), in which case that partner felt cheated. Second, status inequality in a susceptible marriage partner resulted in subjective stress by disrupting four aspects of the couple's interactions, namely, reciprocity, exchange of expressiveness, exchange of affection, and the sharing of values. For example, among those for whom status striving was important, the lower-status partner was judged by the mate as unreciprocating in the relationship; he/she felt like a loser in comparison with the mate who had married up. Likewise, in partners for whom status was important, status inequality created a lack of affection in the relationship, and inadequacy both in the communication and in the sharing of values. For such couples the subjective stress persisted even though there may have been social mobility after the marriage which reduced the original (ascribed) level of inequality for the low-status partner. Pearlin summarizes these findings by stating that:

> To account for marital problems and marital stress it needs to be recognized, first of all, that status inequality by itself is of little or no consequence. The importance of such inequality to marital problems and marital stress depends on the meaning and value that one attaches to it. (p. 356)

We can see in this research not only the explicit mixing of levels of stress analysis, but also how the deliberate step of going back and forth between the social level and the psychological level clarifies what is happening when predicated on independent measurement at both levels. For example, the social variable, status inequality, does not by itself create stress; it does so only in individuals for whom status striving (the psychological variable) is important. Without considering the psychological mediators accounting for individual differences (e.g., individual values, appraisals), we can see that the social variable would not be useful as a predictor of stress in marriage. Moreover, in order to understand adequately the stress reactions generated in individual marriages, it is also necessary to examine the interpersonal or social *processes* that generate them, such as the quality of the byplay between husband and wife. In a situation where the partners feel they have been cheated, and with impairment of their sense of reciprocity, expressive exchanges, affection, and sharing of values, partners experience their marital relationship as stressful.

Also, this is not a one-way street from the social level to the psychological. On the contrary, it would be equally inadequate to try to understand what is going on by looking solely at process and outcome on the psychological level without also viewing the social system matrix as a determinant. Thus the discovery that some couples experience stress in marriage, as expressed in troubled reciprocity, expressiveness, affection, and value sharing, would not be meaningful if we did not also consider the social system variable, status inequality, that makes this stress comprehensible. By noting that the marital stress depended on status inequality between the spouses, we have in effect embedded the reactions in the natural social context engendering the stress in the first place. As we have seen earlier, the relationship between the two sets of levels is not by any means automatic; quite the contrary, only careful attention to both levels simultaneously makes it possible to make sense out of what is happening.

The second example comes from recent research by Mason (1974; Mason, Maher, Hartley, Mougey, Perlow, and Jones, 1976) on endocrine profiles in monkeys and men under various physical stressor conditions, including exercise, fasting, heat and cold. Mason sought to determine whether these divergent physical stresses produce a general endocrine reaction (in the fashion suggested by Selye's General Adaptation Syndrome), or produce reaction patterns specific to each type of stressor. From our present perspective, the most interesting feature of Mason's research was his attempt to "clean up the independent variable," as he put it. That is, psychological threat reactions are usually confounded with physical stresses, so it is difficult to tell what it is that is producing elevated adrenal corticosteroids.

In exercise trials with young human males, in fasting trials with monkeys, and in heat and cold trials with monkeys, Mason took care to minimize novelty, uncertainty, extraneous psychosocial stimuli, and discomfort, in short, to reduce as much as possible any psychological threat that might be engendered in the physical procedures in the laboratory. For example, by minimizing competitive concerns and avoiding severe exertion, the danger that young men would be psychologically threatened in the treadmill exercise experiment was reduced; and by providing the subject monkeys with a non-nutritive placebo, they were less likely to be upset when bypassed by their trainer, who provided food to the control monkeys in the fasting experiment;

and in the heat and cold exposure experiments, temperature changes were made very gradually rather than suddenly so as not to alarm the monkey subjects.

Under these conditions of minimal psychological threat, it was found that each physical stressor produced its own unique profile of hormonal change, and there was no general or nonspecific hormonal response to all stimuli despite expectations to the contrary based on GAS theory. Even more remarkable, when psychological threats were kept at a minimum, there was no elevation of the 17-hydroxicorticosteroid response except for the cold condition.

Here, as before, there has been a crossing over of two levels of stress analysis, the physiological and the psychological, in this case at the stimulus or stressor end, except that here the mixing of levels had been hitherto inadvertent, the psychological level (threat) being confounded usually with the physiological (heat, fasting, cold, exercise). Such confounding appears to have misled previous researchers about the bodily response to various stress conditions. The corticosteroid response appears to be particularly sensitive to psychological threat which is often confounded with other, physical stressors (Lazarus, 1966, p. 398; see also Lazarus, 1974). By systematically designing a study in which the contribution of each level can be separately distinguished—that is, by eliminating the confounding—Mason seems to have advanced substantially our understanding of the psychophysiological processes related to stress. The lesson to be learned is not only that intentionally mixing levels of stress analysis is desirable because it adds to our understanding, but also that the inadvertent or careless mixing of levels (where the two are not differentiated by stimulus manipulation and/or by measurement) can lead to very serious confusion about what is actually happening.

Ipsative-Normative Ways of Studying People

Traditional psychology has tended to be normative in outlook, seeking principles that apply to all humans alike. That such a stance is often counterproductive has been well understood by clinicians concerned with individual adaptation. For example, a person is said to be ineffectual in adaptation, or to function maladaptively, because he or she falls short when compared with other persons, or with some normative standard of ideal or optimal functioning. But the normative perspective fails to take into account the actual circumstances under which a person develops or functions. If this functioning occurs under severe conditions of deprivation or environmental stress, or in a subculture whose values are at variance with the larger culture in which it is embedded, a strictly normative comparison would be inappropriate in many respects. On the other hand, we also recognize that a person is in trouble with reference to an intra-individual standard of comparison—that is, we note that he or she is doing badly in comparison with him/herself at other, more favorable times. The normative perspective is like that of classical perception theory, which, as I noted at the outset, tried to formulate laws for humans in general or, in an arrogant form of reductionism, even for all organisms (cf. Skinner, 1938). In doing so, it failed to consider person characteristics as well as context variables, which were emphasized by the New Look movement.

Ironically, even personality research has tended to be formulated from a normative standpoint, testing the effect of one or a few variables of personality, usually assessed statically, through single-occasion, trait-centered measurement, on some consequent pattern of behavior. This research style—even when it is correlational and multivariate rather than experimental (Cronbach, 1957, 1975)—fragments the person into one or a limited number of traits, rather than attempting to capture the particular organization of properties (or facets) and functions that make up a total individual. Such fragmentation has been clearly recognized in the vigorous debates about the merits and demerits of the nomothetic versus idiographic research styles (cf. Allport, 1962; Holt, 1962). However, such debates have missed a key point: research need not be designed with *either* nomothetic *or* idiographic extremes in mind. The nomothetic style of research still dominates much of personality research, and this emphasis extends to epidemiological and public health research focused on the origins of maladaptation and disease. Typically, large numbers of cases are studied through survey methods to assess either personal or environmental causal antecedents of illness risk. The emphasis is on people in general rather than on individual differences across encounters or over time.

I believe it is becoming evident to many researchers that the purposes of some research require a mixture of the nomothetic and idiographic analytic styles. More sophisticated and less extreme strategies have been proposed which use the term "ipsative" to express the intraindividual perspective and "normative" or nomothetic for the interindividual (cf. Broverman, 1962; Marceil, 1977). Ipsative refers to the many facets of the same person, or to how that person functions (e.g., coping processes) in a variety of contexts or encounters. Research can be both ipsative and normative at the same time.

As my associates and I have argued elsewhere (e.g., Lazarus, 1978; Lazarus & Cohen, 1976; Lazarus, 1980), we will never be able to examine the ongoing processes underlying the causation of various adaptational outcomes, including somatic health and illness, morale, and social functioning, unless we study these processes as they occur across a wide variety of occasions and within persons. To do so requires that we sacrifice the large numbers of (normative) cases needed for statistical significance when the source of variance studied is weak and one of many causal factors, in favor of more intensive examination of the same persons across occasions or over time. Ipsative-normative research designs, in which a heavy commitment is made to repeated measures, require—for the same cost—that we reduce the N across persons and increase it within persons (across occasions).

If our concern is with effective versus ineffective coping, we must be in a position to determine whether any given group of persons (defined by sex, age, personality, or sociocultural variables) copes with a variety of stressful encounters in some consistent way (i.e., with some consistent pattern), or uses effective or ineffective patterns in certain types of encounters but not in others. To find this out we must study the same persons again and again and over time rather than many persons once or twice. And we must learn how to analyze intra-individual data so that we can extract and compare meaningful patterns across diverse encounters and situational contexts, as well as from group to group. Doing so calls for innovative methods of analysis which presently do not exist or are inadequate. What I have said earlier about naturalistic focus, transactional-process perspective, and the need for simultaneous examination of several levels of analysis comes together in this one methodological tenet or dictum about ipsative-normative research design.

SUBSTANTIVE COGNITIVE AND COPING CONCEPTS

As I noted at the start, the cognitive orientation in psychology has had a marked resurgence in recent years. Psychology has always been concerned with the relations between cognition, emotion, and motivation, but the nature of these relationships has been differently conceived at different times. It is only recently, however, that emotions and motivation have been seen as clearly shaped by the way a person construes ongoing relationships with the environment—in effect, by cognitive processes (cf. Lazarus, 1966; Lazarus, Averill, and Opton, 1970; Lazarus and Launier, 1978). There is a growing group of theorists (Arnold, 1960, 1970; Mandler, 1975), including the cognitive behavior therapists (e.g., Beck, 1971; Ellis, 1962; Goldfried, 1979; Mahoney, 1977; Meichenbaum, 1977), which accepts the premise that emotions are products of cognitive activity. In such a view, emotions are outcomes of, or reactions to, cognitively mediated transactions with the environment, actual, imagined, or anticipated. The term I have consistently employed since 1966 to express this idea is "cognitive appraisal," of which there are two main kinds, primary and secondary.

Primary Appraisal and Reappraisal

The process of evaluating the significance of a transaction for one's wellbeing is referred to as *primary appraisal*. Such appraisals come in three forms—judgments that the transaction is either (1) irrelevant, (2) benign-positive, or (3) stressful. There are three subtypes of stressful appraisals: (a) harm/loss, (b) threat, or (c) challenge. Harm/loss refers to injury or damage already done, as in bereavement, loss of physical function, social esteem, self-esteem, existential meaning, etc. Threat can refer to the same kinds of injuries, but the term signifies also that they have not yet occurred but are anticipated. Challenge means an opportunity for growth, mastery, or gain. The distinction between harm/loss, threat, and challenge may be very important not only in affecting the coping process itself and the effectiveness with which coping skills are utilized in social transactions, but also in their divergent consequences for morale and somatic health (Lazarus et al., 1980a).

We know too little about the kinds of people who typically appraise stressful encounters as challenging rather than threatening and vice versa, the types of stress situations that encourage challenge as opposed to threat appraisals and vice versa, and the adaptational consequences of each of these types of appraisal. A working hypothesis about the causal antecedents of threat and challenge is that the former is more likely when a person assumes that the specific environment is hostile and dangerous and that he or she lacks the resources for mastering it, while challenge arises when the environmental demands are seen as difficult but not impossible to manage, and that drawing upon existing or acquirable skills offers a genuine prospect for mastery. In addition to assumptions about specific environments, people may have very general belief systems about themselves and the environment (cf. Bandura, 1977; Ellis, 1962; Lazarus, 1966), systems that also influence appraisal of specific encounters.

Psychological stress, over all, refers to demands (or conflicts among them) which tax or exceed available resources (internal and external) as appraised by the person involved. Cognitive appraisal by an individual is what makes this definition of stress a psychological one. The key element is that a person senses in some way, consciously or unconsciously, that he or she is in jeopardy. In parallel fashion at the social level, stress involves demands from without or within which tax or exceed the resources of a social system. And at the somatic level, stress consists of proximate physical demands (even when they originate distally at the social or psychological level) which tax or exceed the resources of a tissue system—that is, stress is not an environmental stimulus, a characteristic of a system (e.g., a person), or a response; it is a *relational concept*, a balance between demands and the power to deal with them without unreasonable or destructive costs (as pointed out earlier).

At the bottom line of psychological stress analysis, then, primary appraisal determines the intensity and quality of the emotional response to any transaction. A benign-positive appraisal results in a positively toned emotional reaction, such as joy, exhilaration, love, contentment, relief. A stressful appraisal produces negatively toned emotions, such as anxiety, fear, anger, guilt, envy, jealousy, disgust. Each emotional quality and intensity has its own appraisal pattern (see also Beck, 1971). Anxiety, for example, involves an anticipated harm (threat) that is ambiguous, either as to what is to happen or what can be done about it, and is, compared with fear, largely symbolic (Lazarus & Averill, 1972).

Primary appraisal also involves the possibility of feedback from changes in the person-environment relationship and from reflection as the transaction proceeds, thus potentially allowing for changes in the quality and intensity of the emotion. I have called this cognitive activity *reappraisal*. A research example can be found in a study by Folkins (1970) in which experimental groups of subjects await an electric shock, each for a different period of time varying from 30 seconds to 20 minutes. Their intrapsychic processes were later reconstructed through interviews. Psychophysiological stress reactions were found to differ in magnitude depending on the duration of the waiting period, being highest at about one minute, lowest at three and five minutes, then rising again when the time period for waiting was 20 minutes. The interview evidence suggested strongly that this variation depended on what subjects thought about during the waiting period. For example, one minute was long enough for the subject to assimilate the threatening idea that he was going to feel pain when the shock came, but not long enough to develop doubts about the threat. However, if the subject had five minutes to think about it, he began to reflect on or reappraise the situation, saying to himself, for example, "A college professor surely would not expose me to severe pain," or "I have had shock before from a laboratory inductorium and it was hardly anything to worry about." At 20 minutes, the dimensions of the problem seemed to change. Subjects commonly began to feel anxious, perhaps thinking that so long a wait must portend something of major import. Throughout life we are constantly appraising and reappraising encounters with respect to their relevance and meaning. This is one reason why emotions are always in flux from moment to moment, changing both in intensity and quality depending on how the changing portents of the situation are being "read" by the person.

At this writing I have come across a tragic instance of the appraisal and reappraisal processes that illustrates well how they can work. A 45-year-old woman was supposed, after shopping, to meet her husband and daughter at home to go to a local ball game. On the way home she passed a scene of an auto accident to which she paid little attention, and on arrival home, discovered that her husband was not there. For some reason she felt impelled, with some apprehension, to go back to the scene of the accident with her daughter. On first passing the accident she had apparently noticed marginally that the color of the car was the same as that of her husband's. As soon as she and her daughter arrived at the scene of the accident it was clear that it was, indeed, her husband's car. An ambulance had already taken him away. Even though the policemen at first did not mention it, and although the car did not seem badly damaged, somehow she understood that he was already dead. He had had a heart attack. In retrospect she observes that what gave her the clue was that the policemen seemed in no hurry to do anything, or even to get the wife and daughter to the hospital. In effect, it was all over, and without anything having been said she knew this from the manner in which people were acting.

Here we see an interesting series of appraisal and reappraisal processes based on situational cues. Without knowing more about the person, we cannot identify the personal dispositions and knowledge that might also have shaped the cognitive activity. We do not know, for example, whether she had any intimation of his cardiovascular vulnerability. There was the initial marginally registered recognition that the car in the accident was the color of her husband's. When she had arrived home and her husband, usually a prompt man, was not yet there, the earlier, casual recognition now took on new salience—the accident could have happened to her husband. On arrival, and confirming that it was, indeed, her husband's car, she did not have to be told that he was already dead because of the behavior of the people at the scene of the accident. Further talk could only confirm what she already knew. The whole incident involves, in addition to any emotion felt, a series of appraisals and reappraisals as the events unfolded. A new set of appraisals, particularly related to coping with bereavement, eventually would be set in motion by the discovery of her husband's untimely death.

Secondary Appraisal

Primary appraisal concerns the significance of a transaction for well-being, a question of "Is there anything at stake here?" If the answer is that "I am in jeopardy," that is, facing harm/loss, threat, or challenge, a key adaptational process is called into being, namely, *coping*. Whether consciously and deliberately, or unconsciously and automatically, a decision is made about what to do. Since most important stressful transactions are comprised of numerous specific encounters stretching out over time, as in grieving, in bolstering damaged or threatened self (or social) esteem, or in managing chronic interpersonal difficulties, the person needs information about personal and social resources which can be drawn upon, the adequacy of fit between one or many types of coping and the stressful demands, and the possibility that new problems will be created by coping activities. Obviously, all this requires a set of complex cognitive appraisal processes devoted to coping decisions. I have called these cognitive appraisal processes *secondary appraisal* to distinguish their function of evaluating coping options and resources from primary appraisal functions. A fuller account of this may be found in Lazarus and Launier (1978), in which various types of secondary appraisal are illustrated and their consequences for action indicated.

In a dynamic, time-oriented cognitive system such as I am describing, secondary appraisal and primary appraisal processes are interdependent, and even seem to fuse. Their only difference consists of the contents to which they are addressed. For example, to the extent that one identifies a coping course of action that has a high likelihood of success in overcoming a harm, mastering a threat, or being equal to a challenge, primary appraisal of threat is itself changed. One is no longer greatly threatened when it is realized that a potential harm is readily preventable. On the contrary, if a search for information on which to predicate adaptive action turns up little or nothing, or leads to the conviction that there is nothing to be done, threat is apt to be greatly enhanced, and the options for coping are evaluated accordingly.

One can see such a dynamic interplay in the gradual discovery that an illness is not merely a minor breast cyst but a malignant tumor. Surgical removal may once again alter the intensity of the threat, but later evidence of new growthlike symptoms elsewhere alters the threat appraisal a third time, and if this growth turns out to be metastatic, options for mastery of the illness are now severely curtailed, leading to a greatly enhanced sense of injury and threat, and greater reliance may have to be placed on intrapsychic coping processes of denial, efforts to preserve hope, and efforts at acceptance than on actions to change the situation through action.

The concept of cognitive appraisal troubles some because it appears circular—that is, known only after the fact, by inference or by self-report. That is untrue. When I first discussed this concept (Lazarus, 1966), I pointed out that, as with any psychological process, the determinants of appraisal lie in the interaction of the environmental situation and person variables. A number of possible environmental factors probably contribute to appraisal, including the imminence of harm, its ambiguity (cf. Folkman et al., 1979), the power of the environmental demands to do harm, and the duration of the demands. With respect to duration, for example, chronic stress seems more likely to result in gastric ulcers than acute stress (Mahl, 1952, 1953), and there is much evidence that the hormonal and psychological responses to stress also depend on the chronic-acute distinction (Gal and Lazarus, 1975). Among person-centered determinants, two are particularly important: general and specific beliefs about oneself and the environment, and the pattern and strength of values and commitments.

This is not the place to give additional details on the determinants of appraisal, nor is our knowledge of them great. It is important to point out, however, that the mediating concept of cognitive appraisal is fully capable of cause-and-effect research on its determinants, and to emphasize what is often forgotten in actual research, that it is the interaction of both sets of determinants, person and environment, which determines whether a transaction will be appraised as irrelevant, benign-positive, or stressful, and if the last, then whether harm/loss, threat, or challenge.

Coping

In my view, stress itself as a concept pales in significance for adaptation compared with *coping*. As noted elsewhere (Roskies and Lazarus, 1979), stress is ubiquitous, an inevitable feature of normal living, though some persons do indeed experience more frequent, severe, or sustained stressful encounters than others. What makes the major difference in adaptational outcome is coping, and so we should give special attention to it in our research on human functioning. I will first deal with the main functions of coping, then, in order, offer a rough classification of coping modes.

Functions of coping. One major difference I have with the cognitive behavior therapists, such as Albert Ellis (1962), with writers on coping, such as Haan (1977), and with the traditional psychiatric approach, is that I do not assume that the best coping is necessarily realistic, although I am convinced that coping must be flexible. If, as Ellis does, one assumes that the pathology of emotional life rests on false or irrational assumptions or beliefs about life, then therapy must try to make such beliefs realistic, and coping must ultimately be predicated on accurate testing of reality. I agree, of course, that actions to change a troubled relationship with the environment are often of crucial importance to the outcome, especially so in anticipatory coping under conditions in which there is some possibility of evading or preventing the harmful confrontation. However, there are many encounters in which little or nothing can be done even when one has obtained all the available information about a problem. Under such conditions, living optimally or even adequately requires that we tolerate a high degree of ambiguity, or even that we engage in some self-deception (cf. Hamburg and Adams, 1967). Therefore, to the problem-solving or the instrumental function of coping, we must add another important function, in a sense the antithesis of instrumentality—namely, the self-regulation of emotional distress.

Two major functions of coping must therefore be considered: first, to change the situation for the better if we can, either by changing one's own offending action (focus on self) or by changing the damaging or threatening environment; and second, to manage the somatic and subjective components of stress-related emotions themselves, so that they do not get out of hand and do not damage or destroy morale and social functioning. These functions are not always contradictory, but when they are, there is danger of maladaptation. For example, we make ourselves feel better in the face of harm or threat by such palliative modes of coping as denying, intellectualizing (achieving detachment), avoiding negative thoughts, or taking drugs (e.g., alcohol, pain killers, and tranquilizers). Although these make us feel better, they do not change the actual person-environment relationship. Under certain conditions, when it does not countermand needed adaptive actions, this may help greatly.

For example, in the study cited above by Cohen and Lazarus

(1973) on coping with surgical threat, avoidance-denial modes of coping were associated with better postsurgical outcomes than vigilance. Given the circumstances of being hospitalized, there is no evident value in vigilance because there is no action available to master the problem of recovering. On the other hand, research by Katz, Weiner, Gallagher, and Hellman (1970) reveals the other side of this issue: palliative coping obstructed or delayed actions required to protect people against serious illness. They observed that one of the most common ways women coped with the threat of having discovered a breast lump was a pattern of avoidance-denial which resulted in delay in seeking medical evaluation. If the growth was malignant, excessive delay could result in metastasis and a much poorer medical outlook. Similarly, Hackett and Cassem (1975) observed men who, during symptoms of a heart attack, did vigorous pushups or ran up and down some flights of stairs, on the reasoning that they could not be having a heart attack because the exercise did not kill them. These men were trying to feel better psychologically (palliation) at the expense of taking the adaptive action of getting medical attention. As it turned out, they were, indeed, having a heart attack and they did survive, but the coping process clearly endangered their lives.

The two functions of coping—problem-solving and regulation of emotional distress (palliation)—have been commented on by many writers (e.g., Kaplan, Cassel, and Gore, 1973; Mechanic, 1962; Parsons and Bales, 1955; Pinneau, 1976). Although they are sometimes in opposition, especially when the palliative function preempts adaptationally necessary actions, often one supports the other. For example, if one is not too distressed in an examination or a performance before an audience (because of use of a tranquilizer or engaging in some intrapsychic process that lowers the anxiety), performance can be much improved or at least less impaired. Furthermore, actions that resolve the person-environment problem—say, by preventing the harmful confrontation or compensating for an injury—also reduce or eliminate emotional distress. It is a worthwhile working assumption that, despite our society's value preference for reality testing and direct action, effective copers typically engage in forms of coping that achieve both of these functions, and that effective copers use both direct actions and palliative coping modes.

There are two problems in Ellis's account of cognitively based emotion (and those of cognitive behavior therapists in general), both stemming from a preoccupation with psychopathology. Ellis regards such emotions as the pathological result of irrational beliefs about oneself and the environment. From this perspective, it is natural to conclude that the appropriate treatment is to change such beliefs, to help the person test reality more accurately. However, the emphasis on reality testing leaves little or no room for palliative or emotion-regulatory processes as a valid and healthy form of coping. In my view, all well adjusted persons use these on occasion, and probably quite often, along with instrumental or action-centered forms of coping. Since we know little about normal optimal functioning, we may make the unwise assumption that palliation is necessarily pathological because it produces poor adaptational outcomes, when it is quite possible such a generalization does not fit people who are getting along well. The Alcoholics Anonymous "Serenity Prayer" captures this theme very well. It states: "God grant me the serenity to accept the things I cannot change, courage to change the things I can, and the wisdom to know the difference." A cynic might substitute for the last phrase, "and the good luck not to fuck up too often."

The second problem is that emotions are not always negative or pathological. As Ellis seems to assume, and as is widely assumed in psychology and psychiatry in general, there is no room in such an analysis for positively toned emotions, nor is the positive value of such emotions in general adaptation given widespread credence, a theme that my colleagues and I have strongly opposed elsewhere (Lazarus, Kanner and Folkman, 1980*b*). If we obtain our understanding exclusively from the clinical context of maladaptation and treatment, we are in danger of maintaining a very one-sided and incorrect conception of effective adaptation, as represented in the lives of people who never get to treatment centers. A fuller understanding and appreciation of normal, ordinary adaptation, and even optimal adaptation, requires that we learn much more about the ways people and peoples in our society manage their lives, and about the place of both positive and negative emotional experiences in their lives.

Coping modes. In a recent treatment of coping (Lazarus and

and Launier, 1978), four main coping modes were identified, each serving both problem-solving and emotion-regulatory functions, each capable of being oriented to the self or the environment, and each concerned with either past or present (harm/loss) or future (threat or challenge). The four modes are: information-seeking, direct action, inhibition of action, and intrapsychic processes.

Information-seeking involves scanning the characteristics of a stressful encounter for knowledge needed to make a sound coping decision or to reappraise the damage or threat. In addition to providing a basis of action (problem-solving function), information-seeking can also have the function of making the person feel better by rationalizing or bolstering a past decision (Janis, 1968; Janis and Mann, 1977). Ironically, this palliative function is contrary to the assumptions usually made about decision-making by information-processing researchers (cf. Folkman et al., 1979). Palliation often calls for ignoring the negative implications of what one knows or of information one receives or seeks. Moreover, the regulation of emotional distress often requires accepting ambiguity (the obverse of information) as a natural feature of living. At times such ambiguity or uncertainty is even a balm rather than a source of anxiety.

For example, it is no accident, nor is it necessarily a self-protective conspiracy, for a physician not to provide all the gruesome details of a patient's condition, including the recovery process after surgery and what could go wrong, a negative prognosis, a statement of the probable duration of life in a terminal illness, etc. When little can be done to change the situation, the preservation of uncertainty can facilitate hope, morale, and involvement with living, and help the person tolerate or relieve pain and emotional distress. On the other hand, failure to be totally honest can also do great damage in ultimately destroying credibility, or preventing the patient from coming to terms with death or some other distressing fate. Therefore, the recognition that uncertainty can be used positively should not be read as a prescription for professional deception. The most personally sensitive physicians, I think, look for cues about what is needed by a patient, cues that are presented when the patient turns away from further information that is tentatively proffered or seeks to pin down what is happening more precisely. Such a physician also knows that what might be avoided or sought at one point in the personal crisis might change at a later point. Still, we must not forget that there are other ways of coping with threat than wanting to know all, and that the uncertainty afforded a patient by a lack of detailed information can have utility in his or her overall coping strategy. We know too little about the probably wide variation in successful patterns of coping to make the unequivocal assumption that accurate reality testing is always best for all persons and under all conditions.

Anything one does (except cognitively) to handle stressful transactions falls within the rubric of *direct action*. Such actions are as diverse as the environmental demands and personal goals people have to manage, including expressing anger, seeking revenge, fleeing, suicide, building storm shelters, taking medication, jogging to preserve one's health, etc. The list is virtually unlimited. Direct coping actions can also be aimed at the self or the environment, since either is potentially capable of being changed, thereby altering the stressful person-environment relationship for the better. The action can be aimed at overcoming a past injury—as when a grieving person becomes buried in work or seeks a new love relationship—or at a future danger. In the light of their great importance in human adaptation, too little attention has been devoted to anticipatory coping actions.

It may seem strange to cite *inhibition of action* as a coping mode, since it implies inaction, but effective coping often calls more for holding back action impulses that will do harm than taking action that poorly fits the requirements of a transaction. In a complicated social and intrapsychic world, every type of action is capable of coming into conflict with moral, social, or physical constraints and dangers, and choice is possible only if strong natural impulses to act (as in anger and fear) can be held back in the interest of other values.

All the cognitive processes designed to regulate emotion—in effect, the things a person says to himself or herself, as it were—are included in *intrapsychic modes*, making this, too, a highly varied category. Not only does it encompass self-deceptive mechanisms or defenses, such as denial, reaction formation, and projection, but it also includes avoidance and efforts to obtain detachment or insulation (as in isolation, undoing, and intellectualization) from a threat to achieve a feeling of control over it. These modes are mostly palliative in that they make the person feel better by reducing or minimizing emotional distress. As in the case of the other coping modes, they can be oriented to the past, as in the reinterpretation of a traumatic event, or to the future, as in the denial that one is in danger. They can also be focused on the self ("I am not inadequate or evil"), or on the environment ("This situation is not dangerous").

Difficulties in Assessing Coping

To assess coping processes requires strategies of measurement and research that are very different from those employed by personality assessors to measure coping styles or traits. One must develop means of describing what the person is doing and thinking in specific encounters. Most measures of coping currently available are trait-oriented—that is, they inquire about what a person usually does, rather than what he or she did in a specific encounter (Moos, 1974). They are usually focused on a limited class of coping modes, for example, such specific intrapsychic dimensions as repression-sensitization or, in some cases, a cluster of intra-psychic or defensive modes. Almost never do they cover the full ground of the four modes cited above—namely, information search, direct action, inhibition of action, and intrapsychic processes.

There are a number of difficult problems which must be faced if one is to assess coping as it takes place (as a process) in natural-istic settings. I shall briefly discuss a few major ones, specifically, coping as a constellation of many strategies, getting information about how people cope, ambiguities in the definition of coping processes, and evaluating coping effectiveness.

Coping as a constellation of many acts. As noted earlier, coping is not a single act but a constellation of many acts and thoughts engendered by a complex set of demands that may stretch out over time. There are undoubtedly styles or patterns of coping that are more or less characteristic of an individual, but such styles involve a combination of many acts and thoughts rather than a single one. Thus what is needed is a way of describing the many things a person, or particular kinds of persons, did or thought over the period of an encounter or a series of encounters. Such a pattern description could then be used to compare a person or group with themselves and with others (ipsative-normative). It is one thing, for example, to note that a person used avoidance, denial, or intellectualization and quite another to be able to describe the pattern of thoughts and acts employed in the different stages of an encounter, contexts, and instances.

A stressful encounter can be relatively simple or complex, short lived or extended. But even in relatively simple instances, more than one other person may be involved toward whom thoughts and actions are directed, and there is apt to be more than one interchange in which coping thoughts and actions are brought to bear. Before we can summarize what happened through simplifying generalizations, we must be in a position to say which of many possibilities have actually occurred. For example, in a quarrel with a loved one, the person under investigation may have used humor, denial, threats, assaults, anger, martyrdom, attempted detachment, information-seeking, avoidance of implications, self-depreciation, tears, passive dependency, escape from the situation, expressions of love with or without irony or criticism, and so on.

If we, as systematizers of coping, cannot describe these various interpersonal and intrapsychic maneuvers, we will not be able to take the next step of describing the constellation of coping processes used by an individual in any given encounter, whether this takes place over minutes, hours, days, or months. The assessment task requires recording both details and combinations of details as the process unfolds. Only then can abstracting about an overall constellation and style be made. The clinical setting has a tradition of doing this sort of thing, as in the case of Berne's (1964) transactional analysis, in which types of interchanges are not only described but given interpretive names reflecting the type of interpersonal game (implying the motivation or function) being played. The problem is not that such description has never been attempted, but that what has been done is not systematic or measurement-oriented so that it can ultimately be used in research on the determinants and adaptational outcomes of coping, or on the measurement of stability and flux of coping patterns across diverse stressful encounters. There is currently no existing method for handling this assessment problem systematically, though my associates and I are trying to develop such methods, both for specific encounters and across encounters, intra-individually and inter-individually, and to find ways of analyzing ipsative-normative data effectively.

Getting the information about how people cope. To ask most people to tell us how they coped is probably not fruitful, except perhaps in the case of a limited proportion of persons trained in our concepts of coping and capable of introspection and verbalization in the classic tradition of Wundt. We cannot meaningfully expect most people to tell us whether they used denial, intellectualization, or whatever, in a given encounter. However, we can ask them to tell us whether they did or thought this or that. For example, they can tell us whether they felt the need to act even though such action could not change the situation; whether they joked, tried to put a good face on things, saw the situation as hopeless, tried not to think about the problem, etc. For our research on coping my associates and I have created checklists describing dozens of such tactics based on our own rational classificatory scheme and on research and clinical reports, and we have focused on a specific stressful encounter which our research subject chooses from the immediate past. At the same time, through in-depth interviews we use trained clinicians to observe independently and evaluate what, through their observer eyes and ears, they believed the person was doing.

Assessment of the coping process will always have to face the issue of self-report versus observational and inferential sources of knowledge. This issue can be faced only by being in a position to correlate self-report coping patterns with inferential, observer-based sources. In addition, such patterns can be related to outside criteria, for example, adaptational outcomes like health/illness, morale, and social functioning, general personality description by observers and by the person being studied, and other criteria like reported patterns of emotion, appraisals, etc.

Ambiguities in the definition of coping processes. When we speak of denial, avoidance, and other specific intrapsychic coping processes, it is as though we know clearly what these processes are and how they are to be assessed. Such clarity does not exist, however, and in practice their assessment is filled with ambiguity and confusion. This is easily illustrated in the case of denial and avoidance. The problem has at least two facets, both stemming, I believe, from faulty conceptualization.

First, denial and avoidance are different processes, psychologically, yet they are easily confused and often, as I have above, hyphenated to suggest similarity or a close relationship. *Denial* is the effort, sometimes successful, sometimes not, to negate a problem. The person states in some way that he or she is not angry, not dying, not in danger, or whatever. On the other hand, avoidance involves acceptance of the reality of the threat, but it is a deliberate effort not to think about it. A person may deny that he or she has a serious illness or, when that denial becomes impossible, deny that he or she is dying, and ultimately, if Weisman (1972) is correct, that dying means extinction (in some sense the person believes he or she will live on). On the other hand, in *avoidance* the person does not deny the facts or implications of the illness, but whenever possible refuses to talk or think about it. The assessment problem is that often in research on the subject, especially where the assessment process is superficial or mechanical, the fact of avoidance may lead the researcher to classify the process as denial although there is really no negation.

Second, and more important, the typical trait-centered, static research paradigm leads us to treat denial as an established fact, a coping achievement, in which case we tend to speak of deniers rather than denying. This is misleading, because rarely does a process like denial become so fully consolidated as a mode of coping that it is no longer subject to uncertainty, challenge, or even dissolution in the face of the evidence. This is illustrated by a not infrequent scenario that takes place on a cancer ward of a hospital. The patient spends an entire interview giving direct evidence to the clinical worker (physician, psychologist, social worker, nurse) that he is denying his imminent death. The clinician, having listened to the denial-based affirmations, feels sure that the patient is denying. If he were a research worker, perhaps studying coping, he might then classify the patient as a denier. Yet, almost immediately on leaving the office and turning a corner of the hospital corridor, the same patient sees another professional whom he knows and bursts into tears, now sobbing and crying out that he is dying. What happened to the denier?

We can offer two kinds of speculation. On the one hand,

perhaps, the first clinician tends by his manner and personal vulnerabilities to encourage denial in a manner described insightfully by Hackett and Weisman (1964). Physicians, friends, family, and all manner of visitors to the dying patient encourage denial by being unable to face openly what is happening without evident distress. Instead they mouth platitudes, protecting themselves but believing they are protecting the patient. They are already distancing themselves from the person who soon will no longer be around. This implicitly threatens the patient with the loss of important human relationships at just the time when they are most needed. Seeing a more accepting and less vulnerable person in the corridor releases what is really in the patient's mind. The earlier denial was only skin deep. Weisman (1972) has elaborated richly on the concept of "middle knowledge," in which a patient seems to believe one thing on the surface, but somehow "knows" at some dim and perhaps even unverbalized level that he or she has cancer, that death is imminent. A second possibility is that in the first interview the patient is really trying to see the situation in favorable terms—that is, he or she is making an effort at denial, but an unsuccessful one. Listening to their own statement, however, makes it impossible for the patient to believe what he or she is saying.

Herein lies the conceptual confusion. We treat a process of coping as a static state of mind rather than as a constant search for a way of comprehending what is happening, a way that seeks simultaneously to test reality and to retain hope. Depending on the moment, the circumstances, the evidence, the social pressures, the personality, such a construction remains always in flux, now moving one way, now another. Only severely disturbed persons display well consolidated defenses that constantly resist uprooting. If we look at the problem as a continuous effort at meaning (Frankl, 1955, 1963), we come closer, I think, to the way Erikson (1956) views the struggle in aging to achieve integrity rather than despair. One does not usually arrive fixedly at one or the other pole of thought, but is constantly in tension between the two. As Erikson (1956) states:

Identity *formation* neither begins nor ends with adolescence; it is a lifelong development largely unconscious to the individual and to his society . . . (p. 69)

An *evolving configuration*—a configuration which is gradually established by successive ego syntheses and resyntheses . . . integrating *constitutional givens, idiosyncratic libidinal needs, favored capacities, significant identifications, effective defenses, successful sublimations, and consistent roles.* (p. 71)

Not only does this idea of constant tension between the polarities, of constant struggles to construe what is happening in one's existence, represent a dramatically different view of coping than the more traditional emphasis on trait, style, or achieved structure, but it also calls for a very different research strategy. One must observe the coping pattern employed by an individual again and again, at diverse moments, across different types of encounters, and over time, in order to make an accurate description. Our mistake has been prematurely to freeze people analytically into postures and styles; not that styles cannot be identified, but that for such a style to be a valid representation, one must study the individual in greater depth and breadth of encounter than is possible in a single sampling, and then be ready to recognize the frequently transient nature of the coping process and pattern.

Evaluating coping effectiveness. The final difficulty on which I wish to comment is perhaps the most complex and tenuous of all, and it is also the aspect of adaptation theory that has been given the least attention. The problem is made more simple if we limit ourselves to the reduction of existing pathology, since in the clinical setting we know that the person is hurting and relatively ineffectual, and we can perhaps justify any efforts to ameliorate the unwanted symptoms. Even here, however, we may be treading on dangerous ground. For example, those involved in efforts to eliminate Type A behavior because it predisposes to greater risk of cardiovascular disease than persons less pressured, aggressive, and achievement-dedicated, often forget that for the Type A person the alternative may be to give up a social value to which he or she has made a lifelong commitment in favor of another which, for that person, is anathema. On the other hand, as the findings of Clark (1967) seem to suggest, aging persons who cannot relinquish the forms of coping suitable to youth carry far greater risk of being institutionalized for emotional problems than those who take on coping patterns more suitable for older people.

I think there is no longer any doubt that values are inextricably tied to the evaluation of coping effectiveness. We have to ask, "Coping effectiveness for what?" "And at what cost?" The stakes include somatic health/illness, moral, and social functioning, and sometimes one is achieved at the expense of the other. Thus the virtues of being Type A include living up to a deeply entrenched social and personal value but at an increased risk of somatic illness. On the other hand, being insulated in human relations might facilitate somatic health but also decrease emotional satisfactions and positive involvements that help make life worthwhile.

The great dilemma is that, just as we have little descriptive knowledge of the patterns of coping employed by most people, including diverse subgroups within the society, we also do not know the patterns of coping that work for given types of persons, the ways they do, and the specific sets of circumstances under which they do work. In treatment settings, the issue tends to be almost entirely begged (cf. Roskies and Lazarus, 1979), but the therapist can at least hope for improvement in the dysfunctional areas which brought the patient into treatment in the first place. In prevention, whether primary, secondary, or tertiary, the absence of rational guidelines poses an even more serious handicap. As Bower (1977) has put it:

> Lack of knowledge alone does not seem to deter action [to ameliorate psychopathology]; all kinds of halfway or inadequately documented therapies are visited upon the mentally ill—perhaps because the need is critical and the person is hurting. It is humane to try to help the ill despite our doubts about what we are doing. One cannot make such a case for primary prevention. (p. 29)

We must make efforts in coping theory and research to evaluate the adaptational effectiveness of the diverse patterns of coping, but obviously this can be done only after we have done the basic work of identifying such patterns as they appear in all sorts of individuals, populations, and conditions.

SUMMARY OF IMPLICATIONS FOR THE STUDY OF HUMAN FUNCTIONING

It only remains now to point out the implications of this stress and coping paradigm for research on human functioning. These implications, and others, are already embedded in this paper, but it will help the reader keep them in mind to touch briefly on each of the major implications once more, this time separated from the paradigmatic system from which they arise.

I must point out, too, that much, though not all, of what I have said is reflected in typical clinical practice, and sometimes the approach is referred to as the "clinical method." For example, therapists, as they review a client's problems in repeated therapy sessions, inevitably focus on the transactions of the individual in various stressful encounters and over the time-course of continuing treatment. The clinician is thus usually intra-individual (or ipsative) in outlook, although the perspective also includes consideration of the pattern for a single patient in comparison with other patients (normative). Likewise, the encounters the clinician examines take place in the natural context of the client's entire life, rather than being laboratory analogues. Clinical practice also involves an implicit assessment of dynamics, which takes coping processes and their dysfunctional features into account. Therefore, what I have offered paradigmatically for research has much in common with the traditional clinical approach to an individual in trouble, although this approach suffers perforce from the exigencies of treatment obligations, and the accident of which clients seek help. The clinician, therefore, cannot be selective of who is to be treated, nor can the client afford the luxury of being merely a "subject" in research, since he or she needs help. Though in my view clinical practice has been the major source of concepts about psychodynamics, it can hardly be as systematic as can explicitly designed field research.

As I see it, there are at least seven important implications of what I have said for the study of human functioning. They follow briefly:

1. Stress per se cannot be regarded simplistically as causal in human maladaptation, because it generates a variety of coping processes and, in turn, is as much a product of inept coping as of environmental demands or stressors (cf. Lazarus and Cohen, 1977). Therefore, it is not fruitful to blame pathology strictly on stress, except perhaps in extreme situations of environmental deprivation and human cruelty in which little or no opportunity is allowed for the development or utilization of effective coping.

One example would be the concentration camp (Dimsdale, 1980), wherein coping could have little or nothing to do with survival; that depended heavily on luck and other factors outside the person's control. From the perspective of this paper, to relate stress to maladaptation requires emphasis not so much on stressors as on the cognitive and coping processes mediating the reaction.

2. The view presented here is that the greatest need is for naturalistic research on stress and coping. Such research, however, should not be limited to the clinical context of psychopathology and treatment, but should seek knowledge about the day-to-day stresses as well as positive experiences of ordinary people and those who function optimally, and about how such people cope. There are serious conceptual and empirical dangers connected with an exclusive reliance on the context of pathology or dysfunction, the most serious of which is the tendency to equate effective functioning with accurate reality testing, and to underestimate the value of palliative modes of coping, and positive emotions. Even if one doubts the validity of this assertion, it cannot be evaluated without intensive studies of coping patterns in normal and optimally functioning persons and groups.

3. In such research much more attention should be given to pure theoretical description of the transactions of a person with the environment. In the recent past, description has taken a back seat to cause-and-effect research on determinants (interaction), with the result that we do not know how to describe and measure the fundamental processes whose determinants we also need to identify. We have virtually no process measures of coping and other transactional concepts, such as threat and challenge.

4. With respect to causal determinants of human dysfunction, the transactional perspective shifts our attention from strictly endogenous or intrapsychic variables and processes to exogenous ones. The important Freudian discoveries of unconscious, intrapsychic processes and their impact on thought, feeling, and action also got clinicians frozen into the study of internal processes exclusively, but we now cycle back toward a recognition of the important role played by environmental influences in adaptation and maladaptation. Indeed, it would hardly be suitable to cycle back and forth between either extreme from one period to another. The separation of personality from social psychology is an unfortunate consequence of this either/or pattern in thought

and research. Transaction implies the somewhat banal conclusion that we must look at both, though the banality is somewhat mitigated by the fact that mainly lip service has been given to so obvious a conclusion in actual research and theory.

5. Explanation of and research on human functioning more often should include three levels of analysis: the social, psychological and physiological simultaneously, without reductionism and without the perennial and mistaken tendency to use measurement at one level to stand for events at another level. Only when these levels are simultaneously examined can the principles of their relationships be explored. Studied correctly, the mechanisms of psychosomatic disease, and the links between social system and psychological processes, can be identified. Maladaptation always reflects some form of poor fit between the person (psychologically and physiologically) and the social system, and all levels contribute to a full account of human functioning.

6. Two research styles can be profitably combined in the study of human functioning. One of these (normative) selects large representative cohorts of persons chosen through survey methods and categorized on the basis of social or personality variables of interest to us. In stress research such variables include patterns of life change, daily hassles, cognitive appraisals of these, beliefs, commitments, etc. The second style involves study of a single individual or a few individuals over time or across various life circumstances requiring coping and adaptation. We need an in-depth look at the individual as he or she struggles with the tasks of living, and as the processes unfold that will ultimately determine the adaptive outcome in respect to somatic health, morale, and social functioning.

Survey or assessment approaches are designed to identify very general properties of persons, giving us little or no real chance to observe how a resourceful, flexible individual reacts in a variety of adaptive transactions in a changing environment. They are designed for representativeness and economy—we measure what we want to know in one or two limited testing or survey sessions. If such approaches worked ideally or even well in providing us with a reasonably complete portrait of the person, or with an accurate prediction of how he or she reacts emotionally or copes with the conditions of life that must be faced, there would be no inherent problem with structurally oriented strategies. The economy would, in fact, then be very welcome. However, when we want to construct a working portrait of the stresses to which an individual or class of persons is exposed, modes of coping, and the stability and variation of these processes, there are severe limitations to a nomothetic and survey-oriented approach.

The alternative of studying a single individual or several persons is also unacceptable by itself, since it does not allow us to generalize to others with any assurance. Intensive or in-depth study of many individuals over time and across diverse life situations is very costly. A compromise, however, could permit us to study sufficient numbers of subjects and at the same time give us the in-depth information we should need to describe and analyze the processes of stress and coping. In such a compromise the strategy of large cohorts and survey methods for statistical analysis could be retained, while at the same time selecting limited subsamples for more intensive study. Research designs should be ipsative as well as normative—that is, the individuals studied intensively would be observed time and time again, over many life contexts and encounters. By such ipsative or repeated study of the same individuals, the ongoing processes involved in reacting to and coping with stressful transactions—those leading to health/illness, effective/impaired social functioning, and high/low morale—could be examined as they were taking place. In addition, intensive study could capitalize more fully on the advantages of the human relationship between subject-participant and researcher, encouraging more candor and self-examination, as well as the use of clinical skills to infer defenses, ambivalences, and hidden neurotic agendas.

7. Finally, although I have said little about it, the proper study of human functioning requires the evaluation of such functioning. We must be able to indicate how well a coping pattern used by the person facilitates survival and helps him or her to flourish, or is in some sense counterproductive. To intervene in prevention, treatment, or education in the interests of aiding the development of coping effectiveness and social competence means that we have some notions and evidence about the strategies that are effective and the ones that are ineffective. The answer may vary with the kind of person, the context, or the situation, and depend on our values about health and pathology. Optimal functioning might mean that all three categories of adaptational outcome—namely, social functioning, morale, and somatic health—be in harmony in

the ideal case. The trouble is that some coping strategies may work well for one value—say, morale—but poorly in generating effective instrumental actions. Or an individual's coping actions might provide maximum mileage in getting along or succeeding socially and occupationally, but cost greatly in somatic health. Until we are in a better position to evaluate such matters in varying types of persons and situations, we will be operating almost blindly in our intervention efforts, whether these be directed at prevention, treatment, or education. Although there are plenty of ideas about such matters, they are not well bolstered by empirical observations because little research is being mounted today along these lines. Correcting this state of affairs is more easily said than done.

At the present time no author of a paradigm for theory and research on human functioning has reason to crow loudly. We need to seek innovative approaches and travel pathways not well trodden in the past. There is no single stress and coping paradigm, and certainly not one on which there is substantial agreement. I would like to believe that I have described here a meaningful conceptual analysis and a workable set of methodological principles that could and should be tried out and ultimately judged heuristically.

REFERENCES

Allport, G. W. The general and the unique in psychological science. *Journal of Personality*, 1962, *30*, 405–422.

Altman, I. Environmental psychology and social psychology. *Personality and Social Psychology Bulletin*, 1976, *2*, 96–113.

Arnold, M. *Emotion and personality* (2 vols.). New York: Columbia University Press, 1960.

Arnold, M. (Ed.). *Feelings and emotion*. New York: Academic Press, 1970.

Bandura, A. Self-efficacy: Toward a unifying theory of behavioral change. *Psychological Review*, 1977, *84*, 191–215.

Beck, A. T. Cognition, affect and psychopathology. *Archives of General Psychiatry*, 1971, *24*, 495–500.

Berne, E. *Games people play*. New York: Grove, 1964.

Bolles, R. C. Cognition and motivation: Some historical trends. In B. Weiner (Ed.), *Cognitive views of human motivation*. New York: Academic Press, 1974.

Bower, E. M. Mythologies, realities, and possibilities in primary prevention. In G. W. Albee and J. M. Joffe (Eds.), *Primary prevention of psychopathology, Vol. 1: The issues*. Hanover: University Press of New England, New England, 1977.

Broverman, D. M. Normative and ipsative measurement in psychology. *Psychological Review*, 1962, *69*, 295–305.

Bukowski, C. *Mockingbird wish me luck*. Los Angeles: Black Sparrow Press, 1972.

Byrne, D. The repression-sensitization scale: Rationale, reliability and validity. *Journal of Personality*, 1961, *29*, 334–349.

Byrne, D. Repression-sensitization as a dimension of personality. In B. A. Maher (Ed.), *Progress in experimental personality research* (Vol. 1). New York: Academic Press, 1964.

Carlson, R. Where is the person in personality research? *Psychological Bulletin*, 1971, *75*, 203–219.

Carlson, R. Personality. In M. R. Rosenzweig and L. W. Porter (Eds.), *Annual Review of Psychology*, 1975, *26*, 393–414.

Cassel, J. Psychosocial processes and "stress": Theoretical formulations. *International Journal of Health Services*, 1974, *4*, 471–482.

Child, I. L., and Waterhouse, I. K. Frustration and the quality of performance: II. A theoretical statement. *Psychological Review*, 1953, *60*, 127–139.

Clark, M. M. The anthropology of aging, a new area for studies of culture and personality. *The Gerontologist*, 1967, *7*, 55–64.

Cohen, F., and Lazarus, R. S. Active coping processes, coping dispositions, and recovery from surgery. *Psychosomatic Medicine*, 1973, *35*, 375–389.

Cronbach, L. J. The two disciplines of scientific psychology. *American Psychologist*, 1957, *12*, 671–684.

Cronbach, L. J. Beyond the two disciplines of scientific psychology. *American Psychologist*, 1975, *30*, 116–127.

Dember, W. N. Motivation and the cognitive revolution. *American Psychologist*, 1974, *29*, 161–168.

Dimsdale, J. E. (Ed.). *Survivors, victims and perpetrators: Essays on the Nazi holocaust*. Washington, D.C.; Hemisphere, 1980.

Dollard, J., and Miller, N. E. *Personality and psychotherapy*. New York: McGraw-Hill, 1950.

Easterbrook, J. A. The effect of emotion on cue utilization and the organization of behavior. *Psychological Review*, 1959, *66*, 183–201.

Eibl-Eibesfeldt, I. *Ethology: The biology of behavior* (trans. E. Klinghammer). New York: Holt, Rinehart, and Winston, 1970.

Ellis, A. *Reason and emotion in psychotherapy*. New York: Lyle Stuart, 1962.

Epstein, S., and Fenz, W. D. The detection of areas of emotional stress through variations in perceptual threshold and physiological arousal. *Journal of Experimental Research in Personality*, 1967, *2*, 191–199.

Erikson, E. H. The problem of ego identity. *Journal of the American Psychoanalytic Association*, 1956, *4*, 58–121.

Folkins, C. H. Temporal factors and the cognitive mediators of stress reaction. *Journal of Personality and Social Psychology*, 1970, *14*, 173–184.

Folkman, S., Schaefer, C., and Lazarus, R. S. Cognitive processes as mediators of stress and coping. In V. Hamilton and D. M. Warburton (Eds.), *Human stress and cognition: An information processing approach*. London: Wiley, 1979.

Frankl, V. *The doctor and the soul*. New York: Knopf, 1955.

Frankl, V. *Man's search for meaning*. New York: Washington Square Press, 1963.

Gal, R., and Lazarus, R. S. The role of activity in anticipating and confronting stressful situations. *Journal of Human Stress*, 1975, *1*, 4–20.

Gergen, K. J. Stability, change, and chance in understanding human development. In N. Datan and H. W. Reese (Eds.), *Life-span developmental psychology: Dialetical perspectives on experimental research*. New York: Academic Press, 1977.

Goldfried, M. R. Anxiety reduction through cognitive-behavioral intervention. In P. C. Kendall and S. D. Hollon (Eds.), *Cognitive-behavioral interventions: Theory, research, and procedures*. New York: Academic Press, 1979.

Haan, N. *Coping and defending*. New York: Academic Press, 1977.

Hackett, T. P., and Cassem, H. Psychological management of the myocardial infarction patient. *Journal of Human Stress*, 1975, *1*, 25–38.

Hackett, T. P., and Weisman, A. D. Reactions to the imminence of death. In G. H. Grosser, H. Wechsler, and M. Greenblatt (Eds.), *The threat of impending disaster*. Cambridge: The MIT Press, 1964.

Hamburg, D. A., and Adams, J. E. A perspective on coping: Seeking and utilizing information in major transitions. *Archives of General Psychiatry*, 1967, *17*, 277–284.

Herd, J. A. *Cardiovascular correlates of psychological stress*. Paper presented at Conference on the Crisis in Stress Research, Boston, October 20–22, 1977.

Hinkle, L. E. The concept of "stress" in the biological and social sciences. *Sciences, Medicine, and Man*, 1973, *1*, 31–48.

Holt, R. R. Individuality and generality in the psychology of personality. *Journal of Personality*, 1962, *30*, 377–404.

Janis, I. Stages in the decision-making process. In R. Abelson, E. Aronson, W. McGuire, T. Newcomb, M. J. Rosenberg, and P. Tannenbaum (Eds.), *Theories of cognitive consistency: A sourcebook*. Chicago: Rand McNally, 1968.

Janis, I., and Mann, L. *Decision making*. New York: The Free Press, 1977.

Kaplan, B. H., Cassel, J. C., and Gore, S. *Social support and health*. Paper presented at American Public Health Association Meetings, San Francisco, November 9, 1973.

Katz, J. L., Weiner, H., Gallagher, T. G., and Hellman, L. Stress, distress, and ego defenses. *Archives of General Psychiatry*, 1970, *32*, 131–142.

Klausner, S. Z. *On man in his environment*. San Francisco: Jossey-Bass, 1971.

Klein, G. S. (Ed.). *Assessment of human motives*. New York: Holt, Rinehart, and Winston, 1958.

Klein, G. S., and Schlesinger, H. Where is the perceiver in perceptual theory? *Journal of Personality*, 1949, *18*, 32–47.

Klinger, E. Consequences of commitment to and disengagement from incentives. *Psychological Review*, 1975, *82*, 1–25.

Kuhn, T. S. *The structure of scientific revolutions*. Chicago: University of Chicago Press, 1970.

Lazarus, R. S. *Psychological stress and the coping process*. New York: McGraw-Hill, 1966.

Lazarus, R. S. The concepts of stress and disease. In L. Levi (Ed.), *Society, stress and disease* (Vol. 1). London: Oxford University Press, 1971.

Lazarus, R. S. Psychological stress and coping in adaptation and illness. *International Journal of Psychiatry in Medicine*, 1974, *5*, 321–333.

Lazarus, R. S. A strategy for research on psychological and social factors in hypertension. *Journal of Human Stress*, 1978, *4*, 35–40.

Lazarus, R. S., and Averill, J. R. Emotion and cognition: With special reference to anxiety. In C. D. Spielberger (Ed.), *Anxiety: Current trends in theory and research* (Vol. 2). New York: Academic Press, 1972.

Lazarus, R. S., Averill, J. R., and Opton, E. M., Jr. Toward a cognitive theory of emotion. In M. B. Arnold (Ed.), *Feelings and emotions*. New York: Academic Press, 1970.

Lazarus, R. S., and Cohen, J. B. *The study of stress and coping in aging*. Paper presented at the 5th WHO Conference on Society, Stress and Disease: Aging and Old Age, Stockholm, June 14–19, 1976.

Lazarus, R. S., and Cohen, J. B. Environmental stress. In I. Altman and J. F. Wohlwill (Eds.), *Human behavior and the environment: Current theory and research* (Vol. 1). New York: Plenum, 1977.

Lazarus, R. S., Cohen, J. B., Folkman, S., Kanner, A., and Schaefer, C. Psychological stress and adaptation: Some unresolved issues. In H. Selye (Ed.), *Guide to stress research*. New York: Van Nostrand Reinhold, 1980. (*a*)

Lazarus, R. S., Deese, J., and Osler, S. F. The effects of psychological stress upon performance. *Psychological Bulletin*, 1952, *49*, 293–317.

Lazarus, R. S., Kanner, A. D., and Folkman, S. Emotions: A Cognitive-phenomenological analysis. In R. Plutchik and H. Kellerman (Eds.), *Theories of emotion*. New York: Academic Press, 1980. (*b*)

Lazarus, R. S., and Launier, R. Stress-related transactions between person and environment. In L. Pervin and M. Lewis (Eds.), *Perspectives in interactional psychology*. New York: Plenum, 1978.

Lorenz, K. *King Solomon's ring*. New York: Crowell, 1953.

Luborsky, L., Docherty, J. P., and Penick, S. Onset conditions for psychosomatic symptoms: A comparative review of immediate observation with retrospective research. *Psychosomatic Medicine*, 1973, *35*, 187–204.

Mahl, G. F. Relationship between acute and chronic fear and the gastric acidity and blood sugar levels in macada mulatta monkeys. *Psychosomatic Medicine*, 1952, *14*, 182–210.

Mahl, G. F. Physiological changes during chronic fear. *Annals of the New York Academy of Science*, 1953, *56*, 240–249.

Mahoney, M. Cognitive therapy and research: A question of questions. *Cognitive Therapy and Research*, 1977, *1*, 5–17.

Mandler, G. *Mind and emotion*. New York: Wiley, 1975.

Marceil, J. C. Implicit dimensions of idiography and nomothesis: A reformulation. *American Psychologist*, 1977, *32*, 1046–1055.

Mason, J. W. Specificity in the organization of neuroendrocrine response profiles. In P. Seeman and G. M. Brown (Eds.), *Frontiers in neurology and neuroscience research: First International Symposium of the Neuroscience Institute*. Toronto: University of Toronto Press, 1974.

Mason, J. W., Maher, J. T., Hartley, L. H., Mougey, E. H., Perlow, M. J., and Jones, L. G. Selectivity of corticosteroid and catecholamine responses to various natural stimuli. In G. Serban (Ed.), *Psychopathology of human adaptation*. New York: Plenum, 1976.

Mechanic, D. *Students under stress*. New York: The Free Press of Glencoe, 1962.

Meichenbaum, D. *Cognitive-behavior modification: An integrative approach*. New York: Plenum, 1977.

Moos, R. H. Psychological techniques in the assessment of adaptive behavior. In G. V. Coelho, D. A. Hamburg, and J. E. Adams (Eds.), *Coping and adaptation*. New York: Basic Books, 1974.

Parsons, T., and Bales, R. F. *The family: Socialization and interaction process*. Glencoe, Ill.: The Free Press, 1955.

Pearlin, L. I. Status inequality and stress in marriage. *American Sociological Review*, 1975, *40*, 344–357.

Pervin, L. A. Performance and satisfaction as a function of individual-environment fit. *Psychological Bulletin*, 1968, *69*, 56–68.

Pinneau, S. F., Jr. *Effects of social support on occupational stresses and strains*. Paper presented at American Psychological Association Convention, Washington, D. C., September 1976.

Riegel, K. F. Time and change in the development of the individual and society. In H. W. Reese (Ed.), *Advances in child development and behavior* (Vol. 7). New York: Academic Press, 1972.

Riegel, K. F. (Ed.). *The development of dialectical operations.* Basel: Karger, 1975.

Roskies, E., and Lazarus, R. S. Coping theory and the teaching of coping skills. In P. Davidson (Ed.), *Behavioral medicine: Changing health life styles.* New York: Brunner/Mazel, 1979.

Schaller, G. B. *Year of the gorilla.* Chicago: University of Chicago Press, 1964.

Skinner, B. F. *The behavior of organisms.* New York: Appleton-Century-Crofts, 1938.

Smelser, N. J. *Theory of collective behavior.* New York: The Free Press of Glencoe, 1963.

Spence, J. A., and Spence, K. W. The motivational components of manifest anxiety: Drive and drive stimuli. In C. D. Spielberger (Ed.), *Anxiety and behavior.* New York: Academic Press, 1966.

Stahl, S. M., Grim, C. E., Donald, S., and Neikirk, H. J. A model for the social sciences and medicine: The case for hypertension. *Social Science and Medicine,* 1975, *9,* 31–38.

Tinbergen, N. *The study of instincts.* New York: Oxford University Press, 1951.

Van Lawick-Goodall, J. *In the shadow of man.* New York: Dell, 1971.

Vogel, W., Raymond S., and Lazarus, R. S. Intrinsic motivation and psychological stress. *Journal of Abnormal and Social Psychology,* 1959, *58,* 225–233.

Washburn, S. L., and DeVore, I. The social life of baboons. *Scientific American,* 1961, *204,* 62–71.

Weisman, A. D. *On dying and denying.* New York: Behavioral Publications, 1972.

White, R. W. Motivation reconsidered: The concept of competence. *Psychological Review,* 1959, *66,* 297–333.

Willems, E. P., and Raush, H. L. *Naturalistic viewpoints in psychological research.* New York: Holt, Rinehart, and Winston, 1969.

Yerkes, R. M., and Dodson, J. D. The relation of strength of stimulus to rapidity of habit formation. *Journal of Comparative and Neurological Psychology,* 1908, *18,* 459–482.

3

A Competency Model Must Replace the Defect Model

GEORGE W. ALBEE

Frequently a revolution in scientific thinking occurs when some widely accepted premise, some "historical truth," is seen finally as inaccurate or incorrect. Our minds explore the crowded spaces created by the walls of fixed ideas until eventually we question why the walls are there at all. With the expanse of space that comes into view as the old conceptual walls are torn down, completely new kinds of explorations are possible. The simple step of abandoning an old habitual pattern of thinking often leads to a whole new way of dealing with a problem.

The *sickness* or *defect* or *illness* explanation of disturbed behavior has been ascendant for a century. It has been questioned repeatedly over the years, but only recently has the intellectual climate become favorable to the growth of disbelief. Now the harvest of doubt is ready.

One of the most important factors forcing our reevaluation of the *illness* model is a growing concern with the primary prevention of emotional disturbance. To prevent something we must first identify or describe what it is that we wish to prevent; then we must identify the causative forces that lead to the undesirable state or process, and try to remove them—or, as another strategy, we must do other things that "strengthen the host" to resist successfully the causative agent.

The illness model has come to be seen increasingly as inappropriate to meaningful efforts at primary prevention. Mental illnesses are not objective facts. They are not identifiable diseases to be confirmed in the laboratory through diagnostic tests. There is, with rare exceptions, no organic pathology to be discovered. These conditions are not easily identified and are not reliably diagnosed. They do not follow the usual public health paradigm of prevention where an identifiable disease is traced back to a predictable cause that can be removed or defended against. Rather we are concerned with problems in living, problems often created by blows of fate, by the damaging forces of a racist, sexist, ageist society where preparation for competent adaptation is minimal.

One revealing consequence of this state of affairs is resistance and opposition from psychiatry to efforts at primary prevention. The most frequent argument holds that "We do not yet know enough about the organic causes of mental illness to prevent them—and anyway we must spend our limited financial resources helping those who suffer" (see Carstairs, 1958; Eisenberg, 1975; Henderson, 1975). The opposition to prevention in psychiatry is not much different, however, from attitudes in other areas of medicine—prevention has very low priority generally.

A widely touted myth has it that the medical profession in general is actively interested in prevention. The facts lead to a contrary conclusion. Of the billions of dollars spent in recent years for research into the causes and cure of cancer, for example, only a small fraction of one percent has been devoted to research into prevention. This astounding allocation for a search for "cures" is in direct and stark contrast to the generally agreed-upon fact that 80 to 90 percent of all cancer is environmentally caused and therefore, theoretically, preventable. The most under-funded and underpaid branches of medicine have long been the areas concerned with public health; Schools of Public Health are nearly always at the bottom of the totem pole at major universities in terms of status and funding. This curious neglect is all the more strange because of the generally accepted fact that most of the triumphs of medicine for the past century have resulted from discoveries leading to the prevention of diseases rather than to their cure. Recently one of my radical friends, listening to my puzzled preoccupation with these facts, pointed out to me that when strange and paradoxical social situations existed, Lenin was wont to ask, "Who benefits?" Is it too cynical to suggest that physicians are more interested in treatment than in prevention because it is to their economic benefit to treat?

Or that a selection process screens out of medicine people with a prevention orientation? Medicine is most interested in the treatment of illness. Psychiatry is interested in furthering and defending the argument that emotionally disturbed people are sick. It is in the self-interest of the latter field to hold to these views. (But we *know* that socially acceptable reasons will be found in support of these views.)

Henderson (1975), writing in the *Bulletin of the Menninger Clinic*, sees a "fading" of community psychiatry, decries "the magical notion of 'primary prevention' " (p. 235), and points to "the striking advances of biological medicine" (p. 235) in both treatment and prevention. Persons are naive when they talk about prevention (says Henderson) because there are "only a few conditions in psychiatry (brain syphilis and PKU perhaps) that are well . . . (enough) understood to be preventable" (p. 235). He concludes: "it makes little sense to divert millions of dollars from treatment to a 'woolly' notion of primary prevention" (p. 236).

One of the senior gurus in American psychiatry, Leon Eisenberg (1975), has examined the mental hygiene movement and concludes: "Seven decades later, there is no evidence of even modest success from a multitude of earnest efforts" (pp. 118–119). Eisenberg feels that it is "absurd" to think that mental hygiene programs can eliminate mental illness (p. 119). Rather, each of the variety of separate "psychiatric disorders," each with a separate cause, must be approached separately if prevention is the goal.

Surprisingly the general public has not been fooled into accepting the illness model, despite the best efforts of the propagandists for psychiatry over the years. Most people simply do not believe that "mental illness is an illness like any other."

In spite of one hundred years of increasingly massive attempts at educating the general public about mental illness, the person in the street, in contrast to the highly educated, does not interpret most disturbed behavior as "illness." In the late 1950's the Joint Commission on Mental Illness (sic) and Health (see *Action for Mental Health*, 1961) reported an extensive study, done by Shirley Star, of a nationwide sample survey to determine what is recognized by most people as "mental illness." On the basis of 3500 interviews she concluded that there is a large "tendency to resist labeling anyone as mentally ill" (by the general public) except as a last resort (pp. 74–75).

In interviews with a cross-section of the populace her staff described six separate patterns of disturbed behavior. These were fairly detailed sketches of the behavior that would ordinarily occur in those persons labeled paranoid schizophrenic, simple schizophrenic, chronic anxiety neurotic, compulsive phobic, alcoholic, and juvenile delinquent. After listening to the descriptions of each of these patterns of behavior, the 3500 interviewees were asked to tell whether there was anything wrong with the person, whether the person was mentally ill, and whether it was serious. For five of the six disturbed people described, most of those interviewed were unwilling to label the behavior "mental illness" and were able to give more common-sense explanations. Only in the case of the behavior of the so-called paranoid schizophrenic was a majority inclined to use the mentally ill label.

If the general public has not been sold on the sickness explanation, and if our research data fail to support this explanation, why do we continue to emphasize the illness model in our professional intervention centers and professional training programs? If emotional problems are learned in a social context, why do we continue to pretend that people with these problems are sick? If emotional problems have been and continue to be shown to result from the interaction of environmental stress and learned ability to cope with stress (competence), why is our clinical model still medical? Who benefits?

Bertrand Russell suggested that anything worth *stating* is worth *overstating*. I will be following that principle. First let me state my own position. I believe the *competence model* demands an egalitarian political and moral philosophy. If we believe that every person, female and male, of whatever race, nationality, age, or ethnic origin, deserves every possible opportunity to maximize his or her competence and coping skills, we must free ourselves of the prejudices that are so much a part of Western thought. We must accept the position that everyone has the potential for growth and the right to personal maximization of competence to deal with stress.

This moral position is and will be highly threatening to the authoritarians and to those who accept a defect model. I want to argue that a competency model is incompatible with the position that certain persons are emotionally defective, that certain groups are defective because of genetic or organic factors, that women are inferior to men, blacks inferior to whites, southern Europeans inferior to Nordics, and that there is something *inherently* different about Jews, Orientals, French Canadians, Bantus, or whatever groups. I am not arguing against the concepts of individual differences and statistical variability. I am arguing against prejudice, ethnocentrism, and elitism. A competency model will be opposed, subtly or overtly, by those who favor meritocracy, divine right, or separate and unequal kinds of interventions for separate groups. A competency model is anti-categorical and anti-elitist.

I warn you that acceptance of a competency model will be dangerous to your comfort. There are many powerful forces that are threatened by such a model; and as these forces have the power to punish those espousing it, it will be dangerous if we go too far down this road. There is a safe, dillettantist position we can play: the artificial competency training of persons who are imbedded in an authoritarian system that is loaded with injustice. This is comparable to polishing brass on the *Titanic*. But if you accept the position that most emotional distress develops as a result of the unequal battle between individual resistance to stress and competency to deal with stress, on the one side, and on the other, the overwhelming injustice and dehumanization that is part of our consumer-oriented industrial society, then clearly the strategy is to strive to change the society and its values if we are to make a competency model more promising for success in prevention.

My thesis is that excessive industrialization requires the dehumanization of work and the submergence or elimination of individuality, of individual creativity, of a sense of identity and of personal competence. We are merely dealing with a small part of the problem when we try to build competencies into children who are destined to take their places as workers in endlessly boring and routine jobs in manufacturing, sales, service, and agribusiness. The modern industrial state has defined human existence into rigid poles, emphasizing efficient production and mindless consumption. In the process competent individuality has been all but lost (Albee, 1977).

I hope I am not exhibiting the "Old Oaken Bucket Delusion" when I suggest, for example, that life on the family farm may have provided one of the best environments for the development of individual competency and clear personal identity. Jefferson and his contemporaries based their views of democracy on the independent, self-sufficient, small-farm way of life. We have become what Jefferson most feared—a people crowded into cities. Three quarters of us live on 2 percent of the land. Two hundred years ago 90 percent worked on the land. In 1950 there were 5.5 million farms in the United States. Half of them no longer exist. I need not spell out the nutritional horrors and health hazards that have resulted from the industrialization of agriculture, nor the degradation of the lives of 5 million migrant farm workers.

Let me make clear my position on prevention. In developing a model for primary prevention we should focus our attention on the following formula:

$$\text{Incidence} = \frac{\text{Organic causes and stress}}{\text{Competence, coping skills, self esteem, and social support systems}}$$

I must point out that this model can accommodate efforts in the organic and psychotherapeutic modes as well—it depends on whether the focus is on an individual or a population. The point I want to make is that building competence through increasing coping skills will reduce incidence—so long as we do not assume the presence of an unmodifiable organic defect, as long as we have some control over excessive social and economic stress, and as long as we do not have a society that destroys self esteem and/or social support systems. But focusing on competence, important as it is for prevention, must be part of a larger effort at social and political change.

If the primary prevention of emotional distress can be accomplished through the reduction of stress and the development of competence, why do we continue to direct all our clinical efforts at treating symptoms? Why do we focus on *secondary* prevention? Again, who benefits?

In the face of all of the arguments in opposition to the sickness (medical, illness, defect) model, to what forces can we attribute the continued ascendancy of the sickness explanation of mental and emotional problems? I believe that one answer for the persistence of a defect model is to be found in the same basic ethnocentrism and racism that historically were part of the widespread ideological justification for slavery, the jailing of paupers, the exploitation of women, and the ghastly treatment of foreign-born "lunatics." I am not suggesting that all psychiatrists (and others) who hold the illness model are sexists and racists. But the appeal of the model, in the absence of convincing empirical support, rests in large measure on the attitudes that perpetuate racism and sexism. The best argument for the inhumanity of slavery and the denial of the rights to women and paupers and the warehousing of lunatics was that these people were members of an inferior species and had no more rights than other subhuman species or beasts of burden. It was and is argued that members of these groups each possesses a personal defect that defines them as inferior.

Let us look for a moment at some history. As a result of the potato famine in Ireland in 1850 hundreds of thousands of poverty-stricken and illiterate Irish peasants were dumped into the Eastern cities of the United States. Although they did not have to endure the degradations of slavery that were the lot of blacks in the South, the Irish were exploited as cheap labor, as were the Chinese imported to build the railroads and the Japanese imported to work the pineapple fields of Hawaii. Meanwhile, the American Indians were being slaughtered and/or herded into reservations to make way for the expansion of the industrial society under the thoughtful leadership of the great robber barons of the nineteenth century. All of these groups were defined as members of inferior races—they were incompetent to participate in civilized society—and they could not be made competent.

The widespread conviction that the Irish were constitutionally inferior, and that Irish lunatics were incurable, can be read in Edward Jarvis' *Idiocy and Lunacy in Massachusetts* (1855). This report to the Massachusetts legislature (reprinted by Harvard University Press, 1971) is perhaps the best and most clear-cut delineation of psychiatric opinion of that day. Native-born Yankees were curable through gentle, kindly, and humane treatment, but the coarse and uncouth Irish, who had higher rates of lunacy and idiocy, were made of weaker stuff and had to be housed permanently in separate insane asylums, where they would not contaminate the Yankees who had only temporary aberrations. The development of psychiatry in the United States can be traced directly to the newly formed Association for Superintendents of Hospitals for the Insane. More and more insane asylums sprang up over the next half century to house increasing numbers of mentally disturbed, most of whom were bewildered peasants, first from Ireland, and then from Scandanavia, Eastern Europe, and Southern Europe. Most recently the inmates are overrepresented by blacks, Puerto Ricans, and Chicanos. The interested psychologist should go back and read the *American Journal of Insanity*, beginning about 1860 when it came under the editorship of John P. Gray, who began to preach the message that a defective brain in a constitutionally inferior body was the cause of insanity. Phyllis Chesler (1973) and Albert Deutsch (1944) have added comparable explanations of the frequent incarceration of women, members of another inferior species who could be institutionalized on the word of a husband of father that they were deranged.

Albert Deutsch (1944) reviewed some of the "scientific" evidence about the anatomical and mental peculiarities of the "Negro." He pointed out that the proslavery forces were comforted by the 1840 census. An attempt was made to count all insane persons and idiots. This count was reported separately in statistical tables for white and colored inhabitants of the various states and regions. The results of this sixth United States census revealed an interesting phenomenon. The rate of idiocy and lunacy among "free Negroes" was some 11 times higher than it was among Negroes who were slaves! In Maine, for example, every fourteenth Negro was afflicted with insanity or a mental defect. In contrast, in Louisiana, where slavery was firmly entrenched, only one Negro in 4310 was so afflicted!

Southern Senator John C. Calhoun spoke eloquently on the floor of Congress:

> Here is proof of the necessity of slavery. The African is incapable of self care and sinks into lunacy under the burden of freedom. It is a mercy to him to give him a guardianship and protection from mental death. (Deutsch, 1944, p. 473)

It is to his eternal credit that psychiatrist Edward Jarvis, studying the 1840 census while bedfast with a broken leg, found many discrepancies in the data and published a criticism of the census. He questioned the accuracy of the figures about blacks, but his criticism was ignored or rejected by Calhoun and his group in the Senate. Jarvis, the leading psychiatrist at the time, pointed out that:

Slavery is more than 10-fold more favorable to mental health than freedom. . . the slaves are consoled with the assurance that although another man's will governs them . . . their minds are not bound with insane delusions, nor crushed in idiocy, as are those of their brethren who govern themselves . . . The apparent exemption of the slaves from one of the most terrible disorders that has visited humanity and the 10-fold inability of the free black to do the same, may become not only a fundamental principle in medical science but also one of the elementary principles in political economy. (Jarvis, 1844, pp. 74–75)

These errors indeed found their way into the mass media and into the psychiatric literature. The *American Journal of Insanity* in 1851 asked, "Who would believe, without the fact in black and white, before his eyes, that *every 14th* colored person in the State of Maine is an idiot or lunatic?" (italics in original; cited in Deutsch, 1944, p. 478).

Despite his admirable efforts at correcting the census figures Jarvis was not immune to the defect model. In his classic study of *Idiocy and Lunacy in Massachusetts*, (1855) he obtained names of all idiots and lunatics from the town clerks throughout the state and constructed detailed tables for his epidemiological study. After poring over these figures, he reports that "we find that the pauper class furnishes, in ratio of its numbers, 64 times as many cases of insanity as the independent class" (pp. 52–53). Reviewing other studies from England and Wales, he concluded that the proportion of lunacy among their poor was about 40 times greater than those not supported by public charity. He defines the intimate connection between poverty and lunacy:

In this connection it is worthwhile to look somewhat at the nature of poverty, its origin, and its relation to man and to society. It is usually considered as a single outward circumstance—the absence of worldly goods; but this want is a mere incident in this condition—only one of its manifestations.

Poverty is an inward principle, enrooted deeply within the man, and running through all his elements; it reaches his body, his health, his intellect and his moral powers as well as his estate . . . hence we find that, among those whom the world calls poor, there is less vital force, a lower tone of life, more ill health, more weakness, more early death, a diminished longevity. There are also less self-respect, ambition and hope, more idocy [sic] and insanity, and more crime, than among the independent. (p. 52)

He found, as I noted earlier, that it was the Irish who supplied the largest proportion of insane, paupers, and idiots, and he found that they have "greater irritability, are more readily disturbed" and "unquestionably much of their insanity is due to their intemperance, to which the Irish seem to be peculiarly prone" (p. 62).

In summarizing his findings, Jarvis argued that persons placed in institutions for the insane should be with members of their own social class, not mixed indiscriminately—rich and poor, native-born and foreign. He argues at some length for separate state hospitals for "State paupers."

The underlying fatal flaw or defect that afflicts the pauper group, the inferior classes, cultures, and races, and women was used not only to explain higher rates of feeblemindedness and insanity in these groups but also as an excuse to the subjugate and exploit these peoples. Indeed this belief in defect, enthusiastically supported by both psychiatry and psychology throughout the history of our fields, actually led to laws providing for mass programs of sterilization, and even to malign neglect and extermination. Perhaps these words are too strong for the sensitivities of delicate defenders of the purity of our sciences. Let us see if they are justified.

In recent decades two major streams have mixed within American psychiatry. The sickness or defect explanation for psychosis, and the requirement of medical training for the practice of psychoanalysis, have made allies of the "organic" psychiatrists and the "analytic" psychiatrists and have led to the inevitable medical domination of intervention at both levels of disturbance (psychosis and neurosis). The greatest perpetrators of evil in our society are not masked desperados planning the Great Train Robbery, they are manicured and talcumed pillars of their church and society, respected and admired by their community. They rarely see their victims, and may not even be conscious of the evil they do as they make abstract decisions, manipulate budgets, and protect and enhance the affluence of themselves and their peers. They use the ideologies which support the Establishment, in economics, in social and political philosophy, and in explaining dehumanization and emotional distress.

The illness model of mental disturbance is *evil*. It restricts the field of therapy to a small elite band by setting artifically high, nonfunctional, educational criteria for helpers. If one works directly with *sick patients*, then one must have prestigious training and high status. It demands that every person receiving help be given a medical diagnosis—a damaging label that can be a self-ful-filling prophecy and that may be a life-long Scarlet Letter. It ensures that the large sums of money that a trusting society thinks it is appropriating for the relief of human suffering wind up in the pockets of a small and powerful elite group whose under-lying purpose is to support the status quo. It denigrates and ridicules efforts at prevention that suggest the importance of social change and competence building.

The medical model has other faults. It focuses our attention on one-to-one patchwork symptom reduction as the best way to help. Finding ways to prevent cancer would destroy one of the major American growth industries! Accepted epidemiological doctrine says that no mass disorders afflicting humankind have even been eliminated with one-to-one intervention with afflicted persons. In the case of genuine diseases the principle always operates. Smallpox, typhoid fever, polio, and measles were not dealt with successfully by training enough physicians to treat sufferers individually. These scourges afflicting humankind were brought under control by discovering their causes and by effective efforts at primary prevention. An analogy can be drawn with emotional problems. They are so common, so damaging to effec-tive living, and so endemic that we cannot expect to have enough professional people to intervene with each disturbed person on a one-to-one basis; rather we ought to devote our efforts to docu-menting the social origins of psychopathology and to making the social changes necessary to reduce the incidence of these problems, and to increase the competency of people to deal with problems in living. The defect model diverts our attention from the social origins of disturbance and it camouflages the need for radical social change.

I have another complaint about psychiatry and the medical model; it, too, relates to prevention. One of the several major myths that has been promulgated with great intensity in recent years has it that the deinstitutionalization of persons who have been locked for years in the state hospitals is a result of dramatic discoveries in psychiatry and improvements in the field of psycho-tropic medication. This is unmitigated nonsense, but it affects our attitudes about prevention.

If the decarceration of hundreds of thousands of inmates of mental hospitals has *not* been the result of the effectiveness of the new psychotropic drugs, then what *has* led to it? Scull (1977) gives the answer with devastating clarity: it is *cheaper for the states*. With the gradual shift in the cost of public welfare to the Federal Government, the states, particularly the conservative administrations of certain states, discovered that it is far less expensive to get people out of mental hospitals that are supported by state monies and into communities where they can be sup-ported on medicare, daycare, and the welfare roles. No matter that these poor unfortunates are herded into the poverty ghettos of the city slums, where they are preyed on by others. No matter that they must lead lives of terror, subject to the rapaciousness of profiteering group-home and nursing-home operators. In short, the "revolution in the care of the mentally ill" touted by the mass media as a triumph of modern psychiatric and pharma-cological research is little more than a way for the states to cut their losses and shift the burden onto the Federal Government. Scull (1977) points out: "The pervasiveness, intensity, and mutually reinforcing character of the pressures to adopt a policy of decarceration are shown to be intimately connected to the rise of welfare capitalism" (p. 12).

Mechanic (1969) has also shown that the accelerating tendency in England to release mental cases from institutions was observed *before* the introduction of the psychotropic drugs. Scull sum-marizes a number of studies that make it clear "that the tremen-dous change that took place is due largely to alterations in administrative policies" (p. 82). Data on the length of hospitali-zation make it clear that *before* the marketing of chlorapromazine the average duration of stay in mental hospitals in England had already dropped significantly. At the Vermont State Hospital the number of schizophrenics admitted did not essentially vary between 1948 and 1958, but the number of schizophrenics discharged increased four times during this period—*before* drugs were in use!

Scull cites several examples of the nonsense written in support of the position that the new drugs were responsible for decarceration. He reviews studies that underscore the lack of real therapeutic value of the psychotropic drugs for hospitalized psychotics and concludes:

> But if phenothiazines are ineffective for substantial portions of the target population, and if in any event the types of maintenance doses generally prescribed are largely ineffective, how can anyone seriously contend that the advent of drug therapy is the main reason for the decline in mental hospital populations (the more so since the drugs are apparently *least* effective with the groups whose release has been *most* crucial to the running down of mental hospital populations—the old, chronic cases?) (p. 88)

He further describes the recent history of the "massive medical commercial exploitation of new drugs on the basis of flimsy scientific evidence" (p. 89), citing examples of the amphetamines, which have earned untold millions of dollars for the profit-seeking drug companies as a result of their vigorous promotions to and by the medical profession. He describes the comparable exploitation of the psychotropic drugs that have been pushed enthusiastically through physicians and through articles in the popular media on the basis of the thinnest possible evidence of their usefulness and value.

The point of this seeming digression is that it is argued frequently that prevention efforts must await the more careful delineation of the underlying organic causative mechanisms whose existence has been established by the effectiveness of drugs in treating mental conditions. Clearly persons given psychotropic drugs become lethargic and tractable. There is a reduction in the amount of assaultive and other aggressive acting-out behavior in persons under the influence of heavy psychotropic medication. Such persons often lose interest in their surroundings. As the psychotropic drugs became more widely used on the back wards, the use of other forms of physical restraint dropped off. But the drugs are not curative. They do not establish an organic causation.

In another frightening proposal in the frightening world of organic psychiatry the psychopharmocological drugs are being proposed as being useful in altering behavioral deviance in the areas of crime and delinquency (Klerman, 1974). And if that is not enough, consider the suggestion of Brill and Patton (1966), who believe that we are "in urgent need of a mass therapy for conduct and personality disorder, social incapacity, economic dependence, unemployability and vagabondage . . ." (p. 294). They see these conditions as an indication of "the large number of psychiatric casualities whose primary and presenting symptoms are those of gross economic and social incapacity . . ." They observe that "the problems of these people clearly lie within the field of psychopharmacology." These are leaders of American psychiatry speaking! Are we really to treat crime and unemployment with drugs? Who benefits?

It does not seem to me to do violence to the whole complex pharmacologic issue to suggest that many members of the psychiatric profession have become the conscious agents of social control. They dispense drugs that immobilize but do not cure, and they impose chemical restraints on human beings just as inhumanely and barbarously as those who in earlier days chained the insane and the enemies of society in dungeons.

Of all the professions that have been developed to provide for the social control of deviants, psychiatry has been most successful. By allying itself with medicine and by labeling deviants as having *diseases* based on underlying (as yet undiscovered) organic conditions and defects, psychiatry has achieved great social power. Persons judged insane can be deprived of their liberty without a trial, on the basis of psychiatric testimony about their *dangerousness*—even though research evidence has established clearly the unreliability of such a prediction. Stone (1975), a professor of psychiatry and law at Harvard, studied this evidence and concluded:

It can be stated flatly on the basis of my own review of the published material on the prediction of dangerous acts that neither objective actuarial tables nor psychiatric intuition, diagnosis, and psychological testing can claim predictive success when dealing with the traditional population of mental hospitals. (p. 33)

So far I have had some highly critical things to say about psychiatry. Let me give equal time to the evils of psychology. May I commend to your reading Leon Kamin's incisive book *The Science and Politics of IQ* (1974). Kamin documents in incredible detail the lengths to which prominent American psychologists were willing to go to prove their tenacious beliefs in the inheritance of a fixed entity called intelligence and in the inferiority of non-Nordics and other groups who were so inferior genetically that they threatened to destroy the existence of the early sturdy stock of the United States. The roster of these psychologists is a Who's Who in American psychology. They were leaders of the APA, and their intellectual offspring are still at work in our most prestigious universities today. Terman (1917), for example, was convinced that Spanish-Indian and Mexican families in the Southwest, and Negroes, had deficient intellects.

Repeatedly we find psychologists arguing that poor people are poor because they are defective and not for environmental reasons. Terman favored eugenic solutions and he observed pointedly that organized charities often allow these feebleminded individuals to survive when otherwise they would not be able to live and reproduce. Henry Goddard (1917) in an invited address at Princeton University spelled out the reasons why workmen with low intelligence did not merit the same living standards as persons on higher mental levels. Robert Yerkes, another president of APA, was active in the eugenics movement. His group educated the Congress and the state legislatures on the importance of passing sterilization laws. Kamin (1974) concludes: "The mental testers pressed upon the Congress scientific IQ data to demonstrate that the 'new immigration' from Southeastern Europe was genetically inferior" (p. 12). The evidence from the mental testers was used to change the pattern of immigration, to shut off, insofar as possible, immigration from Southern and Eastern Europe. Goddard in 1912 went to Ellis Island with his Binet test and administered this and other performance tests to a representative sample of what he referred to as the great mass of average immigrants. He found that 83% of the Jews, 80% of the Hungarians,

79% of the Italians, and 87% or the Russians were 'feeble minded' " (Kamin, 1974, p. 16).

The most convincing evidence came from the psychological testing of soldiers during World War I. Yerkes and his consultant, Edward Lee Thorndike (another later president of APA), were largely involved, although it was a book by Carl Brigham (1923) of Princeton University that brought the evidence to the educated public. Brigham's book, based on the tests of soldiers in World War I, found a clear-cut relationship between the proportion of Nordic, Alpine, and Mediterranean blood and performance on intelligence tests. The book was praised by the chairman of the Senate Committee considering immigration law change. Brigham says, near the end of his "scientific" review:

We must face a possibility of racial admixture here that is infinitely worse than that faced by any European country today, for we are incorporating the negro into our racial stock, while all of Europe is comparatively free from this taint . . . The decline of American intelligence will be more rapid . . . owing to the presence here of the negro. (pp. 209–210)

The foreword of the book was written by APA President Yerkes. (It may be of some historical interest to note that Brigham designed the Scholastic Aptitude Test and served as Secretary of the College Entrance Examining Board. Later he was elected Secretary of APA.)

Because the Army IQ tests had shown that Jews, "Negroes," Poles, Italians, Spanish-Mexicans, French Canadians, and other "brunette nationalities" performed at the feebleminded level in at least 80 percent of the cases, the immigration laws were changed to defend (rather late in the day) the purity of the native-born white Protestants. As Kamin points out, "there is nowhere in the records of the Congressional hearings—nowhere—a single remark by a single representative of the psychological profession to the effect that the results of the Army testing program were in any way being abused or misinterpreted" (p. 24). Indeed the Army testing program was officially organized by the American Psychological Association and its then current President Robert Yerkes.

Kamin points to the interesting parallel between the statements made about the Italians by Pintner in his 1923 text *Intelligence*

Testing and the statements made today about blacks. Jensen (1969) argues that "Negroes" average about one standard deviation (15 IQ points) below the average of the white population. Is it not highly probable that this finding is as valid as the earlier observations by psychologists that 83 percent of Jewish immigrants were feebleminded or that the average IQ of the Italian was 84?

The most frightening thing about all of this was the sober and owlish assurance given by these early psychologists that they were presenting scientific facts. They had convincing evidence they said, that intelligence was a fixed entity, that it was inherited, and that certain ethnic and racial groups were genetically inferior. They appear to have been totally unconscious of their biases and prejudices, and that these biases preceded their collection and interpretation of data from the testing of World War I soldiers. Brigham's book in particular was not criticized for the obvious fact that the correlation was strong between intelligence and the length of time that the persons tested and their forebears had been part of mainstream American culture.

The Army Alpha test administered during World War I contained, for example, a multiple choice question asking the name of the Brooklyn Baseball Club, another for the name of the company that manufactures revolvers in the United States, and many similar questions. Failure to answer them by immigrant Jews and Italians meant that they had defective genes for intelligence. Why did no one point out the obvious fact that the higher scoring groups had had time to become acculturated to the motivations, language, facts, and values of the dominant American society? Are our contemporary psychologists as blinded by *their* values? And who benefits?

The Jensen position is a modern version. It is antithetical to a competency model. Jensen's monograph (1969) argued that compensatory education may be considered a failure. For him, some people simply do not have it. He acknowledges that his conclusion, if true, amounts to a death sentence for the ideal of egalitarianism, a powerful influence in contemporary Western society. He says:

There is an increasing realization among students of the psychology of the disadvantaged that the discrepancy in their average performance cannot be completely or directly attributed to discrimination or inequalities in education. It seems not unreasonable, in view of the fact that intelligence variation has a large genetic component, to hypothesize that genetic factors may play a part in this picture. But such an hypothesis is anathema to many social scientists. The idea that the lower average intelligence and scholastic performance of Negroes could involve, not only environmental, but also genetic, factors has indeed been strongly denounced e.g., Pettigrew (1964). But it has been neither contradicted nor discredited by evidence.

The fact that a reasonable hypothesis has not been rigorously proved does not mean that it should be summarily dismissed. It only means that we need more appropriate research for putting it to the test. *I believe such definitive research is entirely possible but has not yet been done.* (Italics added; p. 82)

These paragraphs bear careful study. What Jensen is saying is that there are hints and clues that support the position that there are differences in intelligence between the races that are due to genetic factors. But he makes it clear that definite scientific evidence in support of this hypothesis has not yet been accumulated. He urges more research on the question. Yet having disposed of this scientifically necessary qualification, he goes on to draw conclusions and make recommendations for changes in social policy as if the difference had been scientifically established. In a truly scientific approach one never rejects the null hypothesis until the evidence is in, and then only in terms of stated probability limits. The psychologists referred to seem to be rejecting the null hypothesis (that there are no differences between races that cannot be accounted for by environmental differences) but with no real certainty. This is a cardinal scientific sin.

The organic model of retardation, like the organic model of "mental illness" is contradicted by a great many facts. The first of these is that it is very very hard to find "mildly retarded" children before schooling begins. Frequently someone decides to do early intervention with mildly retarded preschoolers in order to see if such efforts can reduce the child's later learning problems in school. In most efforts of this sort it turns out to be impossible to locate "mildly retarded" preschoolers. If one asks pediatricians in public clinics, or faimly doctors, or public health nurses, all of these professionals can identify the more seriously retarded children in the community. But no one knows (with reliable knowledge) who the mildly retarded are. So researchers must work with groups of "high risk" children—say, all the children of mothers with low IQs—to find *some* children who will receive the label when they get to school.

It has also been observed that the IQs of inner city children often decline while they are in school, and they wind up being called "mildly retarded" when they get to junior high, or high school—having gone through regular classes in elementary school. Lane and Albee (1970) found that inner-city school children tested as part of a routine group testing program in the Cleveland schools showed a decline from second to sixth grade that averaged more than 10 points! These children were in the normal range in second grade and were at the borderline or mildly retarded level four or five years later. Obviously this had to be *pseudo-retardation*.

Jane Mercer (1973) has reported a careful study of the social role performance of children with IQs below 69 in the schools of Riverside, California. She compared Anglo (white middle class) children with black children and Mexican-American children. Basically she found that the Anglo children called *educable mentally retarded* (EMR) were failing in their social roles. Children from the two other ethnic groups classified as EMR were *not* failing socially. Most important, she found a low correlation between behavior described as adaptive or competent, and measured intelligence. Sixty percent of the Chicano (Mexican-American) children who had "failed" their intelligence test were able to pass a measure of good adaptive behavior. They were competent. Ninety percent of the black children in this same EMR group were also able to pass a measure of adaptive behavior. Mercer suggests that the educable mentally retarded should be divided into three groups. The first group would include those children damaged by identifiable organic factors (a relatively small group); the second would be those retarded because of the operation of polygenic inheritance (a large group); the third would be those who were culturally different from the norm. It is in this third group that objective measures of intelligence and objective measures of adaptive competent behavior do not agree. She found that at least half of the Mexican-American adults who might have been classed as mentally retarded in school were leading effective competent lives—they had married, were gainfully employed, and were adapting successfully to their environment.

Women do as well on intelligence tests as men. Those who argue that tests are color blind and class blind and that therefore they open up opportunities for everyone must face the fact that women are paid consistently less than men in the same jobs. Because roadblocks are erected against women in a great number of occupations, women who do succeed in these jobs are usually better qualified intellectually than men in the same jobs; yet the women's income is lower. Obviously factors other than test scores are used to establish pay scales. When it suits the purpose of the employer to use tests to discriminate against minority groups, tests are used—"just not qualified for the intellectual demands of the job." When women do well on the tests, some other basis for discrimination is found.

There is a common pervasive value assumption underlying certain common psychiatric and psychological explanations of the conditions once called *lunacy* and *idiocy* and now referred to as mental illness and mental retardation. This widely held assumption holds that persons who are not members of the middle and upper class groups are biologically inferior and, further, that higher rates of idiocy and lunacy found in these inferior groups are the results of constitutional defect. The defect (or fatal flaw) is not limited, however, to members of these inferior races and cultures. It also applies to women. Similarly, appropriate "effective treatment" goes largely to affluent white males—the elect. Lest this accusation be regarded as having no more than historical relevance, we need only look at the report of the latest President's Commission on Mental Health (Albee, 1978) to see how our underlying values limit appropriate high-quality "treatment" to affluent males.

In a review, Albee (1978) says the following:

Who are the underserved and unserved? They are described in several different places in the Commission's report. They include children, adolescents and the elderly—all of whom are identified repeatedly as underserved. These three groups together represent "more than half" of the nation's population.

Then there are the minority groups that include 22 million black Americans, 12 million Hispanic Americans, 3 million Asian and Pacific Island Americans, and 1 million American Indians and Alaska natives. All of these groups are underserved or, in many instances, inappropriately served by persons insensitive to cultural differences or incompetent in appropriate languages. While clearly these identified groups of 38 million persons overlap somewhat with the earlier groups identified as underserved we are not yet at the end of the statistical complexities. Five million seasonal and migrant farm workers are largely excluded from mental health care. Elsewhere we discover that women also often do not receive appropriate care in the mental health system. Neither do persons who live in rural America, or in small towns, or in the poor sections of American cities. Neither do 10 million persons with alcohol-related problems, nor an unspecified number of persons who misuse psychoactive drugs, nor the very large number of children and parents involved in child abuse nor 2 million children with severe learning disabilities, nor 40 million physically handicapped Americans, nor 6 million persons who are mentally retarded. While the Commission made some very brave statements about the recent improvements in the availability of mental health care in this society, it seems clear that this improved care must have been available largely to those groups not identified as being underserved—they could only be white educated males living in the affluent sections and suburbs of major American cities. (p. 550)

The model we adopt affects directly the kind of people we help and the kind of institutions we develop for intervention and prevention. These in turn dictate the kind of people we use to deliver care. With a social-developmental model focused on social reform and competence building, our state hospitals and public clinics would be replaced by social intervention centers, largely staffed by people at the bachelor's level—more like special education teachers and social welfare workers, potentially available in vastly greater supply than psychologists and psychiatrists. For prevention, people like ourselves would be needed as teachers, researchers, and especially as radical social activists proselytizing for changes in our society to make it more supportive, less dehumanized.

The massive deterioration of the fabric of industrial society and its institutions results in a complex tangle of pathology which includes especially the destruction of the emotional integrity of the family. Let me emphasize something that you already know very well. Many significant research breakthroughs have already been made. Many of the discoveries are already in. We know, for example, that the emotional climate that surrounds the infant and young child is of critical importance in determining his or her future—including the kind, the severity, and perhaps even the biological concomitants of later disturbance.

Such knowledge is dangerous. We usually shut our eyes to its implications. We go on trying to fix up damaged adults in one-to-one relationships when a more proper professional function would be to spend a considerable portion of our energies trying to fix up our society in ways that will increase the strength and stability of the family, thereby affecting positively the mental health of generations to come.

Most efforts at prevention focus on the forces that have produced disturbance. Another approach for investigators is to try to define and measure "adaptive potential." This approach argues that certain individuals develop highly skilled patterns of competent adaptation to a wide range of situations. Offer and Sabshin (1963) did a study of adolescents without gross psychopathology—they all showed a high level of mastery of developmental tasks and effective coping skills in their relationships with others. Grinker, Grinker, and Timberlake (1962) studied mentally healthy young males and found that "homoclites" (optimally adjusted men) tended to be self-confident goal-seekers with a strong sense of self-worth, warm family relationships, and an action orientation. This model would suggest that preventive efforts be focused on the development and competence and coping skills in contrast with the more life-history oriented model that focuses on the elimination of pathological experiences. Obviously the two models are not separate and even complement each other.

Poser (1970) has discussed a behavioral model for prevention. This approach focuses attention on the role of learning processes in the development of adaptive and maladaptive behavior. The approach suggests that specific learning experiences can be identified and that behavioral approaches effective in leading to behavioral change can also be identified. Some persons may actively learn to behave in a maladaptive way, while others may passively learn, through modeling ineffective social and interpersonal skills. Both groups are then more vulnerable to later stress situations and so are at higher psychological risk. This approach stresses more careful delineation of specific behavioral problems and draws heavily on the concepts of behavioral psychology.

Other examples in this area include the work of Seligman (1975), whose study of learned helplessness has had such a widespread impact. He suggests that giving individuals early experience with stress situations that they can learn to control may reduce their susceptibility to later feelings of helplessness in uncontrollable aversive situations. Suinn, Jorgensen, Stewart, and McGuirk (1971) gave groups "anxiety management training," and Meichenbaum (1975) used a cognition-training procedure that he called "stress inoculation" as a defense against later anxiety. All of these approaches involve some form of practice in the management of stress so as to increase the person's ability to deal competently with later stress.

Others in this volume are concerned at greater length with the issue of competence. I remind you that competent persons often are turned into incompetent persons as a result of the operation of social and economic forces outside of their control. Forcing persons into an incompetent role or life style when in fact they are competent in another role or life style has to be a major source of stress contributing to emotional disturbances and other forms of psychopathology. I will cite two examples:

In many parts of the United States, particularly in Southern states, laws are *written* in such a way that competent black farmers can be forced off the land they have long regarded as their own, land that has been in their family for several generations. There is a proper legal mechanism involved. In the past, black farmers have often died without a will, and their land has been inherited, share and share alike, by children and/or other relatives. After two or three such generations the legal title to the land is so clouded that persons and corporations coveting the land (the value of which may be increasing rapidly) can use any of several stratagems to force a Sheriff's sale. As a result, many competent black farmers and their families are being forced out of a way of life in which they are self-respecting and self-supporting into cities where they have few salable skills and where they are forced to become part of the welfare roll. Critics of the "growing welfare burden" do all sorts of dehumanizing things to add to the stresses placed on these families, with resulting emotional disturbance, crime, delinquency, and premature pregnancy.

Here is a second example. Impoverished women throughout our society, and especially throughout the third world, are being encouraged to feed their infants with powdered formula in bottles. Propaganda and social pressure for bottle-feeding by women who are perfectly competent to breast feed their infants is fostered and augmented by the formula manufacturing companies, who often have arrangements with local physicians and governmental health educator officials. These give new mothers free samples of powdered infant formula that last long enough for the mother's breast milk to dry up, after which she is then obligated to pay a significant portion of the family income for the formula. In areas where water supplies are contaminated, infants often receive disease-laden formula, or they are given inadequate quantities of the powdered milk as their mothers seek to stretch the formula because of its excessive cost. As a consequence, thousands of infants are failing to thrive, dying, or not developing proper growth of the central nervous system. A major source of stress, of course, is the sickness and death of these infants. Again we see competent people turned into incompetent people as a result of social pressures and economic manipulation.

Many serious, sober, and far-from-radical observers today believe the problem at the heart of our social malaise is the primacy of corporate profits over long-range planning for the public good. Short-run success is all that is important to the mindless corporation. In pursuit of these immediate rewards our environment is devastated, our people are brainwashed into becoming mindless consumers or thrill-seeking robots, and the pleasures of human contact have been subordinated to the pleasures of material consumption.

One of the most serious mental health problems of any industrial society, and perhaps particularly the uncontrolled, unplanned, devil-take-the-hindmost conglomerate-corporation industrial society, is the lack of joy in work. Most industrial jobs, whether on the assembly line or in management have become so monotonous, boring, and meaningless as to throw an intolerable load on people's leisure time activities and on conspicuous consumption as a source of satisfaction. Eric Fromm (1972) suggests that one of the most important sources of aggression today is to be found in persons with what he terms a "bored character." These individuals, who represent a very large portion of our adult society, lack any profound interest in people or in life as a consequence of their feelings of powerlessness. Fromm feels that many people have become controlled by meaningless jobs, and they fall under extreme social pressure to consume worthless and meaningless goods. People having nothing else to do have become compulsive consumers, using up the enormous outpouring of the industrial machine.

One of the most fearsome aspects of this situation is the seeming hopelessness of the system ever changing itself. Enormous corporations and conglomerates defy government control. The cost of running for federal office has grown to the point where successful candidates must be supported by these giant corporate powers in order to be elected. The conglomerates and cartels are more powerful than governments, and power structure extends around the earth.

Blame is one of the most useless human activities. I do not propose to blame solely the corporations or the people who run them for the dehumanization that is a prominent part of the conglomerate society. But we must all point to them as a major source of our pollution, environmental and human, and then seek, coldly and rationally, to change the system.

Back in the early days of this century, before the psychodynamic-sickness model had assumed its current total primacy, there was little ambiguity among mental health professionals about where evil was to be found. It was clearly recognized that human beings were damaged, dehumanized, and destroyed by the mindless and indifferent forces of free-enterprise-industrialization. And it was clear that social causes of emotional disturbance demanded social action as a remedy.

Jane Addams back in 1910 was merciless in her criticism of professionals who failed to recognize the relationship between industrialization and poverty. She urged those in her own field of social work to come together with "the Radicals" to fight for better social conditions. In her view, social work, to achieve its goals, had to engage in social and political action. It was no accident that the economic reforms and labor legislation proposed in the 1912 platform of Theodore Roosevelt's Bull Moose party read like Jane Addams' program for social action. She was on the platform and seconded his nomination.

When did we switch from an *evil-is-in-the-system* social reform philosophy to the more conservative *evil-is-inside-the-person* individual-treatment philosophy? Probably sometime in the decade of the 1920's. Psychiatry and social work focused on individual need, on psychic determinism, and on the one-to-one intervention method. The early involvement of social workers in social action— storming the citadels of the establishment, organizing the poor, working with the unions, leading and encouraging tenant strikes, gave way to the ascendant psychiatric notion that evil is inside the person, and that if we can get the person across a desk from us, we can somehow patch up the problem. Our training programs all teach this model, which serves as a support for reaction. If evil is inside the person, then we do not need to change anything except the person, and the damaging status quo is left intact.

Let us recognize that these training fictions influence the moral attitudes and ethical values of professional workers, and they in turn significantly influence both the form of intervention and the prevention we choose to use, and the way we are perceived by society. The fundamental professional decision is whether we *represent the client* or whether we *represent the agency*, institution, and society that pays the salary.

The professional worker in the human services fields is faced with severe personal role conflicts which are continuing and inescapable. Each professional worker must decide to whom he or she is responsible, the *Establishment* or the *victim*. Professional workers are overwhelmingly drawn from the middle-class and are notoriously timid about fighting for social change. Middle-class professionals are educated in middle-class colleges and universities and are exposed to an endless indoctrination which rewards conformity and control and punishes extremism and originality. The lock-step system of education from the earliest school years through college and professional training continuously weeds out rebels and deviants so that professionals completing their training are a highly selected group of middle-of-the-roaders. Yet once one begins to work with the emotionally disturbed, the so-called insane, the rebels against the system, the alcoholics, the drug addicts, the juvenile delinquents and criminals, one begins to see that many of these problems are caused by the faults and defects of the economic system. Is this knowledge enough to counteract our years of training in conformity? Is it enough to affect our attitudes toward prevention?

The professional must continuously decide whether he or she is a defender of the established order or must become an advocate for the victims of the established order. Those who opt for the traditional pattern of pinning diagnostic labels on disturbed people and explaining their deviant behavior in terms of a sickness originating in a defective brain or endocrine system or chromosomal defect are clearly defenders of the status quo, particularly in the absence of any compelling evidence for such a defect explanation. This whole approach has been well labeled by William Ryan (1971) as *Blaming the Victim*. The poor are to blame for their poverty, and the insane are to blame for the insanity, and the criminals are to blame for their rebellion.

On the other hand, the professionals who see disturbed people as victims of an exploitative and dehumanizing system are quickly made visible and are themselves labeled as radicals or rebels with emotional problems (probably caused by some internal defect). We need unanimity in these matters, or we will be picked off one by one!

Kenneth B. Clark (1974) has pointed out that "any form of rejection, cruelty and injustice inflicted upon any group of human beings by any group of human beings *dehumanizes* the victims overtly and in more subtle ways dehumanizes the perpetrators" (p. 144). He called on psychology to stop avoiding the moral and survival problems of the human race and try to enhance the human capacity for creativity and progress. He argued that it is imperative for psychology to seek to control the destructive forces within society.

Professionally, we also know that a person with the strongest hunger for power, with power needs that lead to an insatiable drive for authority and control over others, is not ordinarily the most empathic person. If those who avidly seek positions of power are drawn from the more neurotic, then perhaps we should apply what we know about intervention in neurosis (which is to make the unconscious conflicts conscious). This suggests that we continue to interpret to political leaders the causes of their most dehumanizing actions, and that we seek to secure whatever legal checks and balances we can to minimize the damage they do to those who cannot help or protect themselves.

Professionally, we also know something about the development of empathy, that feeling we experience when we put ourselves in the place of others. Those with a mature and well developed conscience are capable of empathy. Empathy is the source of most humanistic actions and concerns. Yet we know, too, that empathy is most likely to appear when specific, real, and concrete objects for empathy are clearly perceivable. Many bomber pilots found it hard to empathize with abstract people who might or might not have been in jungle villages thousands of feet below their planes. Neither can polluters feel empathy for unknown people who might be damaged hundreds of miles distant, or several generations hence. Knowing this, it seems to me that we must find ways to make known the sufferings of people—those who are the victims of human actions and policies.

By all of this I am suggesting that we should consider assuming more active efforts to change society. I make this suggestion with some trepidation because I anticipate protest from those who will point to our lack of enough firm knowledge, at the grandiosity implicit in this proposal, and at the inappropriateness of small and precious groups attempting such a formidable task. But our social problems are all human problems, and we are the experts on those.

We must do more than simply make our knowledge available to the decision-makers of our society. As ethical social scientists, we must advocate, assert, urge, and proselytize. Each of us must decide how he or she can best contribute to the reduction of the dehumanizing forces in our society and the enhancement of the human competence that is possible. But we must first agree that the problem is in the system, not in the victim.

REFERENCES

Albee, G. W. The protestant ethic, sex, and psychotherapy. *American Psychologist*, 1977, *32*, 150–161.

Albee, G. W. A manifesto for a fourth mental health resolution? A review of the Report of the President's Commission on mental health, 1978. *Contemporary Psychology*, 1978, *23*, 549–551.

Brigham, C. C. *A study of American intelligence.* Princeton: Princeton University Press, 1923.

Brill, H. and Patton, R. E. Psychopharmacology and the current revolution in mental health services. In *Proceedings of the Fourth World Congress of Psychiatry*, Amsterdam: Excerpta Medica Foundation, 1966.

Carstairs, G. M. Preventive psychiatry—is there such a thing? *Journal of Mental Science*, 1958, *104*, 63–71.

Chesler, P. *Women and madness.* New York: Avon Books, 1973.

Clark, K. B. *Pathos of power.* New York: Harper and Row, 1974.

Deutsch, A. The first U.S. census of the insane (1840) and its use as pro-slavery propaganda. *Bulletin of the History of Medicine*, 1944, *15*, 469–482.

Eisenberg, L. Primary prevention and early detection in mental illness. *Bulletin of the New York Academy of Medicine*, 1975, *51*, 118–129.

Fromm, E. Boredom and aggression. *The New York Times Magazine*, February 27, 1972, pp. 80, 81, 84, 85.

Goddard, H. H. Mental tests and the immigrant. *Journal of Delinquency*, 1917, *2*, 271.

Grinker, R. R., Sr., Grinker, R. R., Jr., and Timberlake, J. A. Study of "mentally healthy" young males (homoclites). *Archives of General Psychiatry*, 1962, *6*, 405–410.

Henderson, J. Community tranference review: With notes on the clinic-community interface. *Journal of the American Academy of Psychoanalysis*, 1974, *2*, 113–128.

Henderson, J. Object relations and a new social psychiatry: The illusion of primary prevention. *Bulletin of the Menninger Clinic*, 1975, *39*, 233–245.

Jarvis, E. *Idiocy and lunacy in Massachusetts. Report of the commission on lunacy.* Boston: William White, Printer to the State, 1855. (reprinted Cambridge: Harvard University Press, 1971).

Jenson, A. R. How much can we boost I.Q. and scholastic achievement? *Harvard Educational Review Monograph*, 1969, *39*(1), 1–123.

Joint Commission on Mental Illness and Health. *Action for mental health.* New York: Basic Books, 1961.

Kamin, L. *The science and politics of I.Q.* Potomac, Md.: Lawrence Erlbaum Associates, 1974.

Klerman, G. Psychotropic drugs as therapeutic agents. *Hastings Center Studies*, 1974, *2*, 81–93.

Lane, E. A., and Albee, G. W. Intellectual antecedents of schizophrenia. In M. Roff and D. Ricks (Eds.), *Life history research in psychopathology.* Minneapolis: University of Minnesota Press, 1970.

Mechanic, D. *Mental health and social policy*. Englewood Cliffs, N.J.: Prentice-Hall, 1969.

Meichenbaum, D. Self-instructional methods. In F. H. Kanfer and A. P. Goldstein (Eds.), *Helping people change*. New York: Pergamon, 1975.

Mercer, J. *Labeling the mentally retarded*. Berkeley: University of California Press, 1973.

Offer, D., and Sabshin, M. The psychiatrist and the normal adolescent. *American Medical Association Archives of General Psychiatry*, 1963, *60*, 427–432.

Pettigrew, T. *A profile of the Negro American*. Princeton: Van Nostrand, 1964.

Pintner, R. *Intelligence testing: Methods and results*. New York: Holt, 1923.

Poser, E. G. Toward a theory of behavioral prophylaxis. *Journal of Behavioral Therapy and Experimental Psychiatry*, 1970, *1*, 39–43.

Ryan, W. *Blaming the victim*. New York: Pantheon Books, 1971.

Scull, A. *Decarceration*. Englewood Cliffs, N.J.: Prentice-Hall, 1977.

Seligman, M. *Helplessness: On depression, development, and death*. San Francisco: Freeman, 1975.

Stone, A. A. *Mental health and the law: A system in transition*. DHEW Publication No. (ADM) 76–176. Washington, D.C.: U.S. Government Printing Office, 1975.

Suinn, R. M., Jorgensen, G. T., Stewart, S. S., and McGuirk, F. D. Fears as attitudes: Experimental reduction of fear through reinforcement. *Journal of Abnormal Psychology*, 1971, *78*, 272–279.

Terman, L. S. Feeble-minded children in the public schools of California. *School and Society*, 1917, *5*, 161–165.

4

Promoting Competence and Enhancing Development through Life Development Intervention

STEVEN J. DANISH and
ANTHONY R. D'AUGELLI

INTRODUCTION

Paradigms in the sciences die hard, but paradigms in the human services die even harder. In the mental health field recent developments in both strategies for behavior change and methods for service delivery have created an impression of rapid, indeed revolutionary, change. In addition, the ever-increasing literature on prevention appears to document a needed shift in focus from a remediative model whose long-term impact has been uncertain to a preventive model in which psychosocial distress is averted. Despite the flurry of activity, however, the most basic assumption of the mental health model—namely, the notion that psychological normality exists and that deviations from normality are worthy of either treatment or prevention—remains essentially unchanged. Current strategies and delivery systems, no matter how sophisticated, make this basic assumption.

In this chapter, we will present a new paradigm that can direct the future development of mental health services. In particular, the approach presented will be offered as an alternative to primary prevention, a concept with much intuitive appeal which has yet to be consistently operationalized. The promotion of competence through life development intervention, in contrast to the remedial or preventive model, is explicitly based on theories of human development (Baltes and Danish, 1980). Such theories, often implicit in mental health activities, suggest different timing for intervention, goals for intervention, and processes for intervention. There-

We owe thanks to Paul Baltes, Carol Nowak, and Michael Symer for identifying a number of issues presented here, and to Margaret Plantz and Rachel Pruchno for their constructive comments.

fore, before describing our model of intervention, we will elaborate our conceptual framework and the theory of development that guides the framework.

PRIMARY PREVENTION AND HUMAN DEVELOPMENT

What is Primary Prevention?

Emory Cowen (1977*b*), in his own inimitable style, has recently revealed primary prevention to be a confusing concept which most psychologists cannot precisely define, let alone practice. Psychologists attending Cowen's Division 27 presidential address were asked to name the most important psychological contribution to primary prevention in mental health and overwhelmingly chose Cowen's Primary Mental Health Project (1975). Though Cowen maintains that the choice of his own work by attendees was confounded by demand characteristics, the fact that a *secondary* prevention project was such a popular choice leads Cowen to conclude that primary prevention is a vague concept fired by idealism only. He later proposed some "baby steps" that might be taken toward beginning primary prevention activities (Cowen, 1977*a*). Broskowski and Baker (1974), Goldston (1977), and Kessler and Albee (1975), among others, have also raised conceptual questions about primary prevention. Despite the confusions, a general definition is possible. Primary prevention consists of

activities directed toward specifically identified vulnerable high risk groups within the community who have not been labeled psychiatrically ill and for whom measures can be undertaken to avoid the onset of emotional disturbance and/or to enhance their level of positive mental health. Programs for the promotion of mental health are primarily educational rather than clinical in conception and operation, their ultimate goal being to increase people's capacities for dealing with crises and for taking steps to improve their own lives. (Goldston, 1977, p. 20)

In actual mental health settings, the promise of primary prevention, so appealing in this definition, is overwhelmed by the politics of service delivery. Human service agencies, generally inundated by direct service demands, find the allocation of funds to primary prevention problematic. This partly reflects the lack of supportive funding agencies for preventive activities. Such support is not forthcoming because the potential outcomes are so uncertain. Accountability is more difficult in the realm of prevention since the acid test of such programming is the nonoccurrence of cases of psychopathology. Primary prevention is analogous to the train passenger who blows a whistle every 15 minutes. When asked why he blows the whistle, he states that it is to keep away the elephants. When the inquirer replies, "What elephants?", he retorts: "See how effective I am!" Preventive activities are an investment in which future payoffs are to a great degree unpredictable. Such investment seems to compare poorly to the allocation of resources to distressed people whose problems can be addressed immediately and with some benefit.

What Is Psychopathology as It Relates to Primary Prevention?

Psychopathology is the study of mental disorder and illness. It is not our intent to engage in a argument of what is or is not mental illness. It is useful to consider, however, that the concept of psychopathology focuses on maladjustment, maladaption, and misery, in other words, problematic deviations from normality. Such deviations in mental health are difficult to define without controversy, since there are few if any unambiguous norms for human behavior. Nevertheless, "mental health" is often operationally defined as the absence of "mental illness." Prevention activities become enmeshed in this issue, since they strive to prevent mental illness without specification of the dimensions of mental health. Since mental health professionals are so well known for seeing "mental illness" or "mental illness"—producing events behind every tree, it is surprising that primary prevention seems like crying wolf. Although spokespersons for primary prevention support notions of increasing "wellness" (Bower, 1972; Goldston, 1977) or promoting mental health, behavioral referents for these constructs are not provided. In short, in its systemic reliance on psychopathology, the concept of prevention has a fatal flaw. The notion is based on a public health model of disease and illness prevention. Prevention is a viable model for physical health endeavors, since indices of normal functioning do exist, but the lack of clear indices of psychological "health" suggests that it has limited usefulness in the mental health area. In contrast to prevention as the goal of a mental health system, we propose *the enhancement of human development* as a more constructive goal for the development of mental health intervention programs.

Toward Enhancement of Human Development

Most conceptions of primary prevention focus on problem prevention. Although one cannot prevent problems without implicitly identifying goals, most mental health interventions do not have explicit goals other than to alleviate problems or prevent them from recurring. As such, these interventions assume a homeostatic (Danish, 1977) or equilibrium (Riegel, 1975*b*) model of human functioning. In other words, the goal of these interventions is a return to the conditions existing prior to the problem. From this perspective, human development is a steady line interrupted by crisis points. These crises can vary in duration, intensity, and severity, and some are likely to result in psychopathology. The return to a steady line indicates successful problem resolution or coping. Primary prevention theoretically protects an individual from experiencing these crisis periods in such a way that debilitating psychological distress results.

An alternative model of human development must have at least two characteristics. The first is a model of behavior which presupposes continuous growth and change. One such model is a life-span human development orientation. This orientation has been characterized by Baltes (1973) and Danish (1977) as one which:

(1) incorporates statements about desirable goals or end-states of behavior;

(2) focuses on sequential change;

(3) emphasizes techniques of optimization;

(4) considers the individual or system as an integrative bio-psychosocial unit (Ford, 1974) and therefore is amenable to a multidisciplinary focus; and

(5) views individuals or systems as developing in a changing biocultural context.

The second characteristic of an alternative model is that crises are not considered by definition pathological or problematic. Part of the problem lies in the language used to describe crisis. Riegel described the dilemma of labeling and conceptualizing a new model:

> Searching through my vocabulary, I thought for a while that terms like "developmental leaps," "critical choice points," or "existential challenges" might somewhat better describe the condition under concern. Failing to convince myself of the preference for these substitutions, I began to realize that it would be necessary to devote (time) to an analysis of the concept of crisis and its underlying philosophical model and ideology. The concept of crisis is antithetically connected with those of equilibrium, stability, consonance, and balance. The notion of equilibrium as a desirable goal has thoroughly penetrated the thinking of behavioral and social scientists and defines crisis in a negative manner. (1975*a*, p. 100)

A more appropriate view is that growth is preceded by a state or imbalance or crisis which serves as the basis for future development. In fact, without crises, development is not possible. Caplan (1964) recognized this quality of crisis in arguing that the way crises are resolved has a major impact on their ultimate role in mental health. In striving to achieve stability during crises, the coping process itself can result in the achievement of a qualitatively different "stability." Thus, contrary to the view that crises are destructive, we contend that they may initiate a restructuring process toward further growth (Danish, 1977). If crises can result in either negative or positive outcomes, the goal of intervention is not to prevent crises, but rather to *enhance* or *enrich* individuals' abilities to deal constructively with these events. Enhancement activities would be designed to enable individuals to use crises as opportunities for growth.

Incorporating the notion of enhancement in mental health program development introduces a new conception of paradigm-like dimensions, the optimization of human development. Not only is the medical model finally discarded, but the noble intentions of those espousing the need for primary prevention can find a direct avenue for widespread implementation. To provide a concrete illustration, it is likely that attendance at "parent effectiveness training" groups would drop quickly if they were labeled as "child abuse prevention groups" or, for that matter, "neurotic parents' discussion groups."

To espouse enhancement as a framework calls for an elucidation of a theory of human development that describes "desirable" behavioral functioning. Given the view that enhancement activities provide an opportunity to optimize human functioning, it is necessary to identify end-states or markers for the life course. A heuristic concept, that of critical life events, is helpful in this regard.

A Critical Life Events Conception of Development

The concept of critical life events has become central to the study of adult development. Interest in life events comes from diverse sources, and research in the area has grown rapidly. Two divergent lines of research are important to review. The first is the investigation of stressful life events and subsequent illness (Rahe, 1974) or psychopathology (Dohrenwend and Dohrenwend, 1974). The second area is the use of life events as markers for adult development (Neugarten and Hagestad, 1976; Nowak, 1978). Both areas clarify the linkage between the occurrences of events and their consequences for individuals. This linkage is important because enhancement activities are targeted to this causal chain. Only a very brief review will appear here; for more detail, the reader is referred to Datan and Ginsberg (1975) and Hultsch and Plemons (1979).

1. Stressful life events. Attempts to identify correlates of stress in the form of physical illness and psychopathology have comprised many of the available studies on stressful life events and their concomitants. From this viewpoint, Selye (1956) postulated that psychological stress and physical stress are similar in sequence. In the same tradition, Holmes and Rahe (1967) have quantified psychological stress in terms of the numbers and types of significant life changes in an individual's experience. Rahe, McKean, and Arthur (1967) suggest that the additive effects of such life changes can be serious enough to predict the need for medical attention in the near future. They developed a checklist of Life Change Units scaled according to alterations in life style needed to readjust to a life event. The readjustment may be to a positive event (such as marriage or birth of a wanted first child) or a negative event (such as death of a spouse or being fired from a job). From this perspective a negative event does not necessarily require more change than a positive one. Their work has indicated that yearly life-change unit totals correlate positively with the risk of major health problems in the following year.

The Dohrenwends (1973, 1974) have studied the relationship between psychological stress—again, measured by life stress situations, e.g., death of a family member, marital breakdown, job loss—and psychopathology. Dohrenwend (1973) summarizes studies which indicate a positive relationship between exposure to recent stressful life events and psychiatric symptomatology. Although statistically significant, many of the correlations reported between life change events and concomitant distress in these studies are modest. Unfortunately, no normative data are available for the experience of stressful events through the adult years since only cross-sectional data are available.

2. Events as markers of life development. Although the critical life concept is most commonly associated with the stressful life events orientation, its use in the field of adult development has become increasingly significant, for it engenders a conceptual shift from a biological to a social clocking of adult development. Effort has been expended in identifying events as societal markers, checking their occurrence for "correct" or normative timing, placing the event in an individual's social and cultural context, and describing the attitudes and moods of individuals during the events (Neugarten, 1976; Neugarten and Hagestad, 1976; Nowak, 1978). As Neugarten (1976) notes:

> There exists a socially prescribed timetable for the ordering of major life events: a time in the life span when men and women are expected to marry, a time to raise children, a time to retire. The normative pattern is adhered to, more or less consistently, by most persons within a given social group—although the actual occurrences of major life events are influenced by various contingencies and although the norms themselves vary somewhat from one socioeconomic, ethnic, or religious group to another. (p. 16)

She later says:

> The fact that regularities of change through the life cycle are demonstrable along biological, social, and psychological dimensions leads to the question of adaptation and the concept of a normal, expectable life cycle. (p. 18)

When events are a priori defined as debilitatingly stressful, the focus of study has been on the parameters of the event itself, and not on the event within the context of the individual's total development. Events are then less useful as markers along the life course. Nowak (1978) has differentiated between the study of life events as stimuli and the study of the structure of the event. She identifies a number of dimensions that may affect an event's impact: timing, intensity, duration, sequencing, and the degree of interference with other developmental events. When the events are considered within the context of the life course rather than discretely, they become targets for enhancement efforts aimed at optimizing adult development. This is not to imply that everyone encounters each event, or that the events always occur in the same sequence. However, informal norms develop about events and when they are likely to be experienced. Contrasting their own experience with such norms, individuals may expect certain events at certain times and experience dissatisfaction if they are "off time" in experiencing an event (Elder, 1975).

Earlier we noted that a human development orientation must contain desirable goals or end-states of behavior. From the perspective of societal norms, life events serve as markers (Lowenthal and Chiriboga, 1973) to chart adult development. An appropriate set of end-states is the ability to confront the life events successfully regardless of whether they are normative or nonnormative. The intuitive appeal of this approach and the documented stress associated with life events suggests that they are highly appropriate targets for intervention.

ENCOUNTERING CRITICAL LIFE EVENTS

Overview

In previous sections we have stressed that critical life events can have either positive or negative outcomes. This section will review the literature on determinants of the outcomes of life events.

Hultsch and Plemons (1979) have identified three factors which affect an individual's reaction to an event: biological, psychological, and contextual. However, these factors take on different significance depending upon the person's position in the life cycle and the specific event. Thus, authors who have considered certain factors as invariably correlated with a certain kind of outcome may not recognize that a factor which may be a resource for one event may be a deficit in another. For example, Lieberman (1975) reported that older adults who adapted well to new living arrangements tended to be aggressive, irritating, and demanding, behaviors generally not associated with successful life adaptation. A second problem with identifying factors influencing the quality of a response to life event is the difficulty in isolating the effects of individual elements and unraveling dependent from independent variables. Identifying what are resources and what are irrelevant factors, then, is not as clear cut as it seems. Despite the difficulties in partialing out the factors (resources) which influence positive responses to events, to do so is essential, since it may provide guidelines for intervention.

In our review of the work on life events, two factors seem prominent: the individual's past history of responding to events and the individual's social support. These two factors seem consistent with Caplan's (1964) conception of psychosocial "supplies."

Past History of Response to Events

When a stressful life event is encountered, one's history and life style influence the impact of the event. Despite qualitative differences in events, the subjective assessment of threat will decrease with greater experience in dealing with generally complex life situations. For example, Birren (1964) suggests that experience in coping with stressful life events leads to enhanced coping ability in the future. Lawton and Nahemow (1973) propose that an individual's response to an external stressor is dependent on the context of the stressor *and the individual's past history with similar phenomena.* They suggest that experience with similar events increases one's competence, thus providing the capacity to cope successfully with a wider range of environmental demands. In fact, they contend that highly competent individuals may find themselves dissatisfied with low levels of demands, finding moderate or higher levels more challenging. This contention is similar to the concept of optimal discrepancy proposed by Hunt (1961). Atchley (1975) and Janis (1971) propose models similar to Lawton and Nahemow (1973).

In sum, when an individual confronting a critical event, such as loss of a job, bereavement, or marriage, encounters the event with a history of success, the likelihood of a positive outcome increases. The past experience has provided both constructive attitudes about the event and behavioral competencies that were reinforced by the success experience. Because of this, the new event is not perceived as overwhelming because psychosocial resources can be drawn upon. Over the course of the life span, a pattern of successful copings would successively decrease the individual's vulnerability to crises.

The ability of an individual with a past history of effective responses to events to respond well to present events can be partly explained by *intra-individual similarity* in reactions to events. Individuals who respond effectively may recognize the similarity between the event they are presently encountering and both past and future events in their lives. Thus they understand that they have experienced similar situations previously. At a cognitive level, they know they *can* deal with the event. At a behavioral level, they employ a behavioral sequence successful in the past. As such the *psychological* uniqueness of the event becomes deemphasized, and properties common to similar experiences are highlighted. This process avoids internal distress and behavioral disability.

Social Support Systems

The impact of critical life events may also be altered by the quality of the support system available to the individual. Gore (1973) reported that stress associated with unexpected unemployment produced fewer negative consequences for men with highly supportive spouses and friends. In a study of life events and complications during pregnancy, by Nuckolls, Cassel, and Kaplan (1972), support measures such as the marriage relationship, quality of interaction with extended family, and adjustment within the community were examined. The results indicated that while neither the past history of events nor support resources alone predicted ease of pregnancy, women with much event experience and high support had one third the complication rate of women with many events and low support. Adams and Lindemann (1974), Hamburg, Coelho, and Adams (1974), and Maddox (1977) also have pointed out the importance of supportive networks and interpersonal resources for an individual dealing with a life event.

The recognition of the mental health function served by social support underlies the burgeoning self-help and natural caregiving movements. The self-help movement especially capitalizes on the value of support systems and their development (Gartner and Riessman, 1978; Lieberman and Borman, 1976). Indeed, an individual encountering a life event might receive a more useful mental health "service" from a self-help group than from a remedially oriented professional. For example, Riessman (1976), contrasting professional and self-help group treatment processes, has found professional help wanting. In his view, self-help approaches are more consumer-centered, more immediately relevant, demystified, not dispensed in a condescending manner, and nonelitist; they are more directly accountable to the consumer (at least in terms of direct satisfaction) and far less expensive. Regardless of the objective quality of help provided (and not much evidence is available on this point), the support would seem to enable self-help group members to encounter critical life events more effectively. In terms of cognitive structuring alone, such groups strive to relabel problematic behaviors or situations in ways that make coping possible. In addition to avoiding stigmatization, self-help groups encourage the development of group cohesion and a strong group affiliation, and ultimately the espousal of a personal ideology (Back and Taylor, 1976; Blumer, 1969).

Recently, the development of natural care-giving systems has expanded rapidly. These systems have many potential advantages over self-help groups. These advantages will be discussed in a later section.

LIFE DEVELOPMENT TRAINING: A MODEL FOR INTERVENTION

Overview

An intervention model can be derived from the framework developed in the initial sections of the paper. The model must have the following attributes: (1) an enhancement orientation, (2) a central focus on life events, (3) a concern with the experience of encountering a number of life events as a resource to developing competence, and (4) an emphasis on the development of a support system. In the following sections, the model will be detailed in the context of mental health service delivery.

The Present Delivery of Human Services

The current mental health delivery system, based on a problematic paradigm, can be characterized as an overworked, fairly ineffective remedial system. The problems of the system have been duly chronicled elsewhere, but one example is worth noting. In Boston, Ryan (1969) reports, a city with one of the highest concentrations of mental health professionals, most individuals experiencing emotional problems do not receive professional mental health assistance. Ryan found that 150 of every 1000 individuals are experiencing mental health problems and that of this 150, 10 are seen in mental health settings (five in hospitals, four in clinics, and one privately). Of the remaining 140, two fifths are seen by physicians without mental health training. Srole, Langner, Michael, Opler, and Rennie's (1962) Midtown Manhattan survey contains similar findings. Thus in urban settings where professional help is assumedly readily available, most individuals in need of help do not see mental health professionals.

If not even most individuals with "serious problems" worthy of traditional remediation are being seen by professionals, what is happening to individuals undergoing life crises? As mentioned above, such crises may indeed become serious problems. Furthermore, if this pattern of low utilization of professionals exists in urban settings, what is happening in rural areas where professionals are scarce? In other words, if people are not seeing professional helpers, who are they seeing? Warren (1976) in his analysis of community helping in Detroit found neighbors and friends to be the primary source of help. Young, Giles and Plantz (1978) found similar patterns in rural Pennsylvania, where helping is primarily a community activity performed by neighbors and friends. This is true for serious problems, problems of living, or everyday concerns! In conclusion, despite the noble intentions of mental health professionals, most help occurs outside the mental health system through informal social systems. If most helping is done not by professionals but by "natural care-givers," it is essential that the role of these care-givers be maximized. Professionals must avoid suggesting to their communities that such help is ineffective, insufficient, and possibly dangerous. (Restrictive licensure laws may implicitly do this. See Danish and Smyer, 1978.)

Not only does the current pattern of professional helping suggest the need to foster rather than discourage natural care-giving, but it also suggests a reexamination of professional helping. Presently the professional mental health system is like a good smorgasbord restaurant—too many people returning for second and third helpings, not enough people leaving to go home, and large lines waiting to enter. Further, there is a question about how healthy it is. A better alternative is a helping system that enables individuals to learn a system of skills and to obtain other resources so that they can cook for themselves. We are intrigued with a saying which goes something like "Give a person a fish and he/she will eat tonight; Teach a person to fish and he/she will eat forever." Too often helping has short-term goals and may produce dependency on the helper as a friend, supporter, insightful understander, and problem-solver.

Life Development Intervention and Enhancement

Our perspective focuses on the course of adult development using life events as markers. We do not intend, however, that intervention be designed to deal with each life event as it occurs. Not only would this be a prohibitively expensive venture, it also could encourage excessive dependence on human service providers. An alternative that avoids these problems starts with an assumption of significant similarity across life events. Although the *content* of the events is different, the skills, risks, and attitudes necessary to encounter events overlap considerably. For example, the life events of marriage and retirement require different information but call for related skills—making decisions about present and future behaviors, risk taking, and so on.

It is necessary to help individuals recognize the similarity among past, present, and future events. What an individual did to encounter successfully a past event must be recalled. The past success experience can help in the present *if the individual can make the connection between one event and another.* Lazarus (1979) called this anticipatory coping. If the person's past experience was not entirely satisfying, it is worth asking now what he or she might have done to be more effective and *then helping the person make the connection between past and present events.* This *intra-individual similarity* can be a potent factor in helping people to deal with life events. Our perspective, then, is that there are a limited number of generic skills of value in many life events. If the skills are known to an individual, use of these skills will enhance the person's development.

We do not mean to imply that having skills is sufficient to deal effectively with life events. Many individuals lack the necessary information to encounter an event successfully. Currently, much knowledge about life events is provided by mass media: Interpersonal helping as typically defined is not necessary. Rather, the acquisition of knowledge becomes essential, and help becomes defined as information dissemination. *Redbook, Good Housekeeping, Your Erroneous Zones,* and other popular self-help publications all provide information, sometimes very effectively. Another example is a current project to disseminate information about the experiences of people in the second half of life. The information would prepare people for life events encountered in the later years. It would be distributed directly to communities through mass media rather than through the human service network (Danish, Smyer, and Nowak, in press). However, such information efforts do not ensure the acquisition of new behaviors (or skills). As long as there is no assumption that skills to encounter these events will necessarily be learned through reading, mass information dissemination is probably the most effective means of acquiring knowledge.

Clearly knowledge about life events can be disseminated *outside of the professional helping system,* and if skills that accompany the knowledge can be provided, intervention can then proceed more rapidly. The knowledge can be provided via media; generic skills can be taught and used across events. In this way the markers become something one *can prepare for*, and intervention is explicit anticipatory socialization. As one becomes more skillful in encountering each event, encounters with events become opportunities for growth, and the situations (events) become viewed as challenging. *Life Development Intervention* is teaching individuals *planfulness* in dealing with life events. Our end-state, then, is *not* a particular outcome with an event but *the ability to be planful in confronting life events*.

To recapitulate briefly, in our conceptual model individual critical life events can become problems of living if not resolved. If personal goals for any event can be identified, it becomes necessary to determine why goals are not achieved and what the roadblocks to achievement are. We believe only three roadblocks can exist. They are a lack of knowledge, a lack of skill, or an inability to assess the risks involved in changing behavior.

In implementing life development intervention, we subscribe to an educational model of service delivery. Such a model has been described by Danish (1977) and Guerney (Guerney, 1977; Guerney, Guerney, and Stollack 1971/1972; Guerney, Stollack, and Guerney, 1971). The educational model takes the school as its model, and instruction as its method of enhancement (D'Augelli, 1978). The helper acts in a consultative way, working with the individual or group to develop a specific enhancement program or to adapt an existing one. Programs on parenting, marital communication, sexual functioning, and decision-making have been developed using this approach (see Authier, Gustafson, Guerney, and Kasdorf, 1975, for a recent review). What is important here is not the context of the intervention as much as the role of the helper. In other words, not only do we reject a medical-disease orientation for a learning one, but we reject the *clinical treatment model* in favor of a *mass teaching model*.

One way to implement such a model is through training natural caregivers in the delivery of helping services. The authors are currently involved in such a project to enhance the natural helping networks of local communities through life development intervention. The Community Helpers Project* is designed on the

*The Community Helpers Project, headed by T. R. Vallance, S. J. Danish, A. R. D'Augelli, and C. E. Young, is funded by an NIMH grant.

pyramid model of human service delivery described by Seidman and Rappaport (1974), in which mental health skills are disseminated to the local level. The training began with professional educators, who are project staff, teaching trainers (about 15 in each of 2 rural communities) methods for enriching the helpfulness of natural caregivers. Second, these trained trainers (mental health staff, human service agency, staff, ministers, housewives, etc.) train the natural caregivers in the communities (approximately 100 in each community) in basic helping, life development skills, and crisis intervention skills. Finally, these caregivers will be able to help others in their community more effectively.

The goal of the project is to expand the scope of helping activities in communities without either encroaching on the delicate patterns of informal helping or sensitizing community helpers to psychopathology. Rather, the approach is to build upon native helping talent and to provide these helpers with a life-development perspective and skills. An emphasis on life development is preferred to one of mental health. Certainly the treatment of mental illness is not a focus of this project, and every effort is made to avoid the transformation of a good listener who happens to be the local postmaster to a mental health counselor. There are four distinct skill packages that are taught.

1. Basic Helping Skills (Danish and Hauer, 1973). These skills contribute to the ability to develop effective helping relationships with others. The skills taught are:

   —increasing awareness of one's own motivation to be a helper;
   —utilizing effective nonverbal behavior;
   —utilizing effective verbal behavior;
   —utilizing effective self-involving behavior;
   —establishing effective helping relationships.

All six skills include three components involved in being a helper; a) an understanding of oneself; b) some knowledge of helping skills; and c) experience in applying the skills. The program follows a structured format to teach each skill which includes: a) defining the skill in behavioral terms; b) discussing the rationale for the skill; c) specifying a skill attainment level; d) using models to demonstrate both effective and ineffective examples of the skills; e) providing opportunities for extensive supervised practice of the skill; and f) assigning homework to assist the generalization process. This 25 hour training program has been used extensively with professional and paraprofessional helpers around the country, but not with natural caregivers.

2. Life Development Skills (Danish, D'Augelli, and Hauer, 1979). This program embodies the notion of planning for life events. Life development skills encourage independent, planful behavior, which should lead to a more cost-effective service delivery system. Providing helpers with such training entails teaching them to view themselves as skill trainers/consultants to others, rather than as counselors. The life development training program provides this orientation and concrete skills. The specific skills taught are:

—teaching goal assessment
—teaching decision making
—teaching risk assessment
—teaching self-development

The format used to teach these skills is the same as that described in the basic helping skills.

3. Life Crisis Skills. This program is presently in its formative stages. Although the format is similar to the other skill programs described above, the exact skills to be taught have not been refined. Currently, the tentative program includes:

—identifying the source of present stress or crisis
—clarifying feelings associated with the stress
—identifying previous attempts to resolve the problem
—determining behaviors that are changeable and those that are not
—teaching the individual in crisis how to change the changeable
—providing referral skills

4. Teaching Skills. After completing each of the training components just described, two sessions are devoted to developing the skills necessary for teaching each training component to others.

There are several unique aspects of this model. First, human concerns are conceptualized not in terms of mental health problems but in terms of life events. Second, the skills can be taught to large numbers of community residents by other residents in nonthreatening settings like schools, YMCA's, civic clubs, churches, and the like. This increases the community-wide impact of the intervention. Third, the residents are taught skills that can be used after their contact with a natural caregiver has been terminated. For example, the life development skills are taught in a general way and then are applied to a specific life event. Although a person might wish to apply the decision-making skill to a decision about marriage, he or she is taught a skill useful in this *and many other* life decisions. Furthermore, one of the skills, Self-Development, enables an individual to design and teach him/herself a life skill. By employing this model, the helpfulness of community caregivers can be enhanced, and community residents are provided with skills to charter their own development. The spread of effect of this kind of community intervention—community helpers involved in life development training—is considerably more pervasive than traditional service delivery systems.

IMPEDIMENTS TO IMPLEMENTING LIFE DEVELOPMENT INTERVENTION

We began this chapter by discussing the difficulties of initiating change in human services systems. In clarifying our conceptual underpinnings and in providing a model for implementation, we hope to avoid some of the pitfalls human service innovations seldom escape. We anticipate, however, that some of the policies of the mental health establishment will obstruct the implementation of a life development orientation as well. Broskowski and Baker (1974) have identified professional, organizational, and social barriers to the implementation of primary prevention. Some of these same barriers are applicable to life development intervention.

Professional Barriers

Professionals have tended to assign a lower status to attempts to *prevent* rather than to *cure* problems (Danish, 1977; Gurevitz and

Heath, 1969; Snoke, 1969). As reimbursement for mental health activities becomes more common, programs aimed at reducing the number of potential consumers may be administratively counterproductive. Furthermore, the demystification of the helping process by employing an educative focus runs counter to the professionals' needs to maintain a heightened aura of mystery around helping activities.

However, professional barriers extend beyond the negative attitudes of some professionals. Most professionals are untrained to deliver such services. For example, despite evidence that the need for preventive services is increasing and the demand for direct services decreasing (Miller, Mazade, Muller, and Andrulis, 1978), the education and training of most professionals still virtually ignores such indirect activities as consultation, training, and education. Few new professionals have either a conceptual perspective or practical experience with these activities. Therefore, to suggest that agencies adopt a life skills enhancement model raises serious attitudinal and pragmatic problems.

Organizational Barriers

Helping people avoid remedial professional services through proactive intervention poses significant difficulties for mental health administrators. As funding to community mental health centers decreases annually—as much as 10 to 20 percent with the reduction of the federal staffing grants—the costs of maintaining a specified level of operations becomes increasingly difficult. State costs appear fixed, counties find it difficult to increase their share of the cost given other demands, and the burden of maintaining operations is placed increasingly on third-party reimbursements. A community mental health center designed to provide services that are clearly reimbursable becomes very much like a traditional outpatient clinic. Both enhancement and prevention activities may be benignly neglected because they keep people out of the reimbursement system and therefore adversely affect operations. The number of client-hours remains a powerful index of a center's effectiveness when funding is sought. It is conceivable that the problem dictates a radical solution, namely that life development services are best not offered in a mental health context at all. The tendency toward subtlely shaping such services into a referral system for direct services may be too powerful, fueled as it is by historical precedent and staff training backgrounds. In any event, an administrative structure that gives primacy to life development services is a requirement.

Social Barriers

Social impediments are the most damaging for the implementation of life development intervention efforts. Groups concerned about combating mental illness have presented the "disease" through the media as a terrible illness, far more dangerous and damaging than cancer or other dreaded physical diseases. Just as the behavioral and social sciences have begun to reject the concept of mental illness (Szasz, 1961), we are more firmly reinforcing its existence to the public. The disease view of mental illness portrayed to the public may arouse sympathy for the "afflicted"; a more pernicious outcome, however, is that the public will be "protected" from the notion that psychosocial problems result from difficulties in life planning. Therefore, the public will not link "mental illness" and problems of living and consequently will not recognize that they must learn to deal more effectively with the critical events in their own lives to prevent problems of living. The public's view of "mental illness" is such that there is no demand or constitutency for developing programs on life planning.

Life planning services can be made appealing to the public, more so than can remediative or preventive services. Individuals are likely to be eager to deal effectively with typical problems of living if they are provided with relevant skills. When the focus of intervention is either prevention or remediation, the danger of defining problems of living as mental illness is perpetuated. A delivery system orienting around illness must create "patients" to "diagnose" and "treat." Although such a system might "prevent" as well, potential patients at risk must be detected. Our argument has been that progress in mental health service delivery will occur only if this trap is avoided. We must remove problems of living from the mental health/mental illness arena and place them in a context of human development.* When a human

---

*It has been suggested by some (Illich, 1976) that perpetuating the notion that problems of living are mental health/mental illness issues is a self-serving

development perspective becomes accepted, life development enhancement strategies will be used, and the stigma associated with coping with personal problems will be eliminated. A new era of human services for human development will begin.

---

social policy supported by the mental health establishment. To prevent the public from becoming aware of the differences between mental illness/mental health and problems of living, conceptions might be labeled *illnessism*. Certainly in the mental health area, the maintenance of illnessism as a "public relations" message is very powerful, since it links mental health with the expertise and prestige of the medical establishment. Although the mental health establishment typically follows medicine's dubious lead in this area, it is clear that mental health professionals are as myopic as physicians in discarding iatrogenic conceptions. We recognize that the perpetuation of illnessism is not purposeful, as many instances of racism, sexism, and ageism are not purposeful social injustices. Nevertheless, the effects of illnessism may be as debilitating as these other social injustices.

REFERENCES

Adams, J. E., and Lindemann, E. Coping with long-term disability. In G. V. Coelho, D. A. Hamburg, and J. E. Adams (Eds.), *Coping and adaptation*. New York: Basic Books, 1974.

Atchley, R. C. Adjustment to loss of job at retirement. *International Journal of Aging and Human Development*, 1975, *6*, 17–27.

Authier, J., Gustafson, K., Guerney, B. G., and Kasdorf, J. A. The psychological practitioner as a teacher: A theoretical-historical and practical review. *The Counseling Psychologist*, 1975, *5*, 31–50.

Back, K. W., and Taylor, R. C. Self-help groups: Tool or symbol? *Journal of Applied Behavioral Science*, 1976, *12*, 295–309.

Baltes, P. B. Prototypical paradigms and questions in life-span research on development and aging. *Gerontologist*, 1973, *13*, 458–467.

Baltes, P. B., and Danish, S. J. Intervention in life span development and aging: Issues and concepts. In R. R. Turner and H. W. Reese (Eds.), *Life-span developmental psychology: Intervention*. New York: Academic Press, 1980.

Birren, J. E. *The psychology of aging*. Englewood Cliffs, N. J.: Prentice-Hall, 1964.

Blumer, H. Social movements. In B. McLaughlin (Ed.), *Studies in social movements: A social psychological perspective*. New York: The Free Press, 1969.

Bower, E. M. K.I.S.S. and kids: A mandate for prevention. *American Journal of Orthopsychiatry*, 1972, *42*, 556–565.

Broskowski, A., and Baker, F. Professional, organizational, and social barriers to primary prevention. *American Journal of Orthopsychiatry*, 1974, *44*, 707–719.

Caplan, G. *Principles of preventive psychiatry*. New York: Basic Books, 1964.

Cowen, E. L. Baby steps toward primary prevention. *American Journal of Community Psychology*, 1977, *5*, 1–22. (*a*)

Cowen, E. L. Psychologists and primary prevention: Blowing the cover story. *American Journal of Community Psychology*, 1977, *5*, 481–490. (*b*)

Cowen, E. L., Trost, M. A., Lorion, R. P., Dorr, D., Izzo, L. D., and Isaacson, R. V. *New ways in school mental health: Early detection and prevention of school maladaption*. New York: Behavioral Publications, 1975.

Danish, S. J. Human development and human services: A marriage proposal. In I. Iscoe, B. L. Bloom, and C. C. Spielberger (Eds.), *Community psychology in transition*. New York: Halsted, 1977.

Danish, S. J., D'Augelli, A. R., and Hauer, A. L. *Helping skills: A life development training program*. New York: Human Sciences Press, 1979.

Danish, S. J., and Hauer, A. L. *Helping skills: A basic training program*. New York: Human Sciences Press, 1973.

Danish, S. J. and Smyer, M. A. *The unintended consequences of requiring a license to help*. Unpublished manuscript, Pennsylvania State University, 1978.

Danish, S. J., Smyer, M. A., and Nowak, C. A. Developmental intervention: Enhancing life-event processes. In P. B. Baltes and O. G. Brim, Jr. (Eds.), *Life-span development and behavior*, Vol. 3. New York: Academic Press, in press.

Datan, N., and Ginsberg, L. H. (Eds.), *Life-span developmental psychology: Normative life crises*. New York: Academic Press, 1975.

D'Augelli, A. R. Paraprofessionals as educator-consultants: A new training model. *Professional Psychology*, 1978, *9*, 18–23.

Dohrenwend, B. S. Social status and stressful life events. *Journal of Personality and Social Psychology*, 1973, *28*, 225–235.

Dohrenwend, B. S., and Dohrenwend, B. P. (Eds.), *Stressful life events: Their nature and effects*. New York: Wiley, 1974.

Elder, G. H., Jr. Age differentiation and the life course. *Annual Review of Sociology*, 1975, *1*, 165–190.

Ford, D. H. Mental health and human development: An analysis of a dilemma. In D. Harshbarger and R. Maley (Eds.), *Behavior analysis and system analysis: An integrative approach to mental health programs*. Kalamazoo, Mich.: Behaviordelia, 1974.

Gartner, A., and Riessman, F. *Self-help in the human services*. San Francisco: Jossey-Bass, 1978.

Goldston, S. E. Defining primary prevention. In G. W. Albee and J. M. Joffe (Eds.), *Primary prevention of psychopathology. Vol. 1: The Issues*. Hanover, N.H.: University Press of New England, 1977.

Gore, S. *The influence of social support and related variables in ameliorating the consequences of job loss*. Unpublished doctoral dissertation, University of Pennsylvania, 1973.

Gurevitz, H., and Heath, D. Prevention and professional response. In H. Lamb, D. Heath, and J. Downing (Eds.), *Handbook of community mental health practice*. San Francisco: Jossey-Bass, 1969.

Guerney, B. G. Should teachers treat illiteracy, hypocalligraphy, and dysmathematica? *The Canadian Counselor*, 1977, *12*, 9–14.

Guerney, B. G., Guerney, L. F., and Stollak, G. E. The potential advantages of changing from a medical to an educational model in practicing psychology. *Interpersonal Development*, 1971/72, *2*, 238–245.

Guerney, B. G., Stollak, G. E., and Guerney, L. F. The practicing psychologist as educator—An alternative to the medical practitioner model. *Professional Psychology*, 1971, *2*, 276–282.

Hamburg, D. A., Coelho, G. V., and Adams, J. E. Coping and adaptation: Steps toward a synthesis of biological and social perspectives. In G. V. Coelho, D. A. Hamburg, and J. E. Adams (Eds.), *Coping and adaptation*. New York: Basic Books, 1974.

Holmes, T. H., and Rahe, R. H. The social readjustment rating scale. *Journal of Psychosomatic Research*, 1967, *11*, 213–218.

Hultsch, D. F., and Plemons, J. K. Life events and life-span development. In P. B. Baltes and O. G. Brim, Jr. (Eds.), *Life-span development and behavior* (Vol. 2). New York: Academic Press, 1979.

Hunt, J. McV. *Intelligence and experience*. New York: Ronald Press, 1961.

Illich, I. *Medical nemesis*. New York: Random House, 1976.

Janis, I. L. *Stress and frustration*. New York: Harcourt Brace Jovanovich, 1971.

Kessler, M. and Albee, G. W. Primary prevention. *Annual Review of Psychology*, 1975, *26*, 557–591.

Lawton, M. P., and Nahemow, L. Ecology and the aging process. In C. Eisdorfer and M. P. Lawton (Eds.), *The psychology of adult development and aging*. Washington, D.C.: American Psychological Association, 1973.

Lazarus, R. S. The stress and coping paradigm. In L. A. Bond and J. C. Rosen (Eds.), *Primary prevention of psychopathology. Vol. 4: Competence and coping during adulthood*. Hanover, N.H.: University Press of New England, 1980.

Lieberman, M. A. Adaptive processes in late life. In N. Datan and L. H. Ginsberg (Eds.), *Life-span developmental psychology: Normative life crises*. New York: Academic Press, 1975.

Lieberman, M. A., and Borman, L. D. Self-help groups: A special issue. *Journal of Applied Behavioral Sciences*, 1976, *12*, 261–463.

Lowenthal, M. F., and Chiriboga, D. Social stress and adaptation: Toward a life-course perspective. In C. Eisdorfer and M. P. Lawton (Eds.), *The psychology of adult development and aging*. Washington, D.C.: American Psychological Association, 1973.

Maddox, G. L. Community and home care: United States and United Kingdom: The unrealized potential of an old idea. In A. N. Exton-Smith and J. G. Evans (Eds.), *Care for the elderly*. London: Academic Press, 1977.

Miller, F. T., Mazade, N. A., Muller, S., and Andrulis, D. Trends in community mental health programming. *American Journal of Community Psychology*, 1978, *6*, 191–198.

Neugarten, B. L. Adaptation and life cycle. *The Counseling Psychologist*, 1976, *6*, 16–18.

Neugarten, B. L., and Hadestad, G. O. Age and the life course. In R. H. Binstock and E. Shanas (Eds.), *Handbook of aging and the social sciences*. New York: Van Nostrand Reinhold, 1976.

Nowak, C. *Research in life events: Conceptual considerations*. Paper presented at the 31st Annual Scientific Meeting of the Gerontological Society, Dallas, November 1978.

Nuckolls, K. B., Cassell, J., and Kaplan, B. Psychosocial assets, life crisis, and the prognosis of pregnancy. *American Journal of Epidemiology*, 1972, *95*, 431–441.

Rahe, R. The pathways between subjects' recent life changes and their near-future illness reports: Representative results and methodological issues. In B. S. and B. P. Dohrenwend (Eds.), *Stressful life events: Their nature and effects*. New York: Wiley Press, 1974.

Rahe, R. H., McKean, J. D., and Arthur, R. J. A longitudinal study of life-change and illness patterns. *Journal of Psychosomatic Research*, 1967, *10*, 355–366.

Riegel, K. F. Adult life crises: A dialectic interpretation of development. In N. Datan and L. Ginsberg (Eds.), *Life-span developmental psychology:*

Normative life crises. New York: Academic Press, 1975. (*a*)

Riegel, K. F. From traits and equilibrium toward developmental dialectics. *The Nebraska Symposium on Motivation* (Vol. 24). Lincoln: University of Nebraska Press, 1975. (*b*)

Riessman, F. How does self-help work? *Social Policy*, 1976, *7*, 41–45.

Ryan, W. *Distress in the city*. Cleveland: Case Western Reserve University Press, 1969.

Seidman, E., and Rappaport, J. The educational pyramid: A paradigm for training, research, and manpower utilization in community psychology. *American Journal of Community Psychology*, 1974, *2*, 119–130.

Selye, H. *The stress of life*. New York: McGraw-Hill, 1956.

Snoke, A. The unsolved problem of the career professional in the establishment of national health policy. *American Journal of Public Health*, 1969, *59*, 1575–1588.

Srole, L., Langner, T. S., Michael, S. T., Opler, M. K., and Rennie, T. A. C. *Mental health in the metropolis: The midtown Manhattan study*. New York: McGraw-Hill, 1962.

Szasz, T. *The myth of mental illness*. New York: Harper and Row, 1961.

Warren, D. I. *Neighborhood and community contexts in help seeking, problem coping and mental health*. Ann Arbor, Michigan: Program in Community Effectiveness, 1976.

Young, C. E., Giles, D. E., and Plantz, M. *Help seeking patterns in rural communities*. Unpublished manuscript, Pennsylvania State University, 1978.

5

A Model for Promoting Competence and Coping in Adolescents and Young Adults

DAVID F. RICKS

Because adolescence involves rapid change, physiologically, psychologically, and socially, this short period presents special risks for disorder and special opportunities for help. I will summarize the main changes of adolescence and some of the many life events that impinge on young people as they go through the transition from boys and girls to men and women. I will then develop a model for ways in which life events may interact with the special strengths and vulnerabilities of adolescents to produce well-being and competence, or disorder, functional disturbance, and disability. This leads to a description of the methods of two therapists, one of whom seemed especially skilled at coping with adolescent protest, the other with adolescent despair and apathy.

What do I mean by a model? Simply, a framework on which to hang the results from several years of study on how children from child guidance and residential treatment facilities develop enough coping skills to negotiate the tricky paths leading to adulthood. By coping I mean surviving, making a go of life, and growing up, all the while avoiding suicide, hospitalization, jail, and the lesser ways in which people fail to live integrated lives. I do not use much traditional psychiatric and psychological terminology, since our static typologies mislead as often as they aid. I use instead some provisional kinds of developmental thinking which may be useful to us in helping adolescents to avoid getting caught up in the often destructive institutions erected for their incarceration and care. Learning to cope with everyday developmental tasks is the distinguishing characteristic of the adolescent who makes it through to adulthood. The rise in adolescent suicide, the lowered average age in many mental hospitals, and the increasing signs that many young people are depressed are evidence that coping may be getting harder than it used to be.

If we see coping as adequacy, doing "well enough," then competence can be seen as a higher level of coping, a capacity to do things really well, and to feel good about one's abilities and accomplishments. The effects of competent interchanges with the environment are clear—one achieves, is promoted, rewarded, and so on. But the internal, self-reward consequences of self-perceived competence are likely to be even stronger. We continue in those activities in which we feel competent, and this shapes our lives. For young boys, Harter (1978) has shown that one's own sense of athletic competence is likely to be overwhelmingly important, although later on, in adolescence, intellectual and social competence are likely to play larger roles. Crandall (1975) has shown that boys tend to be unrealistically optimistic about themselves, overestimating their future performances relative to their past records. Perhaps this is what keeps them trying, although as I will show later, one of the tasks of adolescence is to adjust aims downward and become more realistic. Crandall's results with regard to women are important. Girls may be as optimistic about themselves as boys early in life, but by adolescence they systematically underestimate their future performances relative to the level that their past work would predict. One solution to this problem is for girls and women to move toward careers where competence is clear and easily assessed—if you can program the computer, it runs, regardless of the shape of your body. Another is to work for formality in the school and job arenas, with defined standards of competence (Epstein, 1975), so that your work can be fairly assessed, both by others and, most crucially, by yourself.

THE ADOLESCENT TRANSITION

The magnitude of the adolescent change can be appreciated if we look at people before and after this period. It is helpful to do so realistically, without the romanticizing of adolescence implicit in thinking of it as a period of rebellion, alienation, growing up absurd, or remaking the conscience of the country (Keniston, 1965; Goodman, 1960). Descriptively, what is the difference between the child at the threshold of puberty and the adult who emerges at the end of adolescence? At the beginning one is still physiologically immature; at the end one is a man or woman capable of adult sexuality and reproduction. At the beginning the child is in the family, with status and place in the world defined by parents; at the end one is out in the world, forging an identity based on one's own skills and relationships.

Stierlin's (1972) seminal work has shown some of the ways in which leaving the family can be delayed, hastened, or misused. The child may be held back from exploring the world outside the family, prematurely expelled, or delegated by a parent to have experiences or achieve goals that the parent has found impossible. Parents are entering a mid-life transition, in most instances, at about the same time their children are entering adolescence. Both are periods of restlessness and crisis (Levinson, Darrow, Klein, Levinson and McKee, 1978). Stierlin's work helps explain why some overly restricted children explode in apparently irrational rebellion, why some children run away but maintain contact with an involved parent through all of their delinquencies, and why others escape into the identities and symbols of a deviant peer group, regarding their family of origin as an increasingly remote part of ancient history. Olweus (1972) has shown that there is a delicate balance between the pull of the family and the pull of the peer group. The child still too much in the bosom of the family is treated by peers as a mamma's boy and a victim, while the youth who has severed ties with the family is often a bully, eager to establish peer status by finding victims for group exploitation.

Erikson (1963) has described—and Marcia (1966, 1967, 1970) has developed operational methods to study—the stages through which an adolescent may move toward a stable identity independent of his parents. Identity may be *foreclosed*, so that one remains frozen in a conferred or dictated self-conception of being forever mother's daughter or father's son. This is a dilemma of many people in highly stable societies—an upper-class Boston Harvard man or an Orthodox Chassidic Jew knows his identity is carved out for him. Identity may be foreclosed for other people as well. A girl whose mother buys all her clothes, who is told who is and who is not an acceptable friend, who would not dare transgress against her parents' sexual mores, or even inquire too much about them, is in a state of identity foreclosure. Identity may be *confused*, so that it is hard to develop a consistent set of beliefs and values, to feel that one is the same person with parents and with boy friends, in school and at work. A fairly consistent theme of adolescent exploration is negation, "I know what I don't like, and what I don't believe, but I can't tell you what I believe." A good deal of informal adolescent peer help consists of long discussions aimed at how to get your head together, how to straighten up your act, how to know where you are going. In college-age adolescents this exploration is often worked at as a conscious long-range task, a kind of *moratorium* in which one strives to keep options open, to experiment with different groups and different identities within those groups, all the while avoiding commitment to long-range identities and intimacies. There is much journalistic interest in new patterns of living together in adolescence—it would be just as reasonable to study the other aspects of moratorium, the tendency to live with a temporary identity or job or educational goal, without making a long-term commitment or getting married to it.

By the end of adolescence most people have reached a relatively stable identity, which Erikson calls *identity achievement*. This term, however, is overly static. A major discovery of life-span developmental psychology (Block, 1971; Levinson et al., 1978; Vaillant, 1977) is that after adolescence people continue to develop and change, although at a slower pace and usually with additional competencies with which to meet life's challenges.

A question about which adolescents think a great deal, but which has received less professional attention, is "How do I find a job, and will it be the right job?" Jordaan, Super, and their colleagues (1974) have described the ways in which the adolescent's self-concept is worked out in his or her young adult vocational drifts and developments. Two of their findings are particularly important for a public health view of adolescence. Most adolescents are to some extent disillusioned as they find that their early vocational aspirations are higher than their competence and opportunities will allow them to reach. They adjust their goals down, the aspiring airline pilot becoming a mechanic and the aspiring business executive learning to sell cars. Their goals also become more focused, so that between the 9th grade and the 12th they learn that one cannot simultaneously work toward becoming a physician and a forest ranger but had better think carefully about such coherent vocational groupings as medicine and dentistry, forestry and agriculture. Not long ago I spent some time with a boy who had been referred for some small thefts. His goal was to "be a boss, with my feet on the desk, giving orders." Aware that he was doing badly in school and had no vocational skills, he thought about the discrepancy between his current competence and that required by his goal, then somewhat shakily told me, "I will hire somebody to *think* for me." The crucial issues to look at are vocational maturity— the young man just mentioned is strikingly low in this—and the ways in which transitions are negotiated, first between school and work, then between early jobs and later. Self-esteem tends to be constructed around one's sense of competence in making these changes.

Summing up, we can say that by the end of adolescence, ideally, one is physiologically and sexually mature, has developed some kind of identity, and has fashioned a career pattern that develops, expresses, and tests that identity. The adolescent has given up the ways and the securities of childhood, has worked through at least part of the transition of leaving the family, and has begun to find an appropriate place in the world of adult work and responsibility.

THE SEQUENCE OF DEVELOPMENT

Many of the life histories of people who have a psychotic episode in adult life contain a note like this: "After George dropped out [or was expelled] from school, he sat at home listening to TV, had no friends, and began behaving oddly . . ." In the histories of children, issues of coping with school, of attendance and competent learning, occur early. Not surprisingly, the issue of school phobia, which may be seen as an optimistic hope that one can avoid school altogether, peaks in the first school year. The peak referral years for school learning problems are 9–11, for mental deficiency 14–16. We often think concretely about such problems, assigning a label like mental deficiency to a child and then acting as if the label had become a part of the child, some immutable trait that would describe him or her from that time on. Even worse, we sometimes confuse mere labeling with helping. It is encouraging, though, to see how well many "retarded" children do once they are out of school and into the world of work. Our task here is to help schools learn to accommodate to children, to protect them from labels that become self-fulfilling prophecies, and to enable them to make use of the full range of support systems that are available. Social skills training, for instance, can keep an adolescent in contact with his peers and so forestall social withdrawal.

Issues of compliance and socialization in the larger society outside family and school peak between 13 and 17, earlier for girls, later for boys. Most girls who have a try at shoplifting do it around 13 or 14, as growing interest in makeup and sexy clothes comes into conflict with parental rules. Most boys who have trouble with the law have it first around 15 to 17, as cars and motorcycles come to have almost magical appeal and growing mechanical sophistication makes theft not only interesting but easy. The methods developed by Spivack and Shure (1974) of teaching kids to stop and think, to recognize alternatives, and to choose among options have a great deal of use at this period. So do vocational kinds of therapy, since these teach kids that they can work and wait, rather than impulsively grab the first thing that catches a newly interested eye.

Most of the problems I have been describing involve the child with two institutions, family and school. Both are concerned with developing competence in children, and conflicts between family and school are often due to different interpretations of competence. Institutions change more slowly than individuals, but they do change. New family patterns are emerging, with fathers more involved in child care. Schools are also learning some lessons about how to promote confidence and social competence as well as the traditional kinds of intellectual skills.

Toward the end of adolescence the issues Levinson calls "leaving the family" and "getting into the adult world" reach a crisis. This is the period of highest risk for schizophrenia. It is worth asking why this most serious of emotional disorders is so late in making its appearance, and whether there are special stresses during adolescence that might help us understand the sequence of adaptational failure leading into serious emotional crises.

STRESS DURING ADOLESCENCE

Coddington (1972a, 1972b) has shown that there is a strikingly consistent curve for the frequency of stressful life events as a function of age, a curve that holds well across sexes and across social classes. After rising slowly during the years between 2 and 12, life events begin to accelerate, reach a peak around 15 to 17, and then begin to level off and decrease. Life for the middle adolescent is a matter of enormous changes at the last minute, as life-change units pile up and demand adjustments to them. And the decisions that guide adjustment are made without a great deal of experience—it is hard to decide such issues as "Should I stay with the gang or drop out of it when they get into rough stuff or some drug that scares me?" or "Should I stay in school or drop out to take a job driving a truck?" or "If I take this, will I get caught?" or "Should I sleep with him or not?"

The sheer number of life events shows no difference for boys and girls, but there is clinical evidence that the timing and the impact of events may differ. All through childhood and up to the middle of adolescence, more boys than girls are referred for psychological treatment. In mid-adolescence the frequencies cross, and from that age onward more women than men come to treatment agencies (Weiner and Del Gaudio, 1976). The reasons for this change are obscure, but some directions for study are becoming clear. Some girls have difficulty in negotiating an end to dependency and establishing independence of mother and home (Allen, 1976). The ambiguities of the dual role of worker and wife make it hard for some women to develop coherent educational and interpersonal careers. Women are trained in patterns of self-denial, expected to participate vicariously in the successes of fathers, husbands, and sons, and given little reinforcement for active or assertive kinds of behavior. Yet, as Lewinsohn (1976) has demonstrated, depression tends to accumulate and to overwhelm the person whose life contains few direct satisfactions, obtained by one's own activity. This puts women in the dilemma described by Radloff (1978) and by Vance in the first Vermont conference (1977). Passivity has some immediate pay-off in adolescence, as girls learn to play dumb to avoid threatening boys. It has very serious long term consequences, since it leads to unsatisfying lives, depression, and a bewildering concern over

"Where did I go wrong?" If women also learn, as society is prone to teach them, that "if anything goes wrong, somebody is responsible" and "if somebody is responsible, it is probably me," the stage is set for the drama of self-blame that Beck (1973) has described in depression. Adolescent female socialization is a crucial issue for public health work. A society that can understand female psychological health as being the same as adult psychological health, rather than something different (Broverman, Broverman, Clarkson, Rosencrantz, and Vogel, 1970), that can accord equal power and income to women (Levitin, Quinn, and Staines, 1971), that can appreciate competence in women without deriding it as being pushy (Johnson, 1974), that can help women enjoy and celebrate success rather than fear it—that society will have within its ranks fewer depressed women.

FAILURE IN COMPETENCE AND COPING: PSYCHOPATHOLOGY IN ADOLESCENCE

If we give up the idea of special creation of discrete psychopathological types, we can ultilize a more dynamic and developmental scheme based on relative degrees of adaptation to stress. Ability to cope has a long history and a characteristic pattern of development, such as that shown by Block's (1971) "cognitive copers" or "ego resilients." Inability to cope, similarly, seems to involve consistent patterns. These are summarized in the proposed model (Figure 1), which is adapted from Timeras (1972). The model assumes that there is a relatively narrow range of stressful life events which the organism can assimilate, and beyond this range the more change units that impinge upon the organism, the more stress that will be felt and be manifested in behavior. Current research (Dohrenwend and Dohrenwend, 1974) indicates that this is particularly true if the life events are negative in tone— losses, disappointments, etc.—and if they require major readjustments in life patterns. Work on learned helplessness (Seligman, 1975) and on depression (Lewisohn, Biglan and Zeiss, 1976) suggests that events over which the person has no control are particularly upsetting. For adolescents the model is counterintuitive. We often think, at about age 16 or 17, that nothing in the world is

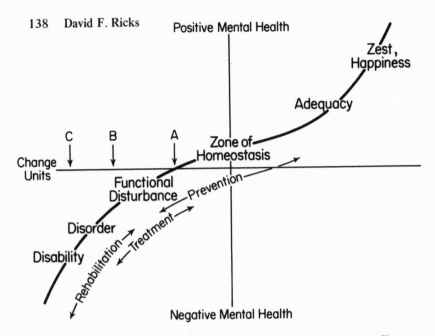

Figure 1. Level of Mental Health as a Function of Life Change Units. Change units are counted as negative events.
A. Threshold of functional disturbance, protest, alarm.
B. Threshold of disorder, despair, learned helplessness.
C. Threshold of disability, apathy.

happening, and that we are going to die of boredom. Research indicates, however, that we can readily adapt to the boredom of everyday life, assimilating small changes easily and maintaining equilibrium, but that when events change very fast or strikingly, we cannot readily adapt to them. The model is also counterintuitive in its long-range implications, showing that strength is a matter of long-term coping with stressful life events, rather than realizing some kind of dream of accumulated positive events. But I will not deal with these long-term implications here.

The dependent variable in the model is the degree of mental health in the individual, beginning in a more or less broad range of homeostasis in the middle and moving up on the positive side toward higher levels of adequacy, competence, and happiness. Maslow (1962) has written extensively about this part of the diagram, and Wessman and Ricks (1966) have reported some of the characteristics of people up on the healthy end of the function. At the lower end of the mental health continuum, life events overwhelm and coping begins to fail. Ranging downward from homeostasis, the model proposes three thresholds: At point A, the person moves from homeostasis into a more or less unstable condition of functional disturbance; at point B the individual moves from disturbance into disorder, and at point C the person moves from disorder into disability, which is to some extent chronic and stable. The three points correspond closely to the transitions between Selye's (1956) stages of alarm, resistance, and exhaustion.

While we are dealing with the zone of homeostasis, where normal function is maintained without significant cost, we can work with methods of primary prevention. Our main goal will be to strengthen the organism, increase skills, develop personal resources and support networks, etc. in such a way as to move point A as far to the left as possible. A highly vulnerable child, say one whose family life has been classically symbiotic or whose neurological integration or intellectual competence is low, will have a very narrow range of psychological homeostasis. Our task is to strengthen him to deal with the inevitable stresses of life, or to help guide him into life patterns with low stress and low demands. Many of our problems in this endeavor come from the fact that neurological disorder, environmental poisons, and other deterrents to competence are more frequent in populations of poor people, and poor people also have more aversive life events with which to cope (Dohrenwend and Dohrenwend, 1974).

Below the level of functional disturbance, at B, the person moves into the range of disorder. Usually this is a new equilibrium, relatively unstable but with some coherence and organization. In the realm of physical disorder, one might think of this as the movement from a nervous stomach to an ulcer. Within the realm of emotional disorder, a comparable movement is from being anxious and alarmed to being depressed and helpless. While symptomatic treatment is often enough for functional disturbances, disorders usually require, in addition, some effort at rehabilitation. How do we keep point B as far to the left as possible? The main issue is one recognized since the Greeks, making sure that we do no harm. Second, we have to recognize that strengthening the individual can go hand in hand with making changes in the environment, an issue I will deal with below in relation to the methods of two therapists for whose competence we have empirical evidence.

At point C we move from disorder to disability. Beyond this point our major efforts must be directed toward rehabilitation. What factors are related to C being closer or further from the range of homeostasis for a given person? It is clear that for some people it is possible to maintain relatively stable levels of disorder for long periods without going into disability. In the individual the major determinants of resistance to disability seem to be the same kinds of skills and competence that maintain homeostasis. For instance, the chief predictor that a person can remain in the community after an episode of hospitalization is the ability to hold a job (Myers and Bean, 1968). In the environment the chief determinants of disability seem to be the degree of undesirableness of life events and their duration. Under the stress of prolonged combat, even relatively healthy people may become disabled.

Can this model help us to understand how emotional disorders develop in late adolescence? Does this sequence of functional disturbance, disorder, and disability have any generality? I think that two similar models suggest its generality and readily available empirical data supports its validity. Bowlby (1969, 1973) and Kubler-Ross (1969) both worked on the psychological effects of the most stressful life events, separation and loss of loved persons. You will probably remember that Bowlby described the equilibrium of the child as including the mother, and he showed the characteristic sequence that occurred when the mother was lost through hospitalization of the child or for some other reason. The child first *protests*, trying to restore his mother-child unity and homeostasis. If this fails, the child goes into *despair*, a condition in which his plainly visible unhappiness calls out to others for mothering and care. If the nurses or others around him are too busy or are unresponsive, he may sink into *apathy*, from which it is hard to restore him. These stages fit rather closely the model I have proposed. Functional disturbance and alarm are the signals that homeostasis has been disturbed, and they correspond to the first unfocused parts of protest. Just as functional disturbance in an unresponsive environment can deteriorate into disorder, protest without response can become despair. And just as disorder and resistance become disability if the organism becomes exhausted, despair can become apathy if it continues too intensely and too long. Kubler-Ross, working with dying patients and their families, has described a similar sequence, ranging from initial denial through anger (protest) and bargaining to grief (despair) and finally acceptance of the inevitable. The outlines of the two sequences are the same, the main difference being that Kubler-Ross, working largely with people who have acquired speech, has been able to describe the additional transitional stages of denial and bargaining, and that she does not interpret the final stage of quiescence as negatively as Bowlby does, or as I do in this model.

This sequence is also similar to the transition from anxiety to learned helplessness (Seligman, 1975) which can be observed in many different organisms when they are faced with inescapable and uncontrollable aversive events. Seligman interprets this as evidence for a particular origin of depression. I think the model is more general, helping us to understand not just movement into depression but also schizo-affective responses and schizophrenia. My evidence is contained in a sequence that anyone with access to large numbers of sequential psychiatric diagnoses can verify. If we put aside the majority of psychiatric diagnoses that agree and concentrate on those where there is disagreement over the years of adolescence and young adult life, we can usually see a characteristic pattern. The first diagnosis is "adjustment reaction of adolescence," "passive-aggressive reaction," or a similar description of a young person in *protest* against the impact of aversive life events. The old idea that schizophrenic patients had been quiet, shut in, and withdrawn since childhood has been disproved, both by follow-up studies of shy children (who turn out to be shy adults, but not schizophrenics) and by follow-back studies of adult schizophrenics, whose childhood records show them to have generally been actively rebellious and protesting (Kohlberg, LaCross, and Ricks, 1972). We can think of protest as a functional disturbance, inherently unstable, tending either back toward homeostasis or down toward despair and disorder. Since every protest involves a complex interaction between real life stress and personal vulnerability, together with more or less successful efforts at self-defense, it is never easy to distinguish between the kinds of healthy protest that lead to growth and competence and protests that fail and lead into disorder.

The second set of diagnoses these young people receive often includes "depressive reaction," "schizo-affective disorder," or some other term suggesting *despair*. Like the despair of infants, their depression often calls out a response from caretaking people, and with that response may come treatment, rehabilitation, and restoration of psychological equilibrium. If not, the next diagnoses may deal with various types of drug or alcohol reactions, types of amateur self-medication sometimes ending in diagnoses of schizophrenia. Once diagnosed schizophrenic, the person tends to stay diagnosed schizophrenic on subsequent hospital admissions. In terms of the coping model, we are at this point at the stage of *disability*, a stage in which social rehabilitation is larger and more important task than psychotherapy. In the model for loss reactions described by Bowlby and by Kubler-Ross, the person is at the stage of *apathy*. This stage was described vividly in the novel *I Never Promised You a Rose Garden*, in which the author writes of the women on the violent ward as "aborted suicides." In the words of Herman Melville, the person who has sunk into apathy is "dead to the world."

Why would a sequence originally described in relation to separation from the mother, and to death, be relevant to adolescence? This is the time when expectations for adult life and leaving the family to establish one's own way become dominant concerns (Blos, 1967). Up until the time of adolescence, most learning has been an unambiguous matter of adding new skills to old. In adolescence, for the first time, new learning requires really major unlearning or it will fail. In order to get into the adult world, one must leave the family, and in order to form new attachments, one must give up the first attachments or redefine them. To those adolescents for whom negotiating separation is impossible, the loss sequence may proceed to various stages. A person given to hysterical defenses may deny the loss, half expecting the mother to come through every door that opens. Or an overly strong tie may lead to violent protest or running away.

Though there is no other loss so overwhelming as that of one's protecting parents, smaller losses may accompany and add to this first. When vocational ambitions are adjusted downward, as they usually are for adolescent boys, the adolescent must give up earlier dreams of glory. One young man in our studies slipped into a catatonic state when a classmate told him that since he wore glasses he could never become a pilot. Another went into an acute panic and identity confusion when a girl with whom he worked, to whom he had apparently never previously spoken, refused to accept a box of candy from him. What I am arguing is that there is a sequence of feeling states leading into schizophrenia, and that it resembles closely the sequence of feelings evoked by response to loss. Fleming (1970) has shown that feelings reported by children in child guidance clinics reliabily distinguish those who later have schizophrenic outcomes from those who do not. The reported feelings that differentiate the groups most strongly are isolation and alienation, anxiety, helplessness and vulnerability, unreality, and discontinuity.

What are the implications of the model for public health approaches to psychological disorders? Our efforts at primary prevention have as their goal expanding the range of homeostasis, strengthening children and families so that they can maintain equilibrium in the face of loss, whether of persons or of hopes and dreams. One way to do this is by helping young people develop support networks, either in advance of crises or as a part of crisis management. To some extent, competence in one area of life can make up for incompetence in others, so promotion of academic or athletic competence can help compensate for social deficits, and vice versa. Since breakdown and passage from homeostasis to disturbance and disorder is often a family matter, we badly need to establish more alternative living arrangements for adolescents, places where they can take some time out from family crises and reestablish their equilibrium. In another article (Ricks, 1970), I described more than twenty other ways of strengthening children to increase coping skills. These methods are often slow going and unglamorous, consisting of such things as help in reading, speech therapy, vocational guidance, and teaching simple social skills. This sort of competence building has results well beyond amelioration of immediate problems. The work combines aspects of strengthening the adolescent, of treating disturbance, and of rehabilitating earlier disabilities. If we can see adolescent protest, no matter how provocative or spiteful it may seem, as an effort to restore one's own health, if we can respond to adolescent despair, no matter how exaggerated or dramatic it may be, as a genuine attempt to call for help, then we may be able to help adolescents avoid moving on to that state of irritable apathy that we call schizophrenia. Even in schizophrenia, if we focus on the feelings of the person in that state, we can find ways to limit the impact of disability, to develop strength and ability to cope, and eventually to help the person back to a functional level of living. Our technical vocabulary tends to isolate us from people who need help. Terms like "sociopath" and "schizophrenia" have a tone of expertise and mystery about them, but I think everyone has some common human sense of how to respond to protest, despair, or apathy.

I am proposing that our greatest task is like that Bettelheim (1967) has described in his work with young "strangers to life"—one of reaching out to the person who has failed to cope, hence has blown up into temper tantrums and protest, or who has alienated people through his or her protests and is now in a state of despair or apathy. Bettelheim once described a frightened child hiding under his covers and reaching out one tentative hand for food left beside his bed. In leaving that food Bettelheim was trying to show the child that he could come out of hiding and find himself in a world that was not too bad after all. Bettelheim, coming from a psychoanalytic understanding of disturbance, and Lewinsohn, coming from a behavioral understanding, reach startlingly similar conclusions about treatment. One has to make the immediate world of the adolescent more rewarding and less condemning and frightening. This is a large task, but like Orpheus, we occasionally bring a person who had been "dead to the world" back to life.

EFFECTIVE INTERVENTION

This last goal may sound overly optimistic, and you may decide that I not only like adolescents but share some of their unrealistic idealism. So I will conclude with a note of hard data. In one of our studies we looked at the adult outcomes of a very large number of children seen in a fine child guidance clinic. Our method of research restricted our sample to a group who were vulnerable to later schizophrenia. Looking at the outcomes of those who saw different therapists, we found that children and adolescents who had seen one therapist, Robert Young, had in general reached levels of adult living that we could see as balanced, adjusted, or, in terms of the model proposed here, in the realm of psychological homeostasis. For the worst therapist, by the criterion of adult outcomes, most of a comparable set of children were schizo-phrenic, a few had escaped with some episodes of disorder, and none was, in adult life, within the area of psychological homeo-stasis. The methods of the more adequate therapist have been described in detail (Ricks, 1974). In summary, the methods were (1) appropriate allocation of effort, giving more time and energy to the more disturbed children rather than to those easier to reach; (2) more effective use of resources outside the immediate therapy situation; (3) firmness and directness in dealing with parents; (4) support of efforts toward autonomy, and stimulation of these when they were absent; (5) anchoring the adolescents in reality through setting up strong therapy relationships on which they tended to rely even after formal termination of therapy, and (6) promotion of competence in handling the everyday problems of life in peer relationships, jobs, and school. These therapeutic methods, which are sometimes thought of as "merely supportive," seem to me the best guides we now have to work with adolescents whose problems have progressed into despair or apathy.

A quite different therapist emerged from studies of "delin-quent" adolescents who were dominated by feelings of protest and anger. There is long-term follow-up data for boys seen by this therapist, Joseph Massimo, for a vocationally oriented intervention designed to help them back into the mainstream of work (Shore and Massimo, 1973). The data are highly convincing. One of the boys, currently a man of about 30, is now doing work similar to that Massimo did, training convicts in a needed vocational skill, auto body repair. While Young seemed at his best in working with adolescents whose retreat had proceeded beyond protest and into despair or apathy, Massimo used active intervention in the community, athletic skills, and knowledge of cars and street life to bind rebellious adolescents to him and to the idea that there were legitimate and reliable ways to get some money in your pocket. Most of the boys seen by Massimo are employed, and few have had further trouble with the law. Most of the matched con-trols have been arrested, some several times. Massimo's work with these boys has had a long-term positive impact.

The arcane language of psychology, both that of varied defenses and that of varied operants and respondents, often hides a certain murkiness of thought. I would like to close this paper with a plea to get back to basics, and to try to express this concern in ordinary language. What we are concerned with in our intervention efforts is how to help people make a go of life, to survive, to reproduce if they want to, to be less vulnerable to extremes of protest, despair, or apathy, to be more competent in learning, work, and social life, and to be better able to deal with stress. Finally, the people into whose lives we reach ought to feel better for our efforts, and their lives ought to show increasing integration and active mastery. There is evidence that the various methods of psychotherapy can have all of these effects (Ricks, Wandersman, and Poppen, 1976), and it is likely that similar results are obtained with better living environments (Wandersman and Moos) and with family interventions (Wandersman and Wandersman, 1976). We still tend to see our work on a scale that is too small—often just as one adolescent in a room with one therapist—and we seldom look at the long-term outcomes of our work. When we do look at long-term outcomes, we find that there are indeed "supershrinks," that their efforts are strikingly cost-effective, and that early intervention often has the spread of effect seen in Massimo's garage mechanic, now a rehabilitation worker in his own right. I do not know who your heroes are, but mine are people like Robert Young and Joseph Massimo, who have reached into the lives of countless adolescents with effects that are still being felt.

REFERENCES

Allen, J. *Identity formation in late adolescent women: An object relations approach.* Unpublished doctoral disseratation, City University of New York, 1976.

Beck. A. T. *The diagnosis and management of depression.* Philadelphia: University of Pennsylvania Press, 1973.

Bettelheim, B. *The empty fortress: Infantile autism and the birth of the self.* New York: Free Press. 1967.

Block, J. *Lives through time.* Berkeley: Bancroft Books, 1971.

Blos, P. The second individuation process of adolescence. *Psychoanalytic Study of the Child,* 1967, *22,* 162–186.

Bowlby, J. *Attachment.* New York: Basic Books, 1969.

Bowlby, J. *Separation.* New York: Basic Books, 1973.

Broverman, I. K., Broverman, D. M., Clarkson, F. E., Rosenkrantz, P. S., and Vogel, S. R. Sex-role stereotypes and clinical judgements of mental health. *Journal of Consulting and Clinical Psychology,* 1970, *34,* 1–7.

Coddington, R. D. The significance of life events as etiological factors in the diseases of children. *Journal of Psychosomatic Research,* 1972, *16,* 1–18. (*a*)

Coddington, R. D. The significance of life events as etiological factors in the diseases of children. II. *Journal of Psychosomatic Research,* 1972, *16,* 205–213. (*b*)

Crandall, V. C. Sex differences in expectancy of intellectual and academic performance. In R. K. Unger and F. L. Denmark (Eds.), *Woman: Dependent or independent variable,* New York, Psychological Dimensions, 1975.

Dohrenwend, B. S. and Dohrenwend, B. P. (Eds.), *Stressful life events: Their nature and effects.* New York: Wiley, 1974.

Epstein, C. F. Encountering the male establishment: Sex-status limits on womens careers in the profession. In R. K. Unger and F. L. Denmark (Eds.), *Women: Dependent or independent variable,* New York, Psychological Dimensions, 1975.

Erikson, E. H. *Childhood and society* (2nd Ed.). New York: Norton, 1963.

Fleming, P., and Ricks, D. F. Emotions of children before schizophrenia and before character disorder. In M. Roff and D. Ricks (Eds.), *Life history research in psychopathology* (Vol. 1). Minneapolis: University of Minnesota Press, 1970.

Green H. *I never promised you a rose garden.* New York: New American Library, 1964.

Goodman, P. *Growing up absurd.* New York: Vintage, 1960.

Harter, S. Effectance motivation reconsidered: Toward a developmental model. *Human Development,* 1978, *21,* 34–64.

Johnson, P. *Social power and sex-role stereotypes.* Paper presented at the meeting of the Western Psychological Association, San Francisco, April 1974.

Jordaan, J. P., and Super, D. E. The prediction of early adult vocational behavior. In D. Ricks, A. Thomas, and M. Roff (Eds.), *Life history research in psychopathology* (Vol. 3). Minneapolis: University of Minnesota Press, 1974.

Keniston, K. *The uncommitted: Alienated youth in American society.* New York: Harcourt, Brace, and World, 1965.

Kohlberg, L., LaCross, J., and Ricks, D. The predictability of adult mental health from childhood behavior. In B. Wolman (Ed.), *Manual of child psychopathology.* New York: McGraw-Hill, 1972.

Kubler-Ross, E. *On death and dying.* New York: Macmillan, 1969.

Levinson, D. J., Darrow, C. N., Klein, E. B., Levinson, M. H., and McKee, B. *The seasons of a man's life.* New York: Knopf, 1978.

Levitin, T., Quinn, R. P., and Staines, G. L. Sex discrimination against American working women. *American Behavioral Scientist,* 1971, *15,* 237–254.

Lewinsohn, P. M., Biglan, A., and Zeiss, A. M. Behavioral treatment of depression. In P. O. Davidson (Ed.), *The behavioral management of anxiety, depression, and pain.* New York: Brunner/Mazel, 1976.

Marcia, J. E. Development and validation of ego identity status. *Journal of Personality and Social Psychology,* 1966, *3,* 551–558.

Marcia, J. E. Ego identity status: Relationship to change in self-esteem, "general maladjustment," and authoritarianism. *Journal of Personality,* 1967, *35,* 118–133.

Marcia, J. E., and Friedman, M. Ego identity status in college women. *Journal of Personality,* 1970, *38,* 249–263.

Maslow, A. H. *Toward a psychology of being.* Princeton, Van Nostrand, 1962.

Myers, J. K., and Bean, L. L. *A decade later: A follow-up of social class and mental illness.* New York: Wiley, 1968.

Olweus, D. Personality and aggression. In J. K. Cole and D. D. Jensen (Eds.), *Nebraska Symposium on Motivation.* Lincoln: University of Nebraska Press, 1972.

Radloff, L. S. Sex differences in helplessness—with implications for depression. In L. S. Hansen and R. S. Rapoza (Eds.), *Career development and counseling of women.* Springfield, Illinois: Charles Thomas, 1978.

Ricks, D. F. Life history research in psychopathology: Retrospect and prospect. In M. Roff and D. Ricks (Eds.), *Life history research in psychopathology* (Vol. 1). Minneapolis, University of Minnesota Press, 1970.

Ricks, D. F. Supershrink: Methods of a therapist judged successful on the basis of adult outcomes of adolescent patients. In D. Ricks, A. Thomas, and M. Roff (Eds.), *Life history research in psychopathology* (Vol. 3). Minneapolis, University of Minnesota Press, 1974.

Ricks, D., Wandersman, A., and Poppen, P. Humanism and behaviorism: Toward a new synthesis. In A. Wandersman, P. Poppen, and D. Ricks (Eds.), *Humanism and behaviorism: Dialogue and growth.* New York: Pergamon, 1976.

Seligman, M. E. P. *Helplessness: On depression, development, and death.* San Francisco: Freeman, 1975.

Selye, H. *The stress of life.* New York: McGraw-Hill, 1956.

Shore, M. F., and Massimo, J. L. After ten years: A follow-up study of comprehensive vocationally oriented psychotherapy. *American Journal of Orthopsychiatry*, 1973, *43*, 128–132.

Spivack, G., and Shure, M. *Social adjustment of young children*. Washington: Jossey-Bass, 1974.

Stierlin, H. *Separating parents and adolescents*. New York: Quadrangle, 1972.

Timeras, P. S. *Developmental physiology and aging*. New York: Macmillan, 1972.

Vaillant, G. E. *Adaptation to life*. Boston: Little, Brown, 1977.

Vance, E. T. A typology of risks and the disabilities of low status. In G. W. Albee and J. M. Joffe (Eds.), *Primary prevention of psychopathology. Vol. 1: The issues*. Hanover: University Press of New England, 1977.

Wandersman, A., and Moos, R. *Evaluating living environments for retarded people*. Unpublished manuscript.

Wandersman, L. P., and Wandersman, A. *Facilitating growth for all the family in the adjustment to a newborn*. Paper presented at the National Conference on Family Relationships, 1976.

Weiner, I. B., and Del Gaudio, A. C. Psychopathology in adolescence: An epidemiological study. *Archives of General Psychiatry*, 1976, *33*, 187–193.

Wessman, A. E., and Ricks, D. F. *Mood and personality*. New York: Holt, Rinehart, and Winston, 1966.

II
Life Satisfaction and Life Stress during Adulthood

Life satisfaction and life stress have too often been characterized as simply the reciprocal of one another. As the papers in the first section have suggested, such an oversimplified model leads to serious misconceptions that in turn result in misdirected research, theory, and application. Although the papers in this section emerge from a variety of perspectives and intentions, all are aimed at clarifying the factors that underlie life satisfaction and life stress.

In the last decade there has been a tremendous surge of activity devoted to delineating contributors to, and social indicators of, quality of life. Which aspects of our lives most affect our feelings of general satisfaction and contentment? To what degree do these factors gain or lose their relative emphases as we age? A prominent figure in this movement has been John C. Flanagan, founder and currently Chairman of the Board of Directors of the American Institutes for Research. Flanagan is well known for Project TALENT, a twelve-year longitudinal study of the talents and careers of a generation of high school students through more than a decade of their post-high school years. He is presently directing an extensive project examining the quality of life of adult Americans. This project has recently been reviewed with the intent of developing an educational program for bettering the quality of life. The conclusions of the review, which included data on a subsample of the Project TALENT population, have been published in a volume edited by Flanagan, *Perspectives on improving education: Project TALENT's young adults look back*.

Flanagan's paper in Part II presents extensive survey data on the perceptions of 30-, 50-, and 70-year-old Americans. Having defined fifteen dimensions that are perceived as critical contributors to quality of life, Flanagan examines the perspectives of men and women across the adult years regarding the adequacy with which their needs and wants are met, estimates of overall quality of life, and dimensions that are most and least important in influencing quality of life. Integrating this information, he empirically identifies reliable predictors of reported quality of life. We are cautioned, however, that although such survey data can prove enlightening, they are limited in the information they can provide for improving the quality of life of *individuals*. To the extent to which the latter is now a priority, Flanagan urges that we supplement our large-scale group analyses with greater attention to individual developmental patterns.

In the second paper of this part, Gisela Konopka offers insight into the stresses and strains particular to adolescent experience. Konopka, an emeritus professor at the University of Minnesota, has made a large number of influential contributions to the field of social work and has written extensively about adolescents. She asserts that adolescence is not a passage, but rather a stage in itself. Drawing from years of experience with adolescents, she illustrates their strong desire for both responsibility and for the facts needed to make their own decisions. In her view, stress results because adolescents are forced to make decisions without experience and are often prevented from acting on their own behalf. Regardless of whether adolescents are assimilated into their world or protest against it desperately, Konopka feels that their underlying motive nevertheless is confirmation of self-value.

Although stress and satisfaction among adults and adolescents are not simply two sides of the same coin, it is clear that certain factors contribute considerably to both. The final paper in this section focuses upon the promotion of physical health as a way of both reducing stress and enhancing a sense of well-being and satisfaction. Primary prevention of psychopathology has its roots in the field of public health, which initiated the notion of decreasing the incidence of a disorder by preventing its causes rather than treating its victims. Now public health itself may help prevent psychopathology by preventing one of its principal causes, physical illness.

Nathan Maccoby is professor and director at the Institute for Communication Research, Stanford University, where he also serves as Co-Director of the Stanford Heart Disease Prevention

Program. Maccoby is noted for his influential work in the fields of public opinion and communication.

Maccoby reviews the link between life style and cardiovascular disease and notes that the prevention of this major health problem depends upon self-management of behavior. How can the behavioral risk factors associated with cardiovascular disease be controlled on a widespread basis but at reasonable cost? He reports on the effectiveness of some of the unconventional health campaign tactics of the Stanford University Heart Disease Prevention Program. Behavioral skills, not just health facts, are being taken out of the clinic, and the message is being brought to the community with the help of the mass media. Maccoby's findings are an encouraging demonstration for other preventive education programs.

6

Quality of Life

JOHN C. FLANAGAN

Interest in the study of quality of life and social indicators has grown markedly in recent years. These studies were stimulated by the report of the President's Commission on National Goals in 1960 and the book *Social Indicators*, edited by Raymond A. Bauer in 1966. These were followed in 1970 by the U.S. Department of Health, Education and Welfare's publication *Toward a Social Report*. A somewhat parallel set of studies focusing more specifically on the individual included a report of a national survey, *Americans View Their Mental Health*, by Gurin, Veroff, and Feld, published in 1960. This was followed by H. Cantril's *The Patterns of Human Concerns* (1965), and N. M. Bradburn and D. Caplovitz' *Reports on Happiness* (1965); subsequently there has been a series of publications (Andrews and Withey, 1976; Campbell, Converse, and Rodgers, 1976; Duncan, 1969; Flanagan and Russ-Eft, 1978; Liu, 1973).

The social indicators movement attempted to develop national and, to some extent, local statistics for major areas of social concern. The effort was to obtain comprehensive coverage, affording an overview of several areas of social needs from a relatively uniform perspective. These types of information were presented in the form of charts and graphs as well as tables in *Social Indicators, 1976*, by the U.S. Department of Commerce. The topics included (1) population, (2) the family, (3) housing, (4) social security and welfare, (5) health and nutrition, (6) public safety, (7) education and training, (8) work, (9) income, wealth, and expenditures, (10) culture, leisure, and use of time, and (11) social mobility and participation.

These presentations included charts showing population change between decennial census years, comparison of the sex and age of persons in selected countries, and also such public perceptions as ideal family size for recent years. Examples on the topic of the family included trends in family size and composition, living arrangements, family stability, and perceptions of marital happiness. For health and nutrition, graphs and tables were included on such topics as changes in life expectancy in this century at ages 20, 40, and 60; admission rates to psychiatric inpatient facilities by race, sex, age, and diagnosis of patients; and food intake by major source of food energy (1957–59 and 1971–72).

Certainly this type of publication with its excellent use of charts and graphs should be very helpful in providing some of the basic data required to study social trends, but these statistical reports cannot be used as normative indicators; the information they present is often ambiguous. Items such as population growth, living arrangements, and food consumption are not easily classified or evaluated. Recognizing this, the government offices made no effort to draw conclusions for policy. However, Taeuber (1978) edited a special issue of *The Annals*, the publication of The American Academy of Political and Social Science, in which a number of social scientists attempted to provide insights into the significance of the patterns and trends presented and to give their personal views on the implications of these data for policy and for the future.

The other series of studies focusing more specifically on the individual's well-being and emphasizing subjective reports of perceived quality of life resulted in a number of national surveys. These surveys concentrated on such factors as morale, satisfactions, happiness, welfare, well-being, and quality of life. Various investigators found that a substantial amount of information was lost if only a single question was asked. Unfortunately, these investigators developed their own set of dimensions, usually on an arbitrary basis.

DEFINING CONTRIBUTORS TO PERCEIVED QUALITY OF LIFE

To obtain more objective dimensions to describe the quality of life, critical incidents were collected from more than 2,800 people in various parts of the country. These incidents were collected from small groups of people using standard response forms. No attempt was made to obtain a precisely representative sample, but the groups were selected to include a wide range of backgrounds and cultures.

The questions used contained references to several different types of circumstances or situations in an effort to identify all of the things that might contribute to a person's quality of life. One example was: "Think of the last time you did something very important to you or had an experience that was especially satisfying to you. What did you do or what happened that was so satisfying to you? Why did this experience seem so important or satisfying?"

Another question was: "Think of a recent time you could *not* do something you very much wanted to do or could *not* have something you very much wanted to have. What exactly did you want to do or to have that you couldn't? Why was this so important to you?"

Other questions involved queries on something that "has given you the most satisfaction in the past year." Still others asked for something "that really was harmful or made your life worse in some way"; "that was a continuing source of pleasure"; "that was a continuing source of trouble"; "that had a strong positive emotional impact"; or "that had a strong negative emotional impact."

There were 6500 critical incidents, which were sorted into homogeneous categories. The final formulation provided 15 types of critical incidents describing all of the experiences and behaviors reported as contributing either positively or negatively to the quality of life of these people. These 15 components were grouped under five headings. They include:

Physical and Material Well-Being

A. *Material well-being and financial security*. Having good food, home, possessions, comforts, and expectations of these for the future. Money and financial security are typically important factors. For most people, filling these needs is primarily a result of their own efforts or those of their spouse.

B. *Health and personal safety*. Enjoying freedom from sickness, possessing physical and mental fitness, avoiding accidents and other health hazards. Problems related to alcohol, drugs, death, and aging are also included. Effective treatment of health problems is a large component.

Relations with Other People

C. *Relations with spouse (girl friend or boy friend).* Being married or having a girl friend or boy friend. The relationship involves love, companionship, sexual satisfaction, understanding, communication, appreciation, devotion, and contentment.

D. *Having and raising children.* Having children and becoming a parent. This relationship involves watching their development, spending time with them and enjoying them. Also included are things like molding, guiding, helping, appreciating, and learning from them and with them.

E. *Relations with parents, siblings, or other relatives.* Having parents, siblings, or other relatives. In these relationships one experiences communicating with them or doing things with them, visiting, enjoying, sharing, understanding, being helped by them, and helping them. The feeling of belonging and having someone to discuss things with is a large component.

F. *Relations with friends.* Having close friends. In these relationships one shares activities, interests, and views. Important aspects of these relationships involve being accepted, visiting, giving and receiving help, love, trust, support, and guidance.

Social, Community, and Civic Activities

G. *Activities related to helping or encouraging other people.* Helping or encouraging adults or children (other than relatives or close friends). This can be done through one's efforts as an individual or as a member of some organization, such as a church, club, or volunteer group, which works for the benefit of other people.

H. *Activities relating to local and national governments.* Keeping informed through the media; participating by voting and other communications; having and appreciating one's political, social, and religious freedom. One component of this includes having living conditions affected by regulation, laws, procedures, and policies of governing agencies and the individuals and groups that influence and operate them.

Personal Development and Fulfillment

I. *Intellectual development.* Learning, attending school, acquiring desired knowledge and mental abilities, graduating, and problem solving. Other aspects involve improving understanding, comprehension, or appreciation in an intellectual area through activities in or out of school.

J. *Personal understanding and planning.* Developing and gaining orientation, purpose, and guiding principles for one's life. This may involve becoming more mature; gaining insight into and acceptance of one's assets and limitations; experiencing, and awareness of, personal growth and development; and realizing the ability to influence the course of one's life significantly. It also includes making decisions and planning life activities and roles. For some people a major component arises from religious or spiritual experiences or activities.

K. *Occupational role (job).* Having interesting, challenging, rewarding, worthwhile work in a job or home. This includes doing well, using one's abilities, learning and producing, obtaining recognition, and accomplishing on the job.

L. *Creativity and personal expression.* Showing ingenuity, originality, imagination in music, art, writing, handicrafts, drama, photography, practical or scientific matters, or everyday activities. This also includes expressing oneself through a collection, a personal project, or an accomplishment or achievement.

Recreation

M. *Socializing.* Entertaining at home or elsewhere, attending parties or other social gatherings, meeting new people, interacting with others. It may include participation in socializing, organizations and clubs.

N. *Passive and observational recreational activities.* Participating in various kinds of passive recreation, such as watching television, listening to music, reading, going to the movies, and going to entertainment or sports events. It also involves appreciating the art and beauty in many aspects of life.

O. *Active and participatory recreational activities.* Participating in various kinds of active recreation, such as sports, hunting, fishing, boating, camping, vacation travel, sightseeing, etc. This may also involve playing sedentary or active games, singing, playing an instrument, dancing, acting, etc.

Predicting Life Satisfaction Across the Adult Years

Although this list of dimensions showed a fair degree of overlap with those used by Andrews and Withey (1976) and Campbell, Converse, and Rodgers (1976), it was believed that its systematic and comprehensive empirical derivation gave it unique credibility for use in studies in this field.

These 15 components were used in surveying representative national samples of three age groups. The 30-year-old cohort consisted of a representative national sample of all 15-year-olds in the United States in 1960. These people were selected from among those 15-year-olds who had participated in Project TALENT. Appropriate weights were used in drawing the sample to give the proper representation to those below the 9th grade at the time of the testing in 1960 and thus correct for the problems of retardation and promotion policies.

The selection of this group made it possible to use the extensive data collected in two days of testing in Project TALENT plus the data from the one-, five-, and eleven-year follow-ups that had been made since that time.

The Field Initiated Studies Program of the National Institute of Education provided the funds for a three-hour interview with each of the 1000 individuals included in this sample when they were about 30 years old. This interview collected information on elementary and secondary school experiences, adolescent development, post high-school training and education, out of high-school activities and development, family relations, personal relations, having and raising children, occupational history, financial situation, health, leisure activities and interests, friends, and evaluation of life to date.

To these data nationally representative cohorts of 50-year-olds and 70-year-olds are being added, with funding from the Administration on Aging of the Department of Health, Education and Welfare. Although longitudinal data are not available for these groups, this population is being requested to supply retrospective data for the earlier age levels. The data analyses being reported here are based on 800 50-year-olds and 800 70-year-olds. The total samples will include 1000 individuals in each of the two cohorts.

Before discussing these people's reports on their quality of life and describing the predictors of life satisfaction, it is useful to look at some of the descriptive data on the various cohorts. For example, in comparison with census statistics, blacks appeared to be about 2 percentage points underrepresented in the 30-year-old cohort for the approximately 85 percent on whom information regarding race was available, and about one percentage point overrepresented in the 50- and 70-year-old cohorts for all of whom we had these data. It is possible that those whose race was not reported contained a larger proportion of blacks. Those not reporting tended to be in the lower socioeconomic categories. About 76 percent of the 30-year-old males and 79 percent of the 30-year-old females were married and living with their spouses. For the 50-year-olds, these figures were 84 and 75 percent respectively. The situation was somewhat different for the 70-year-olds, with 78 percent of the men married and living with their spouses but only 35 percent of the women in this category. Slightly more than half of the 70-year-old women reported they were widowed.

With respect to education, only 2 percent of both the male and female 30-year-olds reported that they never entered high school, but 14 percent of the male and female 50-year-olds and 36 percent of the 70-year-olds reported that they did not enter high school.

Almost all (more than 99 percent) of the 30-year-old men had been employed full time and the remainder employed part time in the year they were interviewed. Among the 30-year-old women, 47 percent were employed full time and 7 percent were employed part time in paid employment. For the 50-year-old men, 81 percent were employed full time and 3 percent part time. Of the 50-year-old women, 34 percent were employed full time and 20 percent part time. Among the 70-year-old men, only 5 percent were employed full time and 13 percent part time. The corresponding figures for 70-year-old women were 3 percent full time and 8 percent part time.

Perceived Importance of Quality of Life Dimensions

What are these groups' perceptions of their quality of life? Members of each of the three age groups were asked how important the 15 quality of life dimensions were to them at the present time. Their responses were made on a 5-point scale (very important, important, moderately important, only slightly important, and not at all important). The results are shown in Table 1. The

Table 1

Percentages of a Sample of 1,000 30-year-olds,
800 50-year-olds, and 800 70-year-olds
Reporting Each of the 15 Quality of Life Components as
for Each of the 15 Quality of Life Components*

Component	Male 30 yrs	Male 50 yrs	Male 70 yrs	Female 30 yrs	Female 50 yrs	Female 70 yrs
Physical and Material Well-Being						
A. Material Comforts	80	86	88	75	84	86
B. Health and Personal Safety	98	96	95	98	97	96
Relations with Other People						
C. Relationships with Relatives	68	64	62	83	76	79
D. Having and Raising Children	84	85	82	93	92	86
E. Close Relationship with a Spouse	90	90	85	94	82	43
F. Close Friends	71	76	74	79	80	88
Social, Community, and Civic Activities						
G. Helping and Encouraging Others	60	73	65	71	75	80
H. Participating in Local and National Government	47	64	65	42	60	57
Personal Development and Fulfillment						
I. Learning	87	69	52	81	68	59
J. Understanding Yourself	84	85	81	92	91	87
K. Work	91	90	58	89	85	60
L. Expressing Yourself Creatively	48	40	37	53	54	60
Recreation						
M. Socializing	48	46	51	53	49	62
N. Passive Recreation	56	45	53	53	56	64
O. Active Recreation	59	52	47	50	52	51

*For all age groups the question read, "At this time in your life, how important to you is ————?"

only component which more than 95 percent of all six groups say is either important or very important is *Health and Personal Safety*. More than 90 percent of the 30- and 50-year-old males give *Work* and *Close Relationship with a Spouse* this importance. *Work* understandably drops to 58 percent for the 70-year-old men, but *Close Relationship with a Spouse* is given this importance by 85 percent of this group. For the women, *Having and Raising Children* and *Understanding Yourself* are given this importance by more than 90 percent of the 30- and 50-year-old groups. These decrease only slightly for the 70-year-old women, to 86 and 87 percent respectively. *Close Relationship with a Spouse* is reported as important or very important to 94 percent of the

30-year-old women. This decreases to 82 percent for the 50-year-old women as a substantial number become widowed and drops much further to 43 percent at age 70 when more than half of them have been widowed.

Although the men do not report *Having and Raising Children* and *Understanding Yourself* to be quite as important to them as do the women, more than 80 percent of all three age groups rate these components as important or very important. Similarly, *Work* is reported as of only slightly less importance to the women than the men at ages 30 and 50. Sixty percent of the 70-year-old women, 2 percent more than the 70-year-old men, give it this importance.

In addition to these five components which are generally reported as important to nearly all of the adults, *Material Comforts* is reported as important by more than 80 percent of all groups except the 30-year-old women. In this latter group, 75 percent report it to be important. It should be noted that for both men and women *Material Comforts* is reported as more important by the older age groups. Two other trends to be mentioned are the decreasing importance given to *Learning* in the older age groups and the increasing importance of *Close Friends*, especially for women, in the three older age groups. As indicated before, half of the 70-year-old women have been widowed.

The five components given least importance by all six age groups are *Socializing, Expressing Yourself Creatively, Active Recreation, Passive Recreation,* and *Participating in Local and National Government.* These components tend to be reported as important by only about half of the persons in each of the six age groups.

To summarize the reports of importance to them, *Health, Work, Close Relationship with a Spouse, Having and Raising Children,* and *Understanding Yourself* are perceived as most important to these adults. Especially at the older ages, *Material Comforts* tends to join this group. Recreational and leisure activities are reported to be important the least frequently of these components, with participation in governmental affairs the next lowest.

Adequacy with Which Needs and Wants are Met

How well, do they report, have their needs and wants been met?

Table 2

Percentages of a Sample of 1,000 30–year–olds,
800 50–year–olds, and 800 70–year–olds Reporting Their Needs
as Moderately, Only Slightly, or Not at All Well Met
for Each of the 15 Quality of Life Components*

	Male			Female		
Component	30 yrs	50 yrs	70 yrs	30 yrs	50 yrs	70 yrs
Physical and Material Well-Being						
A. Material Comforts	26	27	24	24	32	26
B. Health and Personal Safety	14	17	15	14	18	20
Relations with Other People						
C. Relationships with Relatives	19	29	27	19	30	31
D. Having and Raising Children	20	14	18	17	14	16
E. Close Relationship with a Spouse	16	19	13	19	28	31
F. Close Friends	19	19	20	18	21	22
Social, Community, and Civic Activities						
G. Helping and Encouraging Others	39	28	28	38	26	26
H. Participating in Local and National Government	46	38	36	46	38	39
Personal Development and Fulfillment						
I. Learning	42	36	27	50	44	35
J. Understanding Yourself	26	26	24	29	25	20
K. Work	21	26	24	21	32	24
L. Expressing Yourself Creatively	40	32	26	43	32	28
Recreation						
M. Socializing	27	28	27	26	31	27
N. Passive Recreation	29	27	18	30	26	21
O. Active Recreation	36	41	36	37	40	35

*For the 50- and 70-year-olds, the question read "How well are your needs and wants being met in this regard?" For the 30-year-olds, the question read "How satisfied are you with your status in this respect?"

Looking at those which were reported as most important, it is seen (Table 2) that in all age groups only 20 percent or fewer report that their needs and wants are moderately, only slightly, or not at all well met in the areas of *Health* and *Having and Raising Children.* For *Understanding Yourself,* all six groups between 20 and 29 percent reported much dissatisfaction. With respect to *Work,* 32 percent of the 50-year-old females report that their needs and wants are moderately, only slightly, or not at all well met, and for the other five groups these percentages vary from 21 to 26.

Less than 20 percent of all three age groups of men and the 30-year-old women report "much dissatisfaction" with *Close*

Relationship with a Spouse, but 28 percent of the 50-year-old and 31 percent of the 70-year-old women report one or another of the three choices. Of course many fewer of these women have a spouse. Five of the six groups have between 24 and 27 percent selecting one of the three choices for the extent to which their needs and wants are met with respect to *Material Comforts*. The 50-year-old women are slightly less well satisfied, with 32 percent selecting one of these choices.

The areas for which they report their needs and wants are least well met are *Participating in Local and National Government, Learning, Active Recreation,* and *Expressing Yourself Creatively*. The percentages are in very close agreement for the men and women in each of these areas except *Learning,* where 8 percent fewer women than men report that their needs are well met.

Perceptions of Major Contributors to Current Quality of Life

Another approach used to identify areas offering opportunities for improving the quality of life of these adults was tabulating the responses of the 50- and 70-year-olds to a request to name the three areas that tended most to make their quality of life good at the present time (see Table 3). In general, these responses tended to confirm the findings from the previous questions, but with some different emphases. More than half of the 50-year-old and nearly half of the 70-year-old men mentioned *Close Relationship with a Spouse* as something tending to make their life good. Nearly half of the 50-year-old women but only 23 percent of the 70-year-old women mentioned this factor. Of course, only 35 percent of them have a spouse.

The item next most frequently mentioned was *Having and Raising Children.* This item was mentioned as tending to make their life good by 52 percent of the 50-year-old women, 38 percent of the 70-year-old women, 38 percent of the 50-year-old men, and 32 percent of the 70-year-old men. The 50-year-old men cited *Work* next most frequently (26 percent), and about 20 percent included *Material Comforts, Health, Close Friends, Helping and Encouraging Others, Understanding Yourself,* and *Active Recreation.* The other items most frequently mentioned by the 50-year-old women were similar to those mentioned by the men. The major discrepancies were fewer mentions of *Work*

Table 3

*Percentage of 800 Male and 800 Female 50- and 70-year-olds
Mentioning Each Area as One of the Three Areas Tending to
Make Their Quality of Life Good*

15 Areas of	Males		Females	
Quality of Life	At 50 yrs	At 70 yrs	At 50 yrs	At 70 yrs
Material Comforts	22	28	16	19
Health and Personal Safety	21	25	21	28
Relationships with Relatives	10	12	13	22
Having and Raising Children	38	32	52	38
Close Relationship with Husband/Wife	54	46	49	23
Close Friends	20	20	22	33
Helping and Encouraging Others	22	24	21	32
Participation in Government and Public Affairs	4	5	2	2
Learning	12	8	12	8
Understanding Yourself	20	15	24	16
Work	26	17	17	11
Expressing Yourself	11	8	18	16
Socializing	5	6	7	10
Passive Recreation	12	20	14	26
Active Recreation	20	20	11	10

(17 percent), *Material Comforts* (16 percent), and *Active Recreation* (11 percent) and slightly more mentions of *Understanding Yourself* (24 percent) and *Expressing Yourself Creatively*
(18 percent). In addition to *Spouse* and *Children*, the 70-year-
old men cited *Material Comforts* (28 percent), *Health* (25 percent), *Helping and Encouraging Others* (24 percent), *Close Friends*
(20 percent), *Passive Recreation* (20 percent), and *Active Recreation* (20 percent). The 70-year-old women also mentioned
quite frequently several items besides *Spouse* and *Children*.
These included: *Close Friends* (33 percent), *Helping and Encouraging Others* (32 percent), *Health* (27 percent), *Passive
Recreation* (26 percent), *Relationships with Relatives* (22 percent), and *Material Comforts* (19 percent).

A parallel query asked the 50- and 70-year-olds to identify
the three areas that most tended to make their quality of life
poor. These replies gave a somewhat different picture (see Table

Table 4

*Percentage of 800 Male and 800 Female 50- and 70-year-olds
Mentioning Each Area as One of the Three Areas Tending to
Make Their Quality of Life Poor*

15 Areas of Quality of Life	Males		Females	
	At 50 yrs	At 70 yrs	At 50 yrs	At 70 yrs
Material Comforts	27	24	31	31
Health and Personal Safety	22	24	22	30
Relationships with Relatives	8	8	14	8
Having and Raising Children	7	9	8	8
Close Relationship with Husband/Wife	9	6	14	16
Close Friends	6	5	4	4
Helping and Encouraging Others	4	5	4	3
Participation in Government and Public Affairs	16	18	20	17
Learning	27	23	23	18
Understanding Yourself	8	5	8	8
Work	13	14	17	12
Expressing Yourself	18	14	15	9
Socializing	15	14	14	9
Passive Recreation	7	8	8	3
Active Recreation	18	21	15	21

4). Leading the list in frequency of mentions was *Material Comforts* with 27 percent of the 50-year-old men and 31 percent of the 50-year-old women reporting that this factor tended to make their life poor. The comparable figures for the 70-year-olds were 24 percent and 31 percent. *Learning* and *Health* were the next most frequently mentioned items, with *Learning* more frequently mentioned by the 50-year-olds and *Health* by the 70-year-olds. The only other items mentioned by as many as 20 percent of these groups were *Active Recreation* for both the 70-year-old men and women and *Participation in Local and National Government* for the 50-year-old women.

Estimates of Current Overall Quality of Life

Near the end of the interview, the 50- and 70-year-old groups were asked to describe their overall quality of life at the present time (see Table 5). About 21 percent said it was "excellent,"

Table 5

Percentages of Self-Reports of Overall Quality of Life Made by
800 50-year-old Males and Females and 800 70-year-old
Males and Females

Overall Quality of Life	Males		Females	
	at 50 yrs	at 70 yrs	at 50 yrs	at 70 yrs
Excellent	24	22	20	17
Very Good	39	33	36	34
Good	24	27	31	33
Fair	10	15	11	13
Poor	3	3	3	3

35 percent that it was "very good," 29 percent that it was "good," 12 percent said "fair," and 3 percent said "poor." There were about 2 percent more "excellent" in the 50-year-old groups and about 5 percent more "fair" in the 70-year-old groups. There was also a slight tendency for more men to choose "excellent" and "fair" and for more women to choose "good" at both age levels. About 87 percent of both the men and the women at age 50 said their quality of life is "good" or better. At age 70, 81 percent of the men and 84 percent of the women report their quality of life as "good" or better.

Predictors of Quality of Life

Using these self-reports of overall quality of life, the best predictors among the 15 components were obtained by calculating the correlation coefficients between the reports of how well their needs and wants were met for each component with overall quality of life (see Table 6). In carrying out these calculations, the individual's rating for the extent to which needs and wants were met was weighted by the importance assigned this component by the individual. The component having the largest product-moment correlation coefficient between overall quality of life and the extent to which needs and wants were met for the individual by this component was *Material Comforts* for all four groups. The second largest was *Health. Work* and *Active Recreation* also were substantial predictors of overall quality of life. Among the other significant predictors were *Learning, Expressing Yourself Creatively, Close Friends, Under-*

Table 6

*Correlation Coefficients between Self-Reports of How Well
Needs Are Met Weighted on the Individual's Report of
Its Importance and Overall Quality of Life for
800 50- and 70-year-olds*

| | 50-year-olds | | 70-year-olds | |
Quality of Life Components	Males	Females	Males	Females
Material Comforts	.47	.54	.48	.39
Health and Personal Safety	.42	.39	.45	.33
Relationships with Relatives	.20	.13	.20	.10
Having and Raising Children	.30	.20	.25	.01
Close Relationship with Husband/Wife	.31	.38	.35	.18
Close Friends	.32	.25	.31	.21
Helping and Encouraging Others	.19	.12	.23	.22
Participation in Government and Public Affairs	.14	.19	.22	.22
Learning	.31	.38	.32	.22
Understanding Yourself	.32	.22	.24	.29
Work	.41	.49	.38	.30
Expressing Yourself	.30	.30	.35	.23
Socializing	.35	.28	.30	.27
Passive Recreation	.28	.29	.07	.22
Active Recreation	.38	.31	.38	.32

standing Yourself, Socializing, and (except for 70-year-old women) *Close Relationship with a Spouse.*

It is interesting to note that the four poorest predictors of the individual's present report of overall quality of life at ages 50 and 70 included *Having and Raising Children* (this was one of the most frequently reported to be important, one where the needs and wants were well met, and one of the most frequently mentioned as tending to make their quality of life good); *Participation in Local and National Government* (this was not rated as important but was reported as an area in which their needs and wants were not well met, and also was among those components most frequently mentioned as making their quality of life poor); *Helping and Encouraging Others* (this was reported moderately frequently as important to them; they indicated that their needs and wants were fairly well met, and mentioned it moderately frequently as something tending to make their quality of life good); and *Relationships with Relatives* (this was reported in the middle of these components on both importance and the extent to which needs and wants are met, and was one of the components least frequently mentioned as making their life good or poor).

It was clear that the things people considered when asked to rate their overall quality of life were not identical to the items they rated as most important to them and for which they reported their needs are well met. There was a substantial amount of overlap but several discrepancies. Such was also the case for the reports on the things that tended to make their quality of life good or poor. *Health* was consistently evaluated as an important contributor, but the dominant role of *Material Comforts* in predicting the overall quality of life was not apparent from these adults' reports of its importance. *Work* was fairly consistently rated as the important contributor that it appeared to be. The low ratings given its importance by the 70-year-olds did not appear to be borne out by the data. Some type of *Work* activity appeared to remain as one of the better predictors of quality of life for 70-year-olds.

Active Recreation presented probably the biggest surprise among the predictors. With only half of both the 50- and 70-year-olds reporting it to be important or very important to them, about 60 percent indicated that their needs in this area were well met or very well met. Only an average number reported it as something tending to make their quality of life good or poor. Nevertheless, *Active Recreation* was found to be one of the best predictors of the overall quality of life in all four groups. It seems plausible on reflection that an activity that lacks deep commitment and satisfactions may nevertheless be a very important contributor to one's overall feeling of well-being. Three other components that were not reported as high in importance were found to be among the better predictors of the overall quality of life: *Socializing, Expressing Yourself Creatively,* and *Learning.* It seems likely that these contribute to the quality of life in the same way that *Active Recreation* does.

Relationship between Demographic Components and Overall Quality of Life

It is clear that these subjective self-reports have a number of

Table 7

*Correlation Coefficients Between Demographic Components and
Self-Report of Overall Quality of Life for
800 50- and 800 70-year-olds*

Demographic Components	50-year-olds		70-year-olds	
	Males	Females	Males	Females
Family Income	.38	.42	.27	.16
Amount of Education	.25	.30	.26	.16
Marital Status	.35	.35	.35	.13
Employment Status	.54	.26	.08	.04

weaknesses. To supplement the analyses and to provide a somewhat different perspective, some objective measures were compared with the overall quality of life. These included current
family income, current amount of education, marital status, and
employment status (see Table 7).

The product-moment correlation coefficient between self-
report of overall quality of life and total family income was 0.38
for 50-year-old men and 0.42 for 50-year-old women. These
coefficients are not much lower than those found between overall
quality of life and the extent to which they report that their
needs and wants are met in regard to *Material Comforts*, and they
are larger than those for nearly all of the other contributors. The
correlation coefficients between the overall quality of life and
total family income for 70-year-olds are considerably lower than
for 50-year-olds: 0.27 for the males and 0.16 for the females.
The median total family incomes for these four groups were
$18,400 for 50-year-old men, $14,000 for 50-year-old women,
$7,000 for 70-year-old men, and $5,500 for 70-year-old women.
Although these correlations lend further support to the major
contribution of money to overall quality of life, it should also
be noted that the 70-year-old men with much less than half the
income of the 50-year-old group report almost as good an overall
quality of life. Clearly, these judgments are relative.

Expressed in percentage terms, 71 percent of the 50-year-old
men who report their overall quality of life as very good or excellent have total family incomes of $16,000 per year or more.
Conversely, 80 percent of those who report their overall quality
of life as fair or poor have total family incomes of less than

$16,000. Similar results are shown for the 50-year-old women if a cut-point of $12,000 per year is used. The corresponding values are 74 and 83 percent. For the 70-year-old males, 60 percent of those reporting an excellent or very good overall quality of life, report total family income of $8,000 or more and 75 percent of those reporting a fair or poor overall quality of life report less than $8,000. As shown by the correlation coefficients, the prediction is much poorer for the 70-year-old women. There are 67 percent of those reporting their overall quality of life as very good or excellent who report family income of $4,000 per year or more and 44 percent of those reporting their overall quality of life as fair or poor who report total family income of $4,000 or less.

The biserial correlation coefficient between self-report of overall quality of life and whether the individual is married or not married is 0.35 for 50-year-old men. The same coefficient, 0.35, was obtained between these variables for 50-year-old women and for 70-year-old men. For 70-year-old women, the large majority of whom are not married, the coefficient was still positive but much smaller at 0.13.

The same type of biserial correlation coefficient showed a definitely higher report of overall quality of life for the 80 percent of the 50-year-old men who were working than for the 20 percent who were not. This coefficient was 0.54. A few more than half of the 50-year-old women reported they were working full or part time in paid employment. This group reported a slightly better overall quality of life than those not employed as indicated by a coefficient of 0.26. Only about 17 percent of the 70-year-old men and 11 percent of the 70-year-old women had paid employment, and most of these were working part time. They showed only very slightly higher overall quality of life reports, as indicated by biserial correlation coefficients of 0.08 and 0.04 respectively.

The other objective variable was highest level of education reached. This yielded a product-moment correlation coefficient of 0.25 with self-report of overall quality of life for the 50-year-old men. The comparable value for the 50-year-old women was 0.30. The correlation coefficients for the 70-year-olds were 0.26 for the men and 0.16 for the women. These results continue the trend of lower predictability for the overall quality of life of the

70-year-old women on the reports of the extent to which needs and wants were met on the 15 quality of life components.

Sharpening the Picture through Monadic Analysis

Statistical analyses of various reports by representative national samples such as these can provide useful data regarding both basic conditions and trends. However, such analyses contain basic defects as a source of information for improving the quality of life of individuals.

The study of the sample of 1000 30-year-olds reported on here used a group of people who were 15-year-olds when they participated in Project TALENT in 1960. The two days of tests, follow-up studies, and the three-hour interview at age 30 provided a rich data resource that made possible a study of each individual's development and specific insights into the conditions and experiences that either helped or interfered with self-actualization and the attainment of a good quality of life.

The data for each of the 1000 individuals were summarized in a five- to eight-page abstract. In preparing the abstracts, critical factors affecting their development, especially in relation to their educational experiences, were noted. To communicate some of the findings that become evident only when the major facts of an individual's development and present status are known, each of 10 behavioral and social scientists was asked to study the lives, as revealed in these abstracts, of a different set of 100 individuals. Their conclusions along with some of the general findings from the complete sample are included in a book entitled *Perspectives on Improving Education: Project TALENT's Young Adults Look Back* (Flanagan, 1978).

The type of analysis which uses the individual as the unit and tabulates the crucial factors in both development and present status is called *monadic analysis*. Monadic analysis is intended to supplement the types of survey data presented in the preceding analyses. The descriptive characteristics regarding a person collected in typical surveys require no previous history, no specific context, and no other descriptive information about the person. Attitudes, evaluations, preferences, interests, abilities, and events can be tabulated without reference to other characteristics or past history of the individuals involved. Monadic analysis is concerned with studying the history, context, and present status of an individual to determine crucial factors, causes, and possible improvements in a person's life.

Identifying causal factors that determine an individual's present quality of life requires abundant information of both a developmental and historical type, as well as comprehensive information on the influences and context involved in the individual's present life situation. The most useful data from monadic analysis will come from studies of representative samples of important types of populations. The findings from studies of such samples can be generalized to describe the characteristics of the populations on which they are based.

A few of the findings related to improving education from the study of 30-year-olds will illustrate the methods and types of findings that can be obtained by monadic analysis.

A careful examination of the educational experiences, interests, information, abilities, family background, and life histories of this representative national sample of 30-year-olds indicated that lack of adequate educational and vocational guidance in the secondary schools interfered to a significant extent with the development of the present life satisfaction for 65 percent of these young people.

Thumbnail sketches of a few of the cases on which this generalization was based illustrate the way in which crucial factors are tabulated in monadic analysis. The first individual, whom we will call Bill, had very high verbal abilities when tested in the 10th grade, high mechanical and nonverbal abilities, and about average mathematical abilities. He entered a college and enrolled in a science course. After two years he dropped out of school because he was doing poorly in mathematics. While in the service he took a course in computer programming and has been working in this field since. During the interview he said that he would like to get out of programming and move up to a position in middle management. He felt he needed to get his college degree, but he had no definite plans and was still floundering. He clearly needed help in relating his abilities to his career plans.

Mary also was unhappy with her position. When she took the Project TALENT tests in high school, her scores were very high in vocabulary and mechanical reasoning, high in creativity, and fairly high in English, reading comprehension, visualization, and arithmetic computation. Her other scores were a little above average. When interviewed, she reported that in high school "I had a lot of fantasies concerning particular careers, like being in animal science, and I was unaware of the requirements." After working in a variety of jobs, Mary wound up teaching an 8th-grade class. She was not satisfied, however, and wanted to change to another field. She also would have benefited from help in selecting a career.

Although the monadic analysis showed that many of these young people had more than one important factor affecting their development and current life satisfactions, the rich detail contained in the abstracts made it possible for readers not only to identify the crucial factors contributing to their present life satisfaction but also to assess with relatively high inter-judge agreement the level of impact of specific factors on a 4-point scale.

Another illustration of the unique value of monadic analysis was provided by the study of Gary's quality of life. Gary reported that Passive Recreation was important to his quality of life but he also said he was not at all satisfied with the extent to which his needs and wants with respect to this type of activity were being met. He said he liked watching TV, seeing sporting events, and reading newspapers and magazines. However, no amount of massaging the numbers in the report could be expected to reveal that his dissatisfaction came not from the quality of the available viewing or his access to it but was the result of an eye injury he received in an accident. Only monadic analysis brings out the causal factors.

The preparation of abstracts for use in monadic analysis is a very time-consuming activity. The 1000 abstracts prepared for the 30-year-olds represented the expenditure of several thousand hours of effort. Such a procedure is essential, however, since working from the 100- to 120-page interview booklets requires hours to read one life history rather than minutes. With careful training of the abstracters, almost nothing of value is lost in the abstracting process.

It is planned to prepare similar abstracts for the 50- and 70-year-old samples. When this has been completed, a fairly comprehensive data bank consisting of a sample of 3000 representative adults will be available for use in monadic analysis to identify the causal factors determining both the good and bad contributions to the quality of life of adult Americans. The present survey results indicate that only about 15 percent of adult Americans view their quality of life as being only fair or poor. Nearly all of them indicate, however, that there are a number of areas in which it could be improved. It is hoped that the samples and methodology reported here will point the way toward changes leading to greater life satisfaction for all of the country's adults.

REFERENCES

Andrews, F. M., and Withey, S. B. *Social indicators of well-being in America: The development and measurement of perceptual indicators*. New York: Plenum Press, 1976.

Bauer, R. (Ed.). *Social indicators*. Cambridge, Mass.: MIT Press, 1966.

Bradburn, N. M., and Caplovitz, D. *Reports on happiness*. Chicago, Ill.: Aldine, 1965.

Campbell, A., Converse, P. E., and Rodgers, W. L. *The quality of American life*. New York: Russell Sage Foundation, 1976.

Cantril, H. *The pattern of human concerns*. New Brunswick, N.J.: Rutgers University Press, 1965.

Duncan, O. D. *Toward social reporting: Next steps*. New York: Russell Sage Foundation, 1969.

Flanagan, J. C. (Ed.). *Perspectives on improving education: Project TALENT's young adults look back*. New York: Praeger Publishers, 1978.

Flanagan, J. C., and Russ-Eft, D. *Identifying opportunities for improving the quality of life of older age groups* (Progress Report). Palo Alto, Cal: American Institutes for Research, June 1978.

Gurin, G., Veroff, S., and Feld, S. *Americans view their mental health*. New York: Basic Books, 1960.

Liu, B.-C. *The quality of life in the United States: 1970*. Kansas City, Mo.: Midwest Research Institute, 1973.

Taeuber, C. (Ed.). America in the seventies: Some social indicators. *Annals of the American Academy of Political and Social Science*, 1978, *435*.

The President's Commission on National Goals. *Goals for Americans*. Columbia University: The American Assembly, 1960.

U.S. Department of Commerce, Office of Federal Statistical Policy and Standards, Bureau of the Census. *Social indicators, 1976: Selected data on social conditions and trends in the United States*. Washington, D.C.: U.S. Government Printing Office, 1977.

U.S. Department of Health, Education and Welfare. *Toward a social report*. Ann Arbor, Mich.: The University of Michigan Press, 1970.

7

Stresses and Strains
in Adolescents and Young Adults

GISELA KONOPKA

THE CONCEPT OF ADOLESCENCE

It seems to me best to let an adolescent talk first before I say anything about that age group. A girl wrote:

I am a bottle sealed with feeling
too deep for anyone else.
I am a bottle floating in an eternal ocean
of people trying to help.
I am a bottle keeping my fragile contents inside.
Always afraid of breaking and exposing me.
I am a bottle frail and afraid of the rock.
And afraid of the storm.
For if the storm or rocks burst or cracked me,
I would sink and become part of the ocean.

(Konopka, 1976, p. 2)

This 16-year-old expresses clearly that an adolescent is part of humanity, is a person. This should be self-evident; yet in recent years adolescents have been treated often as if they are a species apart, to be feared or occasionally to be flattered.

It is my thesis that the period of adolescence is as significant a period in life for the development of the total personality as are the first years in childhood.

It is a time of rebirth. It is sometimes questioned whether adolescence is purely an artificial concept born out of recent, urban western society. I find this questioning futile. Any division of the life cycle and the conceptualization of various age periods are artificial in the sense that we cannot separate them out, nor are they exactly the same in all cultures. Adulthood, old age, all such periods are different in different cultures. We must look at the life cycle, and the different environments and systems in which human beings grow up, and then try to understand what is specific about these periods.

To me—and here I differ from many textbook descriptions—adolescence does not represent merely a preparation for adulthood, nor should it be a no-man's land between childhood and adulthood. Adolescents are not just pre-adults, pre-parents, or pre-workers but human beings participating in their particular way in the activities of the world around them.

Adolescence is not a passage to somewhere but an important stage in itself, though all stages of human development connect with each other. There is an "adolescenthood."

The key experiences of adolescence (which always include stresses and strains) are certain *firsts* which need to be worked through. They may occur in different individuals at various times with varying intensity, and perhaps not *all* of them apply to every person, but they do exist.

It must be understood that no generalization about human beings ever applies exactly to any one person and that in working with people, we have to take a fresh look at the human being with whom we interact. A 15-year-old said this best:

I used to be . . .
a grape in a bunch
and all the other
grapes were the same.
But now . . .
I'm an apple, crisp
and fresh, and every
one is different.
My, how life has changed!

(Konopka, 1976, p. 7)

Some of the "firsts" of adolescence are:

Experiencing physical sexual maturity. A phenomenon particular to adolescence that never occurs again in the life of the individual is the process of *developing* sexual maturation, different from the state of *accomplished* sexual maturation. Biologically this is a totally new experience. Its significance is due both to its pervasiveness and to the societal expectations surrounding it. It creates in adolescents a great wonderment about themselves and a feeling of having something in common with all human beings. It influences all their relationships with one another, male or female. Entering this part of maturity also stimulates them to a new assessment of the world.

Experiencing withdrawal of and from adult benevolent protection. Along with the biological maturity attained in adolescence come varying degrees of withdrawal of, and from, the protection generally given to dependent children by parents or substitutes. We know that some young people were never protected, even as children; but whatever the degree of previous protection, the adolescent is moving out from the family toward interdependence (not independence, *inter*dependence) in three areas: (a) with peers his or her own generation; (b) with elders, but on an interacting or questioning level instead of a dependent level; and (c) with younger children, not on a play level but on a beginning-to-care-for-and-nurture level. This process of moving away from dependency creates tensions and emotional conflicts.

Consciousness of self in interaction. The development of self and the searching for self starts in childhood, but the intellectual and the emotional consciousness of self in interaction with others is a particular characteristic of adolescence. It is a time when personal meaning is given to new social experiences. Young people define for themselves what they are experiencing in their relationships with others. This is no longer done *for* them by adults, or, if it is done, it is questioned by most adolescents. The categories they used as children to figure out the world begin to break down. What may have been clear and explicable may suddenly become inexplicable. This makes for inner excitement, frightening yet enjoyable.

Reevaluation of values. Though the formation of values is a life-long developmental process, it peaks in adolescence. It is related to both thinking and feeling, and is influenced by human interaction. In our culture, where young people are likely to be exposed to a variety of contradictory values, questioning begins even in childhood. Adolescents engage in reevaluation of values that have been either accepted at an earlier age or simply rejected because of individual resistance. They move beyond simple perception (for example, "if I burn my hand, it hurts") to seeing things in a morally good or bad framework. They become moral philosophers concerned with "shoulds" and "oughts" and they may be subtle or outspoken about it. Value confrontations are inevitable in this age period. The young, because of their intensity, tend to be uncompromising. They may opt clearly for a thoroughly egalitarian value system, or they may give up and become cynics. They often are true believers and therefore feel deeply hurt when others do not accept their value system.

Becoming an active participant in society. Adolescents encounter their world with a new intellectual and emotional consciousness. They meet it less as observers who are satisfied with this role than as participants who actually have a place to fill. I see this wish to *participate* as a most significant "first" in adolescence. In the old, mostly European textbooks it appears as the adolescent quality of rebellion, and for years we have considered rebellion an inevitable attribute of adolescence. I think that this is true in authoritarian societies—and we are still, partially, an authoritarian society—but basically it is not rebellion that characterizes adolescence but an extraordinary new awakening to the fact that one must develop one's values, and not only by imitation. This is a terribly hard task and brings with it enormous stress.

Life Force. Adolescence is an age of extraordinary physical capacity, enormous life force. This is sometimes at variance with the emotional development, and that again makes for great strain. It is an age where the mood swings with utmost intensity from omnipotence to despair. Adolescents can go without sleep for a long time; they run, jump, dance. In one of our Youth Polls done by the Center for Youth Development and Research in which the subject of health was at issue, it became clear that adolescents define health as "activity and energy." One said, "I think I am healthy when I am able to walk and run and run around all day and not be tired." Another, "When you are energetic, lively, active, and not run down." And another, "When you are feeling strong and able to run and laugh."

Being *not* healthy is a total experience because of this extra-ordinary life force: One defined it, "I feel unhealthy when I don't feel like doing anything." And another, "It's when you feel like you don't cope with anything, or feel like you don't have anything to live for" (Hedin, Wolfe, Garrison, and Fruetel, 1977).

CONTENT AREAS OF LIFE SIGNIFICANT TO ADOLESCENCE

The major institutions in which adolescents move have begun to be the same all over the world. Cultures change rapidly. For example, the teenage Bedouin, until recently, had to develop predominantly within the extended family and handle stresses within this system. The boy's work environment was static in terms of its tasks, namely herding goats, but it was changing geographically because of the tribe's nomad existence. The girl had no decisions to make, only to obey. Yet today most of the Bedouin teenagers have to deal with a smaller family unit, with school, with a variety of work tasks, and with less nomadic move-ment. These changes impinge on both sexes.

The most significant institutions in adolescent life today are: (a) the family; (b) the school; (c) the place of work; and (d) the peer group.

The Family

It is a myth that North American young people do not care for the family. In every survey that the Center for Youth Develop-ment and Research has made, the yearning for close family ties emerges clearly. Even a runaway wrote:

The first night was cold—
damn cold.
And walking around the avenues,
we would mock the whores.
The bit man and his badge would
give us a cold eye.
And without hesitation, we
would flip him a bird.
I wished for my mother,

and I wished for sympathy—
For a warm bed, and not the cold
shipyard or the park swings.
I feel really old for 15,
there just isn't any place to go.
Mama, I miss you—
and I just spent my last dollar for cigarettes.

(Konopka, 1976, p. 64)

The major frustration for an adolescent within the family is to suffer the role of an inferior at an age when the wish to be taken seriously, and as an equal, is very intense. Frustrating experiences range from being treated "like a kid" to serious abuse. And additional frustration can result from the youth's keen awareness of problems between the parents. Younger children suffer deeply from strife between parents, but adolescents often feel they have to *do* something about it, that they have to take on the responsibility in the situation. I found again and again a deep resentment of divorce, and at the same time a feeling that the adolescent should have done something to prevent it. Also, adolescents, unlike younger children, begin to look to the future. Many expressed a wish to start a family, but also feared it.

The School

Some of the dynamics in the family apply as well to the relationship of the adolescent to school. Again, the strong sense of self comes in conflict with possible violation of the vulnerable self-integrity. The youth wants to be seen as an individual as expressed by the wishes: "There should be a one to ten ratio of teachers to students." "If the teachers understood the students better, they could help the students with their problems." They should treat young people "like adults, not like two-year-olds, unless students just don't cooperate. Discuss all material that will be tested. Make every effort to answer all questions. Do best to help each student by keeping classes smaller. Not like we are their slaves or workers, and they are the boss." "To understand that we are people too and not just dumb kids to whom they can attach a number" (Hedin, 1978).

There are other stresses in school. It is the place where students expect to learn. Adolescents in their own way begin to question whether they need what they learn. One expressed it this way: "Teach us things that will help us to live in the real world—life and health facts. These are the students' main interests. They should be able to decide what they need to learn along with what the teachers think they have to know" (Hedin, 1978).

I doubt that it occurs to them that the Country Club won't post swim meets because they won't have Blacks swimming in their pool. We were talking about the senior prom, and they wanted to have it at the Country Club.

It's a private school. Well, academically it's all right. But socially it kind of lacks . . . there are 14 Black people there, and 500 or so white people. After four years, that tends to kind of put you out in the cold . . . No, I don't think I have an identity problem. But it doesn't help any to make you feel accepted because you have to fight harder to have friends outside and inside school in order to get along.

The teachers are sort of scared of Blacks here. I'm not the kind of person that shows how much I hate them. I just sit back and do mostly what I'm supposed to do. But teachers are still scared. If I ask a question, some of the teachers just ignore me. And I sit back and I watch this and I feel it. (Konopka, 1976, pp. 114–116)

School experience also includes the questioning of one's intellectual capacity. As students put it: "The students who get the most attention are the ones with special problems, the 'normal' ones get left alone."

I feel the small school should be moved to a general traffic pattern so that the people would be exposed to more socialization which would possibly extract more of their abilities, skills, etc. The people who are higher academically are very seldom allowed to display their full potential under the present majority-based system. (Hedin, 1978)

Sometimes, I don't understand what they are saying. The teachers, they talk but when you go up to the desk and ask what they mean, they don't say nothing. They just say, "Go on and do it!" They don't explain. They just say, "Go back to your desk and do it." (Konopka, 1976, p. 124)

The Place of Work

Many adolescents do work while in school, though others see it as part of the future. We found in our observations a generally strong work ethic. Two students expressed themselves: "looking forward to starting a job because it gives one a sense of responsibility." "Want to work . . . because we've trained for it for so long and we're anxious to start" (Hedin, Wolfe, Bush, and Fruetel, 1977). Contrary to popular assumption, adolescents felt a responsibility for the work they were doing. They frequently regretted not having an opportunity to work on something that would prepare them for a future career. Young people can rarely find work related to special interests. A 16-year-old volunteered to work in the Rape Center of the Attorney General's Office, and saw this as an opportunity not only for feeling significant at that particular time in her life, but also to find out what her specific interests would be. But a study done last summer on CETA jobs showed that usually adolescents felt frustrated because their jobs had no connection with their interests and were not realistic experiences.

They make us work like people in yester-years, like out of the 18th century. With machinery, the government could accomplish something with more speed, efficiency and effectiveness. Instead, they give you old-time machines to do the work; they don't give you a power saw, they give you a hand saw . . . With machinery we could get 50% more work done in a year's time than by hand. They wanted to modernize everything—more power to them—but they don't want to use it. I feel like the work is fine and dandy, it gives us an education on how to use manpower without machinery. We work out-of-doors, but actually this accomplishes nothing because when we get another job in the future, we have no education as to how to use the sophisticated tools there; and we're not here just for the money but for an education also. (Brokering, 1978)

The Peer Group

For adolescents the peer group is most important. In our culture this world exists within organized institutions and in informal encounters. School is seen by practically all adolescents as the major formal institution where they can find friends. But for others, school may mean the unpleasant strain or, for a variety of reasons, painful rejection by one's peers. Youth organizations may also provide friends along with very positive experiences.

On midsummer's eve the moon was high in the sky.
We danced all night in the moon's smiling, gleaming face
We ran about the park with youngness and freedom
We sang songs of old and new.
We played on midsummer's eve as though it were
    never to leave us.
The morning soon followed, so we left.
But we will be back on midsummers'.
                              (Konopka, 1976, p. 129)

The world of peers is the life blood of adolescence. Friendships with both sexes, intensified by growing sexual maturity, are exceedingly important—and complex; they demand decision-making about oneself, about others, about the present and the future. Decision-making is written large all through adolescence, and no decisions are more important than those of peer relationships.

How Do Human Beings in General Cope with Stresses and Strains?

All human beings have to deal with the stresses and strains of life. The answers to life's pain spontaneously range from withdrawal to violent attack on one's self or others. "Coping" means "dealing with." It is more than a reflex; it includes thinking and doing. When we talk about a person being able to cope with life's events, we are not using the term in a neutral sense. We are giving it a value-connected meaning. We do mean the capacity to withstand, to resist, to live through adversity without damage to one's own personality or to the personalities of others. It is important that we are clearly talking about a value judgment. We can cope with stress by denying it and then finally breaking under it, or by blaming others for it and making them miserable, or by demanding incessant support, or by fleeing into drugs or alcohol. We see those ways of "coping" as negative. We wish people to have the capacity to accept stress and strain as an inevitable part of life, to be able to acknowledge it, and then to work their way through it. We do not expect this of the infant. The infant responds to pain and frustration simply by expressing the hurt, by screaming. Increasingly, children learn to handle pain in various new ways, usually with the protective help of adults. This development of new ways, and the acknowledgment of what one can *do* about the stresses and strains, and accepting them as inevitable are the real business of life, and the development of philosophy. These adjustments never end. Only in old age is another ingredient, perhaps reassurance, added to the coping process, namely the knowledge that "it will not be so long anymore."

Coping in Adolescence

The coping process is most significant in adolescence. (A friend of mine said of youth, "They don't yet have anything in the bank," meaning that they have not yet experienced how to live through severe stress.) Because of stresses that are new and because of their intense life energy, adolescents often react to personal or institutional strain with extreme behavior. Some throw off the frustration of an unhappy love experience by totally denying it, by pretending that it never happened. Teachers know the "shrug of the shoulder kid," who seems to be untouched by anything. Some respond to frustration with physical violence. Zvi Eisikovits (1977) studied a number of violent teenage offenders in the State of Minnesota. He found that frequently the victim of violence was not the person who had frustrated the youth, but somebody related to that person whom the adolescent felt more capable of destroying. Adolescents' frustration and anger, and frequently the sense of being totally demeaned, become so overwhelming that sometimes they cannot cope with their emotional and physical revulsion in any way other than to destroy someone.

Despair about life's frustrating events leads to running away, drugs, and suicide. The second leading cause of death in adolescence in Minnesota was suicide (Minnesota Center for Health Statistics, 1975). Drugs and alcohol are frequently taken because of a sense of rejection at home or by a close friend. A 17-year-old said: "I sniffed paint, glue, mainly paint . . . I figure a lot of that happened when I was fighting with my parents" (Konopka,

1976, p. 104). Another said, "I take drugs when I get depressed or when I get upset or when I feel I can't handle a problem, or when I really got a bad problem on my mind" (Konopka, 1976, p. 106).

When there has been no experience dealing with serious life events, the doors seem closed and one cannot cope: "My boy friend, he didn't give me as much attention as I needed so I cut my wrists . . ." (Konopka, 1976, p. 97). And, "I am being pushed around from institution to foster home several times. What have you got to live for? No place to go—no place to stay where you are at? Nothing to want to get up in the morning for. I always feel lonely" (Konopka, 1976, p. 98).

Loneliness is the curse of humans at any time in life. In adolescence the need to have peers who can confirm your own value, and at least one adult whom you can trust, is very great. Loneliness presents a desperate strain then. During our survey of needs of adolescent girls, we often heard them quote a verse: "Loneliness is a silent jail, Without cellmates, parole, or bail" (Konopka, 1976, p. 98).

What are some of the positive ways of coping in adolescence? It rarely is a well thought-out philosophy, but we can speak of four means: (a) communication with contemporaries; (b) communication with adults who understand, often of "the grandparent generation"; (c) religion; and (d) creative expression of emotions, as in songs, poetry, and painting.

Communication with contemporaries. This means talking about one's problems, but also holding each other, crying together, dancing, and sexual relationships. All of these represent some form of coping with problems.

Communication with adults. The wish to find a willing ear of an adult and also to hear what the adult has to say (if he or she is not judgmental) is very great. Again and again, adolescents express a need to be listened to. Among the girls we interviewed, mothers were still the ones that they thought of most often as confidants and from whom they wanted help; if they could not get it from this source, the strain increased. Grandparents, or people of that age group, were often sought out because they seemed to be more patient and less judgmental. Adolescents seemed to understand well that one needs to talk about problems in order to deal with them. In fact, not communicating feelings to others was regarded by them as behavior harmful to one's health.

In general, young people do not consider going to professionals for help, partly because of their own overconfidence and partly because they distrust professionals. As one youth put it: "It's hard to tell your problems to a perfectly strange person. It's hard to let everything out" (Hedin et al., 1977). Adolescents often worry that doctors or nurses might not keep their problems confidential, might tell their parents.

The young person has a very specific difficulty in coping with serious problems, and for two reasons:

(a) They feel that there are many expectations laid upon them and that they will let people down if they do not live up to them.

(b) In spite of these expectations, they are treated as dependent children, and frequently cannot get services by themselves. The wish, for instance, to get medical care without having to go with their parents was expressed very frequently. For instance, the girl who has to cope with a pregnancy out of wedlock deals with an extraordinarily severe life problem. Yet even today she faces not only the problem of how to deal with her own body and the future of her child, but also with the hostility of the human environment. (I know there are exceptions, but this is still the rule.)

Religion. As either a traditional way of dealing with stresses and strains or as a new emotional experience, religion is on the increase among adolescents. The revival of fundamentalist religion and the popularity of various new sects among American youths express a need to deal with a life that is not always happy or satisfying. This renewal also represents an acceptance of authority, but from sources other than the ones with which they grew up.

A society that does not prepare children and young people early for thinking through a problem and making decisions, but considers obedience a higher value, is vulnerable to the embrace by its young of a dangerous authoritarianism.

Creative response. This seems to involve far more youth than we have ever assumed. Young people often keep it hidden. That may be due partly to the fact that art is considered erudite, and they cannot believe that they themselves can produce anything worthwhile, and partly because of impossibly high expectations laid upon them. For example, I found excellent poetry written by girls in delinquency institutions, but they hesitated to share it because the grammar and spelling were not perfect. Yet whether they shared this writing with others or not, for the young people themselves it was a very positive means of coping with frustration and loneliness.

Coping with institutions. When adolescents deal with institutional frustrations (as, for instance, school or correctional institutions) another form of coping is to cheat—a method well known among adults. It is a way of circumventing the source of strain to prevent any further hurt and this is done by "playing the games" that adults expect of them.

For instance, in institutions where constant group involvement or confrontation was the expected form of treatment, adolescents played the game of "involvement," "confrontation," or whatever was demanded and did so superbly. If individual "baring of the soul" was expected, they also knew how to do this. Adolescents are good actors, and they can cope with hurt by pretending to live up to almost any expectations. They know what they are doing. In one institution, a young man asked me cynically: "Well, what do you want me to be or to do, so that you can have success?" Part of their response is based on the philosophy of retaliation which makes it possible to live through frustration: "If teachers would treat us nicely and like adults, we would treat teachers the same way. With respect, etc. A famous saying, An eye for an eye and a tooth for a tooth. That's our philosophy for these questions, about teachers treating us and students treating teachers" (Hedin, 1978).

Many "behavior modification" devices are handled that way by adolescents. The required result is obtained—will the powerful educator or therapist be present? Inside, the stress mounts and breaks out at some time:

I no longer use my mind,
Nor think of anything.
For I am just a puppet,
and my master pulls the strings.

There's just one thing about it
I fear he doesn't know:
Strings are easily broken
and then he'll have to go.

(Konopka, 1966, p. 15)

Help with Coping in Adolescents

It behooves the professional not only to understand, but to use this understanding to prevent illness or to enhance health. To prevent serious damage to the individual adolescent and achieve the human interaction necessary for positive quality of life in our society, we must draw conclusions on how to help young people deal with stress and strain.

We have to accept each specific stage of adolescence with its strength and its problems. The vigorous life force, the wide mood swings, the sense of omnipotence as well as despair—all have to be taken as reality to which one must say "yes." We do not want people to become immune to stress. We want people to be sensitive to whatever life brings, but to be able to cope with it. We therefore do not want to give them drugs to dull their senses. We do not want to develop people who expect life to be a rose garden and are therefore unable to accept imperfection. We should create for adolescents an environment that allows them to be *participating* members of society, so that they actively learn the reality of life. There are many tasks they can fulfill which will give them a sense of worth and accomplishment and strengthen them to work through stress. We must accept their mistakes and let them know it:

You are now on your way, so of course all the mistakes are ahead—all the wonderful mistakes that you must and will make. No matter what the mistakes are that you must make, do not be afraid of having made them or making more of them. (Saroyan, 1943, p. 144)

We adults should also admit mistakes in daily life as well as in clinical encounters with youth. The notion of maturity as a kind of perfection does not help adolescents to learn to cope with life. They must know that coping is a never-ending struggle and that all of us at any time may fail to do it well.

We must let young people know reality not only with its joys but also with its problems. The fiction of a "life of happiness" raises expectations that sap the strength of people.

> Telling lies to the young is wrong.
> Proving to them that lies are true is wrong.
> . . . Tell them the difficulties can't be counted, and
> let them see not only what will be
> but see with clarity these present times.
> Say obstacles exist they must encounter,
> sorrow happens, hardship happens.
> The hell with it. Who never knew the price
> of happiness, will not be happy.
>
> (Yevtushenko, 1962, p. 52)

We have to consciously talk philosophy with young people from their earliest ages. It was a five-year-old with whom I had to discuss death as part of life when my own husband died. It would not have helped this child to develop the capacity to work through other problems in his life if I had put him off with generalities. We had to talk about what it meant to be dead, and also what it meant to keep people alive in memory, and how one gains strength by thinking of other people. Someone else might have discussed this in somewhat different terms. The major point I am making is that I had to work with this child on his level to talk through his own pain and mine as well as to learn about strength in human beings. In adolescence one truly needs to develop a philosophy of life. It should become the basis of thinking, action, and feelings. The sentimental search for a comforting religion that makes no demands arises partially out of experience with an adult world that does not share its problems. Some of us were still very young and comparatively close to adolescence when the unspeakable terror of the Nazi concentration camps and Holocaust came upon us. We could live through those experiences because we had arrived at a meaning in life. This was the basic help that made coping possible. An additional one for some came through their sense of inner creativity. I remember vividly the poetry I quoted in solitary confinement, poetry I had read and poetry I myself created, though there was no way of writing it down. Art and imagination are superb gifts provided for human beings, and we should develop them increasingly in our young people.

Finally, adults themselves will have to accept pain as an important part of life without glorifying it or purposely inflicting it. Yet we cannot let young people grow up thinking that one must avoid it. John Steinbeck wrote beautifully in one of his letters:

> we have learned no technique nor ingredient to take the place of anguish. If in some future mutation we are able to remove pain from our species we will also have removed genius and set ourselves closer to the mushroom than to God.
> (Steinbeck, 1975, p. 604)

I underline that I do no preach death, pain, and stress as ideals, but I see them as necessary ingredients in life; ingredients that cannot be seen merely as catastrophe but also as an opportunity to grow. We will help young people to cope if we form a truly supportive but not sentimental society. A 17-year-old writes it better than I can say it:

> I am growing, world.
> I am reaching and touching and stretching
> and testing
> And finding new things, new wonderful
> Things.
> New frightening things.
> I'm just growing, world, just now.
> I'm not tall, I'm not strong. I'm not
> Right.
> I'm just trying to be.
> I'm a person, I'm me!
> Let me test, let me try, let me reach,
> Let me fly!
> Push me out of my nest (but not too fast).
> There is much I don't know.
> There are things that I want—don't
> hide me from the sight of the world.
> Give me room give me time. There
> are things I'm not frightened
> To try.
> Let me tumble and spring, let me go
> Let me be. Wait and see. . . .
> I am growing, world
> Water me with wisdom of
> Your tears.
>
> (Konopka, 1976, p. 14)

REFERENCES

Brokering, B. *Requirements for healthy development of adolescent youth: With examples from a summer youth employment program* (Center for Youth Development and Research). Unpublished manuscript, University of Minnesota, 1978.

Eisikovits, Zvi C. *Youths committed to the State Department of Corrections of Minnesota for offenses against persons.* Unpublished doctoral dissertation, University of Minnesota, 1977.

Hedin, D., Wolfe, H., Garrison, K., and Fruetel, J. *Youth's views on health* (Minnesota Youth Poll, No. 3, Center for Youth Development and Research). Unpublished manuscript, University of Minnesota, 1977.

Hedin, D. *A poll of Eisenhower High School students on their views of the school's philosophy* (Minnesota Youth Poll, Center for Youth Development and Research). Unpublished manuscript, University of Minnesota, 1978.

Hedin, D., Wolfe, H., Bush, S., and Fruetel, J. *Youth's views on work* (Minnesota Youth Poll, No. 2, Center for Youth Development and Research). Unpublished manuscript, University of Minnesota, 1977.

Konopka, G. *The adolescent girl in conflict.* Englewood Cliffs, N.J.: Prentice-Hall, 1966.

Konopka, G. *Young girls: A portrait of adolescence.* Englewood Cliffs, N.J.: Prentice-Hall, 1976.

Minnesota Center for Health Statistics. *Minnesota health statistics.* Minneapolis, Minnesota,: Author, 1975.

Saroyan, W. *The human comedy.* New York: Pocket Books, 1943.

Steinbeck, J. *Steinbeck: A life in letters.* In E. Steinbeck and R. Wallsten (Eds.), New York: Viking Press, 1975.

Yevtushenko, Y. *Selected Poems* (R. Milner-Gulland and P. Levi, Eds. and trans.) New York: Dutton, 1962.

8

Promoting Positive Health Behaviors in Adults

NATHAN MACCOBY

One of the principal causes of mental illness is physical illness. Multiple sclerosis, which makes people into wheelchair patients, is likely to make people stop trying to function and spend their time bemoaning their cruel fate. Survivors of a heart attack or stroke are similarly inclined to resign from life when it might well be possible for them to continue to make important contributions to self-fulfillment, family, and society: we have had at least two presidents in this century who continued in office long after undergoing severe myocardial infarctions. Other crippling diseases often require a severe mental adjustment.

Although it is frequently possible to succeed in rehabilitating such patients through both physical and mental therapy, how much better it would be if the physical disease could be prevented from happening. Many disabling diseases are to a considerable extent preventable. Interestingly enough, however, changes in life style, a psychological adjustment, are required for such prevention. In other words, reducing the incidence of cardiovascular disease, our single largest cause of premature death, can be accomplished by changes in behavior. The reduction of early deaths would certainly reduce mental illness among closely affiliated survivors. Since about half of the victims of heart attacks survive their first attack, the reduction of such attacks would also help prevent the occurrence among victims of post-heart-attack psychological adjustment problems.

It turns out that the self-management of behavior is the key to prevention of both cardiovascular disease and of psychological maladjustment (Mahoney and Thorensen, 1974). Just as successful adjustment requires self-management of behavior rather than the constant direction of a therapist, so the changes in behavior that can result in reduced risk of cardiovascular disease can be accomplished by self-directed and self-managed behavior changes.

The leading cause of death in this country and, for that matter, in almost all of the other highly developed countries is cardiovascular disease (American Heart Association, 1977). Most of the gains in longevity attained in this century due to advances in public health practices and improvements in medicine have been largely offset by enormous increases in particular diseases (Feinlieb, 1975). Most noticeable among these diseases are the cardiovascular ones, for some time now the leading killer. There has also been a phenomenal risk in the incidence of certain cancers—mainly in lung cancer, an "almost always" fatal disease (Surgeon General's Report, *Smoking and Health*, 1979).

During the last ten years there have been substantial reductions in the number of deaths induced by cardiovascular disease. The reasons for this consistent improvement are not fully known, but the reduction of smoking and reduction of serum cholesterol among middle-aged men may be important factors. Although the causes of atherosclerosis (diseases of the arterial inner walls) the leading form of cardiovascular disease, are not yet fully understood, risk factors and the probable ways in which these risk factors increase the likelihood of occurrence of cardiovascular events are, in at least some instances, clearly identifiable. High blood pressure, smoking, high blood lipids (fats), and particularly low-density lipoproteins (serum LDL cholesterol) are clearly associated with a high incidence of heart attacks and strokes, the leading events in cardiovascular disease. It is important for psychologists to remember that the medical term "hypertension" refers not to stress but to the stretching of the walls of arterial blood vessels due to the filling of the inside openings (lumens) of the arteries with fatty deposits. Stress may in some as yet unknown manner contribute to hypertension, but the term hypertension simply means high blood pressure. Essential hypertension means high blood pressure whose cause is not known.

Epidemiological studies show that combinations of risk factors have a multiplicative relationship to cardiovascular events (Truett, Cornfield, and Kannel, 1967). Thus even a moderately high systolic blood pressure—well below what might be labeled hypertension—when combined with cigarette smoking or moderately high blood cholesterol (LDL) results in considerable risk—much greater than the sum of each risk that these values would suggest. Thus all measures of risk should be regarded as continuous distributions, with some risk beginning at relatively low values and increasing with larger values. The distribution of serum cholesterol indicates that the mean cholesterol value in the United States would be near the top of the distribution in Japan. Almost all of those in the United States have high enough serum cholesterol to have some risk of a cardiovascular event. Secondary risk factors include being overweight, lack of exercise and improper diet—for example, too much salt or sugar—and probably persistent psychological stress.

There is additional epidemiological evidence to support the hypothesis that cardiovascular disease is at least strongly influenced by factors of life style (Intersociety Commission for Heart Disease Resources, 1970). Cross-cultural studies of morbidity and mortality rates assignable to cardiovascular diseases reveals considerable variation from country to country. Finland and the United States lead the list, and Japan, among the developed countries, has very low rates. When the Japanese in California are compared with those in Japan, their rates are much higher, with Japanese in Hawaii showing intermediate values. Dietary factors appear to be strongly implicated in these differences in morbidity and mortality, and cultural hereditary factors seem relatively less important (Kagan, Harris, Johnson, Hiroo, Syme, Rhoads, Gay, Nichamen, Hamilton, Tillotson, and Winkelstein, 1974).

Thus, while the precise mechanisms by which these risk factors contribute to cardiovascular disease is not fully specifiable, the prudent person is clearly wise to take steps to keep blood pressure low, maintain a reasonably lean body, not smoke cigarettes, and observe certain dietary precautions (Keys, Anderson and Grande, 1965). The problem we at the Stanford Heart Disease Prevention Program have undertaken now is to help people adopt and maintain a prudent life style, and how to do this in a reasonably cost-effective and effort-effective manner.

In 1971 the Stanford University Heart Disease Prevention Program undertook a three-community study in order to discover a method for risk reduction which would be generally applicable. Why did we pick a community as the unit of education for reducing risk of cardiovascular disease? (1) If an individual therapist-instructor is used with either one person at a time or even with a small group of persons, the problem of general risk reduction is just too large to manage. Such an undertaking would be very expensive, and the number of therapist-instructors needed would be astronomically high. (2) Risk reduction involves behavior changes that have a very long-term—even a lifetime—duration. Cessation of smoking or not beginning to smoke cigarettes is behavior that has to last if it is going to make a contribution to the reduction of risk of disease. Similarly, changes in diet involving reductions in dietary cholesterol, saturated fats, salt, and calories generally call for changes in eating habits that are permanent for the remainder of the life cycle. (3) These changes need to take place not in the clinic but in the context of the environments in which people live. Furthermore, the community nexus can contribute greatly to the maintenance of changes in life style. The home, the school, the work place (Meyer and Henderson, 1974) and other community settings are the environments in which such behavior occurs, and therefore it must be practiced there. Furthermore, these institutions are potential sources of support for new behavior, or they can constitute obstacles to such change (Farquhar, 1978).

Diffusion of changed behavior and social support are potentially important sources of strength for the formation and maintenance of new habits. Peers can play a very important role in the process. For example, school children can be influenced not to begin cigarette smoking if peer models occupy visible roles as nonsmokers (McAlister, Perry, and Maccoby, 1978).

We were interested in discovering a method for helping people to change their life styles so as to reduce their risk of suffering a cardiovascular event such as a myocardial infarction—a heart attack—or a stroke. We were searching for a method that would accomplish this objective, would not require overwhelming numbers of therapists, and would be relatively inexpensive per person assisted.

In 1972 our group (Farquhar, Maccoby, Wood, Alexander, Breitrose, Brown, Haskell, McAlister, Meyer, Nash and Stern, 1977)—investigators at the School of Medicine and the Institute for Communication Research at Stanford University—began a field experiment in three northern California communities in order to study the modification of risk factors in cardiovascular disease through community education. The major tactical choices for such a campaign are mass media, face-to-face instruction, or combinations of the two. Study of previous mass-media campaigns directed at large open populations has established the potential effectiveness of the media in transmitting information. altering some attitudes, and producing small shifts in behavior, by means of choices among consumer products, but has failed to demonstrate that the media alone substantially influence more complex behavior (Bauer, 1964; Cartwright, 1949; Robertson, Kelley, O'Neil, Wixom, Eisworth and Haddon, 1974; Star and Hughes, 1950). Yet the habits influencing cardiovascular risk factors are very complex and long standing, are often reinforced by culture, custom, and continual commercial advertising, and are unlikely to be very strongly influenced by mass media alone. Face-to-face instruction and exhortation also have a long history of failure, particularly with respect to recidivism, as noted above, in efforts to influence diet (Stunkard, 1975) and smoking (Bernstein and McAlister, 1976).

After considering the powerful culture forces which reinforce and maintain the health habits that we wished to change, and in view of past failure of health education campaigns, we designed a heretofore untested combination of extensive mass media with a considerable amount of face-to-face instruction. We chose this method not so much because it was potentially widely applicable, but because it was a method that we judged most likely to succeed (Mendelsohn, 1973). We could then compare a more generally applicable treatment, though one not quite so promising of results, with the more sure one. Therefore, another community was selected in which we administered treatments via mass media alone. We also chose to include three elements typically ignored in health campaigns: (1) the mass media materials were devised to teach specific behavioral skills, as well as to perform the more usual tasks of offering information and affecting attitude and motivation; (2) both the mass media and, in particular, the face-to-face instruction were designed to embody many previously validated methods of achieving changes in behavior and self-control training principles; and (3) the campaign was designed on the basis of careful analysis of the specific needs and the media consumption patterns of the intended audience. Our overall goal was to create and evaluate methods for effecting changes in smoking, exercise, and diet which would be both cost-effective and applicable to large population groups.

RESEARCH DESIGN

Since our media campaigns were directed at entire communities, random assignment of individuals to the treatment or control condition was not feasible. An equally rigorous experimental method, treating a large number of entire geographically defined populations as single units and randomly assigning some of these communities to treatment and some to control conditions, was prohibitively expensive. Thus we concluded that the most realistic compromise between feasibility and rigor was a quasi-experimental research approach with a small number of experimental units. Three roughly comparable communities in northern California were selected. Tracy was chosen as a control because it was relatively distant and isolated from media in the other communities. Gilroy and Watsonville, the other two communities, share some media channels (television and radio), but each town has its own newspaper. Watsonville and Gilroy received different strategies of health education over a period of two years. Gilroy received health education through the mass media alone; Watsonville also received health education through the mass media, except that there we also carried out a randomized experiment with a sample of persons at higher levels of risk for cardiovascular disease, employing intensive face-to-face instruction for two thirds of this group and using the remaining people in this group, exposed only to health education through the media, as a control against intensive instruction under a mass media umbrella.

To assess the effects of these interventions we gathered baseline and yearly follow-up data from surveys comprised of interviews and medical examinations of a random (multistage probability) sample of 35- to 59-year-old men and women from each of the three communities. The schedule of surveys and educational campaigns is presented in Table 1. Since the measurement process itself may have effects, surveys were withheld from an additional sample ("after-only" sample) in each community until the end of the first year of study, so that effects of the measurement process itself could be judged.

Table 1
Three-Community Study Design

	1972	1973		1974		1975	
Watsonville (W)	Baseline Survey (S1)	Media campaign Intensive instruction (II) for 2/3 of high risk participants	Second Survey (S2)	Media campaign Intensive instruction (II) for 2/3 of high risk participants	Third Survey (S3)	Maintenance (low-level) media campaign II: Summer Follow-up	Fourth Survey (S4)
Gilroy (G)	Baseline Survey (S1)	Media campaign	Second Survey (S2)	Media campaign	Third Survey (S3)	Maintenance (low-level) media campaign	Fourth Survey (S4)
Tracy (T)	Baseline Survey (S1)		Second Survey (S2)		Third Survey (S3)		Fourth Survey (S4)

SURVEY AND MEDICAL EXAMINATIONS

Our annual interviews in the three communities were designed to measure both knowledge about heart disease and individual behavior related to cardiovascular risk. The assessment covered several variables. Knowledge of risk factors was measured with a test of knowledge about dietary and other risk factors associated with coronary heart disease based on 25 multiple-choice items. Of these 25 items, 3 were concerned with the role of smoking in heart disease, 14 with eating habits and heart disease, four with physical activity, 2 with body weight, and 2 with general information about heart disease. Eating habits were assessed in an interview survey which allowed us to estimate daily intake of cholesterol, saturated and polyunsaturated fats, sugar, and alcohol, based on estimates of food composition (Stern, Farquhar, Maccoby, and Russell, 1976). Participants were also asked to report their smoking behavior: whether they smoked cigarettes, pipes, or cigars and what their daily rate of smoking was. Self-reports of smoking status were validated through an assay of plasma thiocyanate concentration which indicated that only about 4 percent of those reporting abstinence may have given inaccurate reports (Butts, Kuehneman, and Widdowson, 1974).

Coincident with the interview, we also collected physiologic data from participants at baseline and after one or two years. These data included values of plasma total cholesterol (we did not yet know of HDL and VDL) and triglyceride concentrations, systolic and diastolic blood pressure, and relative weight (Miller, 1978).

Data were gathered in a survey center set up in each of the three communities, and results were sent to participants and their physicians. The overall risk of coronary heart disease for each of the participants was estimated from a multiple logistic function of risk factors predicting the probability of developing coronary heart disease within 12 years according to the person's age, sex, plasma cholesterol concentration, systolic blood pressure, relative weight, smoking rate, and electrocardiographic findings (Truett, Cornfield, and Kannel, 1967). This calculation allowed us to identify the high-risk study groups described above and to monitor the estimated risk of coronary heart disease for participants in all 12 study groups over the course of the study period.

MASS MEDIA AND INTENSIVE FACE-TO-FACE INSTRUCTION CAMPAIGN

The experimental design involved development and application of a mass media and face-to-face instruction campaign. These communication efforts were designed to overcome deficiencies in previous unsuccessful campaigns to change behavior. Each campaign was intended to produce awareness of the probable causes of coronary disease and of the specific behaviors that may reduce risk. The campaigns also aimed at providing the knowledge and skills necessary to accomplish recommended behavior changes. Lastly, the campaigns were designed to help the individual become self-sufficient in maintaining new health habits and skills. Dietary habits recommended for all participants were those which, if followed, would lead to a reduced intake of saturated fat, cholesterol, salt, sugar, and alcohol. We also urged reduction in body weight through caloric reduction and increased physical activity. Cigarette smokers were educated on the need and methods for ceasing or at least reducing their daily rate of cigarette consumption.

For the mass media campaign a coordinated set of messages was prepared for the lay audiences in Gilroy and Watsonville. Over time these basic messages were transformed into a variety of media (e.g., TV spots, bus cards, etc.) and released to the target audience through a variety of the most generally available media channels. A broad range of materials was produced. For example, about 50 television spots, three hours of television programming, over 100 radio spots, several hours of radio programming, weekly newspaper columns, newspaper advertisements and stories, billboards, printed material sent via direct mail to participants, posters, and other assorted materials. Because of the sizable Spanish-speaking population in the communities, the campaign was presented in both Spanish and English. The media campaign began two months after the initial survey and continued for nine months in 1973, stopped during the second survey, and then continued for nine more months in 1974 and on a very reduced basis in 1975 (Maccoby, Farquhar, Wood, and Alexander, 1977).

The dominant characteristic of the mass media campaign structure was its organization as a total integrated information system such that its primary functions (the creative transformation of the medical risk-reduction messages into media events, the formative evaluation of those events, their distribution in coordinated packages over time, and their cumulative effectiveness in promoting change) could all interact to improve and refine decisions on how best to allocate the remaining available resources. The management of this system was put into operation by a process of continuous monitoring of the target audience's existing knowledge, beliefs, attitudes, risk-related behavior, and media use. At the onset of the campaign, decisions were based primarily on data gathered at the initial survey, from the pretesting on local audiences of various media productions, and on the practical considerations arising from the likely availability of privately owned mass media for our purposes. While the campaign was under way, further guidance was obtained from the second annual survey and from a series of systematic but informal small-scale information-gathering efforts designed to provide media planners with immediate feedback on the public's awareness and acceptance of specified sets of media events, as well as to gauge the progress to date. Thus the total campaign could be seen as a set of phased media events where the information obtained from monitoring was used to refocus priorities, reset directions, and modulate the course of the campaign in the desired direction.

The intensive face-to-face instruction program was directed at a randomly selected two thirds of the Watsonville participants whom we identified as being in the top quartile of risk of coronary heart disease according to the multiple logistic formula. These individuals and their physicians were informed by letter of their relatively high risk status, and this was considered as part of the treatment for the group. Their spouses were also invited to participate. The educational effort was launched six months after the first baseline survey and was conducted intensively over a ten-week period. A less intense effort was conducted during the second year. A total of 107 of 113 participants originally assigned to receive intensive instruction were successfully recruited for treatment, and 77 high risk individuals (and 34 spouses) completed all three interviews and examinations.

The intensive instruction program was composed of education and persuasion in the context of social learning and self-control training procedures designed to achieve the same changes in cholesterol and fat consumption, body weight, cigarette smoking (Meyer, Maccoby, and Farquhar, 1977), and physical exercise that were advocated in the media campaign. It was conducted by a team of graduate students in communication, physicians, and specialist health educators trained in behavior modification techniques. The protocols were pretested in a controlled setting before being applied in the field. The basic sequential strategy was to present information about the behavior that influences risk of coronary heart disease, stimulate personal ayalysis of existing behavior, demonstrate desired skills (e.g., food selection and preparation), guide the individual through tentative practice of those skills, and gradually withdraw instructor participation. The expectation was that the behavior would be maintained in the group setting without the instructor. During the initial stage, intensive instruction was conducted in group classes and home counseling sessions. During the second year the frequency and amount of contact was successively reduced. A less intensive educational campaign was conducted in the summer months of the second year, which consisted primarily of individual counseling in difficult problem areas—for example, smoking (Frederickson, 1968) and weight loss—and such social activities as parties, picnics, and hikes, which were intended primarily to encourage participants to maintain changes that had been produced during the first stage of instruction. Very little follow-up occurred in 1975.

RESULTS

First of all, it is desirable to find out whether our audiences were paying any attention to us. One evidence of this effect is the measure of logo recognition. We used a musical theme to open and close all TV and radio programs and spots. In our TV spots and programs as well as in all our printed materials, we showed a conventional heart drawing with electrocardiographic curves. We found that recognition of our logo increased ultimately to include almost all the population of the two communities in which we carried out a media program.

The results of the education programs may be characterized

Table 2
Knowledge of Risk Factors:
Changes in Total Community Samples
(percentages)

	Tracy n=364	Gilroy n=363	Watsonville Reconstituted n=384	Watsonville n=384
Baseline mean (no. correct)	11.4	11.2	11.3	11.2
End of Year 1	2.1	17.8[a]	30.3[a]	35.4[a]
End of Year 2	6.6	26.8[a]	35.1[a]	40.1[a]
End of Year 3	12.8	35.0[a]	38.2[a]	43.4[a]

[a] $p < .01$

Table 3
Change in High Risk Samples
(percentages)

	Tracy n=89	Gilroy n=85	Watsonville Control n=37	Watsonville Intensive Instruction n=67
Baseline mean (no. correct)	10.8	11.1	11.6	11.2
End of Year 1	2.2	16.6[a]	27.4[a]	51.6[a]
End of Year 2	4.8	28.0[a]	27.7[a]	53.3[a]
End of Year 3	14.0	33.9[a]	27.9[a]	57.0[a]

[a] $p < .01$

in terms of knowledge gained, changes in behavior, and physiological changes.

Knowledge

We employed a twenty-five item test on risk factors in cardiovascular disease as part of the basic interview with our sample in all three communities. Clearly, there were knowledge gains over time everywhere. Even in Tracy, where we did not use the education approach, the general education program for health independent of us had an effect on public knowledge. However, the two communities in which we did campaign showed markedly greater improvements in knowledge.

It is interesting to compare knowledge by the degree of our educational effort. Table 4 demonstrates knowledge gains in dietary risk factors of the various groups.

Table 4
*Knowledge of Changes in Dietary Risk Factors
at the End of Year 1
(percentages)*

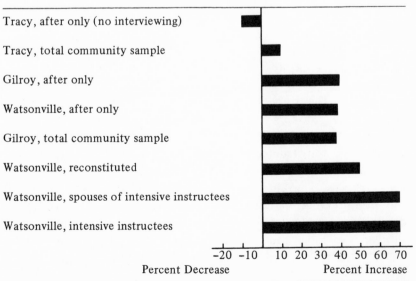

Behavior

Important in the behavior changes that we hoped to help people achieve were those involving cigarette smoking and various aspects of food intake. We assisted people who smoked to learn how to cease smoking, and those who did not yet smoke how to avoid the habit. In diet we tried to educate people to adopt healthier eating habits, particularly to eat foods lower in saturated fats and in cholesterol and to eat less salt and fewer calories. Table 5 shows some of the findings on smoking.

Table 5
*Change in Cigarette Smokers: Total Community Samples
(percentages)*

	Tracy n=364	Gilroy n=363	Watsonville Reconstituted n=384	Watsonville n=384
Baseline (percent of smokers)	29.7	34.7	31.7	33.6
End of Year 1	2.8	– 6.3[a]	–5.5	– 16.3[b]
End of Year 2	1.8	– 5.6	–3.6	– 19.4[b]
End of Year 3	–2.8	– 7.9	–8.2	– 24.0[b]

[a] $p < .05$
[b] $p < .01$

Although some reduction in the number of smokers took place in the communities with mass media only in the total population, the only substantial reductions in the percentage of cigarette smokers occurred in Watsonville, and we can see in Table 6 that those reductions took place primarily among the intensive instructees. The mass-media-only education program did not show evidence of much efficacy in helping people learn to cease smoking. In fact, the secular trend was such that the nonintervention community, Tracy, showed a considerable drop in the number of smokers. However, the intensive instructees showed the most dramatic change of any that occurred in this study. Half of the original smokers were nonsmokers three years after the education program began, and this in the face of very little added instruction during the third year.

Table 6
Change in Cigarette Smokers:
High Risk Samples
(percentages)

	Tracy n=89	Gilroy n=85	Watsonville Control n=37	Watsonville Intensive Instruction n=67
Baseline	52.8	62.4	56.8	59.7
End of Year 1	- 6.4	-15.1	0	-32.5[a]
End of Year 2	-10.6	- 15.1	0	-47.5[a]
End of Year 3	- 14.9	-11.3	0	-50.0[a]

[a] $p < .01$

DIETARY CHOLESTEROL

Table 7 presents our best estimates of the changes in the consumption of cholesterol in the diet in terms of milligrams ingested per day for the three towns. Although small changes (not statistically significant) may have been taking place in the noneducation community (Tracy), the magnitude and stability of the reductions of cholesterol in the diet reported in the two education towns is impressive (all *ps* < .01).

Table 7
Change in Dietary Cholesterol (mg/day):
Total Community Samples
(percentages)

	Tracy n=364	Gilroy n=363	Watsonville Reconstituted n=384	Watsonville n=384
Baseline	491.1	550.7	514.6	508.9
End of Year 1	-10.2	-24.9[a]	-25.5[a]	-28.7[a]
End of Year 2	- 6.1	-28.5[a]	-27.9[a]	-30.7[a]
End of Year 3	- 9.2	-31.5[a]	-031.5[a]	-33.7[a]

[a] $p < .01$

Now examine comparable data for the high risk subsamples (Table 8). Again, while small gains (nonsignificant statistically)

Table 8
Change in Dietary Cholesterol (mg/day)
High Risk Samples
(percentages)

	Tracy n=89	Gilroy n=85	Watsonville Control n=37	Watsonville Intensively Instructed n=67
Baseline	510.7	607.2	492.4	460.9
End of Year 1	-10.1	-29.8[b]	-26.0[a]	-40.7[b]
End of Year 2	- 6.5	-31.8[b]	-22.9[a]	-37.1[b]
End of Year 3	-13.4	-38.6[b]	-27.2[a]	-42.3[b]

[a] $p < .05$

[b] $p < .01$

may be taking place in Tracy, even more substantial and highly significant reductions in dietary cholesterol take place in the mass-mediated (all $ps < .01$ for Gilroy and Watsonville II, and all $ps < .05$ for Watsonville RC) communities. Such is particularly the case among those high risk people, also intensively instructed, whose initial level of cholesterol ingestion was lower than for others at baseline.

Egg yolks are particularly high in cholesterol. It may therefore be instructive to examine the data on egg consumption—a food whose consumption we sought to help people limit (Tables 9 and 10). Differences in the education towns are highly significant both statistically and in amount of change.

Table 9
Change in eggs eaten per day
Total Community Samples
(percentages)

	Tracy n=364	Gilroy n=363	Watsonville Reconstituted n=384	Watsonville n=384
Baseline	0.76	0.85	0.77	0.76
End of Year 1	-15.3	-27.4[a]	-36.0[a]	-40.8[a]
End of Year 2	-15.1	-33.8[a]	-41.7[a]	-43.9[a]
End of Year 3	-20.2	-36.8[a]	-44.0[a]	-46.4[a]

[a] $p < .01$

Table 10
Change in Eggs Eaten per Day:
High Risk Samples
(percentages)

	Tracy n=89	Gilroy n=85	Watsonville Control n=37	Watsonville Intensive Instructees n=67
Baseline	0.87	0.97	0.69	0.65
End of Year 1	–16.1	–36.6[a]	–36.8	–60.1[b]
End of Year 2	–17.0	–36.6[a]	–45.4[a]	–57.5[b]
End of Year 3	–33.3	042.5	–41.4	–58.8

[a]$p < .05$
[b]$p < .01$

Physiology

As before, those at high risk show even greater reductions than is the case for the total communities, and as before, those who were randomly assigned to intensive instruction showed even more change.

It will be recalled that the main object of this study was to discover generally usable ways of helping whole communities to reduce their risk of cardiovascular disease. Risk is best assessed through smoking, blood pressure, and serum cholesterol.

Systolic blood pressure has been found to be a very important precursor of cardiovascular events. In the important lengthy longitudinal study conducted at Framingham, Massachusetts, the predictive value of systolic blood pressure was found to be superior to that of diastolic blood pressure, and the measure was therefore incorporated in their multiple logistic of risk (Truett et al., 1967). See Tables 11 and 12. All educational interventional communities show statistically stable mean reductions in systolic blood pressure. Although this reduction would be clinically insignificant in amount for any given individual, when it is remembered that most subjects evidence moderate or low readings at baseline, the mean differential reductions are important.

Here again, among high risk subjects—many of whom qualified for this classification to a considerable extent because of their relatively high systolic blood pressures—the scores were initially

Table 11
Change in Systolic Blood Pressure:
Millimeters of mercury (mm Hg). Total Community Samples
(percentages)

	Tracy n=364	Gilroy n=363	Watsonville Reconstituted n=384	Watsonville n=384
Baseline (mm Hg)	128.6	131.4	133.4	133.1
End of Year 1	3.2	-2.3[a]	-0.7[a]	-1.4[a]
End of Year 2	1.1	-7.4[a]	-4.7[a]	-4.4[a]
End of Year 3	0.8	-4.4[a]	-4.6[a]	-3.9[a]

[a] $p < .01$

Table 12
Change in Systolic Blood Pressure (mm Hg):
High Risk Samples
(percentages)

	Tracy n=89	Gilroy n=85	Watsonville Control n=37	Watsonville Intensive Instructees n=67
Baseline (mm Hg)	138.4	147.8	148.2	148.1
End of Year 1	1.2	-4.4[b]	-3.2[a]	-6.4[b]
End of Year 2	-2.0	-10.8[b]	-8.5[b]	-7.6[b]
End of Year 3	-2.0	-8.7[b]	-8.9[b]	-6.6[a]

[a] $p < .05$
[b] $p < .01$

higher and show a larger differentiated effect in the mass-mediated communities. Unlike the case in many other findings, however, the reductions among intensive instructees are not greater than for their mass-media-only controls.

Finally, the best overall indicator of risk is the single measure— an adaptation of the Framingham multiple logistic function of risk (Tables 13 and 14). These are substantial and gratifying reductions in the communities in which we conducted our educational campaigns. It may be of interest to note that the mass-media-only conditions showed as much change as the community that contained the subsample group of high risk persons obtaining

Table 13
*Reduction in Multiple Logistic Function of Risk:
Total Community Samples
(percentages)*

	Tracy n=364	Gilroy n=363	Watsonville Reconstituted n=384	Watsonville n=384
Baseline	0.081	0.076	0.093	0.091
End of Year 1	8.8	-3.0[a]	-5.8[a]	-12.3[a]
End of Year 2	6.3	-17.7[a]	-16.1[a]	-17.9[a]
End of Year 3	2.3	-8.4[a]	-14.8[a]	-16.4[a]

[a]$p < .01$

Table 14
*Reduction in Multiple Logistic or Risk:
High Risk Samples
(percentages)*

	Tracy	Gilroy	Watsonville Control	Watsonville
Baseline	.176	.161	.199	.176
End of Year 1	5.4	-7.7[a]	-11.4[b]	-27.6[b]
End of Year 2	-2.6	-25.3[b]	-25.9[b]	-30.3[b]
End of Year 3	-8.0	-16.1	-23.2[a]	-29.0[b]

[a]$p < .05$
[b]$p < .01$

intensive instruction. Some retrogression occurred during the third year in the mass-media-only town when educational programming was sharply curtailed but did not occur in the mass-media town including intensive instructees. Apparently the supplemental value of face-to-face instruction has more staying power.

In previous studies of weight loss, blood pressure detection and control, smoking cessation, and dietary composition changes, selected persons have served as subjects. In this study entire communities were the subjects of education for change. The data reported above were from probability samples of those communities. However, loss of sample subjects in successive waves of measurements may well limit the unbiased nature of the findings. In addition, there were notable lacks of success. Sustained weight loss did not occur, and cessation of smoking occurred primarily among intensive instructees.

In spite of these shortcomings, the changes that did take place are impressive. In general, the changes in knowledge, behavior, and—most important—physiological end points achieved in the first year were maintained and actually improved in the second year of education. Even during the third year, when educational efforts all but ceased, most changes were maintained, especially in the community containing intensive instructees.

This study demonstrates that mass media when appropriately used can increase knowledge and help people to adopt improved health habits. The results led us to believe, however, that the power of this method could be considerably enhanced if we could devise ways of employing the media to stimulate and coordinate face-to-face instructional programs in natural settings in such communities as schools, places of work, and community groups. This study led, therefore, to a further investigation designed to test these ideas.

THE SALINAS AND MONTEREY COMMUNITY HEALTH PROJECTS

At this writing, plans and preliminary community work are well under way for the launching of a new community study. This second study differs from the earlier in that educational strategy for both changes in life style and the long-term maintenance of such changes will be improved. Furthermore, the expensive method of personal intensive instruction by expert staff will be replaced by a more generally applicable method, one potentially less costful per changing person in both money and effort than was the case in the previous investigation. The cities are considerably larger and thus more complex than the towns used in the former study—in fact large enough to enable us to measure changes in morbidity and mortality due to cardiovascular disease. The educational program will be as similar as possible in each of two communities, and there will be three reference or control communities instead of one. The educational program this time will be continued for six or seven years.

A series of independent rather than longitudinal samples of a wider range—12–74 instead of 35–59—will be employed to measure community changes in knowledge, behavior, and physiology looking toward reduction of risk. Smaller longitudinal samples will be employed to trace the course of changes in individuals.

The principal innovation will be the development of the cooperation and participation of the communities in the educational effort. We plan to supplement and extend the mass media efforts through risk-reduction activities provided through the auspices of community organizations. People in these organizations will be recruited and will become active members of the education team.

We believe that media can be powerful, but that their effects can be augmented by community organization. Interpersonal influence can have a multiplicative effect in helping people to change their behavior. Community organizations can expand and improve the educational effort in ways that can improve community-wide risk reduction. They can publicize and support this effort. Most important, community organizations can help the process of community adoption of risk-reduction programs as their own programs and thus increase both the immediate and the long-term educational effectiveness of health education programs in their cities. Our media efforts will include both an improved program of mass media aimed directly at the public and little media packages such as video and audio tapes, booklets, slides, etc. for the use of community educators.

The early part of the human life cycle is clearly the place to begin the development of health habits. To that end our current study includes an emphasis on helping young people to adopt appropriate food consumption, weight control, exercise, and smoking habits. Our strategy is to experiment on a small scale with selected subjects or schools before applying these methods to the communities at large.

The method of temptation-resistance training appears to be a promising approach, especially when the training is conducted by older peers. Studies in schools employing these methods have yielded preliminary findings which suggest that the onset of smoking can at least be delayed and at best, we hope, be prevented from occurring altogether. Training methods for other health habits are being explored similarly in "pre-field" settings.

Although this discussion has been focused on the prevention of cardiovascular disease, it is evident that the methods employed could be adapted to the reduction of other important diseases. The second largest killer in our society is cancer. The etiology of cancer even more than cardiovascular disease, is obscure. As in the case of CVD, however, there are sufficiently identifiable precursors that can be dealt with. Cigarette smoking is not the sole cause of lung cancer, and many people who smoke do not get it, while many who do not smoke do become victims of lung cancer. Clearly, however, from the recent Surgeon General's Report (*Smoking and Health*, 1979), it can be seen that not smoking considerably reduces the risk of contracting lung cancer. It is generally held also that the likelihood of falling victim to other cancers may be decreased by changes in food habits. The linkage of obesity to breast cancer and relation of fiber in the diet to cancer of the colon are two additional examples. The more that we learn about helping people to adopt healthful habits, the more this knowledge can be applied to the reduction of disease generally.

REFERENCES

American Heart Association. *Heart facts.* New York: American Heart Association, 1977.

Bauer, R. A. The obstinate audience: The influence process from the point of view of social communications. *American Psychologist,* 1964, *19,* 319–328.

Bernstein, D. A., and McAlister, A. L. Modification of smoking behavior: Progress and problems. *Addictive Behavior,* 1976, *1,* 89–102.

Butts, W. C., Kuehneman, M., and Widdowson, G. M. Automated method for determining serum thiocyanate to distinguish smokers from nonsmokers. *Clinical Chemistry,* 1974, *20,* 1344–1348.

Cartwright, D. Some principles of mass persuasion. *Human Relations,* 1949, *2,* 253–267.

Farquhar, J. W. The community based model of life style intervention trials. *American Journal of Epidemiology,* 1978, *108,* 103–111.

Farquhar, J. W., Maccoby, N., Wood, P., Alexander, J. K., Breitrose, H., Brown, B., Haskell, W., McAlister, A., Meyer, A., Nash, J., and Stern, M. Community education for cardiovascular health. *Lancet,* 1977, *1,* 1192–1195.

Feinleib, M. Changes in life expectancy since 1900. *Circulation,* 1975, *52* (111), 16–17.

Frederickson, D. T. How to help your patient stop smoking. *Diseases of the Chest,* 1968, *54,* 196–202.

Griffiths, W., and Knutson, A. The role of mass media in public health. *American Journal of Public Health,* 1960, *50,* 515–523.

Intersociety Commission for Heart Disease Resources. Primary prevention of the atherosclerotic diseases. *Circulation,* 1970, *45,* A55–A95.

Kagan, A., Harris, E. R., Johnson, K., Hiroo, K., Syme, S. L., Rhoads, G., Gay, M., Nichamen, M., Hamilton, H., Tillotson, J., and Winkelstein, W. Epidemiological studies of coronary heart disease and stroke in Japan, Hawaii, and California: Demographic, physical, dietary, and biochemical characteristics. *Journal of Chronic Diseases,* 1974, *27,* 345–364.

Keys, A., Anderson, J. T., and Grande, F. Serum cholesterol response to changes in the diet. *Metabolism,* 1965, *14,* 747–787.

Maccoby, N., Farquhar, J. W., Wood, P., and Alexander, J. K. Reducing the risk of cardiovascular disease. *Journal of Community Health,* 1977, *3,* 100–114.

Mahoney, M. J., and Thorensen, C. E. *Self control: Power to the person.* Monterey: Brooks-Cole, 1974.

Mendelsohn, H. Some reasons why information campaigns can succeed. *Public Opinion Quarterly,* 1973, *37,* 50–61.

Meyer, A. J., and Henderson, J. B. Multiple risk factor reduction in the prevention of cardiovascular disease. *Preventive Medicine,* 1974, *3,* 255–236.

Meyer, A. J., Maccoby, N., and Farquhar, J. W. The role of opinion leadership in a cardiovascular health education campaign. In B. D. Ruben (Ed.), *Communication yearbook* (Vol. I). New Brunswick: Transaction Books, 1977.

218   Nathan Maccoby

218   Nathan Maccoby

218   Nathan Maccoby

218   Nathan Maccoby

Miller, N. E. The evidence for the antiatherogenicity of high density lipoprotein in man. *Lipids*, 1978, *13*, 914-919.

McAlister, A., Perry, C., and Maccoby, N. *Systematic peer leadership to discourage onset of tobacco dependency*. Paper presented at American Psychological Convention, Toronto, August 1978.

Robertson, L. S., Kelley, A. B., O'Neill, B., Wixom, C., Eisworth, R., and Haddon, W. A controlled study of the effect of television messages on safety belt use. *American Journal of Public Health*, 1974, *64*, 1071-1080.

Smoking and health: A report of the Surgeon General. Washington, D.C.: Department of Health Education and Welfare, 1979.

Star, S., and Hughes, H. M. Report of an educational campaign: The Cincinnati plan for the United Nations. *American Journal of Sociology*, 1950, *55*, 389-400.

Stern, M. P., Farquhar, J. W., Maccoby, N., and Russell, S. Results of a two-year health education campaign on dietary behavior: The Stanford three-community study. *Circulation*, 1976, *54*, 826-833.

Stunkard, A. J. Presidential address—1974: From explanation to action in psychosomatic medicine: The case of obesity. *Psychosomatic Medicine*, 1975, *37*, 195-236.

Truett, J., Cornfield, J., and Kannel, W. A multivariate analysis of the risk of coronary heart disease in Framingham. *Journal of Chronic Diseases*, 1967, *20*, 511-524.

III
The Role of Work in Competence and Life Satisfaction

Throughout much of our adult lives, the majority of our waking hours are predominantly occupied by our jobs. The sheer amount of time spent in work situations suggests how much work may affect our feelings of satisfaction and competence. Thus, it is not surprising that, as Flanagan demonstrated in Part II, the degree to which people's needs and wants are met by their work is one of the best predictors of reported overall quality of life. Work typically combines a number of roles: it provides a social network that can be both supporting and stressful and an intellectual and/or physical challenge that may be both inspiring and draining; it makes demands on time that may prove both an antidote to boredom and an unwelcome intrusion; and it is a source of income that may offer a sense of independence but that also increases competitiveness and anxiety. Given this broad impact, much interest has turned not only to job satisfaction but also to issues regarding entry and progression through the job hierarchy and absence or retirement from the formal work domain. The papers in this section address these complementary concerns in the context of promoting competence and coping through adulthood.

Harry Levinson is the President of the Levinson Institute and a lecturer at Harvard Medical School. He has written a number of books examining various aspects of work, stress, and mental health. His paper addresses the contradictions that emerge from large sample surveys of satisfaction with work. From a largely psychodynamic perspective, Levinson examines circumstances causing stress, emphasizing the joint contributions of the environment and the individual. He goes on to focus on typically unrecognized factors within individuals which precipitate dissatisfaction and to recommend specific techniques that may promote the ability to cope with such problems.

Grace K. Baruch and Roslind C. Barnett are both Senior Research Associates at the Heller Graduate School, Brandeis University. Baruch, a developmental psychologist, and Barnett, a clinical psychologist, have individually and collaboratively studied a variety of issues concerning female development across the lifespan. Their paper examines the potential role of work in enhancing the psychological well-being of adult women. Baruch and Barnett review certain social changes that have contributed growing significance to the notion of women developing occupational competence and economic independence. By considering self-esteem and role-pattern satisfaction of working and nonworking mothers, they succeed in shattering assumptions that female involvement in multiple roles primarily serves to produce conflict and distress.

Douglas W. Bray is Director and Ann Howard is Manager of Basic Human Resources Research at American Telephone and Telegraph Company. Their past research has dealt with a diversity of such work-related topics as personnel selection, intrinsic motivation and job performance, and the functioning of job assessment centers. Here they discuss the results of an unprecedented longitudinal study, now in its twenty-second year, of the lives and careers of managers in the Bell System. Based upon extensive assessments of a white male sample during its movement from entry-level positions in management through mid-career and middle age, Bray and Howard discuss characteristics that appear to be related to managerial success. Their data provide a rare opportunity for insights into the relationships between life satisfactions and career success and the determinants of adjustment and happiness during adulthood.

Ruth Glick is Co-Founder and Director of the Institute for Retirement Studies, Case Western Reserve University. This Institute was established as an academic program for persons age fifty and over, and has since developed training programs for those in the field of retirement planning and for service providers working in community agencies serving the aged. Glick discusses the faltering emergence of retirement planning in America, arguing that its design is inextricably a function of our basic attitudes toward old age. Retirement has been portrayed as both a traumatic life event eliciting feelings of uselessness and rejection and a rich opportunity to reclaim one's life, develop one's self, and exploit the pleasure of leisure. Glick's analysis of the current social and psychological conditions of older Americans provides a framework for considering the potential role of retirement planning in the promotion of competence and coping.

9

An Overview of Stress and Satisfaction: The Contract with Self

HARRY LEVINSON

Much attention has been given to work satisfaction and its relationship to productivity, accidents, absenteeism, psychological symptoms and the quality of working life. Morale and attitude surveys and climate studies are an organizational commonplace. However, large sample surveys of satisfaction with work seem to be self-contradictory. For the past twenty years 80 percent of the people surveyed by the Institute of Social Research of the University of Michigan say that they are satisfied with their work (Quinn, Mangione, and Baldi de Mandelovito, 1973). Yet up to 60 percent report that they would change to another occupation if they could (Campbell, Converse, and Rodgers, 1976). Job satisfaction as a concept, as expressed in public opinion surveys, has questionable meaning (Campbell, 1977; Kanter, 1978). Why is this so? How then can we speak of satisfaction, and what relationship does it have to stress? There are a number of possible reasons for the contradictions:

(1) A simple one is that people can respond in a perfunctory way. Ask a person walking down the street, "How are you?," and he or she is likely to respond, "Fine" even though he may be suffering from acute intestinal pain or dying of cancer. Most surveys seem to assume that how people *say* they feel is what they really feel.

(2) Asked what they *might* do, for example if they would change jobs, people may well respond in terms of fantasy, even though their responses to their present situations may reflect simultaneously a realistic assessment of the present. As an analogy, to entertain the fantasy of moving to a distant resort area does not necessarily reflect serious discontent with one's present living circumstances.

(3) As Sarason (1977) has pointed out, many people in high status roles are indeed satisfied with their jobs. Even if they are not, they must say so because they are doing so well. However, simultaneously they can be dissatisfied because in an open and mobile society they have developed many competences, and the concurrent expectation that they will do the many things they promised themselves they would do. To have achieved competence in only one occupational role leaves them dissatisfied with that *one*.

(4) When they respond to a question about their present jobs, inevitably people are taking into consideration a configuration of forces: what they expect this job will bring; what lies ahead of them; whether it is a necessary step in a career; their feelings about their work relationships; comparative experiences in their previous jobs; their relative success or failure; their position vis-à-vis peers; and so on.

(5) The questioners have their own, often unconscious, political biases. That somebody asks about a given topic and somebody else responds says nothing about the degree of importance of the topic to the latter person (see, for example, Flanagan, in this volume). Nor does the questioner's interpretation of the responses as reflecting the wish for a given set of conditions necessarily genuinely reflect that wish. For example, highly dependent people might well answer a questionnaire in such a way as to indicate that they want and should have greater autonomy and to actualize themselves. As a matter of fact, probably they would be much more effective, if not much more contented, in a highly structured environment in which they were told what to do. Perhaps both issues could be important to the researcher but less relevant to the respondent.

No doubt there are many other reasons for contradictory findings and why it is difficult to measure satisfaction, to speak about it in any reasonably clear, conceptual way, and to relate it to stress (Zaleznik, Ondrack, and Silver, 1970). The same is true with respect to happiness or well-being (Campbell, 1977). Yet we know from many contemporary circumstances, including strikes and physical symptoms, that there are indeed many dissatisfactions in work situations.

Supervisors and managers at all levels spontaneously speak about the need to treat people differently than was customary a generation ago. When I interviewed a group of first-level foremen in a gas company recently, they said that the newly recruited young people they supervised were quickly bored with routine work. The supervisors felt that they needed to do something to stimulate the recruits because they were going to be doing that same routine work for the next thirty years. With rising levels of expectation as a product of higher levels of education and larger numbers of high school and college graduates now in organizations, not only do people need greater stimulation, but also increasing numbers of them anticipate multiple careers.

Studies of stress indicate that symptoms are inversely correlated with community or organizational status levels (Hollingshead and Redlich, 1958; Kornhauser, 1965; Srole, Langner, Michael, Opler, and Rennie, 1962). Stress seems to be higher, and therefore we must infer that satisfaction is lower, when people feel responsible for others and when there is greater role ambiguity (Kahn, Wolfe, Quinn, Snoek, and Rosenthal, 1964).

In sum we cannot infer much about satisfaction from mass surveys. We often do not know what is being measured in surveys. However, there is much evidence of stress from which we can infer considerable dissatisfaction.

What do we make of all this?

THE EGO IDEAL AND SELF-IMAGE RELATIONSHIP

When we ask people whether they are satisfied, we are asking implicitly about how they see themselves in the present with respect to some ideal anticipated view of themselves in the future. In psychoanalytic terms, we are talking about the difference between the ego ideal (how one perceives oneself at one's ideal best) and the self-image (how one sees oneself in the present). Both have powerful roots in, and evolve out of, unconscious fantasy as well as from developmental circumstances. Certainly both are affected by contemporary events. The greater the gap between the ego ideal and the self-image, the lower the self-esteem and the greater the self-directed aggression or anger with self. This might be expressed in a formula like this:

$$\text{Self Esteem} = \frac{1}{\text{Ego Ideal} - \text{Self-Image}}$$

Thus stress and satisfaction are very closely and inversely related to each other. To be dissatisfied or aggrieved with one's work or job situation is to be angry in varying degrees (disappointment, frustration, disillusionment, defeat) both with the environment (job, organization, career) and with oneself for being in such a position.

THREE CIRCUMSTANCES PRECIPITATING STRESS

There are three circumstances when psychological stress is increased and satisfaction diminished:

(1) When feelings of helplessness or inadequacy increase. This may happen as a product of being moved arbitrarily, of lowered status, of significant deprivations, and of other organizational actions. The fact that people experience being demeaned is reflected in a wide range of studies, expecially those having to do with status. There is also widespread evidence of the significance of loss of support, of life change events, of unemployment, and similar factors which leave the individual feeling more psychologically helpless and alone.

Organizational pyramidal structures, with their heavy emphasis on winners and losers, on one track to success, demean people. People in many specialities must shift from those specialities into managerial ranks in order to attain structural success, although they may be less competent as managers than as specialists. This is as much a problem for teachers who must become principals and superintendents, or nurses who must become nursing administrators, or college professors who must become deans and presidents. This problem is compounded by inadequate appraisal systems which do not speak to people's work performance and behavior on the job but to abstractions like promotability (Levinson, 1976). When, on the basis of inadequate appraisal, people are graded on curves that do not meet the required underlying statistical assumptions, they are arbitrarily defined as successful or unsuccessful when objectively their behavior on the job or their occupational performance is quite acceptable.

Another force that contributes to the lowered self-image in organizations is simply the behavioral consequence of the aging process. Most organizations have no effective or systematic way of describing and defining tasks in such a way as to place people at different ages or life stages in roles which most fit where they are physically and psychologically.

A major problem in many work organizations, if not all, is that phenomena widely recognized in the family tend to get played out in those organizations. Components of organizations, like members of a family, are scapegoated. Frequently, the trained observer sees the splitting phenomenon: people or groups are arbitrarily separated into the black hats and white hats. There is sadistic and overcontrolling behavior, as well as often bitter intra-organizational strife, sometimes chronic, sometimes resulting in the extrusion of some organization members.

Unrelenting pressure for production, managerial inability, or unwillingness to solve frustrating problems, or simple inefficiency, produce feelings of hostility toward the organization and toward the self for putting up with such conditions. The inability of organizations to recognize the devastating effects of change and to build in systematic methods of supporting people through the process of change further compounds the sense of loss, magnifies the feelings of helplessness, and undermines the self-image.

Change takes many forms. A combination of aging and obsolescence may make people less desirable in an occupational marketplace. People who are no longer technically up-to-date feel themselves to be less adequate and more readily threatened. Merger, retirement, transfer, promotion all disrupt previous relationships and produce losses. People do not easily reestablish ties or adapt to new experiences as they age. Therefore they tend to become increasingly isolated as a function of the aging process, making it likely that they will focus more intensely on work. Thus they necessarily develop a greater dependency on work as a source of gratification, and are more vulnerable to the effects of whatever decisions are made about them.

(2) When people's values and personal rules of behavior are

violated. Violations of values precipitate feelings of guilt. People are then angry with themselves or the organizations in which they work. Violation of personal standards occurs repeatedly, and people frequently complain about such violations. Advertising people will write books criticizing their own profession, teachers will complain about schools, and former CIA agents about the activities of their agency. Some people have exposed the dishonesty of their company's actions; others have reported on how they have fudged figures. All respond to internal standards, and the guilt and anger for violation of those standards.

People feel guilty and angry also when they are required to assume responsibilities which they cannot discharge adequately. A significant source of managerial guilt is the appraisal process itself. When managers and supervisors are asked to evaluate or appraise others, they usually feel they are being destructive. This is reflected in the fact that organizations are continuously changing performance-appraisal systems not only because they are unsatisfactory but also because, despite much training and pressure, it is difficult to get managers and supervisors to make evaluations. A fundamental reason is that evaluating others touches off ancient primary process feelings: to think something or to feel it is the same as to do it. Thus to critically evaluate is to be aggressive; unconsciously to be aggressive is to destroy. This problem is exacerbated when younger people are placed in supervisory or managerial roles over older people, as increasingly is the case with higher levels of education and ever more youthful management. Carrying out judgmental criticism under these circumstances becomes much like attacking one's own parents, thus reviving ancient oedipal anxieties, unconscious guilt, and the fear of retaliation. Fear is already exacerbated in organizations by the intense rivalry for places in the organization hierarchy. It is compounded even further by placing people in supervisory positions over others who were previously rivals or supervisors, thus recapitulating the worst fantasies of early childhood.

Changes in organizations which must adapt in turn require people to adopt new styles of behavior. Authoritarian managers are no longer permitted either by their subordinates or by their superiors to be as authoritarian as they once were. Many of us may applaud that phenomenon, but the change is hard on the people involved. There are other less dramatic demands for change in personal style. People who are accustomed to administering by not taking charge, as often is the case in management of mental health clinics or art museums or hospitals, are now being compelled to take charge and to become more efficient, to control people rather than merely consult with them. Employees who formerly were encouraged to be dependent now are frequently being required to become more aggressive as more organizations shift from technical or manufacturing orientations to marketing orientations. Thus the long-term pursuit of the ego ideal for such people is undermined and the fact that they must go off in other occupational directions frequently presents them with a self-image that is anathema to them.

(3) When people feel they are not moving toward their ego ideals. People will be angry with themselves (and therefore depressed) and with their work organizations when they do not have a sense of forward movement. The expected movement toward the ego ideal is implicit in studies that reflect the wish for greater autonomy, opportunity, growth, and challenge.

In addition to negative organizational events, movement toward the ego ideal may be inhibited by social and cultural forces. All cultural units, whether flocks or families, tribes or nations, have pecking orders. The males who are more dominant in the pecking order, presumably for Darwinian reasons, have greater access to food and females. Thus there is a certain inevitability about the way social structures evolve and power is distributed, regardless of economic systems. There is also a certain inevitability about people's willingness to attribute status or "better than" to one kind of work as contrasted with another. The leather workers of India and Japan are drawn only from the lowest castes. In our own country, as well as others in the western world, fewer people are willing to perform personal services, and those who do are now more often immigrants from less developed countries. Repeated surveys of the status of occupations indicate that professions are highest ranked. Within given professions there are also well defined hierarchies. Therefore, even in autonomous professional practices, a sense of hierarchy prevails and people scale themsleves, thereby significantly affecting their own self-images.

Although it is true that one's position in an organization hierarch usually governs one's social position in one's community, nevertheless, even if there were no organizations, there would be competition for social position. As noted earlier, social class studies indicate that the lower a person is in the community social structure, the more likely he or she is to have symptoms of mental and physical illness.

In addition there are, of course, the inevitable socioeconomic forces which go beyond what organizations do of their own accord. When school enrollments decline, some teachers lose their jobs. When brokerage houses merge, there is a surplus of security analysts. When one or another kind of work becomes obsolete, its practitioners are compelled to adapt and to give up their ego ideal pursuits in that particular profession. Then there are problems of racial, ethnic, and educational discrimination which not only do permanent damage to the self-image but also inhibit the move toward the ego ideal.

All this is compounded when there is inadequate information from the organization and repetitive change in organization structures. These result in inadequate support from superiors to deal with both the organization and external reality. Coping both with losses and new demands requires simultaneously taxing adaptation (Holmes and Rahe, 1967). This effort is complicated by role ambiguity. In the absence of information and role definition and without an adequately delegated charge and necessary support, people are more likely to be hyper-self-critical, more defensive, more distressed, more overcontrolled, and increasingly at risk of external criticism from superiors.

People attribute to superiors in their work organizations many of the same qualities they experienced in their relationships with their parents. Superior-subordinate relationships thereby take on powerful psychological overtones, especially these days when young people come to organizations expecting to be helped toward careers. But organizations do not adequately recognize the symbolic representation of superiors as parental surrogates. Nor do work organizations recognize that people can develop mutually supporting work groups around their leadership.

A conspicuous feature in the literature having to do with the precipitants of stress and dissatisfaction to which I have just referred is the assumption in all of these studies that the environment is the problem. Therefore, it follows that if you change the environment, you will change the balance of forces in the equation and people will therefore be better satisfied and have less stress. There is much to this thesis. In fact, if I did not accept the thesis as having a certain validity, I would not do much of what I presently do in organizational consultation. It is clear from all kinds of therapy as well as studies in organizations that people do indeed feel better about themselves when they have a greater effect on the forces that in turn affect them and when they have greater control over their environments. This conviction has led to the contemporary movement loosely labeled "Improving the Quality of Work Life."

But those of us who are clinicians or whose work is rooted in clinical theory and practice, know that people make their own psychological beds, so to speak. All of us are always engaged in maintaining our psychological equilibria, and therefore in making much of our own psychological environments. One way of doing that is by choosing our occupations and the kinds of organizations we work in, however unconsciously. We create psychological contracts with our organizations (Levinson, Price, Munden, Mandl, and Solley, 1962). We are not merely passive agents to be shaped by the organization or the organizational role alone. Furthermore, specific environmental circumstances and events have idiosyncratic meaning for individuals, as reflected in their varying reactions to the same events. Therefore, the sophisticated behavioral scientist must always see a person in context, always engaged in psychological negotiation with his or her environment and key figures in it. However, to assert that the individual has an effect on his or her environment—for example, that the assembly line worker indeed enters into a psychological contract with General Motors—is to risk being accused of blaming the victim, or of taking the extreme position that *everything* that happens to a person is willed by that person. I do not propose to be in either one of those camps.

So while organizations do indeed precipitate dissatisfaction and stress, one cannot take the position that dissatisfaction/stress is altogether the fault of the organization. Not only does the culture have an impact but also individuals bring their own ego ideals and self-images, their own values and expectations to the organization, and thereby their own vulnerabilities. It follows that one cannot readily say that organizations would attain significantly higher levels of satisfaction *if only* they were to change the environment (the organization structure, the political system, the work place, etc.) in a more positive direction.

UNRECOGNIZED FACTORS

Efforts to improve the quality of work life may indeed give rise to greater satisfaction and thereby presumably to less stress. However, there are important factors within individuals which precipitate dissatisfaction and stress which seem to be largely unrecognized. Chief among them is a fundamental phenomenon, primary narcissism (Freud, 1914/1957).

Given the ego ideal/self-image phenomenon, none of us is as good in his own eyes as he or she would like to be. A subtle, unconscious, but nevertheless important aspect of the ego ideal is the wish to attain omnipotence or perfection. None of us comes close. Some think they have a chance and pursue that illusory goal unremittingly in compensatory behavior. To varying degrees, therefore, we will be happy with ourselves for thinking we are coming close. Those who feel they must drive themselves to that end do so in vain. Continuously failing, they are perennially angry with themselves. One of the more commonplace ways of dealing with the obverse of happiness, namely, unhappiness or anger with self, is to displace it onto others. Scapegoating, racial prejudice, and denigration of stereotyped individuals or groups are wisely recognized to be such displacements.

If work in our society is significantly the basis of self-esteem, then dissatisfaction with self is likely to be readily displaced onto work. If by one's own standards one is not as good as one would like to be and one works in an organization, then that organization is likely to be a displacement object. After all, the organization is bigger than the person, has more resources, more information, and more capacity for coping with the environment; and therefore, by definition, it should be more effective than the individual. When the individual sees the organization's ineffectiveness, just as when the child sees the imperfections of the parent, the dissatisfaction with self will be displaced onto the organization. The individual will be easily able to identify those aspects of the organization which "make" him or her feel dissatisfied and therefore be put under stress, when as a matter of fact these elements or forces or events may not be nearly as powerful or stressful as the individual indicates. Indeed, they may be magnified in his or her eyes purely as a product of the individual's psychic conflicts. As an analogy, if a person with an obsessive character structure married another with an hysterical character structure and then they criticize each other for characterological shortcomings, are the shortcomings objective failures or do they lie in the eyes of the respective beholders? How much of the beholders' stress then is self-created? How much do they need each other to live out certain fantasies?

Sarason's (1977) observation, noted earlier, that the higher a person's attainment, even when highly satisfied, the greater the likelihood that he or she will be simultaneously unsatisfied because he or she has not done as much as he or she promised himself he or she would do, supports this point. Again, not having come close to the ego ideal and therefore angry with oneself, one can easily displace such hostility onto the job.

Studies of life stages are now in vogue (Erikson, 1963; Gould, 1978; Levinson, 1977). As adults move through the various stages of adult life, however defined, there are shifts in value emphases and therefore in activities which are more gratifying and more appropriate at different stages of life. There are new and different responsibilities. There are changed expectations of self. For example, now that retirement limits have been lifted for many people, they expect to be able to continue to produce at the same high level as when they were younger. In many instances they will not be able to do so. It will be easier to blame the work organization than to confront that narcissistic injury which is the lowered self-image which accompanies the incapacities of aging.

Finally, we are confronted with another curious dichotomy. Human beings are greatly preoccupied with death. All religions have at their root an effort to understand and cope with death. Great philosophical movements, such as existentialism, have been preoccupied with that issue (Toynbee, 1968). Great authors, too. Isaac Bashevis Singer (1978) says, "in literature, as in our dreams, death does not exist." Alfred Kazin (1978) says of Sylvia Plath, "As a poet, she would not become alive and frightening until she faced her fascination with her own death." The current vogue for counseling the dying (Kübler-Ross, 1969) testifies to another form of the same preoccupation. Historically, the cosmetic business has prospered from the wish to mask one's aging and therefore increasing proximity to death.

Although we are powerfully preoccupied with mortality, we seem not to take this preoccupation into account when we speak of satisfaction in our lives and with our work, which is such a crucial component of both our lives and our satisfaction. Nowhere in the satisfaction/stress literature is this pervasive issue recognized, although it is clear that reported happiness declines with age (Campbell, 1977).

It is a clinical commonplace that primary narcissism is a fundamental protection against the helplessness of the infant and the basis for establishing relationships with others. The infantile wish to be omnipotent, to be able to live forever, never leaves us. We see its effects perennially in the denial of the impact of smoking and similar self-destructive activities. It is this belief in our own omnipotence which is deflated by the aging process, by the vicissitudes of life, and always by the underlying threat of death (nobody knows whether he or she is going to be alive tomorrow). Rubin (1977) remarks on how often working-class men and women, still in their twenties, use the phrase "When I was young." Not only do they feel loaded down early with family responsibilities, but also they feel early on they have "had it" in life. They have to either explode or withdraw, she says. She notes that the men and women she met recall parents, especially fathers, who were taciturn and unresponsive, withdrawing into silence (in my view, dying).

Our anger at the narcissistic injury (the recognition that we are not omnipotent and are not going to live forever) is likely to be displaced onto the most important and easily available activities and social structures in which those activities occur. We see much of this in the middle-age crisis and in the symptoms and the breakup of marriages which follow it.

I contend that much of the dissatisfaction with work is also a displacement from the same phenomenon. Our work, which is the source of so much of our coping effort, ultimately, it turns out, is not going to enable us to master the external environment fully or be fully in control of our fate. In only a few cases is it going to enable us to live forever in the form of great artistic or scientific achievement or great organizational entities. Even then we will endure only symbolically.

In other words, each of us has a contract with himself. Many primitive, infantile elements of that contract having to do with the wish to attain perfection and to live forever are inevitably doomed to nonfulfillment. The underlying disappointment in the failure to understand, let alone fulfill, the contract with the self is a significant component of dissatisfaction and therefore of stress. That fundamental disappointment is exacerbated, in turn, by environmental forces which causes work organizations to violate other elements of that contract (e.g., violations of conscience). It is further magnified by those which become a counterforce or barrier to attaining the more conscious expectations of the self. I say exacerbated because I think the fundamental issues, those of primary narcissim and the wish to endure forever, will not be gratified no matter what happens in the external environment, and therefore there will always be significant elements of dissatisfaction and of stress.

I do not mean to imply that narcissistic injury is all there is to stress or that it is not worth mitigating the precipitating events or configurations of forces that give rise to diminished self-images, problems of conscience, or inhibition of career aspiration. I do mean to say that I think the results people expect from such efforts alone are likely to be both elusive and disappointing. We will continue to find contradictory evidence in morale studies and attitude surveys, and a shift of the focus of discontent from one issue to another as long as the facts of narcissistic injury and displacement are not recognized. The organizational changes that are built on such data will probably continue to yield limited and temporary results.

THE COPING PROCESS

Coping with stress involves coping with one's own character defenses in the face of tasks that are age-specific, stage-specific, and congenial to one's equilibrium-maintaining efforts. Coping involves managing one's drives, the distance between self-image and ego ideal, and focal conflicts, in the face of institutional requirements. Those requirements may magnify or intensify intrapsychic struggles or conversely make certain kinds of defenses incongruous in certain situations. How then do we help people cope with such a phenomenon?

First, by significant public education efforts. We need to help people understand both the sources of and the elements of irrational expectations of self, as well as the consequences of these expectations, e.g., depressive orientations to life, compensatory drives to power, drivenness, unrewarding life experiences despite intense effort to achieve gratification, etc. We need to help them understand the crises of normal development as people pass from one life stage to another, giving up youth and the gratifications of earlier years, and having increasingly to face the realization of mortality as they do so. We need to help them understand the relationship between the consequent disappointment and the appearance of physical, even life-threatening illnesses like cancer. We need to help them understand why there are different value emphases at different points in the life stage curve.

Second, we need to establish better mechanisms through which people can give more thoughtful attention to their careers as they mature. We need to encourage people not merely to seek jobs but to take initiative to develop their own independent occupational activities which they, themselves, may be able to control and, with continuing education, to change as they wish. While this will not cope with the underlying phenomena I have described, it will tend to reduce some of the sense of helplessness and dependency that people feel too often in organizations in which they work. They will be less vulnerable to the feeling of being defeated and destroyed as they age. But they will have to learn to cope with the feeling of being alone in their work, without the comfort of organizational support.

These two together—(1) Greater understanding of the underlying concern with mortality and the displacement phenomenon, and of the transition through life stage events and the experiences of loss, and (2) Greater control over one's work and career—can be fostered through the further development of a contemporary self-help mechanism, namely, mutual-support groups. If we can help people understand and recognize depression, which is anger with self and therefore the core of the emotional stress I have been examining, then we can also help them understand the need for forming more mutual-support groups to deal with specific problems. We already have Weight Watchers, Parents Without Partners, Alcoholics Anonymous, and so on. In only a few instances have there been mutual-support groups of people who have lost their jobs or people who have different kinds of illnesses. These could well proliferate in every community. Indeed, perhaps it should be a major function of community mental health centers to form them.

Finally, we can help bring such understanding into work organizations where it can become part of employee and managerial education. The contemporary vogue of concern with executive stress, relaxation mechanisms and devices, and cathartic relief could well become something more conceptually and professionally solid. For example, there might be systematic education in the formation of various support groups within the organizational structures as well as in the community at large to anticipate, to alleviate, and to ameliorate stress.

Executives, managers, and supervisors could be helped to understand what it means psychologically to be in positions of power over others, and what is required of them as symbolic parental surrogates. Work organizations particularly need to help managers and supervisors understand the guilt involved in performance appraisal and other supervisory actions, and to work out some of those feelings in management training programs.

Executives might be helped to understand the need to evolve multiple paths to achievement, using devices other than the ordinary hierarchical model, and to evolve more structured ways of funneling rivalry into task accomplishment, rather than pitting people against each other. Organizations must increasingly evolve more specific behavioral job descriptions, clearly defining what behavior is to be required of people and how they will know when those requirements are met. I refer specifically to actual behavior rather than to simple objectives.

More organizations might undertake and maintain continuous career counseling—including, particularly, counseling in the middle-age transition and through the preretirement period, specifically taking account of important psychological issues such as those that I have outlined here. They also should have devices for helping people prepare for multiple careers so they can make choices more readily and move into new occupational tracks when they become satiated with the previous work or reach dead ends in their present work or need to seek renewed stimulation.

Organizational leaders need to learn more about managing change in such a way as to alleviate potential stress and enable people to be effectively in charge of what is happening to them.

Finally, work organizations might well provide continuing education programs to support these efforts.

REFERENCES

Campbell, A. Subjective measures of well-being. In G. W. Albee and J. M. Joffe (Eds.), *Primary prevention of psychopathology. Vol. 1: The issues.* Hanover, N. H.: University Press of New England, 1977.

Campbell, A., Converse, P. E., and Rodgers, W. L. *The quality of American life: Perceptions, evaluations and satisfactions.* New York: Russell Sage Foundation, 1976.

Erikson, E. H. *Childhood and society,* 2nd ed. New York: Norton, 1963.

Freud, S. On narcissism: An introduction. In J. Strachey and A. Tyson (Eds.), *The standard edition of the complete psychological works of Sigmund Freud* (Vol. 14). London: Hogarth Press (1957). (Originally published in 1914).

Gould, R. *Transformations.* New York: Simon and Schuster, 1978.

Hollingshead, A. B., and Redlich, F. C. *Social class and mental illness.* New York: Wiley, 1958.

Holmes, T. H., and Rahe, R. H. Social adjustment and rating scale. *Journal of Psychosomatic Research,* 1967, *11*, 213–223.

Kahn, R., Wolfe, D., Quinn, R., Snoek, J., and Rosenthal, R. *Organizational stress: Studies of role conflict and ambiguity.* New York: Wiley, 1964.

Kanter, R. M. Work in a New America. *Daedalus,* 1978, *107*, 47–78.

Kazin, A. *New York Jew.* New York: Knopf, 1978.

Kornhauser, A. W. *Mental health of the industrial worker: A Detroit study.* New York: Wiley, 1965.

Kübler-Ross, E. *On death and dying.* New York: Macmillan, 1969.

Levinson, D. J. *The seasons of a man's life.* New York: Pantheon, 1977.

Levinson, H., Price, C. R., Munden, K. J., Mandl, H. J., and Solley, C. M. *Men, management and mental health.* Cambridge: Harvard University Press, 1962.

Levinson, H. Appraisal of *what* performance? *Harvard Business Review,* 1976, *54*, 30–46.

Quinn, R. S., Mangione, T. W., and Baldi de Mandelovito, M. S. Evaluating working conditions in America. *Monthly Labor Review,* 1973, *96*, 32–41.

Rubin, L. *Worlds of pain.* New York: Basic Books, 1977.

Sarason, S. *Work, aging and social action.* New York: Free Press, 1977.

Singer, I. B. *A young man in search of love.* New York: Doubleday, 1978.

Srole, L., Langner, T. S., Michael, S. T., Opler, M. K., and Rennie, T. A. C. *Mental health in the metropolis: The Midtown Study* (Vol. 1). New York: McGraw-Hill, 1962.

Toynbee, A. (Ed.). *Man's concern with death.* New York: McGraw-Hill, 1968.

Zaleznik, A., Ondrack, J., and Silver, A. Social class, occupational mental illness. In A. McLean (Ed.), *Mental health and work organizations.* Chicago: Rand McNally, 1970.

10

On the Well-Being of Adult Women

G R A C E K. B A R U C H and
R O S A L I N D C. B A R N E T T

The major theme of this paper is that in our society the psychological well-being of women is facilitated: (a) by the development of occupational competence and of the capacity for economic independence; and (b) by involvement in a variety of roles. With respect to the first point, we shall argue that neither psychological well-being nor full social competence in adulthood is compatible with occupational incompetence and economic dependence. Unfortunately, women still fail to grasp this social reality and thus do not prepare for it. Many women, therefore, find themselves unable to cope successfully with the circumstances in which they find themselves. They are at high risk for psychiatric symptomatology, poverty, and diminished well-being, especially as they grow older. As for the second point, we shall argue that when one considers the whole life span, the gratifications provided by multiple role involvement usually outweigh any conflict and stress such involvement may entail.

We begin by discussing the social changes that have made occupational competence and economic independence critical for women's successful adaptation. We then review evidence about the effects of multiple role involvement on psychological well-being in a group of married women with young children who differ in employment status. Women who occupy the traditional pattern of wife and mother are compared with those who combine these roles with that of paid worker, a pattern shared by increasing numbers of women.

The issues to be discussed must be viewed in the context of at least two sets of social changes. The first set includes the ability to control fertility, the problems of overpopulation, and the lengthening life span. An increasing proportion of women need no longer face frequent or unpredictable childbearing (Hoffman, 1977), and the social value of children has decreased. Furthermore, female life expectancy now exceeds 75 years, of which perhaps 10, or no more than about 1/7 of a lifetime, may be spent in intensive child-rearing, and that not for all women. A view of women that focuses on the wife and mother role and socializes girls mainly for such a role reflects serious lags in our perceptions, beliefs, and, perhaps most important, our emotions.

The second set of social changes revolves around what is really not a change at all, but a return to the way things have usually been in human history. We refer to the increasing participation of women, including mothers of young children, in the paid labor force. What is old about this is the restoring to women of their historic role as economic providers. In hunter-gatherer and agricultural societies, which together have constituted the human life style for over 90 percent of our history, women have always provided a substantial proportion of the economic basis for survival and for support of their families through food-gathering, farming, and other economically productive activities.

The East African women studied by the anthropologist Beatrice Whiting (1977), for example, grow crops on small plots, earn cash, and provide food and clothing required by their children. Doing their work in the company of other adults, they spend four or five hours a day away from their children, yet their lives provide what Whiting sees as the critical components of human well-being: a sense of competence—that is, having a valued impact on one's environment; sufficient variation in stimulation; and the assurance of support and comfort. But as their husbands move into stable paid employment in urban settings, the women follow, leaving their family farms. Landless and jobless, they become economically dependent for the first time and must take sole, full-time responsibility for the care of their children in isolated homes. Boredom and irritability increase; self-esteem decreases; well-being suffers. But to take on eight hours a day of poorly paid work in the labor force is not an answer to their demoralization. Such work creates overwhelming difficulties with child care, fatigue, and other problems so familiar to many women in our society. What should strike us is that these new social changes in Kenya that trouble Beatrice Whiting so much are frighteningly similar to our norm, indeed our social ideal, for the American family: the man as sole economic provider, the woman, jobless and in sole charge of children, economically dependent and isolated in her own home.

But for women not to be involved in economically productive work is in fact a new-fangled pattern in human society. With a cross-cultural perspective, we can see that our pattern, which otherwise might appear to reflect some kind of natural law about the division of labor between men and women, may actually be very unstable as well as painful and dysfunctional.

Of course, which patterns are adaptive and which are not depends obviously upon the social context, but given the context we have described, we believe that all adults must be able to function as economic providers. This simple idea is a cliché if one is thinking about men, but it remains controversial when applied to women. When men cannot support themselves or their families, we read about it in the newspapers. And as such cases multiply, they command the attention of social workers and economists, psychiatrists and senators. When a woman is unable to provide for herself and any dependents, that is as expected, unless and until she enters particular social categories of persons who threaten to impinge upon public monies: separated mothers, pregnant teenagers, elderly widows. Like magic, her economic dependence suddenly becomes all too visible and regrettable, attaining the status of a social problem, a label that is a passport to social concern. But this concern should have been present in the minds of parents and educators, mental health workers and public officials from her cradle days on. Yet the situations of the divorced mother, the unmarried pregnant teenager, the poor elderly widow, the battered wife unable to leave home—all are simply visible crises that punctuate the course of an otherwise undetected disease. The twin components of this disease are occupational incompetence and economic dependence; among the various milder manifestations are low self-esteem and depression.

Much current literature on mental health and well-being documents these and other negative impacts of what we might call our recent "traditional" patterns, and conversely, the positive consequences of "nontraditional" lifestyles. For example, when the famous group of gifted children first studied by Terman was followed up recently—they are now in their 60's—the women in the group were asked to describe their life pattern and their satisfaction with it (Sears and Barbee, 1977). The women who reported the highest level of satisfaction were income-producers, that is, they were working for pay, and were heads of households, that is, not currently married. These findings were contrary to expectations, perhaps because our psychological theories (and national mythologies) say that marriage and children are the route to a sense of well-being. These women, of course, were very able and in many cases were relatively successful occupationally. But in a study of working-class women all of whom were married and had children, Myra Ferree (1976) found that despite the routine nature of their jobs, those who worked felt happier and had higher self-esteem than did the unemployed housewives.

A second illustration is the work of George Brown and his colleagues (Brown, Bhrolchain, and Harris, 1975). Their study of the development of psychiatric symptomatology in women living in London showed that among women most at risk—that is, those with small children, who did not have a confidante— employment was a powerful antidote to stress; psychiatric symptoms developed in 79 percent of those women who were not employed, compared with only 14 percent of those employed.

Finally, in a large-scale study of households in the Chicago area, Frederic Ilfeld (1977) found that women have higher rates of symptomatology than do men. However, the only group of women with symptomatology rates as low as those of men were those who worked in high-prestige occupations. The mental health implication, Ilfeld concluded, is to get more women into high-status jobs.

Intellectual well-being, we believe, is also a component of mental health. Consider a very disturbing longitudinal study of children given IQ tests in the 1930's (Kangas and Bradway, 1972). Results of a follow-up when the subjects were in their middle years showed that the brighter a man was as a youngster (in terms of IQ scores), the more he had gained in IQ with age; the brighter a woman, the less she had gained. Since the patterns of "average" women resembled those of men, biological differences are an unlikely explanation for the results found for the bright women. Therefore it may be that their lives had not provided the elements necessary for cognitive growth. On this point, Melvin Kohn and his associates (Kohn and Schooler, 1977) have recently demonstrated that the structure of work affects aspects of personality previously thought to be relatively stable and fixed early in life. The cognitive complexity of the work their subjects did was found to be related both to their intellectual flexibility and to their self-esteem. For those engaged in repetitive work, as are some housewives, the implications for well-being are ominous.

Furthermore, while the family is often viewed as a valuable refuge from the occupational world, we often forget that the workplace can be a valuable refuge from family life, from strong emotions, conflicting demands, petty annoyances. Work can provide variety, challenge, clear-cut responsibilities, even respectful underlings. Certainly if unemployment can contribute to mental illness, employment, for women as well as men, can contribute to mental health. Yet we rarely conceptualize unemployment as a social problem for women. Their unemployment is often hidden; analyses of the National Longitudinal Survey data (Blau, 1978) suggest that the effect of recessions, at least among white women, is to discourage them from entering the labor force. Furthermore, among black women, those who want to work form a larger group than those who actually hold jobs (Sullivan, 1977). When employed women lose their jobs, moreover, the social supports available are minimal (Warren, 1975) compared to those available to men.

It is almost a cliché now for people who work long hours at demanding jobs, aware of what they are missing in terms of time with family, long talks with friends, concerts, all kinds of opportunities for leisure, to express the sentiment that "there is more to life than work." The problem is that life *without* productive work is terrible. We assume this for men in thinking about their unemployment and their retirement, but we do not think about the situation of women in this way. We want to stress here that as Linda Fidell (1978) has shown, for some women the activities associated with child-care and home-making are truly productive and satisfying in terms of engaging their interests and talents, at least for part of their lives, as are volunteer activities. However, for others, the lack of economically productive work is associated with the absence of one or more of the previously mentioned requirements postulated by Beatrice Whiting (1977): a sense of competence; support and comfort; and variations in stimulation.

Many women settle for support and comfort at the expense of their other needs.

Unfortunately, our norm of married women economically dependent upon their husbands is not viable in many circumstances. Husbands lose their jobs or die without leaving an adequate estate; inflation makes two incomes increasingly necessary; and perhaps most important, marriages dissolve. It is projected that 40 percent of current marriages will end in divorce. Divorce too often brings poverty to many middle-class women who thought it could never happen to them. About half of the women now on welfare are separated or divorced, and the situation of divorced and separated women *not* on welfare is precarious. Dorothy Burlage (1978) in a new study of such women asks the question, How do these women manage to avoid welfare? The answer is, barely and painfully, and by being breadwinners. Their major source of support is their own earnings, not alimony or child support. Their economic situation after divorce is much worse than before, and considering income in relation to need, is much worse than that of their ex-husbands. Because of the limitations of their training and experience and the absence of social supports, many are living out Beatrice Whiting's nightmare alternative for mothers: eight hours of paid drudgery. The low pay of women's occupations, the need to work full time to receive not only income but desperately needed health benefits, and barriers to further education constrain both their current and future income. In their book *Time of Transition*, Heather Ross and Isabel Sawhill (1975) report finding that of separated women who are on welfare, only about one quarter could earn even $1000 more a year than welfare provides.

So we return to the question of occupational competence, and to its roots in socialization, because in mentioning such phenomena as divorce and widowhood, one is reciting the list of disasters that young girls are warned may force them to work. Thus they are encouraged to prepare themselves for some sort of fall-back occupation. In this way economic independence is associated not with pride and pleasure but with misfortune, stigma, and failure. For girls to develop maximum occupational competence has been a goal neither for them nor for their parents. The images of girls as future wives and mothers and boys as

economic providers are powerful influences on the values, attitudes, practices, and feelings of parents, who have been very
concerned not to jeopardize the wife-and-mother part of a girl's
future role. We are only now beginning to think about what may
jeopardize optimal development of a girl's occupational life.
The problem may be seen in a study by Barnett (1975), who
found that when one ranks occupations in terms of how prestigious they are, the more prestige an occupation has, the more
boys, but not girls, desired to enter it. For girls the more prestigious an occupation, the more they expressed an aversion to
entering it. Traditional parental values and attitudes can therefore be hazardous for daughters' future occupational options.
Having a challenging and satisfying occupation can be a central
source of self-esteem, identity, and satisfaction and it is increasingly important that women derive these from sources beyond
the roles of wife and mother.

Theoretical and empirical literature relevant to these topics
is unfortunately inadequate. Depending upon whose book one
is reading, one is told that marriage and children are a health
hazard for women, that career-oriented women are unhappy,
neurotic, conflicted about femininity, and so forth. Available
data are limited in various ways, but at least researchers are
asking important questions, such as whether marrying and having children are necessary for well-being.

On the question of marriage, studies of depression indicate
that among married people, women are more depressed than
men; among the unmarried, men are more depressed than women.
In reviewing these data, Lenore Radloff (1975) concluded that
marriage is a mental health advantage to men, but not to women.
However, a large-scale survey by Angus Campbell and his associates (1976) found no evidence that women were less satisfied
than men, and married women were more satisfied and happier
than unmarried women. So far, then, the data on marriage are
mixed.

Data on the relationship between rearing children and well-
being are somewhat clearer. Depression and a lower sense of
well-being are associated with caring for young children; indeed,
women in the so-called empty nest years are in fact lower in risk
for depression and higher in sense of well-being (Radloff, 1975).

Thus intensive involvement in child care is no sure route to happiness for women.

Work, in contrast, has until recently been seen as peripheral to women's well-being. Moreover, even studies that do focus on women's employment status tend to ignore variations among employed women which are due to differences in occupational status and in commitment to work (Campbell, Converse, and Rodgers, 1976; Kanter, 1977). Similarly, Linda Fidell (1978) has recently pointed out that women at home are not all alike; some are committed to the role of housewife, some want to work, and these variations affect well-being.

INVOLVEMENT IN MULTIPLE ROLES

It has been assumed that involvement in multiple roles, a phenomenon particularly relevant to women, is primarily a source of conflict and distress; multiple role involvement is rarely examined as potentially enhancing one's life and one's well-being. Yet in 1973 Gove and Tudor attributed the superiority of men's mental health to their involvement in the arenas of both work and family. The previously mentioned study by Brown et al. (1975) also indicates the benefits of multiple roles, since for married women with children, work was found to mitigate the consequences of stressful life events. And in her study of able women in midlife, Birnbaum (1975) found that compared with educated married women who had not worked since the birth of their first child, married professionals were higher in self-esteem and satisfaction.

In our own research we were able to examine the relationship of multiple role involvement to psychological well-being, indexed by self-esteem and role-pattern satisfaction, in a group of mothers who differed in employment status. Data were collected from women and their husbands, who were parents of preschool girls and boys, all of whom participated in a larger study of family and school influences on the competence-related behavior of preschool girls. Our sample included 142 white, married, middle-class women who had at least one child enrolled in a preschool in the Greater Boston area. All the women were in first marriages, and they were relatively well educated; 62 percent had at least a bachelor's degree. The homogeneity of the sample, while limiting generalizability, allowed us to see important differences that would otherwise be obscured.

Our focus was on comparing employed and unemployed mothers, both to determine any differences in the level of their role-pattern satisfaction and self-esteem and to investigate the differences between the groups with respect to the correlates of each of these outcome variables. The employed women met the criteria of working at least ten hours a week in paid employment for at least the year prior to the data collection. About 35 percent of the mothers in the sample, or 50 women, were classified as employed, and about 60 percent (n = 86) were classified as "at home." The remainder were students and were omitted from this study. The two subgroups of women did not differ with respect to age, education, or number of children. The women at home were occupying the pattern that has traditionally been commended to women, particularly if they have young children, while the group who were employed represented a nontraditional but increasingly popular pattern: that of working at least part time while caring for young children. If involvement in multiple roles is primarily a source of conflict and stress, without compensatory gratification, mothers who work should be lower in psychological well-being than those at home who are not confronted with potential role conflict and who are living out the socially prescribed life style.

Self-esteem was assessed through a modified version of the Coopersmith Self-Esteem Scale (1968), in which subjects indicate whether a series of statements is "like them": for example, "I often wish I were someone else," and "People usually follow my ideas." The women reported their level of satisfaction with their current role pattern by using a four-point scale ranging from 1 = very dissatisfied to 4 = very satisfied.

To examine the correlates of self-esteem and role-pattern satisfaction, we looked at several sets of variables. The first concerned the women's husbands. The profound influence of husbands' attitudes, actual and perceived, upon the role patterns of women (and upon the satisfaction they derive from them), has been demonstrated repeatedly. For example, husbands' actual and perceived attitudes toward wives' employment are related to wives' actual employment status (Macke and Hudis, 1978), particularly among white women. The women were therefore asked to indicate how satisfied they perceived their husbands to be with their (the wives') current role pattern. (Unfortunately, we did not also ask husbands directly how satisfied they were with their wives' role pattern.) Data were collected directly from the husbands about their sex-role ideology, that is, their beliefs about the appropriate roles for women and men, using a modified version of the Spence-Helmreich Attitudes Toward Women Scale, Short Form (1972). In addition, the prestige of the husbands' occupations was rated, using the scale proposed by Treiman (1975). Jean Lipman-Blumen (1973) has argued that women in the traditional role pattern often derive a vicarious sense of achievement and therefore satisfaction from their husbands' occupational achievements. This phenomenon suggests that self-esteem and role-pattern satisfaction should be more strongly correlated with husbands' occupational prestige for women at home than for employed women.

The second set of variables concerned the women's mothers, whom we viewed as possible role models, positive and/or negative. We examined the impact on satisfaction and self-esteem of two aspects of their mothers' lives as reported by the women: (a) the actual employment status of their mothers as they were growing up; and (b) their mothers' role-pattern preferences, that is, whether the mother would have preferred to work or to stay home, regardless of actual employment status.

The third set of variables concerned the role definitions and attitudes of the women themselves. We assessed their sex-role ideology by using the Spence-Helmreich Scale (1972). In order to examine their self-perceptions with respect to competence and femininity, they were asked to rate themselves on two sets of traits taken from the Rosenkrantz Sex-Role Questionnaire (Rosenkrantz, Vogel, Bee, Broverman, and Broverman, 1968). One subset of traits was from the competence subscale and included such qualities as assertiveness, independence, and leadership ability, which were previously determined to be both socially desirable and associated with males. A second subset of traits was previously determined to be socially desirable and associated with females, e.g., kindness, warmth. The first scale was viewed as a measure of a sense of competence, the second as a measure of a sense of femininity. In previous studies (Baruch, 1973, 1976) a sense of competence but not of femininity has been found to be positively correlated with self-esteem.

For the group of women who were employed, several important dimensions of their work were assessed. We measured commitment to work by asking the women to rate how important working in general was to them. They were also asked to rate their satisfaction with their current job. The prestige of their occupations was assessed by using the Treiman Scale (1975).

Finally, women were asked about the number and ages of their children, since several studies have reported a negative relationship between women's mental health and their responsibility for the care of young children. Our sample proved to be relatively homogeneous: all the women had at least one child under six by virtue of inclusion in the sample, and only 14 percent had more than two children. No relationship was found for either group of women between the number or ages of children and role-pattern satisfaction or self-esteem.

Turning to the results, we first present some overall findings and then those concerning the particular subsets of variables (See Table 1).

An important general finding was that there were no significant differences between women in paid employment and women at home with respect to level of either role-pattern satisfaction or self-esteem. Thus involvement in multiple roles, as wife, mother, worker, even when children are young, does not serve to diminish psychological well-being, nor does being at home enhance well-being. Of course, in this relatively well educated and economically privileged sample, the women tended to have the role patterns they preferred; on the four-point satisfaction scale, over 85 percent of the women reported themselves to be either moderately or very satisfied.

A second general finding was of a strong relationship between self-esteem and self-perceptions of competence for both groups of women. For employed women the Pearson product-moment correlation was .48, and for women at home it was .42; both are significant at the .001 level. Thus perceiving oneself as having competence-related traits contributes to the self-esteem of women at home as well as employed women, even though these traits are considered traditionally masculine. It is interesting that sense

Table 1
Summary of Findings

Variables	Employed Women (n = 50)		Unemployed Women (n = 86)	
	Role-pattern satisfaction	Self-esteem	Role-pattern satisfaction	Self-esteem
Husbands of subjects				
Perceived attitude	.58[c]	.39[b]	.74[c]	.31[b]
Sex-role ideology	ns	ns	ns	ns
Occupational prestige	ns	ns	ns	ns
Mothers of subjects				
Employment status	ns	ns	-.29[a]	ns
Role pattern preference	.35[a]	.35[a]	.32[a]	ns
Women's role definitions				
Sex-role ideology	ns	ns	-.25[b]	ns
Self-perception of competence	.28	.48[c]	ns	.42[c]
Self-perception of femininity	ns	ns	ns	ns
Employment characteristics				
Commitment to work	.86[c]	.48[b]		
Satisfaction with current job	.42[b]	.27		
Occupational prestige	-.26	.25		

Note: For correlations without asterisks, $p < .10$.

[a] $p < .05$.

[b] $p < .01$.

[c] $p < .001$.

of femininity was not associated with self-esteem or satisfaction for either group. These data suggest that, in our culture, seeing oneself as possessing competence-related traits is conducive to a high level of self-esteem, while seeing oneself as traditionally feminine is not.

Turning now to the subsets of variables, those concerning husbands were of particular interest. We were surprised by the magnitude of the relationship between women's perceptions of husbands' attitudes toward their role pattern and our indices of well-being. For women at home the correlation between role-pattern satisfaction and husband's perceived attitudes was .74 ($p < .001$); between self-esteem and perceived attitude it was .31 ($p < .01$). Among employed women the correlation for self-esteem was .58 ($p < .001$); for satisfaction, .39 ($p < .01$). Among women at home, then, the degree to which they perceive their husbands as approving their role pattern explains about 55 percent of the variance of their satisfaction with their pattern, compared with 33 percent for employed women. The difference between these groups with respect to the correlation coefficients for role-pattern satisfaction fell just short of conventional levels of significance ($p < .07$). Thus the well-being of women at home appears more dependent upon their husbands than does that of employed women.

Husbands' sex-role ideology was, in contrast, not related to self-esteem or role-pattern satisfaction in either group of women. Since the measure of ideology was administered directly to husbands, it may be that the wives' perceptions of their husbands' attitudes are biased (Bailyn, 1978). It is more likely, however, that a husband's attitude toward his own wife's role pattern may not be identical to his beliefs about the proper roles of men and women in general.

In contrast to expectations derived from the theory of vicarious achievement, the prestige of the husbands' occupations was not related to either outcome variable for either group of women. Thus there was no evidence that self-esteem or role-pattern satisfaction for women at home depended upon their husbands' accomplishments. Occupational prestige is only one index, however, and a fairly crude one, of the husbands' achievements, particularly for a middle-class sample.

The second set of variables concerns the women's mothers.

It is important to note that the employment status of women in our sample was not related to whether their mothers worked. For both groups of women their mothers' actual employment status was unrelated to self-esteem. For employed women, mothers' employment status was also unrelated to role-pattern satisfaction. However, role-pattern satisfaction among women at home was related to having a mother who did not work ($r = .29$, $p < .05$).

Women's reports of whether their mothers would have preferred to work regardless of their actual employment status were related to both indices of psychological well-being. In general, self-esteem and satisfaction were associated with a woman's perceiving her mother as preferring the role pattern she was now occupying. Among employed women, perceiving their mothers as preferring to work was correlated with their own role-pattern satisfaction and self-esteem at the .05 level ($r = .35$ and $r = .35$, respectively). Among women at home, perceiving their mothers as preferring *not* to work was related to satisfaction at the .05 level ($r = .32$); the relationship to self-esteem was not significant. To put it another way, choosing a role pattern contrary to that endorsed by one's mother appears to diminish self-esteem and satisfaction with one's role pattern, perhaps because of feelings of self-doubt, conflict, and guilt about living a life different from that of the mother.

The third set of variables concerned role definitions and attitudes of the women themselves. With respect to sex-role ideology, among employed women there was no relationship to either self-esteem or satisfaction. For women at home, however, having a nontraditional sex-role ideology was negatively related to role-pattern satisfaction at the .01 level of significance ($r = -.25$); there was no significant relationship to self-esteem. A discrepancy between ideology and actual role pattern clearly can contribute to dissatisfaction.

With respect to the work-related attitudes assessed for the employed women, a strong correlation was found between commitment to work and role-pattern satisfaction ($r = .86; p < .001$). Commitment to work was also strongly related to self-esteem ($r = .48$, $p < .01$). The two indices of well-being were less strongly related to satisfaction with current job, which was correlated with satisfaction at the .01 level ($r = .42$) and to self-esteem at a nearly significant level ($r = .27, p < .07$). Thus for employed women the centrality of work to their lives and satisfaction with their current job had a powerful positive impact upon their psychological well-being. These findings directly contradict the idea that when a woman has several roles, the greater her commitment to one role, the more severe the strain and therefore the lower her well-being. In fact, our data suggest that well-being may be enhanced by such commitment.

Finally, with respect to the prestige of women's occupations, the correlations of occupational prestige with satisfaction and self-esteem just failed to attain conventional levels of significance ($r = .26, p < .10$ and $r = .26, p < .10$, respectively). The magnitude of these correlations may have been reduced not only by the small size of the sample but by the relative similarity of the women's occupations with respect to prestige: prestige levels were moderately high.

Perhaps the most important finding of this study concerns the sources of self-esteem and satisfaction available to married women with young children. The well-being of nonemployed women is highly dependent upon their husbands' approval of their pattern, or, more accurately, on their (the wives') perceptions of his approval. Employed women are also sensitive to their husbands' attitudes, although considerably less so. But, in addition, their own commitment to work and their satisfaction with their current job contribute heavily to both indices of well-being. These work-related variables are clearly more under the women's own control, more independent of others, and thus may be more stable bases for well-being. Heavy reliance on external sources, on sources out of one's control, for one's self-esteem is highly problematic, especially in light of the high rate of marital dissolution.

A second important implication of our findings is that even while women are intensely concerned with the demands of young children, involvement in multiple roles need not result in debilitating conflict, strain, and dissatisfaction. At later stages of the life cycle, involvement in multiple roles may even protect against such stress as that associated with the empty nest and aging (Bart, 1972).

Our work supports, at least indirectly, the value of preparing girls from childhood on to develop and exercise occupational competence. In fact, in individual interviews many of the unemployed mothers who had daughters expressed similar sentiments. When asked how they would like their preschool daughter's life to be similar to theirs and how they would like it to be different, they stressed the importance of evaluating life choices before making commitments:

I hope she decides to get into some career *before* marriage, or at least before she has children—it would just make things a lot easier on all concerned.

I would like her to find a satisfying career which she can combine with being married and having a family, if she chooses to have one. I feel it is extremely important for her to have a fulfilling career for her to establish a real sense of worth as an adult woman. I do not feel I am as career-oriented and ambitious as I would like to be. I would like Debbie to be more so.

REFERENCES

Bailyn, L. Personal communication, 1978.

Barnett, R. C. Sex differences and age trends in occupational preference and occupational prestige. *Journal of Counseling Psychology*, 1975, *22*, 35–38.

Bart, P. Depression in middle-aged women. In J. M. Bardwick (Ed.), *Readings on the psychology of women*. New York: Harper and Row, 1972.

Baruch, G. K. Feminine self-esteem, self-ratings of competence, and maternal career-commitment. *Journal of Counseling Psychology*, 1973, *20*, 487–488.

Baruch, G. K. Girls who perceive themselves as competent: Some antecedents and correlates. *Psychology of Women Quarterly*, 1976, *1*, 38–49.

Birnbaum, J. A. Live patterns and self-esteem in gifted family-oriented and career-committed women. In M. Mednick, S. Tangri, and L. W. Hoffman (Eds.), *Women and achievement: Social and motivational analysis*. New York: Hemisphere-Halstead, 1975.

Blau, F. D. *The impact of the unemployment rate on labor force entries and exits*. Paper presented to Secretary of Labor's Invitational Conference on the National Longitudinal Surveys of Mature Women, Washington, D.C., 1978.

Brown, G. W., Bhrolchain, M. N., and Harris, T. Social class and psychiatric disturbance among women in an urban population. *Sociology*, 1975, *9*, 225–254.

Burlage, D. *Divorced and separated mothers: Combining the responsibilities of breadwinning and childrearing*. Unpublished doctoral dissertation, Harvard University, 1978.

Campbell, A., Converse, P. E., and Rodgers, W. L. *The quality of American life*. New York: Russell Sage, 1976.

Coopersmith, S. *The antecedents of self-esteem*. San Francisco: Freeman, 1968.

Ferree, M. M. The confused American housewife. *Psychology Today*, 1976, *10*, 76–80.

Fidell, L. *Employment status, role dissatisfaction and the housewife syndrome*. Unpublished manuscript, California State University, 1978.

Gove, W. R., and Tudor, J. F. Adult sex roles and mental illness. *American Journal of Sociology*, 1973, *78*, 812–835.

Hoffman, L. W. Changes in family roles, socialization, and sex differences. *American Psychologist*, 1977, *32*, 644–657.

Ilfeld, F., Jr. *Sex differences in psychiatric symptomatology*. Paper presented at American Psychological Association meeting, San Francisco, 1977.

Kangas, J., and Bradway, K. Intelligence at middle age: A thirty-eight-year-follow-up. *Developmental Psychology*, 1972, *5*, 333–337.

Kanter, R. M. *Work and family in the United States: A critical review and agenda for research and policy*. New York: Russell Sage Foundation, 1977.

Kohn, M. L., and Schooler, C. *The complexity of work and intellectual functioning*. Paper presented to American Sociological Association meeting, Chicago, 1977.

Lipman-Blumen, J. *The vicarious achievement ethic and non-traditional roles for women.* Paper presented to Eastern Sociological Association, New York, 1973.

Macke, A. S., and Hudis, P. M. *Sex-role attitudes and employment among women: A dynamic model of change and continuity.* Paper presented to Secretary of Labor's invitational conference on the National Longitudinal Surveys of Mature Women, Washington, D.C., 1978.

Radloff, L. Sex differences in depression: The effects of occupation and marital status. *Sex Roles*, 1975, *1*, 249-265.

Rosenkrantz, P., Vogel, S., Bee, H., Broverman, I., and Broverman, D. Sex-role stereotypes and self-concepts in college students. *Journal of Consulting Psychology*, 1968, *32*, 287-295.

Ross, H. L., and Sawhill, I. V. *Time of transition: The growth of families headed by women.* Washington: The Urban Institute, 1975.

Sears, P. S., and Barbee, A. H. Career and life satisfaction among Terman's gifted women. In J. Stanley, W. George, and C. Solano (Eds.), *The gifted and the creative: Fifty year perspective.* Balitmore: Johns Hopkins University Press, 1977.

Spence, J., and Helmreich, R. The attitudes towards women scale: An objective instrument to measure attitudes towards the rights and roles of women in contemporary society. JSAS *Catalog of Selected Documents in Psychology*, 1972, *2*, 66.

Sullivan, T. A., *Black female breadwinners: Some intersections of dual market and secondary worker theory.* Paper presented to American Sociological Association, Chicago, 1977.

Treiman, D. J. Problems of concept and measurement in the comparative study of occupational mobility. *Social Science Research*, 1975, *4*, 183-230.

Warren, R. B. *The work role and problem coping: Sex differentials in the use of helping systems in urban communities.* Paper presented at meeting of American Sociological Association, San Francisco, 1975.

Whiting, B. B. Changing life styles in Kenya. *Daedalus*, 1977, *106*, 211-225.

11

Career Success and Life Satisfactions of Middle-Aged Managers

DOUGLAS W. BRAY and
ANN HOWARD

Some 22 years ago, the Bell System began a long-term study of the lives and careers of managers called The Management Progress Study. The participating managers, originally 422 young white males from six telephone companies, are now middle-aged and in mid-career, and a new phase of research is in progress to determine what this stage of life means to them. The preliminary data from this midlife research allows the exploration of the relationship between career success and life satisfactions reported here.

The Management Progress Study (MPS) participants have undergone a rigorous schedule over the years. Their introduction to the study brought them in groups of twelve to a three-day management assessment center between 1956 and 1960. At the assessment center, the first of its kind in industry, the participants underwent a series of individual and group exercises. These included simulations (an In-Basket exercise, a short business game, and a leaderless group discussion), interviews, aptitude tests, attitude and personality questionnaires, and projective techniques (the Thematic Apperception Test and sentence completion blanks). Behavior in the exercises was observed by a trained staff of psychologists and reported in an "integration" session, where each participant was evaluated individually. The assessors pooled their judgments and rated the assessees on a number of dimensions like leadership skills, planning and organizing ability, and primacy of work. Finally, overall predictions were made about each participant's future as a Bell System manager.

The data from the original assessments were securely filed away

The authors thank Louise DuBois for her conscientious research assistance in the analyses of these data.

and individual results kept confidential from both management and the participants themselves. Annually, for the next seven years, each participant was interviewed by a psychologist while a representative of the company was interviewed about him independently. Eight years after the start of the study, the participants were reassessed in a center similar to the one they had gone through initially. Following this, the interviewing program became triannual with the participants and with their bosses, and was expanded to include telephone interviews with participants who had terminated their employment with the Bell System.

Twenty years after the first assessment another close look at the participants was in order. The original plans had called for another management assessment center to evaluate changes in their management skills over the twenty-year span. But as the time drew near, it appeared that a great opportunity would be missed by merely continuing the study in the same direction. For this was the mid-1970's, when midlife and its crises were consuming the attention of writers and theoreticians, and the middle-aged male was threatening to replace the white rat and the college sophomore as the dominant research subject in psychology. The Management Progress Study was redirected toward studying its participants as middle-aged people and not just managers. Thus a new assessment center was developed, entitled MPS:20.

THE MPS:20 ASSESSMENT CENTER

The purposes of the MPS:20 assessment were as follows:

(1) to evaluate the work motivation, company commitment, career satisfaction, and retirement proneness of mid-career managers.
(2) to measure changes in their abilities, attitudes, and personality characteristics over a twenty-year span and explore the reasons for those changes.
(3) to assess the effects on them of plateauing promotional and salary opportunities, affirmative action, and outside pressures on and challenges to the Bell System.
(4) to appraise the quality of life in the middle years—its rewards and hazards, and possible crises and reorientations.

(5) to develop an assessment center procedure for the study of middle life.

The accomplishment of these purposes depended on an orderly structuring of the midlife assessment center.

Assessment centers are designed around a number of dimensions to be evaluated for each participant. In the original management assessment center 26 different dimensions related to managerial effectiveness were rated, and these were repeated in the MPS:20 assessment. They included the following:

Administrative Skills:
  Organizing and Planning
  Decision Making
  Creativity

Work Motivation:
  Primacy of Work
  Inner Work Standards
  Energy
  Self-Objectivity

Interpersonal Skills:
  Leadership Skills
  Oral Communication Skills
  Behavior Flexibility
  Personal Impact
  Social Objectivity
  Perception of Threshold
    Social Cues

Career Orientation:
  Need for Advancement
  Need for Security
  Ability to Delay Grati-
    fication
  Realism of Expectations
  Bell System Value Orienta-
    tion

Intellectual Ability:
  General Mental Ability
  Range of Interests
  Written Communication
    Skill

Dependency:
  Need for Superior Approval
  Need for Peer Approval
  Goal Flexibility

Stability of Performance:
  Tolerance of Uncertainty
  Resistance to Stress

Because the MPS:20 assessment was refocused beyond managerial concerns and into midlife concerns, an additional set of assessment dimensions was required. A literature review pointed to 21 new dimensions related to the interests and concerns of mid-career and middle age. These were:

Work Satisfaction:
  Job Satisfaction
  Career Satisfaction
  Retirement Proneness

Philosophical Attitudes:
  Conservatism
  Cynicism
  Involvement
  Religiosity

Financial Concerns:
  Absence of Financial Worries
  Financial Motivation

Family Concerns:
  Stability of Marriage
  Marital Satisfaction
  Absence of Familial Worries

Self Concerns:
  Advocational Interest
  Self-development
  Escapism
  Adjustment
  Happiness
  Feelings of Crisis
  Concern with Health
  Concern with Aging
  Selfishness

A primary principle of assessment centers is the use of multiple assessors. At the integration sessions following the MPS:20 assessments the 47 dimensions are rated for each individual by a minimum of four assessors. For the data presented here, the assessors were the two authors of this paper, both industrial psychologists, and two clinical psychologists who have worked with the study for over 20 years: Dr. Joseph Rychlak of Purdue University and Dr. Walter Katkovsky of Northern Illinois University. The four staff members took turns reading aloud all the data from each case and then rated the 47 dimensions independently. Each announced his or her rating for each dimension; where there was disagreement of two points or more on the five-point scale, discussion ensued until consensus within one scale point was achieved.

After rating the dimensions, the staff members made independent predictions about each individual. In the career realm these included whether the man's job performance and commitment to the company would change between the present and his retirement, if he would retire early, how well he would adjust to retirement, and how satisfied he would feel with his career when it is over. In the personal arena, forecasts were made as to how satisfied he would feel with his life as he reaches old age and whether he would experience a critical disturbance in his personal adjustment or a significant value reorientation between the present and retirement. These predictions were in contrast to those made at the original management assessment center, which concerned how successful the man would be in terms of advancing within the management hierarchy and whether he would remain in the Bell System.

In addition to being organized around dimensions and using multiple assessors, assessment centers are characterized by the use of a number of redundant but different exercises to measure the qualities to be rated. At the MPS:20 assessment two different group techniques are used to measure some of these characteristics. The first is a leaderless group discussion entitled, "The Being Who Fell to '195'". This involves a simulation in which it is posited that a creature from another universe has taken over as the chairman of the board of AT&T at the world headquarters at 195 Broadway in New York City. This Being from outer space is an expert in telecommunications but knows nothing of human life. It wants to find out what life is like as a manager in the Bell System, and the group undergoing assessment has been appointed as a task force to report to the Being. The group must discuss who reaches top management and how, the character of communications within the organization, techniques for managerial motivation and control, the status of good will and cooperation among managers, and the rewards and stresses of being a Bell System manager. The participants are expected to come to some consensus about what they will report to the Being. These discussions are transcribed and used not only for evaluating individual assessees or participants in the study, but to analyze the content as an informational tool for management.

A second group technique in the MPS:20 assessment center is also a leaderless group discussion, this time directed at problems of living outside the corporate structure. The participants are asked to play the roles of senior advisors in a counseling center. They are to read and discuss cases the junior counselors have brought to them, and to give the junior counselors some advice on how to handle the clients. Each case is described in a short paragraph. Participants must make recommendations on such issues as relocation to company headquarters, care for an elderly in-law either at home or at a nursing home, marital infidelity, a hippie son who does not want to go to college, and a young man contemplating marriage with a career-oriented young woman.

The individual techniques used in MPS:20 are administered in two separate sessions. In a preliminary one-day session (Phase I) a number of questionnaires and paper-and-pencil exercises are repeated; these exercises were administered to each participant at least twice before, in the initial management assessment center and in the reassessment eight years later. A number are personality or motivation questionnaires, including the Edwards Personal Preference Schedule (EPPS), the Guilford-Martin Inventory of Factors GAMIN, the Survey of Attitudes Toward Life (a measure of need for upward mobility), the Opinion Questionnaire (a version of the California F-Scale measuring authoritarianism), and a Q-sort, which gets at self-perception. Three projective tests are used, including the Rotter Incomplete Sentences Blank, the Business Incomplete Sentences Test directed at business situations, and six cards of the Thematic Apperception Test. Two job attitude measures, the Management Questionnaire and the Expectations Inventory, were administered annually during the first seven years of the study; these are repeated at MPS:20. Also repeated at MPS:20 are two cognitive tests, the School and College Abilities Test (SCAT) and a General Information Test.

The remaining individual techniques are presented at a two-day session (Phase II) a few weeks after the administration of the one-day session. These individual techniques were newly developed by the authors for the twentieth-year reassessment and focus on mid-career and middle life.

One highlight for the participants is an interview with feedback on their own test scores for the first time in the history of the study. An interviewer presents each participant with scores on the personality and attitude questionnaires he completed in the Phase I session and contrasts them with his results from the same exercises taken 12 years previously and 20 years previously. The participant is asked if he can identify with the findings and explain them, especially changes over time. This method thus attempts to identify the causal links in these individual diaries of change.

About a week of work per interviewee is required to prepare the materials for the feedback interview. To help orient the interviewers, the sequences of interviews with the participants over the last 10 years are summarized and combined with material from the first two assessments and intervening interviews in a case review outline. A report describing the man's responses to the projective tests taken in Phase I is also written. For actual presentation to the participants, graphs are prepared with scores on the various management questionnaires and self-concept measures. To supplement this, on the sentence completion tests responses to stems are selected which illustrate changes over time.

In another exercise, also discussed in the feedback interview, participants fill in a series of Time Lines representing each year since the beginning of the study. They are asked to think retrospectively about the highlights of their lives, distinguishing between their pleasures and their misfortunes. There are three Time Lines; one for job and career, one for home and family, and one for other aspects of the self.

The Sunny/Stormy Exercise brings the time line idea into the present. The participants fill in lines around a sunny face to indicate events and circumstances in their lives at the present time that are positive or favorable. Around the stormy face they fill in aspects of their lives that are negative or unfavorable. Following this, they are asked to write essays about the six most salient issues, no more than four emanating from the same face.

Two new projective tests were also developed for MPS:20 Phase II. The Adult Development Incomplete Sentence Test (ADIST) has 108 sentence stems drawn from major areas of concern to middle-aged people. For example, to get at feelings and motivations in the financial area, a sample stem begins "Making ends meet . . ." In the area of family relationships, a sample stem is "The problem with my children . . ."

Because the TAT was not designed for people over forty, there are few middle-aged characters to stimulate identification processes. Consequently, the Middlescent Male Picture Test (MMPT) was developed with eight drawings of middle-aged people in typical but ambiguous life situations. As with the TAT in Phase I, the participants write a story about each picture, indicating what is happening in the picture, who the characters are, what led up to the circumstances pictured, and what outcome will likely result.

THE SUCCESSFUL MANAGER

Because the original assessments in the Management Progress Study were conducted over a five-year period, the twentieth-year reassessments will span the years 1976 to 1980. At the time of this writing, MPS:20 assessments have been completed for the 1956 and 1957 samples, a total of 80 college graduates. These men had varying degrees of success in advancing from the first level of telephone company management to a possible maximum of seventh level, which is the President. Of the 80, 22 had been promoted to the fourth and fifth levels and can be counted as definitely successful. Another 39 participants had made the third level, which is the entry into middle management, and might be called moderately successful. The less successful were still at the first and second levels of management; there were 19 of these men. A comparison of results for these three groups of managers permitted an investigation of factors associated with managerial success.

A cross-sectional sample of successful managers was also obtained for corroborating data. This consisted of 35 participants in the Bell Advanced Management Program (BAMP). This group of high potential fourth and fifth level managers (all but two were white males) had been selected to participate in a one-month advanced training program at the University of Illinois in 1978. Although time constraints did not permit a full assessment of these managers, some of the same paper-and-pencil exercises used in the Management Progress Study were administered. This second sample permitted identification of any results in the Management Progress Study which seemed to be atypical; it turned out that this was seldom the case. Thus data were available for two groups of managers identified as "successful": 22 from the Management Progress Study and 35 from the BAMP program.

The typical successful manager at MPS:20 was, by virtue of sample selection, a white male college graduate with 20 years in the Bell System. He was married, had three children, and was 44 years of age. In contrast, the BAMP managers were slightly younger, with an average age between 39 and 40. Average tenure for the BAMP managers was 16 years.

Management Progress Study results have previously identified high levels of managerial abilities and motivations that characterize successful managers (Bray, Campbell, and Grant, 1974). Factor analyses of ratings of the dimensions in the managerial assessment centers showed seven major categories of success-related characteristics. Compared to less successful managers, successful men have greater administrative skills, stronger interpersonal skills as shown in face-to-face leadership, and greater intellectual ability. Their performance is more stable in that they are less likely to suffer performance decrements due to stress and uncertainty. Their work motivation is high, meaning that they get a lot of satisfaction from the work area compared to other areas of life, and they have their own high work standards. Their career orientation is toward advancement in management, and they are relatively independent of others.

Analyses of scores from individual exercises provide more specific data about the characteristics of successful managers. The Edwards Personal Preference Schedule showed similar personality/motivational structures for the fourth and fifth level MPS:20 men and the BAMP managers. Their average scores on six scales were notably different from the Bell System norms of 585 college recruits surveyed in 1958. The successful managers were particularly high on needs for achievement (accomplishing difficult tasks), dominance (the need to lead and direct others), aggression (the tendency to express hostility), and autonomy (the need to be independent of others). Both groups scored rather low on need for deference (desire to please others) and affiliation (need for friendships).

It is not really surprising to find that successful managers describe themselves as independent men who do not want to be controlled by the organization or bosses. Moreover, they respond to the challenge of doing a difficult job well and seem to enjoy taking leadership roles. Their tendency not to need or value friendships was less obvious, however. Although the men often appeared quite sociable in casual encounters, deep and meaningful friendships do not seem to be one of their major sources of life satisfaction.

Another unanticipated finding was the high average score on need for aggression. This is not just an assertiveness scale, but implies being rather nasty, hostile, and willing to tell people off.

The notion that middle-aged people or managers who have achieved success then relax and nurture their subordinates as they move into a fatherly or mentor-like role is certainly not supported by these data, at least not for men in their forties.

Another strong characteristic of the successful manager is that his job involvement is quite high. When sequences of interviews with the MPS men were rated by a clinical psychologist on "life themes" (Rychlak and Bray, 1967), the successful managers were found to be highly involved on the occupational life theme. In other words, their interviews revealed that they were highly concerned with and talked a lot about their jobs, their bosses, salary, promotions, the company, and other work-related events. On a questionnaire administered with their 19th-year interview, these men rated career as one of the most important things in their lives, and they indicated that they work more hours at home than do less successful managers. The BAMP managers responded similarly to the same questionnaire items.

Successful managers are not just involved with the company, however, but are apt to expand their lives more than do other managers. As reported earlier (Bray et al., 1974), the type of man known as the "enlarger" seems to extend himself toward achieving in many areas of life, and this was more characteristic of the successful men. In contrast, the less successful were more likely to be "enfolders," those who stabilize and build on existing life structures.

As evidence of the successful men's enlarging tendencies, ratings of the MPS:20 dimensions showed them to have a broader range of interests. They were also rated higher on involvement in affairs of the world and the community. Analysis of the sequences of interviews found that the successful men rated higher on what was called the ego functional life theme—that is, they were more concerned with improving their intellectual abilities and emotional and physical health. Finally, on the 19th-year questionnaire the successful men reported a greater interest in current events, a finding replicated with the BAMP managers.

DETERMINANTS OF CURRENT CHARACTERISTICS OF SUCCESSFUL MANAGERS

Given this farily clear description of what the successful manager is like, the next question is, "How does he get that way?" Three major sources of current characteristics of successful managers were identified.

Initial Status

The first source investigated was initial status, or characteristics that differentiated the men when they first entered the Bell System 20 years previously. Predictions of career progress by the assessors at the original MPS assessment centers were excellent indicators of which new managers would reach the fourth level of management or higher. About half of the new college recruits did notably well in the management assessment, although the remainder did less well. Some 16 years later, 46 percent of those who assessed well were at the fourth or fifth level or higher. Only 19 percent of those who assessed poorly had progressed that far. That such long-range prediction was possible implies that important managerial characteristics were apparent at the time of employment.

Many managerial qualities differentiated the potentially more successful candidates at the start of their careers. A selected sample of some test scores and ratings on assessment dimensions which predicted management level after 20 years is shown in Table 1.

Cognitive ability differences are apparent in the first three entries. The successful managers had higher levels of general mental ability and planning and organizing ability from the start, and they were more likely to give creative solutions to management problems. Their greater range of interests indicates broader application of their intellects as well.

Greater managerial motivation was also in evidence, since the future successes were more likely to have their own high work standards, want advancement in the company (although for many these needs declined over time), and to enjoy a leadership role. They were less likely to be dependent on authority figures, however, as shown by ratings on need for superior approval and scores

Table 1

Some 20-Year Predictors of Management Level

	N	r
General mental ability (SCAT)	50	.39[a]
Planning and organizing ability (rating)	49	.33[a]
Creativity (rating)	79	.22[b]
Range of interests (rating)	80	.26[b]
Inner work standards (rating)	80	.29[a]
Need for advancement (rating)	80	.43[a]
Dominance (EPPS)	80	.21[c]
Need for superior approval (rating)	80	-.25[b]
Deference (EPPS)	80	.21[c]

[a]$p < .01$ [b]$p < .05$ [c]$p < .06$

on the EPPS deference scale. To a large extent, then, the die had already been cast when these recruits first appeared at the doors of the telephone company.

Developmental Changes

Other characteristics of successful managers were traced to general adult development. Some personal qualities seem to develop over time with age and experience; a number of these did not differentiate the successful from the unsuccessful managers but were equally characteristic of both. One of these attributes was the need for autonomy on the Edwards Personal Preference Schedule as shown in Figure 1. When the 80 managers in the Management Progress Study were first assessed 20 years ago, their average score was at the 49th percentile of the Bell System norms. When reassessed 20 years later, the average was at the 83rd percentile, a significant shift upward and one that appeared continuous in light of the intermediate rise at year 8. This shift was no more typical of the successful than of the less successful managers; moreover, the average of the BAMP managers, another successful group, was about the same—at the 82nd percentile.

A pertinent question, however, is whether the rise in need for autonomy is indeed a developmental change, or whether it represents a general culture change. An alternative hypothesis might

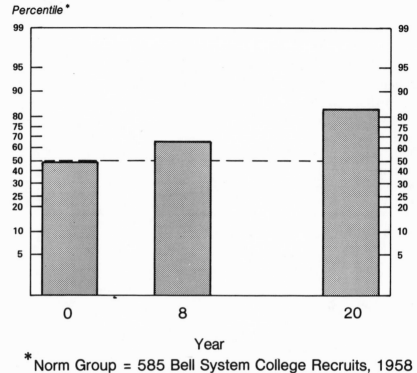

*Norm Group = 585 Bell System College Recruits, 1958

Figure 1. Mean Scores on EPPS for Autonomy (N = 80)

be that everyone in our culture is simply more oriented to independence, or "doing your own thing" in the '70's than in the '50's. The most appropriate method for disentangling these two types of explanations is to employ another sample in a cohort analysis. Fortunately, such a sample was at hand in the first wave of the new Management Continuity Study.

The Management Continuity Study (MCS) is intended to be a longitudinal study of today's management recruits. Its major purpose is to determine the abilities and motivations of these new additions to management, but an important by-product is to add perspective to the findings of the Management Progress Study. Only 47 participants have as yet been assessed in the new study, and white males are in the minority. Nevertheless, results so far have provided valuable comparisons, and no race or sex differences characterize the data reported here.

Table 2
Average Motivation Scores

	New Managers		Middle-Aged Managers		
Needs For:	MPS 1956–60	MCS 1977	MPS:20 1976–77 Levels 1–3	MPS:20 1976–77 Levels 4–5	BAMP 1978 Levels 4–5
Autonomy	57%	66%	82%	85%	82%
Achievement	63%	67%	78%	89%	84%
Affiliation	56%	58%	36%	29%	24%
Aggression	55%	55%	69%	71%	76%
No. tested	274	47	58	22	35

Source: Edwards Personal Preference Schedule. Resulted expressed in percentiles; norm group = 585 Bell System college recruits, 1958.

Table 2 shows the average percentile score of five groups of managers relative to the norm group of Bell System college recruits tested in 1958. The first column of the table shows the average percentile for all college graduates in the Management Progress Study when they were tested as new recruits in the years 1956–1960. The second column shows the results for the college recruits of today, those in the Management Continuity Study, tested in 1977. It is apparent that the percentile scores for these two groups of new managers differ very little from each other. Young people today score about the same as young people did 20 years ago. This does not support the notion of societal changes in need for autonomy, or any of the other three needs in the table.

The remaining three columns in Table 2 are made up of middle-aged managers: the MPS:20 men who had gone no further than the lowest three levels of management in 1976–1977; the MPS:20 men who had arrived at levels four and five; and the 4th and 5th level BAMP managers, tested in 1978. Scores of the three middle-aged groups are similar to one another but significantly different from those of the two new recruit groups. Thus successful managers had changed in these traits over time, but so had the less successful. This leads to the conclusion that the successful middle manager is independent, achievement-oriented, unaffiliative, and hostile, not because he is a successful manager, but because he is a middle-aged manager.

Some of the reasons for these changes were explored with

each man in the feedback interview at MPS:20 Phase II. The increase in the need for autonomy was tied to such things as increasing self-confidence and a growing awareness that it was possible to disagree with superiors without grave consequences. In response to feedback on increased needs for achievement, demands for results and competition on the job were frequently cited as causal factors. As the men achieved, they found that they enjoyed it, and intrinsic motivation seemed to develop. Their competence increased their self-confidence, which in turn encouraged them to tackle more difficult problems. This turning toward the job, along with increased involvement with families, resulted in a decrease in the importanct of friendships. Although fraternities and military experiences had promoted affiliation, the need for friendly interactions declined in the first few years in the Bell System.

Perhaps less easy to explain is the increase in need for aggression, which was more pronounced in the last 12 years than in the first 8 years of the study. A frustration-aggression hypothesis was entertained at first, since it was speculated that the total group of managers was frustrated from not having risen higher in management and was reacting with hostility. But since the fourth and fifth level managers in both MPS and BAMP scored as high as the lower-level managers on this scale, such a hypothesis was not supported.

More tenable explanations are tied to the experiences and cricumstances that accompany the trek from youth to middle age. As the years go by, responsibilities abound while social restraints on somewhat aggressive behavior are found to lack teeth. Aggravations increase, patience decreases. By middle age the balance tips and there is an eruption of intolerant hostility. A frustration-aggression hypothesis may be warranted, but it seems more likely that it is the little frustrations of living that get men down, not lesser degrees of career success.

Differential Development

The changes just discussed are characteristic of managers regardless of the level they have reached in the organization. There remains the question of changes that accompany success itselv. One of the most dramatic of these changes concerns the importance that work takes on. Evidence of this comes from an important assessment dimension rated 20 years ago, 12 years ago, and again today in the Management Progress Study called, "Primacy of Work." The definition is "To what extent does this individual find satisfactions from work more important than those from other areas of life?" The ratings on this dimension were almost identical twenty years ago for men who have wound up at the 1st and 2nd level of management, men who have achieved the 3rd level, and men who have achieved the 4th level or higher. But the MPS:20 ratings sharply differentiate these groups, with those who have reached higher levels much more likely to give work a top place in their lives. An analysis of variance among the three assessment ratings of Primacy of Work showed a highly significant interaction between time and management level by the 20th year ($F = 4.89, p < .001$).

This finding was strongly supported by an analysis of the interviews conducted over the years with the same three groups of managers. Figure 2 shows the dramatic differences that have taken place.

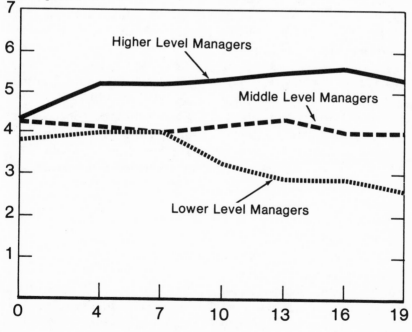

Figure 2. Occupational Life Theme Ratings

When the initial interviews were scored on a seven-point scale by a clinical psychologist rating involvement with the "occupational life theme," there was little difference between the three groups. By the time of the most recent interviews, the differences are wide indeed, and the Time X Level interaction highly significant ($F = 3.61, p < .001$).

Explanations for these findings are not difficult to formulate. There is no doubt that success in management brings rewards. These include not only pay, recognition, and power, but the satisfaction of achieving on more challenging assignments. It is highly likely that such rewards intensify one's involvement in work (which in turn leads to even greater rewards).

But perhaps this increased work involvement is not without its price. Some have asked, "Isn't success in management achieved at the expense of the rest of life, such as involvement with families, recreational activities, and service to the community?" The interview data in the Management Progress Study provide some answers to such questions.

Higher-level managers showed almost no change in their involvement with their wives and marital families over the two decades of the study, and they evidenced only a small decline in involvement in recreational activities, such as hobbies, sports, and partying. The least successful managers, however, showed a substantial increase on both of these nonwork themes, perhaps because they did not find as many rewards in the world of work. Hence, even though all managers began at about the same level of involvement in these two activities, by the 20th year the less successful men were at higher levels. (Analysis-of-variance results showed a Time X Level $F = 1.96$, $p < .01$ for Marital-Familial life theme and $F = 1.72$, $p < .02$ for Recreational-Social life theme.) Thus the impression that successful managers are sacrificing other important parts of life may be only in contrast to those who have not risen as far in the business hierarchy and are investing more in family and recreational pursuits.

As far as service to the community is concerned, all groups suffered some decline in this activity over the 20 years of the study. But the decline for the most successful managers was slight, whereas the less successful dropped precipitously (Time X Level $F - 1.90$, $p < .008$). It seems reasonable to believe that the most successful managers are also the most competent in service organizations and derive rewards there similar to those at work, thus maintaining their interest. These findings also argue against the notion that all of the successful managers' energy is consumed by the job. It seems more likely that this is more evidence of the "enlarging" life style of the successful manager, whereby his energies and interests expand into other areas of life.

One other group of characteristics possibly related to moving up in management concerns face-to-face leadership motivation and behavior. The most successful group, initially higher in the desire to lead as shown by the dominance scale of the Edwards Personal Preference Schedule, rose still higher in this desire over time, while the less successful group declined over the years. There was a similar finding for ratings of forcefulness by the assessors who interacted with these men face to face for three days at the three different assessments. Analysis-of-variance results for the interaction of time and management level did not quite reach traditional levels of statistical significance, however (for dominance, $F = 2.16$, $p < .08$; for forcefulness, $F = 2.21$, $p < .07$). In the same vein but more conclusive were significant interaction results for ratings of the men on leadership skills at the assessment centers ($F = 5.53$, $p < .001$). In the two leaderless group discussions that were part of the 20th-year reassessment, the higher-level men tended to take over, organize things, and lead their groups toward the assigned goals. This was true even for the nonbusiness-oriented Counseling Center Group Discussion, where the higher-level men could not be considered any more knowledgeable.

LIFE SATISFACTIONS

A critical next question is whether career success is related to life satisfactions. Eleven of the dimensions rated at the 20th-year assessment reflected aspects of life satisfactions. The correlation of each of these with management level is presented in Table 3.

The most significant correlation was between management level and career satisfaction, or the extent to which the participant had positive feelings about the series of work-related experiences that comprise his career with the Bell System. The more successful

Table 3

Correlations of Life Satisfaction Dimensions and Management Level

	r
Career Satisfaction	.52[a]
Job Satisfaction	.31[a]
Absence of Financial Worries	.20
Marital Satisfaction	−.03
Marital Stability	−.02
Absence of Familial Worries	−.03
Avocational Interest	−.08
Cynicism	.02
Feelings of Crisis	−.06
Adjustment	.19
Happiness	.11

[a] $p < .01$, $N = 80$

men felt better about their careers, as might be expected. Success was less strongly, but still significantly, related to job satisfaction, reflecting feelings about the present job. Although one would expect financial worries to be related to salary, and salary is related to management level, the correlation between level and "absence of financial worries" did not quite reach statistical significance ($p < .08$). Other sources of income are a possible explanation, although there is also a restriction of range; even first-level managers in the Bell System can hardly be called poverty stricken, especially after 20 years of service. Variability in expenses suffers from less restriction; family size differed widely. But another explanation is that the extent of concern over finances did not co-vary perfectly with the ratio of income to expenses; some people just worry more.

Beyond the first three lines in Table 3, which are the most job-related dimensions, the correlations between career success and life satisfactions are nearly all negligible and approach zero. It might have been expected that the three dimensions related to marriage and family (marital satisfaction, marital stability, absence of familial worries) and the avocational interest dimension would be related negatively to career success, given the greater preoccupation of lower-level managers with these life themes in the later years. It is notable that even though the lower-level managers were becoming more invested in the marital-family situation and with recreational-social activity, they were not seen as deriving more satisfaction from those activities than do those at higher levels of management.

The last two dimensions in Table 3, adjustment and happiness, are global measures of life satisfactions. Adjustment was defined as the extent to which the person has changed or adapted himself to his life situation in an emotionally healthy way, while happiness was concerned with the extent to which he indicated feelings of great pleasure and contentment with his life. The four psychologist-assessors rating the men on these dimensions at the MPS:20 assessment considered adjustment and happiness in all the significant aspects of the men's lives, including the work area. Thus it is surprising that the corrleations of these dimensions with management level, which related strongly to career satisfaction, were not statistically significant.

In summary, with the exception of career and job satisfaction, the dimensions of life satisfaction were not related to career success. If career success is not the major determinant of life satisfactions, then what is?

DETERMINANTS OF ADJUSTMENT AND HAPPINESS

As with the investigation of career success, initial status was the first source of adjustment and happiness investigated, followed by differential development. The general developmental changes described in the section on determinants of current characteristics of managers were primarily unrelated to adjustment and happiness.

Initial Status

Several types of data collected at the original assessment center can be used to predict life satisfaction 20 years later. Those showing statistically significant relationships are presented in Table 4.

Three scales of the Guilford Martin Inventory of Factors GAMIN related significantly to later adjustment and happiness.

Table 4
20-Year Predictors of Life Satisfactions

	r with Adjustment	r with Happiness
Ascendancy (GAMIN-A)	.25	.23
Self-Confidence (GAMIN-I)	.38	.35
Emotional Stability (GAMIN-N)	.37	.31
Expectations Inventory	.21	.27
Mental Ability (SCAT-T)	−.13	−.26
Mental Ability (rating)	−.30	−.34
Heterosexuality (EPPS)	−.29	−.27

Note: $r \geqq .22$, $p < .05$; $r \geqq .28$, $p < .01$; $r \geqq .36$, $p < .001$, N = 80.

The Ascendancy or A scale measures social assertiveness and has items reflecting a willingness to stand up for one's rights and a lack of fearfulness of standing out in a crowd, taking action in a troublesome situation, or confronting disagreement. The Self-Confidence or I scale reflects a lack of inferiority feelings. High scorers believe they can cope with most situations and that people will treat them well; they feel worthy as individuals without the approval of others. The Emotional Stability or N scale contains items reflecting a lack of nervousness and possession of a steady temperament. These three scales of the GAMIN are intercorrelated and have in common characteristics of a positive self-concept.

The Expectations Inventory is a Bell-System-designed measure of favorability of expectations about one's career. At the original assessment, participants were asked to indicate what they thought would be true for them five years hence. The questionnaire items referred to such things as salary, promotions, supervision, colleagues, type of work, and working and living conditions. The men who were rated higher on happiness 20 years later were more positive and optimistic in outlook from the start of their careers.

The significant values of the remaining predictors in Table 4 came as somewhat of a surprise. General mental ability was negatively correlated with life satisfactions, whether measured by a test score (School and College Ability Test—Total) or an assessment rating. There is a restriction of range here, since all participants are college graduates and their average score on a mental ability test is above that of the general population. But within this range of intelligence, the less bright had impressed the assessors as being better adjusted and happier. One might speculate that the more intelligent men perceived (or created) more complexities in their lives and found more things to react negatively to and fret about.

A second surprising finding was the negative correlation between need for heterosexuality on the Edwards Personal Preference Schedule and later adjustment and happiness. This scale reflects a need for social and sexual activities with the opposite sex as well as enjoying discussions, stories, and jokes involving sex. An interpretation of "sexiness" as bad for your mental health does not seem warranted, on logical or common sense grounds. Rather, higher scorers on this scale are probably reflecting a certain amount of dependency and irresponsible hedonism. Scores on this measure of heterosexuality in the 20th year were concurrently correlated with ratings of escapism and selfishness.

The implication of these initial status predictors of adjustment and happiness is that adjustment at the early adult stage of life is probably a good sign of adjustment in middle age. Relating this to the prevention of psychopathology, one technique to help assure that you will be happy and self-satisfied in middle age is to be that way when you are young!

Differential Development

Other aspects of adjustment and happiness among the MPS men seemed to develop differentially over time, however. That is, those highly adjusted in middle age changed over the 20 years in ways different from those who were poorly adjusted in middle age.

The need for succorance scale of the Edwards test illustrates one such differential development (see Figure 3). This scale reflects a desire for understanding and encouragement, including having others provide help in times of illness or trouble, react sympathetically about personal problems, and offer affection and favors. The highly adjusted declined in this need by year 8, and the moderately adjusted had dropped to a similar level by year 20. The poorly adjusted men did not show such a decline with time, however. These differences were reflected in analysis of variance results, which showed a significant Group X Time

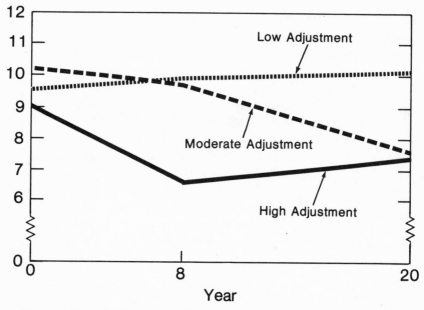

Figure 3. Need for Succorance (Understanding and Encouragement)

interaction ($F = 3.28, p < .01$). The retention of high succorance needs by the less adjusted men may indicate a somewhat childlike desire to be taken care of by others which did not diminish with maturity and the responsibilities of adulthood.

Another Edwards scale showing differential development with respect to adjustment was the need for dominance. Items here reflect liking leadership roles and having an influence on others. As shown in Figure 4, men low in adjustment declined in this need over time, while those who were moderate and high in adjustment by the 20th year increased in this need (F for Group × Time = $3.22, p < .01$).

A possible explanation of these results is that a certain amount of self-assurance is required to function in the position of leading rather than being led. Thus well-adjusted people are more likely to feel rewarded by leadership roles, while the poorly adjusted may feel somewhat inadequate to the task.

Another set of variables related to differential development of adjustment involves attitudes toward work and the company. It will be recalled that need for achievement on the Edwards test increased over time for the group as a whole, particularly in the first eight years. Scores continued to rise for the moderately

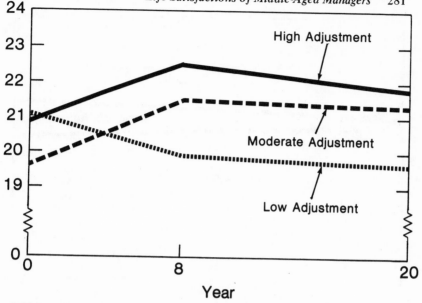

Figure 4. Need for Dominance (To Lead and Direct Others)

and highly adjusted people over the next 12 years, but the poorly adjusted men dropped back to their initial levels (F for Group $\times$ Time = 2.44, $p < .05$). Further evidence is shown in Figure 5, which illustrates the assessment rating of primacy of work, or the extent to which work is a primary source of satisfaction in life. The least adjusted group showed a progressive decline over the 20 years, while the most adjusted showed a slight increase (F for Group $\times$ Time = 3.13, $p < .02$).

The differentially developing attitudes toward work in general were paralleled by changes in feelings about one's career in the Bell System. An attitude questionnaire was administered to the Management Progress Study participants annually during the first 7 years of the study and again at year 20. A General Management Attitude scale from that questionnaire, indicating general satisfaction with the company and one's life in it, showed gradually declining scores for the group as a whole as their youthful idealism gave way to realistic experiences. However, the greater one's level of adjustment at year 20, the smaller the slope of the curve of decline, so that the least well adjusted people ended up considerably more pessimistic and sour about the company (F of Group $\times$ Time = 1.90, $p < .03$).

A related assessment dimension, called Bell System Value

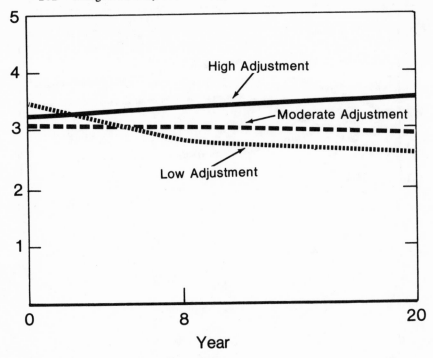

Figure 5. Assessment Rating of Primary of Work

Orientation, was used to evaluate organizational identification, or acceptance of the company's values and posture on major issues. Ratings by the assessors of the three adjustment groups at the original assessment showed no significant differences between them, but by the 20th year the high-adjusted group had risen substantially, while the low-adjusted had fallen off (F for Group $\times$ Time = 5.94, $p < .001$).

The composite picture presented by the differentially changing work attitudes is that the high-adjusted people tended to maintain or increase their interest and involvement in work and achievement over the years and to be among the more positive supporters of the company and what it has offered them. The low adjusted, though initially as work-involved and positive toward the company as their peers, became increasingly less so as time went on. They seemed to tune out of achievement and turn away from work as a primary satisfaction in life as they fell out of love with Ma Bell.

A final variable reflecting differential development was the assessment rating of energy, or ability to sustain a high level of work effort. The lowest adjustment group showed a progressive decline in this rating over the 20-year period, while the moderate and high adjusted increased slightly (*F* for Group × Time = 4.75, *p* < .001). One might interpret this finding as "neurotic fatigue," since low adjusted people often get bogged down in their troubles and drain off their energy fighting internal wars.

RECAPITULATION

What then do we conclude of career success and life satisfactions among middle-aged managers? The major tie, and apparently the only tie, between them is career satisfaction. As shown in Figure 6, career satisfaction acts as a bridge between career success and life satisfactions. Although career satisfaction relates significantly to both career success (measured by management level achieved) and life satisfactions (measured by ratings on happiness), the two primary concepts are not significantly related to each other. The more successful are more apt to be satisfied with their careers and the happier people are more likely to be satisfied with their careers as an important aspect of life, but this link is not strong enough to establish a significant relationship between advancement and general life happiness. Other considerations intervene.

Various assessment dimensions and test scores that form the substance of the ratings on career satisfaction help show the composition of the small area of overlap in the three circles diagrammed in Figure 6. Both the highly successful and the highly satisfied with life show increasingly positive attitudes toward work and the company as a place to work, as evidenced by ratings on primacy of work, scores on the need for achievement scale of the Edwards test, ratings on Bell System Value Orientation, and scores on the General Management Attitude scale. Both derive pleasure from leading others: the most successful were initially higher on the dominance scale of the Edwards and became increasingly so; the happiest and best adjusted were not initially higher but became so over time. Both the successful and the happy tended to have fewer financial worries also; the

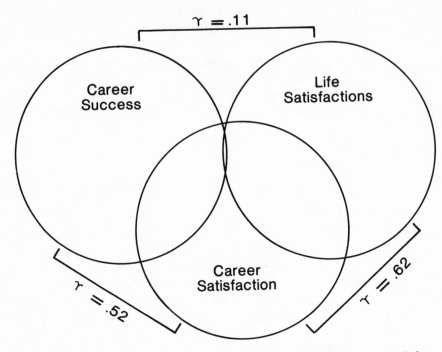

Figure 6. Career Satisfaction as a Bridge Between Career Success and Life Satisfactions

successful presumably because they have more income, the happy because they have fewer worries in general.

But beyond the bridge of work-related pleasures and pains, career success and life satisfactions are essentially not related in our group of middle-aged managers. The correlates of these two end states as of the 20th year which are not represented by the overlapping circles in Figure 6 are shown in Table 5.

Related positively to career success but not adjustment and happiness were cognitive abilities and administrative skills—intellectual ability, planning and organizing ability, and creativity in the solution of business problems. The more successful tended to enlarge their lives by their interest in a variety of fields of activity and were concerned with expanding their skills, knowledge, or personality. They tended to function independently of others, as shown by lower ratings on need for superior and peer approval by the assessment staffs and by low scores on the need for deference scale of the Edwards Personal Preference

Table 5

*Non-Overlapping Correlates of Career Success
and Life Satisfactions*

	r with Level	r with Adjustment	r with Happiness
Cognitive Abilities:			
Mental ability (rating)	.30[a]	−.22[a]	−.30[a]
Mental ability (SCAT-T)	.26[a]	−.16	−.25[a]
General Information Test	.10	−.26[a]	−.31[a]
Administrative Skills:			
Planning and Organizing (rating)	.55[a]	.20	.13
Creativity (rating)	.50[a]	.04	−.05
"Enlarging" characteristics:			
Self-Development (rating)	.22[a]	−.02	−.08
Range of interests (rating)	.31[a]	−.05	−.09
Independence of others:			
Need for superior approval (rating)	−.22[a]	.12	.12
Need for peer approval (rating)	−.24[a]	.09	.08
Need for deference (EPPS)	−.27[a]	.03	−.01
Positive self concept:			
Ascendancy (GAMIN-A)	.17	.29[a]	.30[a]
Self-confidence (GAMIN-I)	.14	.43[a]	.49[a]
Emotional stability (GAMIN-N)	.08	.49[a]	.49[a]
Other characteristics of self:			
Cynicism (rating)	.02	−.42[a]	−.38[a]
Conservatism (rating)	−.01	.39[a]	.34[a]
Selfishness (rating)	.05	−.51[a]	−.43[a]
Need for heterosexuality (EPPS)	.09	.25[a]	.30[a]
Drop in General Management Attitude (questionnaire score)	.04	−.30[a]	−.27[a]

[a]Statistically significant. For $r = .22$, $p < .05$; $r = .28$, $p < .01$; $r = .36$, $p < .001$.

Schedule. The most successful managers were "organization men" only in the sense of dedication to work and organizational identification; they did not kowtow to authority but remained their own men.

The two right-hand columns of Table 5 show a different and somewhat contradictory picture of the well-adjusted and happy manager. His intellectual abilities are more constricted than his peers; and he had acquired less knowledge, according to scores on a General Information Test administered in the 20th year. Still, these men have a positive self-concept, as shown in particular on the GAMIN scales. Ratings by the MPS:20 assessment staff showed them to be less cynical, which can be interpreted as a positive attitude toward others as well.

One interpretation of this constellation of scores is that the best adjusted and happiest individuals are not particularly evaluative or critical about life. Their outlook is positive, whether directed toward themselves, their careers, others, or life in general. Although they obviously must attend to problems in order to resolve them, they do not ruminate about what life is all about but accept it as it is.

The last four rows in Table 5 indicate that the best adjusted seemed also to be stable and responsible individuals. Their values tended to be traditional, as evidenced by higher assessment ratings of conservatism. Selfishness or hedonism was out of character for them. Stability and persistence were also indicated by their higher endurance scores on the Edwards tests and the relative lack of decline in their General Management Attitude and Expectations Inventory scores.

The implication of these results with middle-aged managers is that career success does not necessarily lead to happiness. Contrary to those who find all good things in the same baskets (cf. Vaillant, 1977), these results indicate that career success relates to satisfactions only in the career area of life. Since work is increasingly being found a highly critical area of life, this relationship is not to be discounted. These data show, however, that the most successful at work are no more likely to be the most successful in marriage and family life or in recreational pursuits. Nor are they more likely to feel more positive about life and the nature of man or be able to avoid the feelings of crisis that sometimes accompany middle age.

On the other hand, there are no apparent detrimental effects of career success on life satisfactions. Although some would have us believe that success in one's vocation can be achieved only by sacrificing other aspects of one's personal life, the data here do not support this contention.

From the standpoint of our own biases, then, we have concluded that you might as well be successful in your work, because there is no guarantee that you will be happier any other way.

REFERENCES

Bray, D. W., Campbell, R. J., and Grant, D. L. *Formative years in business: A long-term AT&T study of managerial lives.* New York: John Wiley and Sons, 1974.

Rychlak, J. F. and Bray, D. W. A life-theme method for scoring of interviews in the longitudinal study of young business managers. *Psychological Reports*, Monograph Supplement 1–V21, 1967.

Vaillant, G. E. *Adaptation to life.* Boston: Little, Brown, 1977.

12

Promoting Competence and Coping through Retirement Planning

RUTH GLICK

The people so peculiar in renewal and comeback
You can't laugh off their capacity to take it.
—*Carl Sandburg, "107"*

The title suggests that retirement planning as a piece of social programming is important enough to warrant inquiry into its background in search of some set of guiding principles or a statement of policy.

We have programs variously called retirement planning, retirement counseling, retirement preparation, retirement education. They are not different conceptually or in practice as the names might imply. One cannot tell by the rubric what the content and format are. They all more or less claim the same basic goal of helping older people who are leaving the labor force to prepare for a time when employment is over.

Most of the programs extant are carried on in major corporations and financial institutions, many of which were slow to respond to the need expressed by employees for help in planning. One explanation for the foot dragging is that management did not want workers to know how niggardly their pensions would be or whether in fact there was any guarantee of a pension at all. A more generous view is that employers were not sure what retirement programs were supposed to accomplish. A United States Civil Service Commission Study (1961) stated their case: "Many employers, both public and private, have a watchful, wait-and-see attitude, accompanied by a strictly limited program or none at all, because they think that the right or wrong answers have not been found in this relatively new area of personnel management" (p. 6).

To be fair, one problem may have stemmed from the failure to make a clear distinction between retirement counseling and retirement planning. Today the words tend to be used synonymously in the context of retirement preparation, a term which was adopted to avoid the ambiguity. The term "counseling" itself, as we know, covers a wide range of procedures. Dictionary definitions include information giving, as well as advice giving and a mutual exchange of opinions and ideas, discussion and deliberation; and all of this goes on in varying amounts in retirement planning programs. But counseling also has psychiatric connotatins, and a powerful assumption underlying the process was that retirement is a traumatic event sometimes precipitating a serious emotional crisis, the aftermath of which might be a downward and maybe irreversible path. Much has been written about the work ethic, the roleless role, the identity crisis, and retirement shock. All have been explored and explained (Atchley, 1972). Retirement, especially mandatory retirement, has been linked to serious psychological disorders, like depression; to alcoholism; to physical deterioration; and to overwhelming despair culminating in a high rate of suicide in older males. This in itself was enough to call industry off. Counseling such a population was seen as dangerously close to psychotherapy, and an intrusion into the private lives of employees. Clearly, it was not within the province of personnel management.

Also stalling the implementation of programs was the accelerating trend toward early retirement, a phenomenon still not well understood. Between 1960 and 1974 well over half of all retirements occurred at the age of 62 and were apparently voluntary. This may have been a flurry tied to monetary incentives not yet neutralized by high inflation, but it hardly confirmed the bad reputation of retirement. Therefore while industry waited for the right and wrong answers, the proponents of planning tried another stratagem. If management could not be persuaded to act in behalf of the workers, it ought to act in its own interest. This notion was pitched to improved workers' morale, which was linked in turn to increased productivity, hence to profits. A fine hypothesis—and it was widely promulgated, although there was no data in support of it, not even testimonials. People just used to say: "As is well known." Research was vaguely alluded to, but this phantom literature never materialized. Meanwhile the world was not standing still. The Employment Retirement Income Security Act, commonly known as ERISA, came into being, and since it mandated periodic disclosure of the status of pension plans to employees, the secrecy angle was knocked out. Management did a turnabout, and planning programs, now called any of the alternative names listed above, were seen as the treatment of choice for easing senior workers into acceptance of mandatory retirement. Today no one argues morale and productivity. The programs are understood to be a function of corporate social responsibility.

To put it another way, the Director of Retirement Planning of one of the *Fortune* 500 corporations, during a recent conference in Washington on "Work and Retirement," said to his colleagues, "Listen, if the companies don't do it, the government is gonna step in and say you gotta do it." So much for policy.

Company programs appear to be taking hold. A national survey of *Fortune* 500 Retirement Plans and Policies conducted in 1975 (Prentis, 1975) indicated growing awareness of the need to help people plan. Since these pathfinders employ more than three quarters of the employees working for all United States corporations, it seems safe to say that if one half of the responding companies at that time were either already sponsoring programs or intending to do so shortly, the idea has arrived. Thousands of group leaders have been trained. Hundreds of companies have instituted programs. As a matter of fact, however, I frequently meet personnel who have been through one training program at the University of Michigan, another at the University of Southern California, or at Drake, or at Case Western Reserve University— who have yet to conduct a single program.

For most people retirement is a major economic, social, and psychological event. This is true whether it is welcomed or dreaded; whether it is, as officially defined, departure from the labor force or a silent and unconscious shifting down as in the case of a wife who has never worked outside the home but now enters with her retired husband into the new status.

There is no longer an institutional role to carry out. Income is reduced by a half to two thirds. Day to day routines are dramatically altered. The old center of life is gone, and another must be carved out if days are not to be shapeless. Finally in our culture retirement formally ushers in the period of life called old age, and the knowledge of death lurking must somehow be worked through.

It seems logical to prepare for so new and different a status; to seek and process needed information; discuss it with others; understand ramification, risks, and realities; consider the options; weigh the trade-offs; and create bridges for a successful transition. It appeals to our common sense that this should be done. (I once had a professor who used to snarl: "Don't bring common sense into my class. I want evidence.")

Is retirement planning a means of promoting competence and coping in later life? To reply at all, it is necessary to cast the issue somewhat differently, because the crucial question is not what effect will this program or that legislation or such-and-such a policy have on older people, but rather how should old people live?

I am indebted to Harry Moody (1976) for giving us a way of looking at the matter which takes it out of the everyday realm of social planning or intervention models or increased services to older people. It is Professor Moody's thesis that the kind of social policy which a society adopts for its old is a function of the importance it gives to the very existence of old people, its view of human life as a whole, the significance it assigns the experience of aging. For Moody, public policy on old age in any society is rooted in basic attitudes toward old age, in certain assumptions about old people, and in systems of belief about human potential and human values.

Moody has set forth four patterns or stages or ways in which old people are perceived, and has tied these to corresponding characteristics of policy, treatment, and consequence. His Stage I is called *Rejection*. Here the old are seen as a drag and a drain, a parasitical body that consumes rather than produces and is useless in a technological society. Stage I stops just short of the ice floe. Its axiom, if it had one, would be: "No deposit, no return." The old are like the empty bottles thrown into the trash heap or tossed out of moving cars into the gutter.

Stage II is *Social Services*. It developed in reaction to the devastation wrought by Stage I. Remedial measures born of the liberal ethic and social conscience produced relief in the form of social security, welfare, food stamps, nursing-home care, senior centers, day care, nutrition programs, subsidized housing, and so on. Under this ethos the elderly become a special constituency with their own bureaucracy, their own lobbyists and professional service providers. The style of Stage II is prescriptive, its message simple—stay busy, there are 1001 things to do. These are called leisure time activities.

Stage III is *Participation*. It rejects the interest group liberalism of Stage II and its domination by middleman policies and programs, feeding the horses to feed the chickens. It rejects the passivity engendered by social services and advocates wide-randing changes within the society which have brought the old to their present pass. It demands, for instance, that the goals set forth in the Older Americans Act be carried out forthwith. It asks for an end to poverty, a comprehensive national health care program, the abolition of mandatory retirement, the opportunity for new careers, and the right of older persons to participate as they wish and can in the mainstream of the culture. Stage III is sometimes radical, always activist. *Priorities and Options* is its axiom. It says that if you need 1001 things to do, it is because you cannot find a few that have meaning. Following Simone de Beauvoir (1972), Stage III states that "There is only one solution if old age is not to be an absurd parody of our former life, and that is to go on pursuing ends that give our existence a meaning—devotion to individuals, to groups and to causes—social, political, intellectual and creative work" (p. 540).

Stage IV is called *Self-Actualization*. Moody wonders how this can be described in a society such as ours which has no image of life at full length, no role unique to the old, no philosophy of old age, as in ancient India, for example, where the old retreated in the final stage of life into the forest for contemplation and meditation in quest of spiritual deliverance—moksha. He reminds us of the patriarch, the guru, the archetype of the wise old man in many traditional societies. In these the old person symbolizes the completeness of the life cycle, the spiritual goal of existence, something more than a middle-aged person who has had a long, long, life—however productive. Only Stage IV acknowledges old age on its own terms.

Looking back over these stages, I suggest that in view of the greater visibility of the aged in recent years, and massive government expenditure, it may seem that Stage I is gone, and only tiny pockets of extreme deprivation and neglect have survived. But this is not the case. Fifteen percent of the aged still live in devastating poverty (Brotman, 1978). Most of these elderly poor are women who have worked all of their lives in low-paying jobs or as housewives. Some of these old women, especially the black isolates of the inner city—the poorest of the poor—live in danger of victimization and violence by hoodlums and junkies. A more recently revealed atrocity against the frail elderly is physical abuse by their own adult offspring. The calamitous conditions of nursing homes and the misuse of commitment procedures are documented. Despite staggering amounts of money spent, Stage I has not been obliterated.

It is true, however, that a wide variety of Stage II benefits have been made available to older people. Many, not old and needy, have benefited—the pharmaceutical companies, the medical profession, nursing home operators, politicians, the aging bureaucracy, researchers in the field of gerontology, and those who provide the social services of Stage II. The beneficiaries of this charitableness of a benevolent government and a rich society are everywhere.

The Stage II ethos fosters segregation, caretaking, and dependency, and weakens the natural support systems—family, church and synagogue, neighbors, friends, community. Much Stage II programming for the elderly, however well meant, also deals them out of the game, limits their freedom, limits their autonomy, limits their dignity. And some policies, although alleged to be in the best interests of the elderly, are not well meant. In the years preceding the fight against the 1978 amendment for the Antidiscrimination in Employment Act, which raised the age of retirement to 70 and abolished it altogether for federal employees, the powerful lobbies for industry and business and the labor unions which fought the new legislation argued that mandatory retirement is in reality an act of kindness, because it protects all workers from the shock of sudden retirement; if the workers know what to expect they can plan ahead with certainty, and the unfit and incompetent are protected from the humiliation of being weeded out because all men and women are treated equally.

Most retirement planning is a Stage II operation. One form of the art consists mainly of a series of pamphlets to be read and digested. The purpose is to give information—in some cases, it seems, all the information the individual is going to need in the next twenty years. This material, which is sold to industry and mailed at regular intervals to the worker's home, also sells a postretirement gift program to which many companies subscribe for their already retired employees.

In some large and prestigious organizations, everyone due to retire within the next year or two is herded into an auditorium. There, over a period of one, two, or three days, a panel of "resource people" has assembled to funnel into the pre-retirees' heads information about financial matters, health, Social Security, Medicare, physical fitness, consumer fraud, housing, peace of mind, wills. They talk about budgeting and about recreation and about volunteerism, and they tell them and tell them and tell them.

In a great many companies, maybe in the majority, preretirement counseling is one to one. Typically in the individual approach, a month or two before the big event, the prospective retiree is called in and informed about company benefits—pension, and insurance etc.—Social Security, Medicare, and whatever general information the teller happens to have. I met a union fellow at a retirement conference who told me he "counsels" 2500 prospective retirees a year, a half-hour at a time. I asked: "What do you tell them?" He said: "I tell 'em everything."

The economist Malcolm Morrison (1976) has shown that employees are seriously handicapped with respect to planning ahead for income adequacy, the number one problem in retirement. They lack the necessary information as well as the necessary skills to interpret and make use of the information. A recent study of trends in planning early retirement (Barfield and Morgan, 1978) reports that the number of respondents professing ignorance about the amount of retirement pension they could expect was so great that the investigators could not use the amount in the analysis. Many people still believe that pension, Social Security, and savings will yield enough for comfortable living to the end of their days. But only about 20 percent of retirees even receive a pension today (Morrison, 1978). Furthermore, early retirement means about a 20 percent permanent reduction in Social Security benefits. And then there is inflation. Morrison's blue collar workers are not the only ones who do not know that a $600 pension at age 62 in 1978 will be worth $306 at age 72 and $155 at age 82, given an expected continuing 7 percent rate of inflation. Many people say that they expect to earn money after retirement, as though the labor market is all that accessible to aging workers. Furthermore, the projected replacement earnings are as unrealistic as the projected accumulated savings. Listen, my friends, it may be that in old age money is one's best friend.

Better to go down dignified
With boughten friendship at your side
Than none at all. Provide, provide!

—Frost, "Provide, provide"

We are in Stage II on the growing edge of Stage III. Stage III concepts grow out of respect for the capacity of older people to take responsibility for themselves. The new legislation raising the age of retirement to 70, or abolishing it altogether, is a Stage III concept. The last of the legalized discriminations is on its last legs. Workers will be employed as long as they can do a job. The waste of healthy vigorous people will stop. Talent and experience will be valued. Competent workers will be able to decide for themselves whether, when, and how they will leave the labor force, rather than having to make the best of someone else's decision.

Stage III advocates treatment of older workers which is equitable with other workers; training and retraining; job redesign; and job development. It advocates alternatives to retirement which permit greater flexibility and increased opportunities for choice between leisure and work. Stage III options include retiring, taking early retirement, continuing to work full time, phasing out gradually from work, job shifting as people's ages and capacities changes, increasing the availability of part-time work, and providing the opportunity for a person to take time off for a while and then return to work (Morrison, 1978).

The new law finds many workers not prepared to make the most of the freedom to choose between options. This should have been built in over the years. Many workers are not prepared for flexible work schedules. In a study of the Steel Workers Union's extended vacation plan for older workers with seniority (Parker, 1971), it was found that most of the workers did not know what to do with their bonus time. They used it as regular vacation time and many admitted to boredom and were glad to get back to the job. George Steiner says we have not begun to understand the vacuum that is going to come on society given the glut of leisure it does not know how to use (Hall, 1973).

Stage II's conception of leisure is a mishmash of taking it easy while keeping busy. A little this, a little that. Busy. Busy. The more activities, the richer the life. Maggie Kuhn says that we are the only society that sends its babies to school and its old people out to play. What is interesting about these "leisure" activities is that they are usually the same pursuits that were carried on during the work life in a relatively small amount of free time. Why they should still be called leisure-time activities in the retirement years is a mystery, since in one sense it's all leisure. A vacuous design for living is conveyed in the popular retirement rhetoric: Golden Days, Harvest Years, the Next Promotion, Retire to Life, Retire to Action, The Best Is Yet to Be. Reading, you think you will drown in a sea of golden age garbage. Life itself is ultimately a leisure-time activity.

Pre-retirees also need substantive information about aging to which retirement is ineluctably linked, and here again they receive little help. Growing old. People are not sufficiently awed by how tough it is until they come to it themselves. Several months ago I was asked to speak at a conference, the title of which was "The Bright, Bright Future of Aging." I asked the 33-year-old program chairman who had invited me if he did not think one "Bright" would do it. He did not. I tried again: "E. M. Forster wrote a book called *Two Cheers for Democracy*. If he could knock out a "Cheer," can't you knock out a "Bright?" But he would not yield, so I had then to set to the task of ferreting out the possible sources of these brightnesses. I had to think long and hard on it, seek out the evidence, weigh it, and keep an open mind. Because I am not by nature cheerful and optimistic, I had to guard against a bias.

What can we say about old age in America today? What is the condition of the old among us? Are they the victims of neglect, resentment, and discrimination? Is the distance between the generations growing? That Americans hate old age is clear enough. Do they also hate old people? Is the society agist through and through?

Or as some believe, is there gradually evolving a more just system in which most older people are receiving a fair share? Does the fact that the young old (55–75) and an increasing minority of the old old (75 plus) are stronger, healthier, better educated, more vigorous, and more independent than their parents and grandparents ever dreamed of—does this mean that older people in the richest society in the world are better off than ever before?

One eminent student of aging, Leonard Hayflick, says to be old in America is unpleasant; to be old and poor, a tragedy (Hayflick, 1977, p. 9). Another gerontologist, perhaps even more eminent, Bernice Neugarten, says the old are in good shape today and getting better (Neugarten, 1974, p. 198). It is the worst of times. It is the best of times.

An unemployed school teacher applied for a position in a small midwestern city. A member of the school board interviewing him asked: "Do you believe that the world is round or that the world is flat?" The school teacher answered: "I can teach it both ways."

Old age is hard—and the people cope. Even when the last decades are not a catastrophe, even may be good, for the majority the rewards dwindle, social isolation increases in the wake of retirement, the loss of friends, the fading of emotional support, as children live their lives and grandchildren move away. Health, vigor, and perceptual acuity decline in varying degrees. Loss, loss. Worst of all is the threat of diminished intellectual competency, the specter of dependence, the possibility that one may not make it to death's door in control of one's own body and one's own mind.

What can talkative retirement planning accomplish in view of this? It can do some things. It can inform, it can advise, it can teach. How it informs and what it advises, what information it gives is, as I have tried to suggest, more than a matter of teaching styles.

Who will teach? I am surprised at how little even educated people know at this late date about aging. Full professors, including psychologists, still ask questions revealing that they do not know the difference between gerontology and geriatrics. The people in industry who are designated to conduct the retirement planning programs are ignorant as owls about the subject. You can imagine. Typically the job is passed to some young person from Pensions and Benefits or maybe to a superfluous person in the late fifties whom the company is trying to dump. As in medicine and psychology, anything to do with aging is low status. These trainers are not exceptional in their ignorance. I give a true-false questionnaire to university students of all ages, to young and old service providers to the elderly, to decision-makers in the aging bureaucracy, to individuals training to be retirement planners, and to planners who have been in the business for years, and I find the picture of older Americans drawn by them not too different from that revealed by the now famous Harris Poll Survey (National Council on Aging, 1975), an utterly false portrait of old people rotting away in poor health without proper medical care or enough money to live on: 30 percent are incarcerated in institutions, senility is a common condition, old people think a lot about death, we lose 100,000 brain cells a day. All false but frequently marked true. One item is detected as false every time— "Old people have little or no interest in sex." An odd picture this, of a population of demented, poverty-stricken, sick, old people, obsessed by death and apt to end up as vegetables in a nursing home, but jumping into bed to make love despite all the adversity. It is not really hard to understand. The sexual act is life itself. We should not be surprised that people in the last years of life cherish it as much for its symbolic as for its more obvious values. Schopenhauer (1928) said that the sexual impulse in itself is the expression of the will to live.

Retirement planning could debunk a lot of this stereotypy and misconception. There is no way to talk meaningfully about retirement without discussing aging. People need to know what is error and what is reality and what is as yet unknown. We are battling centuries of antipathy. Research into aging by the social historians and other humanists tells us that what is felt and said today about old age is no different than what has come down through the ages. There is no pattern, no progression whether we look at children's literature or history or philosophy from Plato to Sartre. There never was a Golden Age.

Against ignorance, fear, and anxiety, however, the sober realistic initiating of the planning process with accurate information can be corrective. Stage III programs can heighten the awareness of their situation and encourage older people to take action.

One example of the difference between a Stage II and a Stage III approach to a single problem illustrates this well. Older people often need drugs and medication, the cost of which is beyond their means. A Stage II solution is the enlistment by politicians of pharmacists who will give discounts to the elderly. Scrounging for discounts from all merchants and purveyors is Stage II's idea of a social invention. Stage III, also recognizing that older people need drugs and medication the cost of which is beyond their means, advocates political action. In Cleveland a group of mostly older people calling themselves "Active Clevelanders Together" banded together and, armed with irrefutable evidence that generic drugs could safely replace name-brand drugs, pushed through the legislation making it legal for every pharmacist in Ohio to dispense the generic drug at a fraction of the cost unless the physician has handwritten instructions disallowing it. And this is for people of all ages, not only for the elderly.

Can retirement planning programs help older people to cope more effectively with the problems of retirement? Well yes, but that is because they are already coping. That is how they come to be in the program.

Research (Kasschau, 1974) tells us that those who fare best in retirement are those who are favorably disposed toward it, and those are precisely the ones who tend to prepare ahead. The participants in the programs are all volunteers. Individuals with negative attitudes are unlikely to attend. A commonly reported problem by the researchers is that satisfaction or adjustment levels were initially so high on pre-program tests that there was nowhere to go on the post tests.

There is no scholarly body of research on retirement planning. The subject is not listed in the index of the *Handbook of Aging and the Social Sciences* (1976), nor is it mentioned in the chapter on work and retirement by Harold Sheppard in that volume.

A few studies have attempted to measure changes in attitude or behavior. Kasschau (1974, p. 47), summing them up, said, "The hit or miss character of the evaluation research seems intimately tied to the hit or miss fashion in which these programs are administered." Elsewhere she writes (p. 46): "Even the best company programs involve only one and one half to two hours weekly group sessions for five to twelve weeks. How can individual attitudes toward life, work, and retirement change from such brief impersonal encounters?" In the same article she reviews the retirement adjustment literature, most if not all of which reveals a high degree of satisfaction with retirement. A warning from Carl Eisdorfer (1977) about the discrepancy between self-estimates of health and objective criteria may be relevant here. Despite moderate to severe chronic illness as measured by objective criteria, a great majority of old people in the studies he reviewed did not identify themselves as significantly impaired but rather saw their symptoms as the limitations of normal old age. So it is with self-estimates of adjustment or life satisfaction. What does it mean if a 65-year-old person checks good or very good or excellent on a scale when asked how he finds life in retirement? The old joke serves us well—compared to what? To Joe who has terminal cancer? To Alice who has been dead a year?

The Moody model does not quite work. Stage III presents a conceptual problem. Participation seems to be a substage of a larger, more generic progressive principle. It is only one option, one avenue in the direction of self-actualization. Moody himself admits that Stage III denies the aging process with its insistence on continued activity in later life.

There is a general tendency today to decry solitude as unhealthy and looking inward, and disengaging as morbid. But a good measure of solitude is necessary for reflection. Introspection is a requisite of psychological growth, and the constructive use of experience depends first of all on one's awareness of that experience in some focused, holistic way. Stage III points to Arthur Rubinstein and Miz Lillian as examples of the ideal. Indeed, many gerontologists believe that the ideal old age is an extension, a stretching out of a good middle age. But Moody suggests that there is something *uniquely possible* in old age that is possible only at this point in the life cycle.

Self-actualization reaches its fullest explication in the thinking of the psychologist Abraham Maslow (1954). Maslow early in his career thought that self-actualization was the ultimate development of one's capacities and abilities. He thought it was the goal to be sought. In his maturity he said he realized that self-actualization could not be sought, but that like happiness it would elude us if we made its search the objective of our lives. Self-actualization comes as a by-product of something else that we do or that we are.

Maslow early in his career thought that self-actualization could occur in young people. In his maturity he wrote that this could not happen. Why? I give you his answer (1970, Preface, xx):

Because in our culture at least, youngsters have not yet achieved identity or autonomy, nor have they had time enough to experience an enduring, loyal, post-romantic love relationship, nor have they generally found their calling, the altar upon which to offer themselves, nor have they worked out their own system of values; nor have they had experience enough (responsibility for others, tragedy, failure, achievement, success) to shed perfectionist illusions and become realistic; nor have they generally made their peace with death; nor have they learned how to be patient; nor have they learned enough about evil in themselves and others to be compassionate; nor have they had time to become postambivalent about parents and elders, power and authority; nor have they generally become wise; nor have they generally acquired enough courage to be unpopular; to be unashamed about being openly virtuous . . .

In the final analysis the best thing about old age is experience. It is incontrovertibly the one thing old people have more of than young people. You do not live two thirds of a century for nothing. You learn how to cope.

Ethel Shanas (1975) says that when one interviews the old old, the very old in their 80's and 90's, a common statement is: "I never expected to live so long." These old pioneers reached extreme old age unexpectedly, you might say, and so had to invent coping mechanisms and behaviors and styles.

Do not reckon without the host The old person is not at this party as a pauper, but as a survivor. "Sobre viviente" the Spaniard says. He has continued to live in spite of, and after.

Could better, earlier, longer, more rational planning promote coping and competence in older adults? Again, yes. One thinks of long-term financial planning, health education, education about life span development, and the constructive uses of time. But if one thinks about the creative uses of experience, of self-knowledge, changing human relationships, life tasks, and values and meaning, then we are not talking about retirement planning.

Da capo. How do we view life as a whole? What significance do we assign the experience of aging? How should old people live?

REFERENCES

Atchley, R. C. *Social forces in later life: An introduction to social gerontology*. Belmont, Cal.: Wadsworth, 1972.

Barfield, R. E., and Morgan, J. N. Trends in planned early retirement. *The Gerontologist*, 1978, *18*, 13–18.

Beauvoir, S. de. *The coming of age*. (P. O'Brian, trans.). New York: Putnam, 1972.

Binstock, R., and Shanas, E. (Eds.). *Handbook of the aging and the social sciences*. New York: Van Nostrand Reinhold, 1976.

Brotman, H. *Money income and poverty status of family and persons in the United States: 1977*. Current population reports, consumer income series (P-60, No. 116), advance report. U. S. Dept. of Commerce, Bureau of the Census, July 1978.

Eisdorfer, C. The meaning of retirement. In R. A. Kalish (Ed.), *The later years*. Belmont, Cal.: Wadsworth, 1977.

Frost, R. Provide, Provide. In E. C. Lathem (Ed.), *The poetry of Robert Frost*. New York: Holt, Rinehart and Winston, 1969.

Hall, E. The freakish passion: A conversation with George Steiner. *Psychology Today*, February 1973, pp. 56–58, 60, 62, 64, 66–69.

Hayflick, L. Perspectives on human longevity. In Committee on Human Development, *Extending the human life span: Social policy and social ethics*. Chicago: University of Chicago Press, 1977.

Kasschau, P. L. Reevaluating the need for retirement planning programs. *Industrial Gerontology*, 1974, *1* (1), 42–59.

Maslow, A. H. *Motivation and personality*. New York: Harper and Brothers, 1954.

Maslow, A. H. *Motivation and personality* (2nd ed.). New York: Harper and Row, 1970.

Moody, H. R. Philosophical presuppositions of education for old age. *Educational Gerontology: An International Quarterly*, 1976, *1*, 1–16.

Morrison, M. H. Planning for income adequacy in retirement. *The Gerontologist*, 1976, *16*, 538–543.

Morrison, M. H. *The retirement revolution*. Unpublished manuscript, 1978.

National Council on Aging. *The myth and reality of aging in America*. Washington, D. C. 1975.

Neugarten, B. Age groups in American society and the rise of the young-old. *Annals of the American Academy of Political and Social Sciences*, 1974, *415*, 198.

Parker, S. *The future of work and leisure*. London: MacGibbon and Kee, 1971.

Prentis, R. S. *National survey of Fortune's "500" pre-retirement plans and policies*. Ann Arbor and Detroit, Mich.: University of Michigan and Wayne State University Institute of Labor and Industrial Relations, July, 1975.

Sandburg, C. 107, *The people, yes*. New York: Harcourt Brace, 1936.

Schopenhauer, A. [The metaphysics of the love of the sexes.] In W. Durant (Ed., R. B. Haldane and J. Kemp, trans.), *The world as will and idea* (Vol. 3). New York: Simon and Schuster, 1928.

Shanas, E. Aging in the year 2000; A look at the future. *The Gerontologist*, 1975, *15* (1), 38.

United States Civil Service Commission. *Retirement planning: A growing employee relations service*. Washington, D. C.: U. S. Government Printing Office, 1961.

IV
Coping, Competence, and the Family

The papers in this section examine the family in the light of a concern for primary prevention. What we have seen to be true of many social institutions is true of the family too. It may simultaneously provide support and enhance coping and at the same time be a source of stress and conflict. Furthermore, such factors as the rapid increase in divorce and second and third marriages, living at great distances from kin, and cohabitation and parenting without marriage have led us to attempt to improve our understanding of the ways in which evolving family structures affect the individual's daily functioning. The authors of the papers in Part IV consider two distinct aspects of the relationship between coping and competence and the family.

Lillian B. Rubin is a Research Associate at the Institute for the Study of Social Change, University of California, Berkeley. Trained as a sociologist and as a marriage, family, and child counselor, Rubin has focused on women's development through adulthood, American social class structure, and the interplay of these domains. In her paper, taken from her latest book, *Women of a certain age: The midlife search for self*, Rubin goes beyond the assumptions and stereotypes of the "empty nest syndrome" to analyze the ways in which women in fact deal with the midlife transition surrounding the end of their "active mothering years." Her analysis is based on in-depth interviews of 160 working class to professional upper-middle class mothers. In her attempt to decipher the nature of the problems which women face at this life transition point, Rubin offers some insight into the experiences of men as well.

Henry P. David is the Director of the Transnational Family Research Institute and is an associate clinical professor of psychology in the department of psychiatry at the University of Maryland School of Medicine. He is former Associate Director of the World Federation for Mental Health in Geneva and acts as a consultant to the World Health Organization. Within the context of a prevention model, David presents an extensive integration of the literature relevant to strengthening family capabilities for coping. Taking a transnational perspective, he considers concepts of family and healthy family functioning and the relationship between coping with conception, quality of life, and socioeconomic development. David suggests the merits of focusing upon fertility choice behavior and decision-making processes in developing a theory of healthy family functioning. He highlights the need for cooperative cross-cultural research into the behavioral attributes of recently formed family units.

13

The Empty Nest: Beginning or Ending?

LILLIAN B. RUBIN

For many years, we have been hearing of the *empty-nest syndrome*—a package of depressive pathology that supposedly afflicts middle-aged women when their children leave the family fold (Bart, 1968, 1970, 1971; Curlee, 1969; Deykin, Jacobson, Klerman, and Solomon, 1966; Harkins and House, 1975; Jacobson and Klerman, 1966; Powell, 1977; Spence and Lonner, 1971; Weissman, Pincus, Radding, Lawrence, and Siegel, 1973; Weissman and Paykel, 1974). Until quite recently, this stage of women's lives was the province of clinicians. If a woman became depressed after her children left home, the relationship was assumed to be one of cause and effect. Children's leave-taking, they said, causes depression, a particular kind of depression that even warranted its own name. The empty-nest syndrome, they called it. Nothing to worry about, they assured us. It is a loss like any other. And as with any loss, the normal processes of grief and mourning would produce their healing effect. Sometimes the healing did not come. Instead the women were characterized as neurotic—pathological in their inability to separate from their children, in their incapacity to manage internal conflict without breakdown. Even then few questioned the theory.

There are some notable exceptions in the work of Deutscher (1969) and Neugarten (1968a, 1968b, 1974), Neugarten, Wood, Kraines, and Loomis (1968), and Neugarten and Datan (1974). Over a decade ago they showed that most women accept the departure of their children with equanimity, if not relief. But

The material presented here is taken from the author's book, *Women of a Certain Age: The Midlife Search for Self* (New York: Harper and Row, 1979). It is based on research supported by the Behavioral Sciences Research Division, National Institute of Mental Health, Grant No. MH 28167.

these findings were paid scant attention, probably because they flew in the face of established stereotypes and preconceptions. As recently as 1974 Neugarten noted that regardless of what the stereotype indicates, in reality we do not hear women mourning the loss of their role as mother, or their reproductive capacity. Yet, so pervasive are notions about the empty-nest depression that researchers continue to express doubt about their own findings when their data contradict the preconception. Thus Glenn (1975) found that women in the postparental stage reported greater marital happiness than those who were in the parental stage, but tempered his conclusion with the caution that "the empty-nest syndrome may still be prevalent enough to warrent concern." And Lowenthal, Thurnher, and Chiriboga (1975) heard the women they interviewed say they were looking forward to the children's departure, and concluded that their anxiety and despair about the empty-nest was too deep to be tapped by their interviews.

As consciousness heightened about the nature of the life problems that women face, as more women moved into the social sciences, where such theories are born, the empty nest depression underwent a reinterpretation. Now the pathology was located not in the woman, but in the system of social roles and arrangements that makes it always difficult, sometimes impossible, for a mother to develop an identity that rests on alternative roles.

An important shift in understanding this, but not yet enough, for these new formulations still rest on the same unspoken assumptions as the old ones—assumptions that depression in mid-life women is linked to the departure of their children, that it is the loss of the mothering role that *produces* the sadness and despair. Like the old ideas, these new ones too often take as given the belief that a woman is little more than the builder of the nest and the nurturer of the young, that her reason for being is in that nesting and nurturing function.

Bart (1968, 1969, 1970, 1971) is an important exception to these comments. Her pioneering work offers a complex and subtle analysis of social role which few of those who followed her have matched.

Think about the language we unquestioningly use to characterize this period of life: *the empty nest*. Not the *awakening*, not the *emergence*, not words that might suggest that inside that house all those years there lived someone besides a mother. No, we say the *empty nest*. And think, too, about the associations of those words. When we hear the phrase *empty nest*, we do not think of a father, because the "nest" is so intimately associated with mother that it is difficult to separate the two. Indeed, the very words "empty nest" conjure up a vision of a lonely, depressed woman clinging pathetically and inappropriately to a lost past—a woman who has lived for and through her children, a woman incapable of either conceiving or desiring a "room of her own."

That is the stereotype that permeates the culture, dominates our image of women at midlife. It is so consonant with our view of Woman-as-Mother—a view so widely shared and, until recently, so unconsciously held—that the phrase *empty-nest syndrome* has slipped into the language as if it speaks to an enternal and unvarying truth. What we have failed to notice, however, is that most of the ideas we have about depression in midlife women come from research done on hospitalized patients (Bart, 1968; Deykin, Jacobson, Klerman, and Solomon, 1966; Jacobson and Klerman, 1966; Weissman and Paykel, 1974).

Over the last few years other investigators have begun to suggest that in fact the departure of the children brings both an increase in marital satisfaction for women and an increased sense of well-being (Fuchs, 1977; Glenn, 1975; Lowenthal, Thurnher, and Chiriboga, 1975; Lowenthal and Weiss, 1976; Maas and Kuypers, 1975; Sales, 1977). These new research findings have received relatively little attention compared to the old ones, which are closer to the myth and stereotype about the nature of woman and the naturalness of motherhood.

Does this sad creature of the stereotype exist in the larger world where women live their lives and dream their dreams? This was one of the questions I brought to my study of midlife women. I wanted to know how women handle the midlife transition—how they respond to the end of their active mothering years, whether this life stage catches them unaware, as so much writing suggests, or whether, in fact, the process of living, growing, changing itself provides some preparation even if not consciously planned.

To this end I conducted intensive, in-depth, focused interviews with 160 women whose average age was 46.5 years—women who were or had been married, had borne and raised children, and (except for ten) had none under thirteen years old left in the home. They were and are women whose class backgrounds range from working class to professional upper-middle class. But they share in common the fact that they all gave up whatever jobs or careers they may have had in their youth to devote themselves to full-time mothering and housewifery for at least ten years after the first child was born.

Currently, almost half work in paid jobs outside their homes. Most are secretaries, clerks, receptionists; a few are factory workers, a few professionals. Of the rest, about a quarter are heavily committed volunteers, fewer than 15 percent have returned to school to prepare for a career, and most—well over half—call themselves "homemakers."

All have children in varying stages of leaving the nest. For some, the children have all been gone for a few years, and for others, only several months. A few still have one or more children living at home, but most can anticipate their departure within the next year or two.

It is true that some are sad, some lonely, some even depressed. It is true also that some are hesitant, some are unconfident, and most are frightened as they face an uncertain future. But except for one, none suffers the classical symptoms of the empty-nest syndrome (Bart, 1968, 1970, 1971; Deykin et al., 1966; Jacobson and Klerman, 1966). Those symptoms are a profound clinical depression, usually characterized by several serious psychiatric symptoms, such as deep sadness and despair; sleeplessness; loss of appetite; loss of sexual desire; retardation of initiative, thinking, and motor abilities; severely low self-esteem and self-confidence; little or no interest in daily life and ordinary affairs; an incapacity to experience pleasure or joy; and an inability to engage in anything that requires sustained effort or attention.

Certainly, there are differences among them—differences related to how long the children have been gone or whether they are yet gone (Harkins and House, 1975), differences related to how successfully a woman feels she handled the tasks of mothering, how she feels about her adult children (Spence and Lonner, 1971); differences related to how a woman has lived her life until this period, how she has prepared for the transition, how she feels about her marriage—or her divorce—as the case may be (Powell, 1977). Important differences, these, which merit attention and examination. But underlying all those differences is a more important similarity. *Almost all the women I spoke with respond to the departure of their children—whether actual or impending—with a decided sense of relief.*

Among those whose children are already gone, almost every one is unequivocal in those feelings:

I can't tell you what a relief it was to find myself with an empty nest. Oh sure, when the last child went away to school, for the first day or so there was a kind of a throb, but believe me, it was only a day or two.

Even those most committed to the traditional homemaker role—women who have never worked outside the home in the past and do not intend to in the future—speak in the same vein:

When the youngest one was ready to move out of the house, I was right there helping him pack. We love having the children live in the area, and we love seeing them and the grandchildren, but I don't need for any of them to live in this house ever again. *I've had as much as I ever need or want of being tied down with children.*

A few—generally those who are a little closer to the time of the transition—are more ambivalent:

It's complicated; it doesn't just feel one way or the other. I guess it's rather a bittersweet thing. It's not that it's either good or bad, it's just that it's an era that's coming to an end and, in many ways, it was a nice era. So there's some sadness in it, and I guess I feel a little lost sometimes. But it's no big thing; it comes and goes.

Even women who have not yet watched a child leave home speak with hunger of their readiness to turn their attention to their own lives:

From the day the kids are born, if it's not one thing, it's another. After all these years of being responsible for them, you finally get to the point where you want to scream, "Fall out of the nest already, you guys, will you? It's time." It's as if I want to take myself back after all these years—to give me back to me, if you know what I mean. Of course, that's providing there's any "me" left.

But what about women who are divorced? Although just over 20 percent of the women in this study are divorced, see Rubin (1979) for more detailed discussion of divorced women at this stage of the life cycle. Would not women who have no husbands around to claim their attention—perhaps no prospect of marriage in sight—find the departure of the children more troubling? Surprisingly, the answer is *no*. For whatever the problems divorced women suffer, the departure of the children is not high among them. Like their married sisters, they are relieved to be freed of the responsibilities of mothering, glad to be able to call their lives their own:

> I thought it would be hard when they left, but it's not. I was talking to a friend about it just yesterday, and she said, "Why should it make a difference if the kids are home or not? They don't warm up the bed."

Are there no women, then, who experience feelings of loss at their children's departure, none who feels the grief and sadness that inevitably accompanies such loss? Of course there are. Most women do. But there is wide variation in the duration of those feelings—some speaking of days, or weeks, much more seldom of months. And whatever the intensity of the feelings, they rarely devastate women, rarely leave them depressed and barely functional.

Sometimes the leave-taking is more problematic for working-class than for middle-class mothers (Bart, 1968, 1971; Weissman and Paykel, 1974; Weissman, Pincus, Radding, Lawrence, and Siegel, 1973). But notice first the word "sometimes." And notice also that this says nothing about depression. In fact, in those instances where such problems exist for working-class women, they are almost always short-term and of limited intensity. Still, there *is* a difference—a difference related to the *process* by which the children of each class generally leave home.

Almost from birth, most middle-class parents know when the big break from the family will come—at eighteen, when the child leaves for college. There is plenty of warning, plenty of time to get ready. But in working-class families, college attendance is not taken for granted—often these days it is not even desired (Rubin, 1972)—and children are expected to live at home until they marry. Indeed, even among those working-class girls and boys who are college bound, most know they will live at home during those years—both because it is part of the family expectations, and because generally they cannot afford to do otherwise (Rubin, 1976). Because the age of marriage is not clearly fixed, the time of departure is also indefinite, for both parents and children—somewhat like living with an indeterminate prison sentence rather than a firm release date that has been agreed upon and understood by all. That difference alone, the unpredictability of the departure date, makes preparation for separation more difficult in working-class families. Indeed, often middle-class mothers speak of the child's senior year in high school as the year in which much of the separation work was done—what sociologists call "anticipatory socialization."

By the time my daughter left for college, I had already dealt with the issues. From time to time in her senior year in high school, I'd get a pang thinking about what was coming. I must admit, though, that by the time it actually happened, even I was surprised at how easy it was. I guess I had just grown accustomed to the idea by then.

But for the working-class woman there is no such clear marker, no date known years in advance when she can expect a child's departure. For her, therefore, preparation is different, separation perhaps more difficult for some brief period of time. Almost always the difficulty *is* brief, however, and it surely does not approach anything that could rightfully be called a depression.

In fact, regardless of class, those who suffer most are women who are disappointed in their children, whose relationships with them are unsatisfactory, whose disapproval of their life style makes the relationship difficult and tenuous, at least for the moment. Those are the most difficult times for a mother—the times when she looks inside herself and thinks, "It didn't work out the way I planned." Partly, that is because it is almost impossible for a mother to experience that disappointment in her children without blaming herself. After all, if her main task in life is to raise the children and it does not come out right according to her standards, whom else can she blame? Indeed, who else will be blamed? (Abramowitz, 1977; Bernard, 1975; Rich, 1976). On the other hand, Bart (1967, 1971) suggests that whether mothers have satisfactory or unsatisfactory relationships with their children makes little difference in their adjustment and suffering at the time of the children's departure. The difference between us may be due to the fact that the women she studied were hospitalized patients suffering a severe clinical depression, while the women I talked to were coping well and functioning normally. In a recent telephone conversation with Bart, she suggested that the changed cultural context—that is, the difference between the experience of being a midlife woman in the 1960's and the 1970's, after the changes wrought by the women's movement—could also be a factor in accounting for the differences in our findings about the prevalence of the empty-nest depression. Although this is reasonable speculation, it is not convincing, since it does not take into account that even in the 1960's research findings challenged the belief in the empty-nest syndrome.

I lie awake many a night wondering what I did wrong that my daughter lives the way she does—the dope and the living together, and all that kind of thing. I don't know; I couldn't stop her. God knows, I tried. I try to tell myself it's a different world and it's not my fault. But it's hard to believe that. It just feels like I failed at my job.

It may not be reasonable that women shoulder that burden. There are, after all, fathers who, by their absence if not by their presence, must take some responsibility for how their children grow and develop, for what kinds of adults they become. And there is a society outside the family with which children interact from very early childhood—schools, classmates, peer groups, each with a culture that helps to shape and mold its members. Yet from all sides the finger of blame is pointed at mothers—blame that, until now, they have accepted and internalized unquestioningly.

But there is more than pressure from external sources, there is more involved than blame and its companion, guilt. When most midlife women became mothers, they aborted their own hopes and dreams and invested them in their children—an investment whose costs lie heavily on both mothers and children, since it asks nothing less than that the child validate the mother's life.

My only career has been my children. If I can't find success in raising them, then what? Where am I going to look for any sense of pride or fulfillment? There's nothing else I've done that I can judge myself by. My husband has his career, and he finds success and fulfillment in that. He's proven himself someplace, so he doesn't feel the disappointment the way I do. For me, it's the only thing I tried to do, and I failed. You know, when you look at your children and see that they're not going to be what you dreamed, when those fantasies and illusions go out the window, it's hell.

"My only career has been my children"—words that suggest that if a woman has another "career," she can more easily tolerate the disappointement of her dreams for her children, that it will not be such "hell." And if it is possible to measure hell, that is probably true. Women who have work from which they get substantial independent gratification *can* more easily avoid the pain by burying themselves in this work. They have other things to think about, other ways of relating to the world and to themselves. They have at least the beginning of another identity, an emerging sense of their own separateness. That developing identity may not yet stand firmly, but its existence alone is enough to make a difference. It is demonstrable proof that a self lives apart from the children, clear evidence that a future exists.

Important though it may be, however, who suffers more from such disappointments and who less is not the central issue here. The question is: How do women handle the departure of their children under these circumstances? The answer: With pain, but also with relief:

It hurts that he's gone because things are terrible between us now, and he doesn't come around much any more. But, I don't know, I think it's better since he's gone. It's a relief, you know, not to have to see him every day. Oh, I don't know. What can I say? It hurts not to see him, but it hurts more to see him and be reminded.

She is relieved that he has gone—glad not to be burdened by his presence, not to be reminded daily of her pain. But it hurts, too—hurts because even though he is not there, she cannot help remembering, cannot help believing she failed, cannot help reflecting on the past with regret, cannot help wondering how it could have been otherwise.

There is something else. Those memories, those questions, mean also that the separation from the child is more difficult than usual, because she is stuck with feelings of incompletion—with the sense that one of life's tasks is not finished, yet is now outside her control. It is akin to dealing with the death of a parent with whom conflicts remain unresolved. Even though the departing child is not dead, the psychological experience of the loss can be the same; the last chance to heal the divisions, the last chance to make peace. The departure of a child with whom there is conflict means that the loss is experienced even more keenly, and the grief is more difficult to manage and work through.

With all this—whatever the disappointments, the sense of failure, the loss, whatever the time span of the suffering or the intensity of the pain—one thing is certain: The women I met are not debilitated by it. Indeed, they cope quite well with whatever feelings of failure, disappointment, and loss they may suffer, for alongside them, there exists another, at least equally powerful set of feelings which helps to neutralize the pain. Alongside them there is the longing for freedom, the wish to find and claim a well defined and differentiated self, and the belief that finally this may be possible. These are the feelings which dominate the transition period and beyond, a struggle that engages women perhaps for the rest of their lives. "If it's hard now, it's because I don't know what I'll be doing, not because the children are gone. Their going is a blessing; it's time. But I'm scared."

How then can we account for the persistence of the myth that inside the empty nest lives a shattered and depressed shell of a woman—a woman in constant pain because her children have left her roof? Is it possible that a notion so pervasive is, in fact, just a myth? No simple questions, these; and no easy answers, for they touch the deepest layers of social structure and personality, and the interconnections between the two.

To start, let us grant that, as with all stereotypes, there is a kernel of truth in this one. The midlife transition is, in fact, difficult for most women—a time often filled with turmoil and self-doubt, a time when old roles are being shed and the shape of new ones are not yet apparent; a time of reordering long-held priorities, of restructuring daily life. From that small truth, however, has grown a fabrication based on the one-sided and distorted view of women and womanhood; a view that insists that womanhood and motherhood are synonymous, that motherhood is a woman's ineluctable destiny, her sacred calling, her singular area of fulfillment. Until recently (Bernard, 1975; Easton, 1976; Lazarre, 1976; McBride, 1973; Rich, 1976; Wortis, 1974), this view has remained largely unchallenged—one of the accepted verities on which our social and economic system is built. Man worked outside the home, woman inside. Her biological destiny was to nurture, his to provide the safety within which she could do it.

Never mind that it did not really work that way, that the ideology and the structure of the economy are at odds. Never mind that most men in this society cannot provide that safety, not because they do not want to or are lacking in skills, but because there are not enough jobs. Never mind that even where jobs exist, most do not pay enough to ensure much safety for the family. Never mind that poor women have always had to work, or that among married women with children under six years old, well over one third now work outside the home— most of them because of economic necessity. Never mind that this represents a threefold increase over the last two and a half decades, and continues to rise as inflation pushes the cost of living even higher. The myth lives—a kind of cultural conspiracy that blinds us all to such realities.

That myth—the image of the madonna-mother—has prevented us from knowing that just as men are more than fathers, women are more than mothers. It has kept us from hearing their voices when they try to tell us of other aspirations, other needs; kept us from believing that they share with men the desire for achievement, mastery, competence—the desire to do something for *themselves* (Baruch, 1976; Laws, 1976). It has aided and abetted the distortion of feminine consciousness—a distortion that makes it difficult, indeed, for women to accept and acknowledge their inner experience, whether in relation to their own aspirations or to their feelings about the end of their active mothering years. "I felt terrible when I didn't feel bad enough when the last of my children left. I'd walk around wondering 'What kind of mother are you?' "

But even when a woman can say clearly that she is glad it is over, rarely can she let the statement stand without qualification or equivocation. Instead, she covers it at once with some "evidence" that she really is a good and loving mother: "I mean, I really love them. You know, I gave them my life for all those years. And I miss them, too; I really do."

Why the hasty retreat? Partly, it is because she is concerned about the impact of her words on her listener. More importantly, it is because the acknowledgment of those sentiments—the act of speaking them aloud—activates her own guilt and discomfort, violates her own expectations about how a good mother should feel. Still, the relief is so powerfully felt that she cannot help adding with a self-conscious smile and a self-deprecating air— a manner suggesting that *these* words about to be spoken are not to be taken too seriously: "It's just that it's nice to have the house to ourselves."

By such comments we can come to understand a woman's yearning to comprehend the totality of the experience of motherhood and the profound ways in which it colors daily life. By such comments we come to know something of the things she holds dear. Yet because they are so incongruent with the set of expectations we bring to the situation, these are the very words we too often fail to hear; these are the words whose real meaning eludes us.

Often enough, as well, we are not told. It is difficult to speak of such feelings in the face of the myth. Often they are repressed and denied long before they ever surface into consciousness. When that does not work, the guilt that attends them can be excruciating, and the fear of being found deficient—"unnatural"—is felt keenly enough to still the tongue. A 51-year-old mother whose last child had left home a year before speaks compellingly about just those fears:

> I sometimes worried that I was unnatural, so I didn't really like to talk about it. You know, when you hear all around you that women are pining for their children, you feel as if there's something wrong with you—that you're not a natural mother—if you don't.

What do women mean by "natural mother"? Why is it that about one fourth of the women I met admitted guiltily, almost fearfully, that they do not consider themselves "natural mothers," do not feel that they were "made for motherhood"?

Perhaps because the ideal we all hold is anything but "natural." In our minds lives the madonna-image—the all-embracing, all-giving tranquil mother of a Raphael painting—one child at her breast, another at her feet; a woman fulfilled, one who asks nothing more than to nurture and nourish. This creature of fantasy is the model—the unattainable ideal against which women measure not only their performance but their feelings about being mothers. Who, under those circumstances, is "made for mother-hood"? And who, under those circumstances, can acknowledge— let alone speak easily—of her real feelings?

Everyone knows there is more talk now about such issues, more public discussion, more critical examination of long-cher-ished ways of thinking about women and femininity. If the new feminist movement has done nothing else, it has raised these issues and forced us into a national dialogue about them. And, indeed, often enough women now say that they know others who feel relief at the departure of the children. But whether speaking of self or friends, rarely is it said without some sign of distress. Always there is the sense that perhaps it is true that other women share these feelings, but no one can be quite certain that it is right. Thus, when discussing the subject, women often look about uncertainly, lower their voices, and generally give signals of discomfort—as if they fear being overheard. Typical is a forty-five year-old who leaned forward in her chair as if to bestow an important confidence, dropped her voice to just above a whisper, and said:

> To tell you the truth, most of the time it's a big relief to be free of them, finally. I suppose that's awful to say. But you know what, most of the women I know feel the same way. It's just that they're uncomfortable saying it because there's all this talk about how sad mothers are supposed to be when the kids leave home.

"Most of the women I know feel the same way." How is it, then, that this woman, like so many others, does not really know what she knows? Why the discomfort with her own feelings? Why the guilt? Some women respond to those questions by denying the reality of what they hear: "Well, people say that now because, you know, women aren't supposed to be such gung-ho mothers any more. We're supposed to be liberated and

322 Lillian B. Rubin

all that stuff." Others simply label themselves and their friends
as deviant or aberrant, assuming that the rest of the world is
different:

> I don't think my friends are typical or representative, or any-
> thing like that. I think most women still are in very traditional
> places, and most women really do miss their children terribly
> when they go. It's as if their lives just end. I'm different, and
> so are my friends. That's because I picked them, I suppose.

All this suggests the enormous complexity of interaction between cultural expectations, their internalization, and personal
experience. For what I have been saying is that, at one level,
it is no big news to women who live it that the empty-nest syndrome does not exist for most of them. At another level, however,
they are so mystified by the ideology of motherhood that they
deny their own inner experience as well as the evidence their
eyes and ears bring to them from the outer world.

It should come as no surprise to anyone that the end of the
active mothering function is greeted with relief. Only someone
who has never been a mother would fail to understand how
awesome are the demands of motherhood as they are currently
defined in our culture—demands and obligations that, for most
women, are rooted deeply enough to color not only their living
in peace but their prospects for dying in peace:

> Maybe you'll think I'm crazy, but when they were younger,
> I used to worry about what would happen if I died. Don't
> misunderstand me, I'm not ready to die. But if I have to die
> now, at least I can go knowing my kids could tolerate it, and
> that they don't really need me any more. *What a relief to
> know that!* It would be a tragedy, wouldn't it, to be a mother
> and die before you thought your kids were ready?

A tragedy? Perhaps. But at least equally tragic is the burden
she carries. One might ask: What is so special about *her* burden?
Do fathers not also feel keenly their parental responsibilities?
We all know men, after all, who are encumbered with the need
to plan for death as well as for life—men who struggle not only
to make a living today, but to provide for tomorrow as well.
Insurance companies grow rich as they offer to protect against
just those fears—fears that are the price men pay for their un-

questioning acceptance of the present division of labor in the family. With a wife and children wholly, or even largely, dependent upon him, a man works all his life partly, at least, to ensure their support when he dies. And that, of course, is the crucial difference. A mother fears leaving her children before they are emotionally ready, a father before they are financially ready.

This is not to suggest that mothers feel more deeply about their children than fathers, nor that the differences in their responses—the nature of their concerns—belong to natural differences between women and men. There is nothing natural about mothers being caregivers and fathers being money-givers. Rather, these are social arrangements—both women and men responding to long-established, socially defined roles and functions within the family. As a consequence of this family structure, however, a father can feel he has fulfilled his responsibility if he leaves enough dollars behind him. But what replaces a mother? What can she plan to leave behind to help her children until they become emotionally independent adults?

They carry with them heavy costs, these social arrangements— burdening both women and men in painful, if different ways. Mothers suffer when they bear the burdens of child-rearing alone, it is true. But the reward is an intimate connection with their children. And fathers? Contrary to all we hear about women and their empty-nest problems, it may be fathers more often than mothers who are pained by the children's imminent or actual departure—fathers who want to keep the children in the home for just a little longer:

> For me, it's enough! They've been here long enough—maybe too long. It's a funny thing, though. All these years, Fred was too busy to have much time for the kids, and now he's the one who's depressed because they're leaving. He's really having trouble letting go. He wants to gather them around and keep them right here in this house.

Another, 48 years old, whose first child was married a year before we met, says:

> My son's marriage was very hard on my husband—very hard on him. He was terribly upset. I was so shocked, I could hardly believe it. She's a beautiful girl and we both love her, so it

wasn't that. I couldn't figure it out for a long time, but after a couple of months, we finally talked it out. It turned out he was suffering because he felt like it was the end of our little family. He felt terrible because it would never be the same again. He doesn't say much about it any more, but I can just tell it's still hard for him. My daughter is going with a very nice young man now, and it's quite possible that they'll get married. But Alex ignores it; I mean, it's like he pretends it isn't happening; you know, like if he doesn't look, it'll go away.

Interesting observations, these. And surprising—until I stopped to reflect on the different experiences men and women have in the family in general and in parenting in particular. Then it seemed reasonable that fathers would suffer the loss of children, sometimes even more than mothers. Foremost among those differences, perhaps, is the fact that for mothers the departure of their children comes as the culmination of a developmental sequence, the result of a natural process in which they have participated, rather than a sudden break—a fact that empty-nest theorists generally ignore: "Mother nature had it all figured out. By the time they're ready to go, you're ready to see them go." Indeed, she figured it out well from first separation to last. By the time the ninth month of pregnancy arrives, a woman does not object to birthing the child. She does not suffer from an empty womb, she rejoices in a full crib. This is not to deny the existence of postpartum depression in some women. It simply asserts that no matter how much a woman may enjoy and appreciate the experience of pregnancy, no matter what feelings the separation of the birth may eventually evoke, by the time she has carried a child to term, she is ready to give it up. So it is through all the stages of a child's development. Each stage brings with it some loss, some sadness. Each brings also some joy, some pride, some sense of accomplishment—another step taken, another phase negotiated successfully. And in each there is preparation for the next—an ending, but also a beginning—not alone for the child, but for the mother as well. Children crawl before they walk, walk before they run—each generally a precondition for the other. And with each step they take toward more independence, more mastery of the environment, their mothers take a step away—each a small separation, a small distancing. The child moves from its mother's arms, to the floor, to its own two feet—for mother and child a shared miracle which is, also, a shared separation. By the time a mother sends a little one off to school for the first time, she is ready—a readiness born of the experience of hundreds of such small separations, of her intense involvement in each stage of the child's growth which already foretells the next. For her, then, the preparation for the child's eventual departure is continuous, even if not always experienced consciously, its inevitability long ago etched in her psyche.

I've been thinking a lot about how I'll feel when they go because it seems as if it won't be hard for me. I've been wondering about that, and thinking about whether I'm just kidding myself. But you know, you grow toward it all the time you're raising your children. Where I wasn't ready to lose them a few years ago, I've grown now to where I look forward to it.

It is this developmental process that too often is missed by those who write and speak of the pain of the empty-nest stage— this process which makes it possible for a mother to speak of relief while acknowledging the sadness; this process which suggests that there are no shocks, no surprises, no sudden jolts. Certainly, there are moments of heightened realization, when the knowledge of change in the family is hammered home—a child goes to camp for the first time, an older one to college, another marries. But even these moments of high drama take place in the context of a long and subtle process that usually happens outside the immediate awareness of the people who live it, one they may understand only in retrospect.

Compare this with father's experience in the family. While mother has been feeding, tending, nurturing, teaching, watching, and sharing inside the home, father has been working outside. Sometimes he spends most of this time at work because work is the major emotional commitment in his life, sometimes simply because it is his job to ensure the family's economic stability. More often, it is probably some mix of the two.

But whatever his feelings about his work, he generally spends most of his life at it—most of his emotional and physical energy is spent in the pursuit of economic security for the family. Consequently, he is not there when his children take that first step, or when they come home from school on that first day. He is not there to watch their development, to share their triumphs and pains. Then, one day, it is too late: they are gone—before he had a chance really to know them. For him, indeed, it must seem sudden. For him there is nothing natural about the process because he has not watched it, has not shared in it. One can almost see him passing his hand over his eyes wearily, wondering, "How did it all happen so fast?"

Long ago he had a dim sense of being cheated, a wish to relate more and differently to his children. Long ago he promised himself he would—some day, when he was not so busy, not so tired. But there was never the time or the energy, and he never quite knew how to relate to them, what to say; how to play with them when they were little, how to talk with them as they grew.

Over and over, women—paradoxically, even those married to child psychiatrists and psychologists—tell of being the interpreter between father and children, the buffer, the mediator, the one whose task is to explain each to the other.

> I always felt as if I had a foot in two different worlds, as if I was the one who walked across that no-man's land that always seemed to exist between them. Oh, it was better at some times than others; I mean, they were able to talk to each other some of the time. But even at its best, I was always there as mediator and explainer, the one who knew what the other wanted and tried to explain it.

True, women complain a good deal about this: "I *hated* always to have to explain the kids to him. They're his kids too. Why couldn't he take the trouble to get to know them?" And it is true also that, with all their complaints, it is a role they often hold onto because it gives them a sense of power, of mastery in a world where, in fact, they have little:

> *Was it only that you resented being in that position, or were there elements of it that you also liked?*
> Well, when I could make it work, I have to admit it could be very satisfying. It's like in a job you set out to do—when it works, it's just fine. You feel challenged and useful and important, as if there's at least one thing you can do that nobody else can. I guess in order to give up that role, you have to know there's something else waiting for you; I mean, you have to know there's something you can do as well.

On the surface it looks like a functional division of labor—
both parents get what they want or need at the moment. She
gets to feel important; he gets left alone to do his work. But
the cost, especially for the father, is high. Just when he has more
time, just when the children are old enough to be talked to like
real people, just when he is beginning to notice what he has
missed—they are gone.

Since mothers usually do not miss any part of the process,
the end of active mothering does not come with any sudden
wrench. Indeed, for women who can look at their children and
think, "There a job well done," the sense of accomplishment
transcends any feelings of loss; the relief is unequivocal. For those
who suffer disappointment, the relief is mixed with painful
feelings of failure. Yet not one of those women yearned for
another chance. For good or ill, they were glad the job was done,
ready to move on to the next stage of life.

That does not mean there are no problems with this life transition; it means only that the problems are in contemplation of
and confrontation with the next stage of life, only that the problems have to do with anxieties about the future, not nostalgia
for the past.

Some women talk of fears for the marriage. It has been so
long since there were just the two of them, will they know how
to relate to each other without the children mediating?

I'm fond of saying, "You start with the husband. Then, the
kids are around for a few years. Then, you pick up with the
husband again." So intellectually, I feel my first role should
be as wife, but when you think of how much time being a
mother takes, I know it hasn't been that way. Now, when the
last of my kids go, I'm going to have to learn to be a wife
again—just a wife. I don't know how graceful I'll be at it; I'm
not very practiced.

Will they be able to talk? "It isn't that I want to hold the
children here, it's just that I worry about what our life will be
like. I don't know what we'll talk about, just the two of us,
after all these years."

Alongside those fears there is excitement—each vying with the
other as women contemplate an unknown future. For many
families, especially those in the working class, there is some

financial freedom for the first time in their years together—
sometimes for the first time in their life together. That means
there are possibilities for adventure, freedom, travel—possibilities that until now existed only in fantasy. And there is more.
The departure of the children also means the possibility for the
flowering of the marriage relationship in new, even undreamed-
of ways, and for the development of a self only hinted at until
now. Recall the woman who said: "I want to take myself back
after all these years—to give me back to me." And recall, also,
her fearful caveat, that inner voice warning her against expecting
too much: "That's providing there's any 'me' left."

All these possibilities are exciting, yet frightening. How will
it be? What kind of changes will it require, in him, in her, in
their marriage? For her, the greatest unknown—and the central
problem of her life right now—is what the next thirty or forty
years will look like. What will be their shape and texture? What
will be their daily flavor? Frightening questions, exciting possibilities.

> The children's leaving hasn't been traumatic at all. What has
> been and still is traumatic is trying to find the thing I want to
> do, and being able to pursue it to a successful conclusion.
> I'm an artist—a good one, I think. But it's hard to make the
> kind of commitment that real success requires. I'm afraid of
> what it'll do to my marriage, and also to the rest of my life.
> And I suppose I'm afraid to really try and fail. But that's the
> stuff that's so hard and painful right now; it's not knowing
> what I'll be doing, or even what I *can* do. And from forty-
> five to seventy-five is a lot of years if I don't have something
> useful to do.

The ending, then, is difficult, not because the children are
gone, but because it brings with it a beginning with the potential for adventure and excitement, but at the same time the
possibility of failure. Some will negotiate it successfully, some
will not. Sometimes the failure will be theirs; more often it will
lie in the social constraints by which women's lives have been and
continue to be hemmed in. But for all women whose central
life task has been bearing and raising children, one question is

heard like an urgent demand: "What am I going to do with the next thirty years of my life?" It is not an empty nest that plagues them, but the problems that stem from one that has been full too long.

REFERENCES

Abramowitz, C. F. Blaming the mother: An experimental investigation of sex-role bias in countertransference. *Psychology of Women Quarterly*, 1977, *2*, 23–34.

Bart, P. B. Depression in middle-aged women: Some sociocultural factors. (Doctoral dissertation, University of California at Los Angeles, 1967). *Dissertation Abstracts International*, 1968, *28*, 4752-B (University Microfilms No. 68–7452).

Bart, P. B. Why women's status changes in middle age. *Sociological Symposium*, 1969, *3*, 1–18.

Bart, P. B. Portnoy's mother's complaint. *Trans-action*, 1970, *8*, 69–74.

Bart, P. B. Depression in middle-aged women. In V. Gornick and B. K. Moran (Eds.), *Women in sexist society*. New York: Basic Books, 1971.

Baruch, G. K. Girls who perceive themselves as competent: Some antecedents and correlates. *Psychology of Women Quarterly*, 1976, *1*, 38–49.

Bernard, J. *The future of motherhood*. Baltimore: Penguin Books, 1975.

Curlee, J. Alcoholism and the empty nest. *Bulletin of the Menninger Clinic*, 1969, *33*, 165–171.

Deutscher, I. Socialization for postparental life. In R. S. Cavan (Ed.), *Marriage and family in the modern world*. New York: Thomas Y. Crowell, 1969.

Deykin, E. Y., Jacobson, S., Klerman, G. L., and Solomon, M. The empty nest: Psychosocial aspects of conflict between depressed women and their grown children. *American Journal of Psychiatry*, 1966, *122*, 1422–1426.

Easton, B. L. Industrialization and femininity: A case study of nineteenth century New England. *Social Problems*, 1976, *23*, 389–401.

Fuchs, E. *The second season: Life, love and sex—women in the middle years*. Garden City, N. Y.: Anchor Books, Doubleday, 1977.

Glenn, N. D. Psychological well-being in the postparental stage: Some evidence from national surveys. *Journal of Marriage and the Family*, 1975, *37*, 105–110.

Hammer, S. *Daughters and mothers: Mothers and daughters*. New York: Signet Books, 1975.

Harkins, E. B., and House, J. S. Effects of empty-nest transition on self-report of psychological and physical well-being. *Gerontologist*, 1975, *15*, 43.

Jacobson, S., and Klerman, G. L. Interpersonal dynamics of hospitalized depressed patients' home visits. *Journal of Marriage and the Family*, 1966, *28*, 94–102.

Laws, J. L. Work aspirations of women: False leads and new starts. *Signs*, 1976, *1*, 33–49.

Lazarre, J. *The mother knot*. New York: Dell Publishing, 1976.

Lowenthal, M. F., Thurnher, M., and Chiriboga, D. *Four stages of life*. San Francisco: Jossey Bass, 1975.

Lowenthal, M. F., and Weiss, L. Intimacy and crises in adulthood. *The Counseling Psychologist*, 1976, *6*, 10–15.

Maas, H. S., and Kuypers, J. A. *From thirty to seventy—a forty-year longitudinal study of adult styles and personality*. San Francisco: Jossey Bass, 1975.

McBride, A. B. *The growth and development of mothers*. New York: Harper and Row, 1973.

Neugarten, B. L. The awareness of middle age. In B. L. Neugarten (Ed.), *Middle age and aging*. Chicago: University of Chicago Press, 1968a.

Neugarten, B. L. Adult personality: Toward a psychology of the life cycle. In B. L. Neugarten (Ed.), *Middle age and aging*. Chicago: University of Chicago Press, 1968b.

Neugarten, B. L. The roles we play. In American Medical Association (Eds.), *The quality of life: The middle years*. Acton, Mass: Publishing Sciences Group, 1974.

Neugarten, B. L., Wood, V., Kraines, R. J., and Loomis, B. Women's attitudes toward the menopause. In B. L. Neugarten (Ed.), *Middle age and aging*. Chicago: University of Chicago Press, 1968.

Neugarten, B. L., and Datan, N. The middle years. In S. Arieti (Ed.), *American handbook of psychiatry* (2nd ed., Vol. 1). New York: Basic Books, 1974.

Powell, B. The empty nest, employment and psychiatric symptoms in college-educated women. *Psychology of Women Quarterly*, 1977, *2*, 35–43.

Rich, A. *Of woman born: Motherhood as experience and institution*. New York: W. W. Norton, 1976.

Rubin, L. B. *Busing and backlash: White against white in an urban school district*. Berkeley: University of California Press, 1972.

Rubin, L. B. *Worlds of pain: Life in the working-class family*. New York: Basic Books, 1976.

Rubin, L. B. *Women of a certain age*. New York: Harper and Row, 1979.

Sales, E., with the assistance of R. B. Katz. In I. Frieze, J. Parsons, P. Johnson, D. Ruble, and G. Zellman (Eds.), *Women's adult development*. New York: W. W. Norton, 1977.

Spence, D., and Lonner, T. The empty nest: A transition within motherhood. *The Family Coordinator*, 1971, *20*, 369–375.

Weissman, M. M., and Paykel, E. S. *The depressed woman: A study of social relationships*. Chicago: University of Chicago Press, 1974.

Weissman, M. M., Pincus, C., Radding, N., Lawrence, R., and Siegel, R. The educated housewife: Mild depression and the search for work. *American Journal of Orthopsychiatry*, 1973, *43*, 565–573.

Wortis, R. P. The acceptance of the concept of the maternal role by behavioral scientists: Its effects on women. In A. Skolnick and J. H. Skolnick (Eds.), *Intimacy, family and society*. Boston: Little, Brown, 1974.

14

Healthy Family Coping: Transnational Perspectives

HENRY P. DAVID

INTRODUCTION

Orientation

In collecting material for this paper it was sobering to read in Volume I of the Vermont Conference reports Kessler and Albee's (1977) assessment of the extensive literature on primary prevention as having to do with "conditions which are not clearly defined, which vary in rate enormously as a function of community tolerance for deviance, which change frequencies with changing social conditions, and which may not even exist as identifiable defects" (p. 355). Similar reservations have been expressed by others (e.g. ADAMHA, 1977; Klein and Goldston, 1977). Nor was my task made easier by Kessler and Albee's (1977) observation that "everything aimed at improving the human condition, at making life more fulfilling and meaningful, may be considered to be part of primary prevention of mental or emotional disturbance" (p. 351).

At the first Vermont Conference and on subsequent occasions Goldston (1977a; 1977b; 1977c) ably defined the meaning of primary prevention of psychopathology for individuals. I would add only that programs for the promotion of healthy family functioning, or healthy family coping, are primarily educational, socioeconomic, and development oriented rather than providing clinical/curative services. The objective is to strengthen family

This paper is based, in part, on an overview developed under contract with the Division of Mental Health, World Health Organization, Geneva, Switzerland. No endorsement from WHO is assumed or implied.

capabilities for coping with crises and with perceived environmental or emotional stress. There is a "proactive" component to healthy family coping, acting rather than waiting for something to happen and then treating the symptoms (e.g. Huntington, 1975; Vaughn, Huntington, Samuels, Bilmes, and Shapiro, 1975).

Transnational Perspective

In offering a transnational perspective, I propose moving beyond the U.S. scene, without, however, ignoring it. The term "transnational" is preferred because it has a wider scope than "international," which is usually interpreted as dealing primarily with issues between nations (Kennedy, 1977). Many of my comments are based on discussions with colleagues abroad, WHO consultations, and personal observations. I will begin with an overview of the global mental health situation, followed by some discussion of prevailing concepts of the family, family health, and healthy family functioning amidst environmental stress. Family life cycle concerns will be briefly noted. A major portion of the paper will focus on the interrelationship between healthy family coping, conception control, and socioeconomic development. Prevention promotion requires a recognition of sociopolitical realities and a redirection of resources, a social revolution which is already occurring in many parts of the world. There is an urgent need for better utilization of already available knowledge. Finally, I want to propose a theory of healthy family functioning and suggest a program of cooperative transnational research with newly married couples. There are obvious biases in what I will be saying, and I look forward to further discussion.

Global Trends

In his Report to the 1978 World Health Assembly, the Director-General of the World Health Organization Mahler (1978a) estimated that some 40 million people in the world suffer from severe mental illness and that twice as many are seriously disabled by drug dependence, alcohol-related problems, mental retardation, and organic disorders of the nervous system. The Director of the WHO Division of Mental Health (Sartorius, 1977) estimates that 200 million persons have emotional handicaps that are socially crippling and economically significant. In many countries mental disorders are the major cause of disability for two of every five disabled individuals. In economically advanced nations, every third hospital bed is for psychiatric care. In developing lands nearly 20 percent of all people seeking help in general health services have some form of mental disorder.

In considering global trends it is important to remember that about 80 percent of the world's population live in rural areas of developing countries, often under conditions of considerable economic deprivation and limited health resources, amidst rapid socioeconomic and cultural change. For the approximately 800 million persons residing in Southeast Asia there are probably fewer than 1000 mental health workers with graduate university degrees. In much of Africa south of the Sahara a similar scarcity of qualified professionals in all the mental health disciplines exists. This is in contrast to a rate of about one clinical psychiatrist per 80 to 150 patients in most developed countries (WHO Division of Mental Health, 1977). The socioeconomic constraints on expanding mental health services are being experienced everywhere in developed as well as in developing countries (Fowlie, 1978). A reorientation and rethinking of mental health services and professional roles are required if preventive programs are to have a meaningful impact (Mahler, 1975b; Sartorius, 1978).

FAMILY, FAMILY HEALTH, AND FAMILY FUNCTIONING AMIDST ENVIRONMENTAL STRESS

The Family

The concept of the family is probably universal and has existed throughout recorded history, although its form varies and is changing within societies (Carballo, 1975; Elliot, 1970; Johnson, 1975). Although there is a well established tradition of studying the family as a sociocultural institution, interest in its role within the context of mental health and coping with stress is of far more recent origin (Fleck, 1975a; Lidz, 1963).

During the past several years traditional family roles have been reexamined and redebated (Leslie, 1976). While some social scientists believe that the U.S. family is in decline (e.g. Bronfenbrenner, 1977), others hold a more positive view (Bane, 1976;

Glick and Norton, 1977). Although divorce rates are higher, divorced women have increasingly better economic opportunities to support themselves; fewer children are being sent to grand-parents, foster homes, or orphanages. A more pressing problem is what happens to a child while the mother works. Increasing numbers of children are coming home from school to empty houses and remain unsupervised until the mother or father returns from work. Throughout the early and mid 1970s the standard feminist solution was federally funded day care, but the concern of child experts about possible psychological damage helped de-feat recent legislation (Roberts, 1978). More flexible working hours may help resolve the impasse. Men and women have many more options today on whether to marry, have children, or stay married. Still, the ties experienced in family life between parents and children, between two adults making a long-term commitment to each other, are central to living in our society. There is no ready substitute for the family as an institution.

Family Health

Although widely discussed, the concept of family health is seldom linked with health care delivery (Manciaux, 1975; Miller, 1975). The ambiguity of the term is apparent in its definitions, ranging from the health of individual family members to the health of a family as a unit or the sum of the health statuses of individual family members (WHO, 1976). The designation "family physician" is usually applied to the doctor providing health care for all members of a family. The recognition of health as a social value, linking family health with community health and social action, is of relatively recent origin.

During the past two decades there has been a growing apprecia-tion of the family as one of the most significant social forces in human development. Systematic attention is now given to the role of the whole family in individual illness, the impact of en-vironmental stress on family life, and the way the family contri-butes to health care (Litman, 1974; WHO, 1976). However, the family's traditional role as a support system is being reexamined as more liberal definitions of gender roles and alternative life styles are increasingly discussed (Carballo, 1976; Glick and Norton, 1977; Macklin, 1978).

Environmental Stress

Stress may be defined as a nonspecific physical and/or emotional response to a variety of psychosocial and environmental conditions of modern life (Levi and Andersson, 1975; Selye, 1956). The effects of stressful events in the family life cycle are well documented in the clinical literature, particularly the impact on such high risk groups as the young and the uprooted. Coping consists of efforts to solve problems by an individual or family faced with demands highly relevant to their welfare but taxing adaptive resources (Lazarus, 1966; Lazarus, Averill, and Opton, 1974).

The public health concept of being "at risk" has been adopted by the behavioral sciences. What makes for strength and mastery of risk? There is little available knowledge about multimodal coping strategies or common responses to varied stress categories. Coping behavior is influenced by the situation in which it occurs, but there is a paucity of information about how families develop coping ability. What kinds of experiences promote such ability? How can coping skills be identified and taught? There are few suggestions in the biomedical, sociological, and anthropological literature.

Family Functioning

It is curious that the notion of family functioning or coping behavior has seldom been systematically assessed in family sociology (Otto, 1971). Such terms as Family Health, Family Mental Health, Healthy Family Functioning, or Family Coping do not appear in the indices to the 12,850 references on marriage and the family published between 1900 and 1974 (Aldous and Hill, 1967; Aldous and Dahl, 1974; Olson and Dahl, 1975). There is, however, a definition of Family Problems as "any situation that threatens the family's values" (Aldous, 1971).

Sociologists have long thought in terms of resources and role structures that might help families avoid a panic crisis in a stressful situation (Nye, 1976). There is, however, no compilation of what is known about the dynamics and determinants of healthy family functioning and healthy family coping. One reason is the considerable difficulty in developing comparable social indices of family health (McEwan, 1975). As Speer (1970) observed nearly a decade ago, "We know almost nothing about the satisfaction, closeness, meaning achieving, autonomy, problem solving, communication, change, and basic relationship-organizing processes of exceptionally well-functioning, broadly and deeply satisfied families" (p. 273–274).

Psychiatrists and clinical psychologists have also not been of much help. There are numerous examples in the literature of studies of mental disorders affecting poor families living in urban slums. The latest therapeutic technique centers on social network concepts, derived from anthropological research in Africa (Mitchell, 1971) and Europe (Boissevain, 1974). Network intervention is a therapeutic approach which *temporarily* mobilizes family and friendship support systems in a collaborative effort to resolve a family crisis (Caplan and Killilea, 1975; Rueveni, 1977). There is very little research on the reasons or factors that allow a majority of slum families to cope with environmental stress without experiencing mental dysfunction. The academic tradition continues to favor studies of morbidity, of exceptions to the rule, preferring to indulge in the reverse logic of trying to understand the normal as a variation of the pathological (Gadpaille, 1978).

Over the years there has been much discussion of "positive mental health," a concept introduced 20 years ago by Jahoda (1958). Strategies for preventive programs have ranged from parental education (e.g. Charny, 1972) and school services (e.g. Bower, 1969) to specific facilities for low-income or minority groups (e.g. Christmas, 1969) and coping with death of family members (e.g. Goldston, 1977c; Stoddard, 1978). Unhappily, there continues to be a striking gap between service recommendations and illustrative programs (e.g. Cowen, 1977), in part because of the discrepancy between the U.S. political process and the optimal goals of prevention (Brown, 1977).

The concept of healthy family functioning or healthy family coping has also posed problems for the World Health Organization. For example, the Report of the 1975 WHO Study Group on Statistical Indices of Family Health noted that over the past two decades the family has variously been perceived as an independent, dependent, and intervening variable, as well as a precipitating, predisposing, and contributing factor in the etiology, care, and treatment of both physical and mental illness, and as a basic unit of interaction and transaction in health care. It was concluded that "no satisfactory measure of family effectiveness has yet been developed" and that the concept of family functioning "remains ill defined" (WHO, 1976). While there are, as yet, no reported comparative cross-cultural studies of well-functioning families, the impression persists that cohesive family life does reduce stress and improves family coping capabilities (e.g., Buckle, Hoffmeyer, Isambert, Knobloch, Knoblochova, Krapf, Lebovici, Pertejo de Alcami, Pincus and Sandler, 1965; Lewis, Beavers, Gossett and Phillips, 1976).

Despite the reservations, the World Health Organization has given and continues to give priority to improving health care delivery systems strengthening the family, especially in rural areas of developing countries (Newell, 1975). Innovative mental health programs have been reported from every continent (e.g. Baasher, Carstairs, Giel, and Hassler, 1975; David, 1977; Giel and Harding, 1976). It is, of course, realized that any definition of priority needs involves value judgments (Draper, 1973), that health care is an important ingredient for improving the socio-economic conditions of the family (Smith, 1975), and that the structure and operation of preventive services are influenced by a country's political system and ideology as well as realities of health manpower and economic resources (Diop, 1974).

A Proposed Definition

How then can or should healthy family functioning or healthy family coping be defined? I would propose a definition in terms of a family unit (whatever its concept in a given society), effectively coping with cultural-environmental, psychosocial, and socio-economic stresses throughout the diverse phases of the family life cycle. With different ideological views on health and well-being in different societies, it is recognized that there is likely to be more than one model of healthy family functioning or coping.

Although perceptions of families coping with stress have been sensitively portrayed in the arts and in clinical reports, there is as yet no widely accepted theory of healthy family functioning. Few testable hypotheses have emerged, and only a beginning has been made toward developing assessment procedures adaptable to different cultures (Campbell, 1977; Cantril, 1965). Social researchers are still groping toward a better understanding of the complex interrelationships between individuals, family, health, and society, while public health administrators are exploring new ways of responding to service demands generated by rapid social and environmental changes (Lalonde, 1975; Meyer and Sainsbury, 1975; Newell, 1975). Of particular relevance are potentially transferable experiences from developing countries representing different sociopolitical structures and recognizing the influence on family well-being of changes in socioeconomic sectors of society, the priority given to primary prevention over curative medicine, and the enhancement of self-reliance while accepting reduced levels of comprehensiveness and professional skills (Djukanovic and Mach, 1975; Wilenski, 1976; Wolfson, 1976).

THE FAMILY LIFE CYCLE

Structure

Each family experiences its own dynamics of formation, growth, maturation, and dissolution (WHO, 1975b) Crises confronted may be divided into those that are transitional in the family life cycle (e.g. birth of first child or loss of spouse) or nontransitional (e.g. acts of war, uprooting, etc.). Family sociologists have studied effects of sudden shifts in economic status, migration, uprooting, disasters, physical change or incapacity of a family member, and the impact of crises at various stages of the family life cycle. It has been suggested that stress and health hazards are likely to increase when environmental changes occur at critical developmental periods, such as adolescence, first pregnancy, menopause, and retirement. The ability to cope in given situations depends, in part, on perception of threat, motivation, and readiness to respond creatively, available emotional and social supports, and cultural provisions (Coelho, Hamburg, and Adams, 1974; Moos, 1976; Weiss, 1975).

Compared with other social organizations, the average family has distinct disadvantages. Its age composition is heavily weighted by dependents and is of uncertain sex distribution. No other institution is so exposed to crises and stress but so potentially capable of resolving frustration and releasing tension. Yet there are few reports in the literature on successful approaches to providing emotional security for family members, attaining socialization of children and transfer of social values, and achieving a productive and responsible adult life.

Childhood

As noted by several observers (e.g. Huntington, 1975; Rutter, 1976; Vaughn, Huntington, Samuels, Bilmes, and Shapiro, 1975), the literature on delinquency, psychiatric conditions, mental disorders, and other childhood disorders has produced considerable knowledge on *in*security and *in*competence, and on the damage done by marital discord, parental rejection, and institutional rearing. Much less is known about conditions facilitating normal development or why some children with a variety of unfortunate disadvantages still manage to develop a healthy personality, emotional security, and social competence.

In 1976 the WHO Expert Committee on Mental Health considered current trends in childhood mental health and psychosocial development. Persistent and socially handicapping mental disorders affect between 5 and 15 percent of all children aged 3–15 years—and there are 1.3 billion children in the world under 15. Concern with childhood mental disorders is especially appropriate in developing countries, where children under 15 years of age account for about 40 percent of the population, compared to 25 percent in developed countries. Poverty and low socioeconomic status appear to be associated with a greater incidence of mental disorder. The Committee recommended that immediate steps be taken to forestall the rise in psychosocial problems that can be expected to occur in developing countries with increasing industrialization, urbanization, and affluence, and that "this can be done only if decision-makers are made aware of the psychosocial repercussions of socioeconomic policies." It was noted that the majority of effective interventions in childhood mental health are based on human interaction, and that efforts should be made to involve families in treatment and to increase parental skills and confidence. "The aim is to enhance normal family functioning by helping parents to help their children" (WHO, 1977a).

Adolescence

The onset of puberty and physical maturation does not vary

greatly throughout the world, but adolescence as a stage of psychological growth and stress is more closely associated with patterns of a country's economic development, social and cultural values, and historical conditions. In recent years the World Health Organization has given increasing attention to the special problems associated with adolescent development, from pregnancy and abortion (WHO, 1975a) through physical and psychosocial health issues (WHO, 1977b) to societal support services (Shore, Robert, and Jeanneret, 1977) and service-oriented research in adolescent fertility (David, 1978b).

Parenthood

In modern society, preparation for parenthood is a complex and changing task. Parental skills do not necessarily come easily and naturally. In part, parents behave the way they do because of their own childhood experiences. Persons reared in unhappy, discordant, or disrupted homes are more likely to marry in their teens, to have out-of-wedlock children, and to experience unhappy marriages and difficulties in child rearing (Rutter and Madge, 1976; WHO, 1977c). Such links between childhood experiences and subsequent parental behavior are not inevitable. There appears to be considerable capacity for modification of parental behavior, as shown most frequently in the differential treatment of the second child.

The stereotype roles of parenthood are losing their validity amidst cultural changes (Farber, 1973). For example, there appears to be growing social sensitivity to parent-child communication when one parent dies, the death of an infant in the family, and the needs of single-parent families headed by women. Not nearly enough is known about the factors that modify parental behavior or how to help parents improve their relationships with their children, who comprise nearly half of the world's population.

Middle Age and Beyond

Psychosocial research on family coping in the second half of life is only beginning to elicit more interest, although demographic projections indicate that by the year 2000, for example, one in every twenty Europeans will be 75 years or older, a 100 percent increase over the comparable situation in 1950. Similar increases in the population of older persons can be anticipated in other regions of the world (Carballo, 1975). While gerontologists have become increasingly concerned with patterns of social adaptation and the role of the family in the lives of older persons (Fleck 1975b; Troll, 1971), the literature on family coping with midlife crises is particularly sparse (Levinson et al., 1978; Neugarten, 1968).

Self-Reliance

The inherent strengths of the family for coping with stress are being rediscovered in many areas of the developed and developing world. Governments are being advised to meet family needs rather than take over family functions. The impetus is to help families help themselves. Mutual help is an alternate method of coping, involving positive aspects of the family and the community. Mutual help groups typically develop around critical transition points in the family life cycle and are oriented toward shared concerns (Katz, 1976). A related trend is the increased emphasis on family self-care, accompanied by a consumer demand for demystifying medicine, less imposed authority, and greater self-reliance (Illich, 1977; Levin, 1976, 1978; Levin, Katz, and Holst, 1976). An illustrative example is the People's Republic of China with its emphasis on primary prevention rather than curative medicine, training and utilization of large cadres of health auxiliaries in urban and rural settings, and common identification and resolution of problems through fostering family self-reliance (Akhtar, 1975; Sidel and Sidel, 1975; Wolfson and Kane, 1976).

One of the task panel reports to the President's Commission on Mental Health suggests that the rapid growth of community support systems, self help, and alternative services stems only in part from the failure of traditional services to address more than a limited segment of mental health needs. There is also a growing awareness within mental health fields of the importance of inter-relationships among individuals, groups, and society. The Commission's recommendations include identifying and strengthening natural networks, such as families, and initiating research to span knowledge of the ways and effects of support systems, such as the public schools, for example. The task panel conceded that while community support systems are not in competition with professional and formal institutional caregiving systems, they do pose a challenge for mental health professionals who must assume the role of facilitator rather than undisputed authority (APA *Monitor*, June, 1978). The strength of the family is being rediscovered.

COPING WITH CONCEPTION

Conception Control

A particularly salient example of how modern technology has enhanced family coping capability is the development of coitus-independent contraceptive methods and the availability of legal abortion. In most countries the present generation of families is perhaps the first to engage in the conscious process of deciding on the timing and spacing of children, or, indeed, whether to have children. For many couples such deliberate decisions are at times difficult to make, requiring a balancing of personal values, anticipated costs and benefits, and perceived societal pressures (David and Johnson, 1977).

Fertility regulation, whether by pre- or postconceptive means, is neither a socially progressive nor a reactionary idea when viewed in historical perspective (David, 1980). Although many individual physicians have made outstanding contributions and consistently championed the rights of women, organized medicine has often been reluctant to advocate family planning services unless established and operated under medical control (Mohr, 1978; Reed, 1978). It is rarely mentioned that motivation for conception control is not a symptom of illness or a major health issue. Pregnancy termination does involve medical skills but may soon come under increasingly personal control as technology moves closer toward the goal of safe, self-induced early abortion.

Mental Health Aspects

That family planning can be one of the most effective preventive tools in the mental health arsenal was recognized by

Freud (1898) before the turn of the century. Reducing the numbers of unwanted children was one of the major objectives motivating Margaret Sanger and other pioneers of the planned parenthood movement (Reed, 1978). Although often recommended (David, 1971, 1972; Lieberman, 1964), active cooperation between mental health centers and family planning facilities appears to be rare. Extensive searches of government and voluntary association files in 1966 yielded only minimal linkages (Brown, 1966), a situation essentially unchanged in 1971 and 1974 (Goldston, 1977c). Even the risk of unintended pregnancy faced by mentally handicapped persons going on home visits has elicited only limited institutional interest (Abernathy and Grunebaum, 1972; David and Lindner, 1975; David, Smith, and Friedman, 1976). Failure to provide contraceptive counseling is usually ascribed to restrictive interpretations of existing policies, institutional inertia, or other people's presumed sensibilities, thus leaving the family concerned to cope as best possible. Insistence by policy-makers and practitioners on procreative rights seems illusory, given the lack of power and/or competence which frequently impair individual freedom of choice and informed consent for many handicapped persons. Indeed, it seems more unethical not to try to dissuade such couples from unprotected sexual activities, the unintended results of which increase their already disadvantaged position in society (Brody, 1976).

It may well be a truism that there is no psychologically painless way to cope with an unwanted pregnancy. Although an abortion may elicit feelings of guilt, regret, or loss, alternative solutions such as adding a baby to an already strained family situation are also likely to be accompanied by psychological problems for the woman, the child, the family, and society (David, 1978a). This is one of the findings in a longitudinal case control study of 220 children born to women twice denied abortion for the same pregnancy in Prague, Czechoslovakia, during 1961–63. The control group consisted of 220 children born to mothers who had not requested an abortion. The children were matched for sex, birth order, number of siblings, and school class (often in the same school); the mothers were matched for age, marital status, and socioeconomic situation as determined by the husband's occupation and presence in the home. Data were obtained from clinic records and school reports, medical and psychological examinations of the children, and structured interviews with the parents by a team of professionals. Schoolroom sociograms, rating scales, and questionnaires were also used. Analysis of all the findings suggest that the psychosocial development of the unwanted children was more problem prone than the accepted children; boys and only children seemed to be particularly effected (David, Matejcek, Dytrych, Schuller, and Friedman, 1977; Dytrych, Matejcek, Schuller, David, and Friedman, 1975; Matejcek, Dytrych, and Schuller, 1978). Further adolescent development of these children will continue to be monitored.

In considering rapid developments in conception control, one needs to recall that courses in human sexuality and discussion of fertility regulation are a relatively recent phenomenon in medical and nursing schools (Lief and Karlen, 1976). Protected by conscience clauses in prevailing statutes, many physicians and nurses decline to staff abortion services. As one consequence, eight out of ten counties in the United States did not have a single abortion facility in 1976 (Sullivan, Tietze, and Dryfoos, 1977), a situation little changed in 1978. A similar trend prevails in those Western European countries which legalized abortion on request in recent years. As long as a significant number of health service providers remain personally ambivalent, it is not surprising that outmoded attitudes toward sex education and contraceptive practices become major determinants in responding to women's requests for terminating unwanted pregnancies.

Women's Choice

The World Plan of Action adopted by 135 governments at the 1974 World Population Conference in Bucharest (David, 1975) states that "all couples and individuals have the basic human right to decide freely and responsibly the number and spacing of their children and to have the information, education, and means to do so." Such a declaration by official representatives of more than 95 percent of the world's population would have been unthinkable even a few years ago. When society has reached the stage in which all pregnancies are planned and wanted, abortion services may well become obsolete. Until that time, access to all safe means of conception control should be a choice a woman is free to make without undue restrictions imposed by a still largely male-dominated governing structure.

It has not been widely reported that the April 1978 Report of the President's Commission on Mental Health (1978) included a firmly worded position in favor of "selective and optional termination of pregnancy when medically indicated." (Medical indications were not defined but presumably include psychosocial factors.) The Subpanel on the "Mental Health of Women" further recommended that, "given the mental health implications of abortion, all restrictions on federal funding for abortion services be eliminated," underscoring the need for reproductive freedom "because of its particular importance in the prevention of mental disorders among women." Within the Panel on "Mental Health and American Families," subpanels on "General Issues and Adult Years" and on "Infants and Children" addressed issues of contraception and abortion for adolescents. One of the recommendations was that "efforts to discourage pregnancy and early parenthood should be given highest priority." The Panel further recommended programs to "make the public aware of adolescent sexuality and help parents to deal with it." It will be of interest to see what happens to the recommendations on abortion which are contradictory to present federal policy (Rosoff, 1978).

QUALITY OF LIFE AND DEVELOPMENT PLANNING

Quality of Life

Although there are multiple definitions of the diverse components comprising the concept "quality of life," there appears to be consensual agreement that personal well-being and successful family coping are among the key factors (Campbell, 1977; Flanagan, 1978). Population issues and quality of life concerns interact and affect each other causally and consequentially (Zeidenstein, 1978). For example, as couples perceive an improvement in their quality of life, the desire to limit family size frequently increases. Conversely, rapid population growth can aggravate the socioeconomic stressors that lower quality of life, make it more difficult to cope, and increase the potential for family disruption, mental ill health, and psychopathology. The evidence from developed and developing countries is persuasive that effective family planning improves the quality of life and family coping capabilities (e.g. Katz, 1972; Lieberman, 1975; Mukherjee, 1975; Munandar, 1970; Omran, 1974; Park, Chung and Hans, 1975; Wishik and Bernard, 1969).

One of the most promising global trends is the gradual slowing of population growth (Freedman, 1978). Available data from the World Fertility Survey indicate that 10 of 13 developing countries with a population of 35 million or more reported significant declines in the crude birth rate from 1965 to 1975, as well as a marked rise in age at marriage (Mauldin, 1978). Still, high fertility makes economic and social sense in rural areas where a surviving child is expected to produce more than it consumes (Arnold, Bulatao, Buripakdi, Chung, Fawcett, Iritani, Lee, and Wu, 1975) and where a woman's status is primarily dependent on her bearing sons who are viewed as assuring family lineage and providing economic security for the parents in their old age (Williamson, 1976).

The economics of large versus small families, or the desire of women to have fewer children, is not significantly different between major countries currently experiencing quite diverse population swings, e.g. India and Indonesia. What *is* different is the motivation of political leaders and the willingness of governments to support effective policies and voluntary programs across the entire country; these are usually designed to reduce infant mortality to assure the survival of more children, provide more educational and employment opportunities for women, thus developing alternative status roles, and communicate the availability and accessibility of all methods of family planning to those couples who want them. That is what has helped to reduce the birth rate and family size so dramatically in, for example, Indonesia (Hull, Hull, and Singarimbun, 1977) and in Thailand (O'Donnell, 1977; U.S. Bureau of the Census, 1978). When viewed in historical perspective, these movements toward achieving a better quality of life have been extraordinarily rapid (Freedman, 1978).

Observations from recent psychosocial research suggest that there are differences in planning behavior and future time orientation between successful contraceptors and nonacceptors of available services, whether poor illiterate Indian villagers (Friedman and David, 1977) or literate urban adolescents (e.g. Miller and Godwin, 1977; Mindick, Oskamp, and Berger, 1977). There are important differences between couples in the way in which they believe they can control their own destinies and the degree to which they have aspirations for a more modern life style. As rural couples see more evidence of successful planning in agriculture, economic development, and health care, they are likely to become better family planners. In the more developed countries of Europe and North America the ever-escalating costs of child rearing and the family need for the woman's income may explain the current preference among young couples for two or fewer children (David and Johnson, 1977). The increase in stable marriage-like nonmarital cohabitation and in child-free families may herald a further realignment in couple relationships and quality of life values (Glick and Norton, 1977; Trost, 1978b).

Development Planning

To guard against oversimplification it is important to remember that rapid population growth is not the sole source or even main cause of an impoverished quality of life in the developing world. Fertility is only one of several threads in the complex tapestry of people's lives (Zeidenstein, 1978). Programs advocating conception control, touching upon the most intimate aspects of a couple's private behavior and their strategies for family survival, well-being, and quality of life, must be associated with other culturally sensitive socioeconomic health care and nutritional development efforts designed to improve the community's quality of life. When supported by an actively committed national leadership, local community efforts can foster self-reliance, enhance the quality of life, and strengthen family coping capability.

A major priority for encouraging international action is the improvement of the social and economic status of women. Although advances are often trumpeted in the media, it is seldom acknowledged that modernization programs in developing countries have generally tended to enhance the role of men at the expense of women. In the economically most deprived nations, women are the poorest of the poor. Until the well-being of these women is improved, particularly those now reaching the fertile years, family coping capabilities are likely to be further eroded amidst societal upheavals. Enlightened development planning requires that priority be given to removing the attitudinal, conceptual, and political barriers erected by male-dominated societies and fully recognizing and supporting women's educational needs, career potentials, and changed roles (Buvenic, 1976; Naur, 1976; Zeidenstein, 1978).

PREVENTION PROMOTION

An Emerging Social Revolution

Recognition of the impact on the health sector of environmental changes and stress is accompanied by a global concern with the eroding quality of life and awareness that family well-being and coping are linked to progress in socioeconomic development. The relevance of conventional health services is being increasingly reconsidered. There is greater awareness that issues of socioeconomic development were not a major consideration in the evolution of the Western model of medicine, with its emphasis on individual care by a highly trained physician or medical staff. The concept of service is being redefined, reversing the traditional reactive posture of responding to requests for assistance. Different concepts of health promotion, primary prevention, and health care delivery are being explored, especially in the rural areas of developing countries, where most of the world's population reside. Citizen participation and community self-reliance are encouraged as policy-makers are forced to decide between different options in the allocation of scarce resources, evaluating the impact of health sector priorities on the rate of national economic development, ideological values, and political goals (Meyer and Sainsbury, 1975; Ugalde, 1978).

In many countries promotion of primary prevention is used as a leading edge for experimentation with new social forms designed to change society's structure. In his Report to the 1975 World Health Assembly, the Director-General (Mahler, 1976a) postulated a model of primary health care which emphasizes self-reliance and improved living conditions for individuals, families, and communities. Promotion of prevention headed the list of measures, which also included curative, rehabilitative, and community development activities. Later that year in a report to the WHO Executive Board, the Director-General (Mahler,

1975a) emphasized the importance of psychosocial factors, particularly in services for uprooted families and those living under conditions of rapid social change. Among the recommendations were studies of family functioning, which would link family health and mental health programs. In a subsequent address to WHO Regional Committees, the Director-General (Mahler, 1975c) reemphasized the relationship of health improvement to social and economic development. The theme of prevention was restated in the Report to the 1976 World Health Assembly, termed "a social revolution in public health" (Mahler, 1976b), and further stated in the address to the 1978 World Health Assembly (Mahler, 1978b). The Deputy Director-General of WHO similarly noted that health services too fequently lack relevance to people's needs and that "there is room for social revolution in health which should pave the way for more equitable distribution of health resources" (Lambo, 1975a, 1975b, 1976).

Migration and Uprooting

Problems of uprooting and migration have long been of special relevance to the World Health Organization, the High Commission for Refugees, and the World Federation for Mental Health (David, 1968). The concepts of migration and uprooting have many meanings. Migration may be intercontinental, intracontinental, internal (e.g. within one country), or local (within the community). Movements may include brief visits, seasonal work, and/or seeking of a new habitat in the city or the country. Reasons for migration and uprooting range from environmental catastrophes, economic deprivation, and political and religious persecution to social and psychological upheavals and industrialization and urbanization often associated with temporary or longer-term family separation (Zwingmann and Pfister-Ammende, 1973).

Men and women have been on the move since the dawn of human existence. Changing from one social environment to another is often provocative of social dislocation, with family adjustment becoming more difficult with the increasing complexity of urbanization and industrialization (Bernard, 1974). Studies of mental health/adaptation problems of involuntary migrants have usually been concerned with prevalence, incidence, etiology, and symptomatology, seldom with coping and family adjustment (Brody, 1970; David, 1970). Particularly sparse is the literature on healthy family functioning among voluntary migrants moving from the country to a city.

By 1970, about 864 million (24 percent of the world's population) lived in 1777 cities, each of more than 100,000 inhabitants. By the year 2000, about 40 percent of the population is expected to live in urban areas, with 25 percent of the cities having a population exceeding one million. In developing countries about one third of the city dwellers live in slums and shantytowns; 50 percent are children (UNICEF, 1975). With the accelerated process of urbanization and industrialization in these countries, traditional social systems are changing more rapidly than was the experience in developed nations. Patterns of family structure and control are being invalidated (WHO Assembly, 1975).

Considering the long history of migration and the magnitude of the problem, there is a surprising lack of systematically accumulated knowledge (Shaw, 1975). Discussions with representatives of international, national, and local service organizations suggest that field workers are often aware of likely adjustment problems, and are interested in helping families to cope. There is, however, only a limited record of experience gained in different cultures with recommendations for assisting future migrants.

SOCIOPOLITICAL REALITIES

There is a growing awareness that the promotion of primary prevention programs, like other elements of health care, reflect a society's political, social, economic, and cultural history as well as current structure (Sidel and Sidel, 1977). In the thirty some years since the end of World War II and the founding of the United Nations and its specialized organizations, the sociopolitical character of health policy has gradually attained increasing recognition, despite the massive opposition of organized medicine in industrial and developing countries.

In the developing world with its shortages of professional resources amidst growing populations, there is today greater discussion among health planners of the relationship to family coping capability of inequitable income distribution, employment, and economic opportunities. This is often accompanied by a political insistence on social relevance in technical assistance, whether in the delivery of improved health services to the rural poor or in university-based social science research in fertility behavior. The notion of the impartiality and implicit value of research for the sake of new knowledge is seriously questioned. The fierce defense by United States academic researchers of their freedom to neglect sociopolitical realities is perceived as incredibly naive by colleagues abroad.

If the knowledge of differences among people and countries is to be used constructively, such observations cannot be swept aside as insignificant variations from some theoretical norm, whether based on the postulates of a Viennese physician writing early in this century or a latter-day theoretician. The recognition that there is more than one perception of the world and that there is no implicit correctness in any one (apart from the difficult-to-achieve test of usefulness in its own setting) is a necessary first step for the development of any scientific discipline in the mental health field. "The need to share resources must be accompanied by a willingness to accept that no particular philosophical, ethical, and cultural system is inherently better than any other" (Sartorius, 1977).

Utilizing Available Knowledge

It has been said that "the road to political inaction is paved with unused research reports" (Henry, 1976). Discussions at international meetings and regional seminars confirm that serious problems exist in bringing already available and cogent social science research findings to bear in a continuous and systematic way on the refining of priorities and implementation of policies, whether the area be primary prevention of psychopathology or unintended adolescent premarital pregnancy. While researchers shrug their shoulders about the "underutilization" of their findings, policy-makers and government planners complain that social science research is rarely relevant to immediate policy issues or couched in an "employable" format.

The effectiveness of dissemination methods and the barriers to the use of policy-relevant information by decision-makers have been well reviewed (e.g. Batscha, 1976; Caplan, 1975). Innovative approaches have come from the East-West Communication Center (e.g. Kar, 1977) and particularly from the Research Utilization Projects of the Population Center Foundation in the Philippines (e.g. Reyes, 1976). There is clear need for fostering dialogue between policy-makers and social science researchers. Involving those close to decision-making in the process of establishing research priorities and the early phases of research planning is likely to enhance better perception of realities and eventual utilization of service-oriented recommendations. At the international level, information centers and clearinghouses have demonstrated the utility of fostering transnational communication and regional awareness of factors making for success or failure in prevention-promotion programs.

TOWARD A THEORY OF HEALTHY FAMILY FUNCTIONING

Choice Behavior

Individuals comprising a family unit are constantly faced with choices and alternative courses of action that will determine, at least in part, healthy family functioning and coping with stress. Awareness of these points, the extent to which alternative courses are recognized, and the degree to which choices are based upon realistic appraisals of different costs and consequences are believed to be keystones of healthy family functioning. Public policies and their implementation, the provision of information, education, and services, and the social-motivational factors that encourage or discourage various alternatives are subjective aspects of the environment which must be appraised by family members along with their own needs and desires. Family functioning involves more than one person and is subject to change with time; understanding the communication process and the perceptions of family members is essential to an understanding of healthy family functioning.

The Decision-Making Process

In nearly all sociocultural contexts, an individual's awareness of his or her partner's perceptions is of critical importance. However clever social scientists may be in unearthing valid information about knowledge, attitudes, and even the individual practices of one person, false conclusions may be drawn about the behavior of this individual in conjunction with his/her partner and, consequently, on how healthy family-functioning behavior or coping is determined or modified. Valuable lessons can be drawn from the psychosocial model of fertility-choice behavior, which emphasizes the subjective assessment of the environment by the individual and the importance of the two partners in determining each other's choice behavior (Friedman, Johnson, and David, 1976).

Research Planning

In studies of healthy family functioning and coping, it is critical to know not only what is available in the environment but, especially, what family members believe to be available. Receptiveness to information can be restricted by conceptually elusive yet nonetheless powerful psychological forces, such as alienation. Similarly, decisions have to be reached on how study populations might be defined, the stage in the family life cycle of the population group studied, the nature of the data to be collected, and methodological design factors.

The possibility of defining populations for study on the basis of self-selecting biopsychosocial factors makes cross-cultural comparisons more meaningful. While cultural and environmental factors differ, the principles of healthy family functioning and coping do not. It is these principles that form part of the theory of healthy family functioning and, in a classical pattern, the development of new hypotheses for behavioral testing.

THE YOUNG FAMILY: A PROPOSAL FOR COOPERATIVE CROSS–CULTURAL RESEARCH

The Basic Unit of Healthy Family Functioning and Coping

Although much attention has been devoted to the relationship between sociodemographic variables and indicators of dysfunction, relatively little consideration has been given to mutable psychosocial variables such as healthy family functioning, health maintenance, and coping behavior. Already available knowledge is used primarily by a minority of families who appear to engage in planning behavior encompassing all parts of family life, including health. To gain a comparative cross-cultural perspective, it is proposed that coordinated research be conducted into the behavioral attributes of healthy family functioning in the early years of marriage (or consensual unions or other marriage-like relationships). What distinguishes the young families who plan effectively from others who do not, at similar stages of the life cycle and in different cultures experiencing rapid social change? What information and practical recommendations can be provided to policy-makers to enlarge this group of effective early planners and copers? How can successful coping be defined, taught, and communicated?

The basic unit of successful coping and healthy family functioning is likely to be the young family. Categories of variables of seemingly universal relevance will have to be delineated and a set of structured data needs prepared in order to test hypotheses concerned with coping behavior in developed and developing countries. The focus could be on coping with specific concerns ranging from migration and uprooting to fertility regulation. Although cultural differences exist, comparisons within and between cultures offer tests for hypotheses, especially if selected families can be followed through the family life cycle.

Methodological Advantages

There are major methodological advantages to studying recently formed family units. This population is relatively small in any given society, is usually definable, and (with proper precautions) can be approached. It is likely that a proportionately large, representative, and relatively good sample can be obtained in countries willing to cooperate. Since in most societies nearly all individuals "marry," the proposed group usually represents a thorough cross-section of the population (albeit at one point in their life cycles) so that information about them is likely to cut across all socioeconomic classes and provide useful information for the nation as a whole. At this stage in the life cycle, the couple is also a self-determining social unit, comparable across cultures, because the basis for the group is a universal stage in a person's existence. By letting the group "self-select" rather than selecting them on the basis of age or other variables, which have different social significance in different cultures, more cross-culturally comparable populations are obtained. Pilot studies are currently in progress in Geneva, Switzerland (Kellerhals, 1977), and Gävle, Sweden (Trost, 1978a), both using separate but simultaneous interviews with marital partners.

SUMMING UP

In its recent Report, the President's Commission on Mental Health (1978) observed that "the history of public health in the past century provides ample evidence that programs designed to prevent disease and disorder can be effective and economical. The mental health field has yet to use available knowledge in a comparable effort." The Commission's Report described efforts to prevent mental illness or promote mental health as "unstructured, unfocused, and uncoordinated," commanding "few dollars, limited personnel, and little interest at levels where resources are sufficient to achieve results" (p. 53). As a first step toward achieving increased visibility of prevention as a national policy, the Commission recommended that a Center for Prevention be established within the National Institute of Mental Health to support prevention research, evaluate existing programs, and replicate effective prevention approaches.

If the Commission's recommendations are implemented, I hope that consideration will be given to the lessons already learned and that we do not reinvent the wheel. I urge a long and practical look at what has been accomplished by different ideological approaches in other lands and the applicability of transnational experience to what is administratively possible and politically feasible in the United States. Within such a framework, strengthening healthy family functioning and healthy family-coping resources would be among society's best investments.

REFERENCES

Abernathy, V. D., and Grunebaum, H. Toward a family planning program in psychiatric hospitals. *American Journal of Public Health*, 1972, *62*, 1638-1646.

Akhtar, S. *Health care in the People's Republic of China*. Ottawa: International Development Research Centre, 1975.

Alcohol, Drug Abuse, and Mental Health Administration. *Summary proceedings: Tripartite conference on prevention*. Rockville, Md.: ADAMHA, 1977, DHEW Publication No. (ADM), 77-484.

Aldous, J. A framework for the analysis of family problem solving. In J. Aldous, T. Condon, R. Hill, M. Straus, and I. Tallman (Eds.). *Family problem solving: A symposium on theoretical, methodological, and substantive concerns*. Hinsdale, Ill.: Dryden Press, 1971.

Aldous, J., and Dahl, N. *International bibliography of research in marriage and the family: 1965-1972* (Vol. 2). Minneapolis: University of Minnesota Press, 1974.

Aldous, J., and Hill, R. *International bibliography of research in marriage and the family: 1900-1964*. Minneapolis: University of Minnesota Press, 1967.

APA *Monitor*, June 1978.

Arnold, F., Bulatao, R. A., Buripakdi, C., Chung, B. J., Fawcett, J. T., Iritani, T., Lee, S. J., and Wu, T. S. *The value of children: A cross-national study* (Vol. 1). Honolulu: East-West Population Institute, 1975.

Baasher, T. A., Carstairs, G. M., Giel, R., and Hassler, F. R. (Eds.), *Mental health services in developing countries*. Geneva: World Health Organization, 1975. Offset Publication No. 22.

Bane, M. J. *Here to stay: American families in the 20th century*. New York: Basic Books, 1976.

Batscha, R. *The effectiveness of dissemination methods for social and economic development research*. Paris: OECD Development Centre, 1976.

Bernard, W. S. Orientation and counseling; their nature and role in the adaptation and integration of permanent immigrants. *International Migration*, 1974, *12*, 182-200.

Boissevain, J. *Friends of friends—networks, manipulators, and coalitions*. New York: St. Martin's Press, 1974.

Bower, E. M. *Early identification of emotionally handicapped children in school*. Springfield, Ill.: Thomas, 1969.

Brody, E. B. (Ed.). *Behavior in new environments: Adaptation of migrant populations*. Beverly Hills, Cal.: Sage Publications, 1970.

Brody, E. B. Reproductive freedom, coercion, and justice. *Social Science and Medicine*, 1976, *10*, 553-557.

Bronfenbrenner, U. The erosion of the American family. *Psychology Today*, May 1977.

Brown, B. Quoted in *Family planning and mental health*. Washington, D.C.: Population Crisis Committee and NIMH, 1966.

Brown, B. The politics of prevention. In *Summary proceedings of tri-*

partite conference on prevention. Rockville, Md.: ADAMHA, 1977. DHEW Publication No. (ADM)77-484, 85–88.

Buckle, D., Hoffmeyer, H., Isambert, A., Knobloch, F., Knoblochova, J., Krapf, E. E., Lebovici, S., Pertejo de Alcami, J., Pincus, L., and Sandler, J. *Aspects of family mental health in Europe*. Geneva: World Health Organization, Public Health Papers, 1965, No. 28.

Buvenic, M. *Women and world development: An annotated bibliography*. Washington, D.C.: Overseas Development Council, 1976.

Campbell, A. Subjective measures of well-being. In G. W. Albee and J. M. Joffe (Eds.), *Primary prevention of psychopathology. Vol. 1: The issues*. Hanover, N.H.: University Press of New England, 1977, 321–337.

Cantril, H. *The patterns of human concerns*. New Brunswick, N.J.: Rutgers University Press, 1965.

Caplan, G., and Killilea, M. *Support systems and mutual help*. New York: Grune and Stratton, 1975.

Caplan, N. The use of social science information by federal executives. In G. M. Lyons (Ed.), *Social research and public policy*. Hanover, N.H.: Dartmouth College, 1975.

Carballo, M. Need for adaptation. *World Health*, September 1975, 34–37.

Carballo, M. A promise unfulfilled. *World Health*, August/September 1976, 16–21.

Charny, I. Parental intervention with one another on behalf of their child: A breakthrough tool in preventing emotional disturbance. *Journal of Contemporary Psychotherapy*, 1972, *5*, 19–26.

Christmas, J. J. Philosophy and practice of socio-psychiatric rehabilitation in a black urban ghetto. *American Journal of Orthopsychiatry*, 1969, *39*, 651–661.

Coelho, G. V., Hamburg, D. A., and Adams, J. E. (Eds.), *Coping and adaptation*. New York: Basic Books, 1974.

Cowen, E. L. Psychologists and primary prevention: Blowing the cover story. *American Journal of Community Psychology*, 1977, *5*, 481–490.

David, H. P. (Ed.). *Migration, mental health and community services*. Geneva: American Joint Distribution Committee, 1968.

David, H. P. Involuntary international migration. In E. B. Brody (Ed.), *Behavior in new environments*. Beverly Hill, Cal.: Sage Publications, 1970.

David, H. P. Mental health and family planning. *Family Planning Perspectives*, 1971, *3* (2), 2–23.

David, H. P. Unwanted pregnancies: Costs and alternatives. In C. F. Westoff and R. Parke, Jr. (Eds.), *Demographic and social aspects of population growth*. Washington, D.C.: U.S. Government Printing Office, 1972.

David, H. P. Report from Bucharest: The World Population Conference, 1974. *Journal of Psychiatric Nursing*, 1975, *13*, 32–34.

David, H. P. Healthy family functioning: An overview. Geneva: World Health Organization, 1977, Document MNH/77.7.

David, H. P. Psychosocial studies of abortion in the United States. In H. P. David, H. L. Friedman, J. van der Tak, and M. Sevilla (Eds.), *Abortion in psychosocial perspective: Trends in transnational research*. New York: Springer, 1978. (*a*)

David, H. P. Adolescent fertility: needed service oriented research. Invited keynote paper presented to the WHO European Region Meeting on "Service Oriented Research in Adolescent Fertility in Europe," Warnemünde, German Democratic Republic, April 1978. (*b*)

David, H. P. Abortion policies. In P. J. Huntingford (Ed.), *Techniques of abortion and sterilization*. London: Academic Press, 1980.

David, H. P., and Johnson, R. L. Fertility regulation in early childbearing years: Psychosocial and psychoeconomic aspects. *Preventive Medicine*, 1977, *6*, 52–64.

David, H. P., and Lindner, M. A. Family planning for the mentally handicapped. *Bulletin of the World Health Organization*, 1975, *52*, 155–161.

David, H. P., Matejcek, Z., Dytrych, A., Schüller, V., and Friedman, H. L. Developmental consequences of unwanted pregnancies: Studies from Sweden and Czechoslovakia. In Y. H. Poortinga (Ed.), *Basic problems in cross-cultural psychology*. Amsterdam: Swets and Zeitlinger, 1977.

David, H. P., Smith, J. D., and Friedman, E. Family planning services for persons handicapped by mental retardation. *American Journal of Public Health*, 1976, *66*, 1053–1057.

Diop, S. M. B. *The place of mental health in the development of public health services*. Brazzaville: World Health Organization, AFRO Technical Papers, No. 8, 1974.

Djukanovic, V., and Mach, E. P. *Alternative approaches to meeting basic health needs in developing countries*. Geneva: World Health Organization, 1975.

Draper, P. Value judgements in health planning. *Community Medicine*, 1973, *129*, 372–374.

Dytrych, Z., Matejcek, Z., Schüller, V., David, H. P., and Friedman, H. L. Children born to women denied abortion. *Family Planning Perspectives*, 1975, *7*, 165–171.

Elliot, K. *The family and its future*. London: Churchill, 1970.

Farber, B. *Family and kinship in modern society*. Glenview, Ill.: Scott, Foresman, 1973.

Flanagan, J. C. A research approach to improving our quality of life. *American Psychologist*, 1978, *33*, 138–147.

Fleck, S. The family and psychiatry. In A. Freedman, H. Kaplan, and B. Sadock (Eds.), *Comprehensive textbook of psychiatry* (2nd ed.). Baltimore: Williams and Wilkins, 1975. (*a*)

Fleck, S. Unified health services and family-focused primary care. *International Journal of Psychiatry in Medicine*, 1975, *6*, 501–515. (*b*)

Fowlie, H. C. *Constraints in mental health services development: Report of a working group*. Copenhagen: World Health Organization Regional Office for Europe, 1978.

Freedman, R. Social science research in population in Asia. Prepared for presentation to the House Select Committee on Population, April 27, 1978.

Freud, S. Sexuality in the etiology of neuroses. *Wiener klinische Rundschau*, 1898, Nos. 2, 4, 5, and 7. Also in *Collected Papers*, Vol. 1. New York: Basic Books, 1959.

Friedman, H. L., and David, L. H. Family planning among rural Indian couples: A psychosocial comparison of acceptors and non-acceptors. Unpublished paper, 1977.

Friedman, H. L., Johnson, R. L., and David, H. P. The dynamics of fertility choice behavior: A pattern for research. In S. Newman & V. Thompson (Eds.), *Population psychology: Research and educational issues*. Bethesda, Md: Center for Population Research, 1976.

Gadpaille, W. J. Commentary. *Medical Aspects of Human Sexuality*, February 1978, p. 177.

Giel, R., and Harding, T. W. Psychiatric priorities in developing countries. *British Journal of Psychiatry*, 1976, *128*, 513–522.

Glick, P. C., and Norton, A. J. Marrying, divorcing, and living together in the U.S. today. *Population Bulletin*, 1977, *32*(5).

Goldston, S. E. Defining primary prevention. In G. W. Albee and J. M. Joffe (Eds.), *Primary prevention of psychopathology. Vol. 1: The issues*. Hanover, N.H.: University Press of New England, 1977. (*a*)

Goldston, S. E. Primary prevention: A view from the federal level. In G. W. Albee and J. M. Joffee (Eds.), *Primary prevention of psychopathology. Vol. 1: The issues*. Hanover, N.H.: University Press of New England, 1977. (*b*)

Goldston, S. E. An overview of primary prevention programming. In D. C. Klein & S. E. Goldston (Eds.), *Primary prevention: An idea whose time has come*. Rockville, Md: National Institute of Mental Health, 1977. (*c*)

Henry, P. M. Preface to R. Batscha, *"The effectiveness of dissemination methods for social and economic development research."* Paris: OECD Development Centre, 1976.

Hull, T. H., Hull, V. J., and Singarimbun, M. Indonesia's family planning story: Success and challenge. *Population Bulletin*, 1977, *32*(6).

Huntington, D. S. Learning from infants and families. *Journal of the Association for Care of Children in Hospital*, 1975, *4* (1), 5–38.

Illich, I. *Medical nemesis*. New York: Bantam, 1977.

Jahoda, M. *Current concepts of positive mental health*. New York: Basic Books, 1958.

Johnson, B. C. A. Changing patterns. *World Health*, September 1975, 16.

Kar, S. B. *Management and utilization of population communication research*. Honolulu: East-West Communications Institute, 1977.

Katz, A. H. with Bender, E. *The strength in US: Self help in the modern world*. New York: Franklin-Watts, 1976.

Katz, J. Family planning, mental health, and preventive psychiatry. *Mental Health in Australia*, 1972, *4*, 138–143.

Kellerhals, J. Personal communication, 1977.

Kennedy, P. W. International grant making and U.S. foundations. *Foundation News*, 1977, *18*, 40–47.

Kessler, M., and Albee, G. W. An overview of the literature of primary prevention. In G. W. Albee and J. M. Joffe (Eds.), *Primary prevention of psychopathology. Vol. 1: The issues*. Hanover, N.H.: University Press of New England, 1977.

Klein, D. C., and Goldston, S. E. (Eds.). *Primary prevention: An idea whose time has come*. Rockville, Md.: National Institute of Mental Health, 1977.

Lalonde, M. *A new perspective on the health of Canadians*. Ottawa: Information Canada, 1975.

Lambo, T. A. Foreword to *Promoting health in the human environment*. Geneva: World Health Organization, 1975. (*a*)

Lambo, T. A. Total Health. *World Health*, December 1975, No. 3. (*b*)

Lambo, T. A. The world situation. *Royal Society of Health Journal*, 1976, *96*, 243–245.

Lazarus, R. S. *Psychological stress and the coping process*. New York: McGraw-Hill, 1966.

Lazarus, R. S., Averill, J. R., and Opton, E. M., Jr. The psychology of coping: Issues of research and assessment. In E. V. Coelho, D. A. Hamburg, and J. Adams (Eds.), *Coping and adaptation*. New York: Basic Books, 1974.

Leslie, G. R. *The family in social context* (3rd ed.). New York: Oxford, 1976.

Levi, L., and Andersson, L. *Psychosocial stress: Population, environment, and quality of life*. New York: Spectrum Publications, 1975.

Levin, L. S. Self-care: An international perspective. *Social Policy*, 1976, *7*, 70–75.

Levin, L. S. Self-care: An emerging component of the health care system. *Hospital and Health Services Administration*, 1978, *23*, 17–25.

Levin, L. S., Katz, A. H., and Holst, E. *Self-care: Lay initiatives in health*. New York: Prodist, 1976.

Levinson, D. J., with C. N. Darrow, E. B. Klein, M. H. Levinson, and B. McKee. *The seasons of a man's life*. New York: Knopf, 1978.

Lewis, J. M., Beavers, W. R., Gossett, J. T., and Phillips, V. A. *No single thread: Psychological health in family systems*. New York: Brunner/Mazel, 1976.

Lidz, T. *The family and human adaptation*. New York: International Universities Press, 1963.

Lieberman, E. J. Preventive psychiatry and family planning. *Journal of Marriage and the Family*, 1964, *26*, 471–477.

Lieberman, E. J. Family formation and development: The primary institution. In E. J. Lieberman (Ed.), *Mental Health: The public health challenge*. Washington, D.C.: American Public Health Association, 1975.

Lief, H. I., and Karlen, A. (Eds.). *Sex education in medicine*. New York: Halsted, 1976.

Litman, T. J. The family as a basic unit in health and medical care: A social behavioral overview. *Social Science and Medicine*, 1974, *8*, 495–519.

Macklin, E. D. Nonmarital heterosexual cohabitation. *Marriage and Family Review*, 1978, *1*(2), 1–12.

Mahler, H. Psychosocial factors and health: Report to the 57th Session of the Executive Board. Geneva: World Health Organization, 1975, Document EB 57/22. (*a*)

Mahler, H. A moral revolution. *World Health*, September 1975, No. 3. (*b*)

Mahler, H. Health for all by the year 2000, *WHO Chronicle*, 1975, *29*, 457–461. (*c*)

Mahler, H. *The work of WHO, 1975*. Annual report of the Director-General to the World Health Assembly. Geneva: World Health Organization Official Records, 1976, No. 229. (*a*)

Mahler, H. A social revolution in public health. *WHO Chronicle*, 1976, *30*, 475–480. (*b*)

Mahler, H. Report of the Director-General to the 31st World Health Assembly. Geneva: World Health Organization, 1978; Document WHA/9. (*a*)

Mahler, H. *World health is indivisible*. Geneva: World Health Organization, 1978, Document WHA/5. (*b*)

Manciaux, M. The health of the family. *World Health*, September 1975, Nos. 4–9.

Matejcek, Z., Dytrych, Z., and Schüler, V. Children from unwanted pregnancies. *Acta Psychiatrica Scandinavia*, 1978, *57*, 67–90.

Mauldin, W. P. Patterns of fertility decline in developing countries, 1950–1975. *Studies in Family Planning*, 1978, *9*, 75–84.

May, J. T. (Ed.). *Family mental health: Annotated bibliography*. Rockville, Md.: National Institute of Mental Health, 1974.

McEwan, P. J. M. *The search for social indices of family health*. Geneva: World Health Organization, 1975, Document DSI/WP/75.6.

Meyer, E. E., and Sainsbury, P. (Eds.). *Promoting health in the human environment*. Geneva: World Health Organization, 1975.

Miller, F. J. W. The target. *World Health*, September 1975, 10–15.

Miller, L. (Ed.). *Mental health in rapid changing society*. Jerusalem: Academic Press, 1971.

Miller, W. B., and Godwin, R. K. *Psyche and Demos*. New York: Oxford, 1977.

Mindick, B., Oskamp, S., and Berger, D. E. Prediction of success or failure in birth planning: An approach to prevention of individual and family stress. *American Journal of Community Psychology*, 1977, *5*, 447–460.

Mitchell, J. C. (Ed.). *Social networks in urban situations: Analyses of personal relationships in African towns*. Manchester, England: Manchester University Press, 1971.

Mohr, J. C. *Abortion in America*. New York: Oxford, 1978.

Moos, R. H. (Ed.). *Human adaptation: Coping with life crises*. Lexington, Mass.: Heath, 1976.

Mukherjee, B. N. Marital decision-making and family planning. *Journal of Family Welfare*, 1975, *21*, 77–101.

Munandar, S. C. U. Family Planning. *Psychologi* (Jakarta), 1970, *2*, 38–47.

Naur, M. Population policy: An escape, politically and scientifically, using India as an example. *Acta Sociologia*, 1976, *19*, 137–145.

Neugarten, B. L. *Middle age and aging*. Chicago: University of Chicago Press, 1968.

Newell, K. W. (Ed.). *Health by the people*. Geneva: World Health Organization, 1975.

Nye, F. I. *Role structure and analysis of the family*. Beverly Hills, Cal.: Sage Publications, 1976.

O'Donnell, M. How to start a social revolution: Blow up a concom. *World Medicine*, 12 January 1977.

Olson, D. H., and Dahl, N. S. (Eds.). *Inventory of marriage and family literature*. St. Paul, Minn.: University of Minnesota, 1975.

Omran, A. R. Health benefits for mother and child. *World Health*, January 1974, 6-13.

Otto, H. A. A new light on human potential. In Iowa State University (Ed.), *Families of the future*. Ames, Iowa: Iowa State University Press, 1971.

Park, H. J., Chung, K. K., and Han, D. S. A study of some behavioral problems in sequential processes of adoption in family planning. *International Journal of Health Education*, 1975, *18*, 229-240.

President's Commission on Mental Health. *Report to the President* (Vol. I). Washington, D.C.: U.S. Government Printing Office, 1978.

Reed, J. *From private vice to public virtue: The birth control movement and American society since 1880*. New York: Basic Books, 1978.

Reyes, F. A. *Using information for problem solving*. Manila: Population Center Foundation, 1976.

Roberts, S. V. The family fascinates a host of students. *New York Times*, 23 April 1978.

Rosoff, J. President's Commission Backs "Selective, Optional" Abortion for Mental Health. *PP/WP Washington Memo*, 19 May 1978.

Rueveni, U. Family network intervention: Mobilizing support for families in crisis. *International Journal of Family Counseling*, 1977, *5*, 77-83.

Rutter, M. *Early resources of security and competence*. Unpublished lecture, February 1976.

Rutter, M., and Madge, N. *Cycles of disadvantage*. London: Heinemann, 1976.

Sartorius, N. Priorities for research likely to contribute to better provision of mental health care. *Social Psychiatry*, 1977, *12*, 171-184.

Sartorius, N. WHO's new mental health programme. *WHO Chronicle*, 1978, *32*, 60-62.

Seyle, H. *The stress of life*. New York: McGraw-Hill, 1956.

Shaw, R. P. *Migration theory and fact: A review and bibliography of current literature*. Philadelphia, Penn.: Regional Science Research Institute, 1975.

Shore, M. R., Robert, C.-N., and Jeanneret, O. *Patterns of youth advisory services*. Copenhagen: World Health Organization Regional Office for Europe, 1977, ICP/MNH 016 III.

Sidel, V. W., and Sidel, R. The health care delivery system of the People's Republic of China. In K. W. Newell (Ed.), *Health by the people*. Geneva: World Health Organization, 1975.

Sidel, V. W., and Sidel, R. Primary health care in relation to socio-political structure. *Social Science and Medicine*, 1977, *11*, 415-419.

Smith, K. A. Health priorities in the poorer countries. *Social Science and Medicine*, 1975, *9*, 121-132.

Speer, D. C. Family systems: Morphostasis and morphogenesis, or is homeostasis enough? *Family Process*, 1970, *9*, 259-278.

Stoddard, S. *The hospice movement: A better way of caring for the dying*. New York: Stein and Day, 1978.

364   Henry P. David

Sullivan, E., Tietze, C., and Dryfoos, J. Legal abortion in the United States, 1975-1976. *Family Planning Perspectives*, 1977, *9*, 116-129.

Troll, L. E. The family of later life: A decade review. *Journal of Marriage and the Family*, 1971, *33*, 263-290.

Trost, J. Personal communication, 1978. (*a*)

Trost, J. Attitudes toward and occurrence of cohabitation without marriage. *Journal of Marriage and the Family*, 1978, *40*, 393-400. (*b*)

Ugalde, A. Health decision making in developing nations: A comparative analysis of Columbia and Iran. *Social Science and Medicine*, 1978, *12*, 1-7.

UNICEF. Twelve facts about the state of children in developing countries. *International Child Welfare Review*, 1975, No. 25, p. 24.

U.S. Bureau of the Census Country Demographic Profiles: Thailand. Washington, D.C.: Bureau of the Census, 1978 (ISP-DP-15).

Vaughn, W. T., Jr., Huntington, D. S., Samuels, T. E., Bilmes, M., and Shapiro, M. I. Family mental health maintenance: A new approach to primary prevention. *Hospital and Community Psychiatry*, 1975, *26*, 503-508.

Weiss, S. M. (Ed.) *Proceedings of the National Heart and Lung Institute Working Conference on Health Behavior*, Bayse, Va.: May 1975. Washington, D.C.: DHEW Publication No. (NIH)76-868.

Wilenski, P. *The delivery of health services in the People's Republic of China*. Ottawa: International Development Research Centre, 1976.

Williamson, N. E. *Sons or daughters: A cross-cultural survey of parental preferences*. Beverly Hills, Cal.: Sage Publications, 1976.

Wishik, S., and Bernard, V. W. Family planning, population policies, and mental health. In S. E. Goldston (Ed.), *Mental health considerations in public health*. USPHS Publication No. 1898, May 1969.

Wolfson, M. Environment: A key to health. *People*. 1976, *3*(3), 12-14.

Wolfson, M., and Kane, P. Learning from the Chinese lesson. *People*, 1976, *3* (3), 22.

World Health Organization. *Pregnancy and abortion in adolescence*. Geneva: WHO Technical Report Series, No. 583, 1975. (*a*)

World Health Organization. *Report on consultation of family health*. Geneva, 5-12 November 1973. Geneva WHO, Document FHE/75.4, 1975. (*b*)

World Health Organization. *Statistical indices of family health*. Report of a WHO Study Group. Geneva: WHO Technical Report Series, No. 587, 1976.

World Health Organization. Child development: Separating fact from fiction. *WHO Chronicle*, 1977, *31*, 18-22. (*a*)

World Health Organization. *Health needs of adolescents*. Report of a WHO Expert Committee. Geneva: WHO Technical Report Series, No. 609, 1977. (*b*)

World Health Organization. *Chile mental health and psychological development*. Report of a WHO Expert Committee. Geneva: WHO Technical Report Series, No. 613, 1977. (*c*)

World Health Organization Assembly. *Psychosocial Factors and health*. WHO Executive Board, Document EB 57/22, 20 November 1975.

World Health Organization, Division of Mental Health. Protecting populations at risk: A new strategy. Brochure inserted in *World Health*, December 1977.

Zeidenstein, G. Population processes and improving the quality of human life. Testimony before the Select Committee on Population, U.S. House of Representatives, 20 April 1978.

Zwingmann, C., and Pfister-Ammende, M. *Uprooting and after.* New York: Springer Verlag, 1973.

Name Index

Abelson, R., 72
Abernathy, V. D., 344, 357
Abramowitz, C. F., 315, 330
Adams, J. E., 53, 71, 73, 115, 126, 127, 339, 358, 361
Addams, J., 99, 100
Akhtar, S., 342, 357
Albee, G. W., 4, 7, 70, 93, 94, 103, 106, 127, 128, 149, 239, 332, 358, 360
Alcohol, Drug Abuse and Mental Health Administration (ADAMHA), 332, 357
Aldous, J. A., 336, 357
Alexander, J. K., 198, 203, 217
Allen, J., 136, 147
Allport, G. W., 45, 70
Altman, I., 36, 70, 72
American Heart Association, 196, 217
American Medical Association, 331
Anderson, J. T., 197, 217
Andersson, L., 336, 361
Andrews, F. M., 156, 161, 177
Andrulis, D., 123, 128
APA *Monitor*, 343, 357
Arieti, S., 331
Arnold, F., 347, 357
Arnold, M., 47, 70, 72
Aronson, E., 72
Arthur, R. J., 110, 128
Atchley, R. C., 114, 126, 289, 302
Authier, J., 119, 126
Averill, J. R., 31, 47, 49, 72, 336, 361

Baasher, T. A., 338, 357
Back, K. W., 115, 126
Bailyn, L., 252, 256
Baker, F., 106, 122, 126
Baldi de Mandelovito, M. S., 224, 239
Bales, R. F., 54, 73
Baltes, P. B., 105, 108, 126, 127
Bandura, A., 48, 70
Bane, M. J., 334, 357
Barbee, A. H., 243, 257
Bardwick, J. M., 256
Barfield, R. E., 294, 302
Barnett, R. C., 222, 256
Bart, P. B., 254, 256, 309, 310, 311, 312, 314, 315, 316, 330
Baruch, G. K., 222, 250, 256, 319, 330
Batscha, R., 352, 357, 360
Bauer, R. A., 156, 177, 199, 217
Bean, L. L., 140, 148
Beauvoir, S. de, 292, 302
Beavers, W. R., 338, 361
Beck, A. T., 47, 48, 70, 137, 147
Bee, H., 249, 257
Bender, E., 342, 360
Berger, D. E., 348, 362
Bernard, J., 315, 319, 330
Bernard, V. W., 364
Bernard, W. S., 350, 357
Berne, E., 59, 70
Bernstein, D. A., 199, 217
Bettelheim, B., 144, 147
Bhrolchain, M. N., 243, 247, 256
Biglan, A., 136, 137, 148
Bilmes, M., 333, 340, 364

Binstock, R., 128, 302
Birnbaum, J. A., 247, 256
Birren, J. E., 113, 126
Blatt, B., 11, 27
Blau, F. D., 244, 256
Block, J., 133, 137, 147
Bloom, B. L., 126
Blos, P., 142, 147
Blumer, H., 115, 126
Boissevain, J., 337, 357
Bolles, R. C., 31
Bond, L. A., 128
Borman, L. D., 115, 128
Bower, E. M., 64, 70, 107, 126, 337, 357
Bowlby, J., 140, 141, 142, 147
Bradburn, N. M., 156, 177
Bradway, K., 243, 256
Bray, D. W., 222, 266, 267, 287
Breitrose, H., 198, 217
Brigham, C. C., 90, 91, 103
Brill, H., 88, 103
Brim, O. G., Jr., 127
Brody, E. B., 344, 350, 357, 358
Brokering, B., 185, 194
Bronfenbrenner, U., 334, 357
Broskowski, A., 106, 122, 126
Brotman, H. 292, 302
Broverman, D. M., 46, 70, 137, 147, 249, 259
Broverman, I. K., 137, 147, 249, 257
Brown, B., 198, 217, 344, 357
Brown, B. S., 337, 357
Brown, G. M., 73
Brown, G. W., 243, 247, 256
Buckle, D., 338, 358
Bukowski, C., 33, 34, 70
Bulatao, R. A., 347, 357
Buripakdi, C., 347, 357
Burlage, D., 245, 256
Bush, S., 185, 194
Butts, W. C., 202, 217
Buvenic, M., 349, 358
Byrne, D., 38, 70

Calhoun, J. C., 82, 83
Campbell, A., 156, 161, 177, 224, 225, 235, 239, 246, 247, 256, 338, 358
Campbell, R. J., 266, 267, 287
Cantril, H., 156, 177, 338, 358
Caplan, G., 109, 113, 126, 337, 358
Caplan, N., 352, 358
Caplovitz, D., 156, 177
Carballo, M., 334, 335, 342, 358
Carlson, R., 33, 70
Carstairs, G. M., 76, 103, 338, 357
Cartwright, D., 199, 217
Cassel, J., 41, 54, 70, 72, 115, 128
Cassem, H., 54, 71
Cavan, R. S., 330
Charny, I., 337, 358
Chesler, P., 82, 103
Child, I. L., 30, 70
Chiriboga, D., 112, 128, 310, 311, 330
Christmas, J. J., 337, 358
Chung, B. J., 347, 357
Chung, K. K., 347, 363
Clark, K. C., 101, 103
Clark, M. M., 63, 70
Clarkson, F. E., 137, 147
Coddington, R. D., 136, 147
Coelho, G. V., 73, 115, 126, 127, 339, 358
Cohen, D., 28
Cohen, F., 38, 53, 54, 70
Cohen, J. B., 35, 40, 41, 46, 47, 65, 72
Cole, J. K., 148
Condon, R., 357
Converse, P. E., 156, 161, 177, 224, 239, 246, 247, 256
Coopersmith, S., 248, 256
Cornfield, J., 196, 202, 211, 218
Cowen, E. L., 106, 126, 337, 358
Crandall, V. C., 131, 147
Cronbach, L. J., 45, 70
Curlee, J., 309, 330

Dahl, N. S., 336, 357, 363
Danish, S. J., 4, 5, 105, 108, 109, 117, 118, 119, 120, 121, 122, 126, 127

Darrow, C. N., 132, 133, 148, 342, 361

Datan, N., 71, 110, 127, 128, 309, 331

D'Augelli, A. R., 4, 5, 119, 121, 126

David, H. P., 308, 338, 341, 343, 344, 345, 347, 348, 350, 354, 358, 359, 360

David, L. H., 347, 360

Davidson, K. S., 11, 27

Davidson, P., 74

Davidson, P. O., 148

Deese, J., 29, 30, 32, 73

Del Gaudio, A. C., 136, 149

Dember, N. N., 31, 71

Denmark, F. L., 147

Deutsch, A., 82, 83, 103

Deutscher, I., 309, 330

DeVore, I., 35, 74

Deykin, E. Y., 309, 311, 312, 330

Dimsdale, J. E., 66, 71

Diop, S. M. B., 338, 359

Djukanovic, V., 339, 359

Docherty, J. P., 35, 73

Dodson, J. D., 30, 74

Dohrenwend, B. P., 110, 111, 127, 128, 137, 139, 147

Dohrenwend, B. S., 110, 111, 127, 128, 137, 139, 147

Dollard, J., 31, 71

Donald, S., 34, 74

Dorr, D., 126

Douglas, M., 19, 27

Downing, J., 127

Draper, P., 338, 359

Dryfoos, J., 345, 364

DuBois, L., 258

Duncan, O. D., 156, 177

Durant, W., 303

Dytrych, Z., 345, 359, 362

Easterbrook, J. A., 30, 71

Easton, B. L., 319, 330

Eibl-Eibesfeldt, I., 33, 71

Eisdorfer, C., 28, 128, 299, 302

Eisenberg, L., 76, 77, 103

Eisikovits, Z., 187, 194

Eisworth, R., 199, 218

Elder, G. H., Jr., 112, 127

Elliot, K., 334, 359

Ellis, A., 47, 48, 53, 55, 71

Epstein, C. F., 131, 147

Epstein, S., 38, 71

Erikson, E. H., 62, 63, 71, 132, 133, 147, 234, 239

Evans, J. G., 128

Exton-Smith, A. N., 128

Farber, B., 341, 359

Farquhar, J. W., 198, 202, 203, 205, 217, 218

Fawcett, J. T., 347, 357

Feinlieb, M., 196, 217

Feld, S., 156, 177

Fenz, W. D., 38, 71

Ferree, M., 243, 256

Fidell, L., 244, 247, 256

Flanagan, J. C., 153, 174, 177, 221, 225, 246, 346, 359

Fleck, S., 334, 342, 359

Fleming, P., 143, 147

Folkins, C. H., 49, 71

Folkman, S., 30, 31, 35, 47, 52, 55, 56, 71, 72, 73

Ford, D. H., 108, 127

Forster, E. M., 296

Fowlie, H. C., 334, 359

Frankl, V., 62, 71

Frederickson, D. T., 205, 217

Freedman, A., 359

Freedman, R., 347, 359

Freud, S., 16, 66, 233, 239, 344, 359

Friedman, E., 344, 359

Friedman, H. L., 344, 345, 347, 349, 354, 358, 359, 360

Friedman, M., 132, 148

Frieze, I., 331

Fromm, E., 99, 103

Frost, R., 295, 302

Fruetel, J., 182, 185, 194

Fuchs, E., 311, 330

Gadpaille, W. J., 337, 360

Gal, R., 52, 71

Gallagher, T. G., 54, 72
Garrison, K., 182, 194
Gartner, A., 115, 127
Gay, M., 197, 217
George, W., 257
Gergen, K. J., 39, 71
Giel, R., 338, 357, 360
Giles, D. E., 117, 129
Ginsberg, L. H., 110, 127, 128
Glenn, N. D., 310, 311, 330
Glick, P. C., 335, 348, 360
Glick, R., 222, 223
Goddard, H., 89, 103
Godwin, R. K., 348, 362
Goldfried, M. R., 47, 71
Goldstein, A. P., 104
Goldston, S. E., 106, 107, 127, 332,
  337, 344, 360, 361, 364
Goodman, P., 131, 147
Gore, S., 54, 72, 114, 127
Gornick, V., 330
Gossett, J. T., 338, 361
Gould, R., 234, 239
Gove, W. R., 247, 256
Grande, F., 197, 217
Grant, D. L., 266, 267, 287
Green, H., 142, 147
Greenblatt, M., 71
Grey, J. P., 82
Griffiths, W., 217
Grim, C. E., 34, 74
Grinker, R. R., Jr., 96, 103
Grinker, R. R., Sr., 96, 103
Grosser, G. H., 71
Grunebaum, H., 344, 357
Guerney, B. G., 119, 126, 127
Guerney, L. F., 119, 127
Gurevitz, H., 122, 127
Gurin, G., 156, 177
Gustafson, K., 119, 126

Haan, N., 53, 71
Hackett, T. P., 54, 62
Haddon, W. A., 199, 218
Hagestad, G. O., 110, 111, 128
Haldane, R. B., 303
Hall, E., 295, 302

Hamburg, D. A., 53, 71, 73, 115, 126,
  127, 339, 358, 361
Hamilton, H., 197, 217
Hamilton, V., 71
Hammer, S., 330
Hans, D. S., 347, 363
Hansen, L. S., 148
Harding, T. W., 338, 360
Harkins, E. B., 309, 312, 330
Harris, E. R., 197, 217
Harris, T., 243, 247, 256
Harshbarger, D., 127
Harter, S., 131, 147
Hartley, L. H., 43, 73
Haskell, W., 198, 217
Hassler, F. R., 338, 357
Hauer, A. L., 120, 121, 126
Hayflick, L., 297, 302
Health, D., 123, 127
Hedin, D., 182, 183, 184, 185, 190,
  194
Heider, F., 32
Hellman, L., 54, 72
Helmreich, R., 249, 257
Henderson, J., 76, 77, 103
Henderson, J. B., 198, 217
Henry, P. M., 352, 360
Herd, J. A., 34, 71
Hill, R., 336, 357
Hinkle, L. E., 41, 72
Hiroo, K., 197, 217
Hoffman, L. W., 241, 256
Hoffmeyer, H., 338, 358
Hollingshead A. B., 226, 239
Hollon, S. D., 71
Holmes, T. H., 110, 127, 231, 239
Holst, E., 342, 361
Holt, R. R., 45, 72
House, J. S., 309, 312, 330
Howard, A., 222
Hudis, P. M., 249, 257
Hughes, H. M., 199, 218
Hull, T. H., 347, 360
Hull, V. J., 347, 360
Hultsch, D. F., 110, 113, 127
Hunt, J. McV., 114, 127
Huntingford, P. J., 359

Huntington, D. S., 333, 340, 360, 364

Ilfeld, F., 243, 256
Illich, I., 124, 127, 342, 360
Intersociety Commission for Heart Disease Resources, 197, 217
Iowa State University, 363
Iritani, T., 347, 357
Isaacson, R. V., 126
Isambert, A., 338, 358
Iscoe, I., 126
Izzo, L. D., 126

Jacobson, S., 309, 311, 312, 330
Jahoda, M., 337, 360
James, W., 30, 31
Janis, I. L., 56, 72, 114, 128
Jarvis, E., 81, 83, 84, 103
Jeanneret, O., 341, 363
Jensen, A. R., 91, 92, 103
Jensen, D. D., 148
Joffe, J. M., 70, 127, 149, 239, 358, 360
Johnson, B. C., 334, 360
Johnson, K., 197, 217
Johnson, P., 137, 147, 331
Johnson, R. L., 348, 354, 359, 360
Joint Commission on Mental Illness and Health, 77, 103
Jones, L. G., 43, 73
Jordaan, J. P., 133, 147
Jorgensen, G. T., 97, 104

Kagan, A., 197, 217
Kahn, R., 226, 239
Kalish, R. A., 302
Kamin, L., 89, 90, 103
Kane, P., 342, 364
Kanfer, F. H., 104
Kangas, J., 243, 256
Kannel, W. A., 196, 202, 211, 218
Kanner, A., 31, 35, 47, 55, 72, 73
Kanter, R., 224, 239, 247, 256
Kaplan, B., 115, 128
Kaplan, B. H., 54, 72
Kaplan, H., 359

Kar, S. B., 352, 360
Karlen, A., 345, 361
Kasdorf, J. A., 119, 126
Kasschau, P. L., 299, 302
Katkovsky, W., 261
Katz, A. H., 342, 347, 360, 361
Katz, J., 347, 360
Katz, J. L., 54, 72
Katz, R. B., 331
Kazin, A., 234, 239
Kellerhals, J., 355, 360
Kellerman, H., 73
Kelley, A. B., 199, 218
Kelly, G., 32
Kemp, J., 303
Kendall, P. C., 71
Keniston, K., 131, 148
Kennedy, P. W., 333, 360
Kessler, M., 106, 128, 332, 360
Keys, A., 197, 217
Killilea, M., 337, 358
Klausner, S. Z., 36, 72
Klein, D. C., 332, 360, 361
Klein, E. B., 132, 133, 148, 342, 361
Klein, G. S., 31, 33, 72
Kleinman, A., 28
Klerman, G. L., 88, 103, 309, 311, 312, 330
Klinger, E., 31, 72
Klinghammer, E., 71
Knobloch, F., 338, 358
Knoblochova, J., 338, 358
Knutson, A., 217
Kohlberg, L., 141, 148
Kohn, M. L., 243, 256
Konopka, G., 154, 173, 179, 183, 184, 186, 187, 188, 191, 193, 194
Kornhauser, A. W., 226, 239
Kraines, R. J., 309, 331
Krapf, E. E., 338, 358
Kübler-Ross, E., 140, 141, 142, 148, 234
Kuehneman, M., 202, 217
Kuhn, M., 296
Kuhn, T. S., 28, 72
Kuypers, J. A., 311, 331

LaCross, J., 141, 148

Lalonde, M., 339, 361
Lamb, H., 127
Lambo, T. A., 350, 361
Lane, E. A., 93, 103
Langner, T. S., 116, 129, 226, 239
Lathem, E. C., 302
Launier, R., 47, 51, 56, 73
Lawrence, R., 309, 314, 331
Laws, J. L., 319, 330
Lawton, M. P., 113, 114, 128
Lazarre, J., 319, 330
Lazarus, R. S., 3, 4, 29, 30, 31, 32,
    34, 38, 40, 41, 44, 46, 47, 48,
    49, 51, 53, 54, 55, 56, 64, 65,
    70, 71, 72, 73, 74, 118, 128,
    336, 361
Lebovici, S., 338, 358
Lee, S. J., 347, 357
Lenin, V. I., 76
Leslie, G. R., 334, 361
Levi, L., 72, 336, 361
Levi, P., 194
Levin, L. S., 342
Levine, M., 16
Levinson, D. J., 132, 133, 135, 147,
    234, 239, 342, 361
Levinson, H., 221, 227, 232, 239
Levinson, M. H., 132, 133, 148, 342,
    361
Levitin, T., 137, 148
Lewin, K., 32
Lewinsohn, P. M., 136, 144, 148
Lewis, J. M., 338, 361
Lewis, M., 73
Lidz, T., 334, 361
Lieberman, E. J., 344, 347, 361
Lieberman, M. A., 113, 115, 128
Lief, H. I., 345, 361
Lindemann, E., 115, 126
Lindner, M. A., 344, 359
Lipman-Blumen, J., 249, 257
Litman, T. J., 335, 358
Liu, B-C., 156, 177
Lonner, T., 309, 312, 331
Loomis, B., 309, 331
Lorenz, K., 33, 73
Lorion, R. P., 126

Lowenthal, M. F., 112, 128, 310, 311,
    330, 331
Luborsky, L., 35, 73
Lyons, G. M., 358

McAllister, A. L., 198, 199, 217, 218
McBride, A. B., 319, 331
McEwan, P. J. M., 336, 362
McGuire, W., 72
McGuirk, F. D., 97, 104
McKean, J. D., 110, 128
McKee, B., 132, 133, 148, 334, 361
McLaughlin, B., 126
McLean, A., 239
Maas, H. S., 311, 313
Maccoby, N., 154, 155, 198, 202, 203,
    205, 217, 218
Mach, E. P., 339, 359
Macke, A. S., 249, 257
Macklin, E. D., 335, 361
Maddox, G. L., 115, 128
Madge, N., 341, 363
Maher, B. A., 43, 70, 73
Mahl, G. F., 52, 73
Mahler, H., 333, 334, 349, 350, 361,
    362
Mahoney, M., 47, 73
Mahoney, M. J., 195, 217
Maley, R., 127
Manciaux, M., 335, 362
Mandl, H. J., 232, 239
Mandler, G., 47, 73
Mangione, T. W., 224, 239
Mann, L., 56, 72
Marcia, J. E., 132, 148
Marciel, J. C., 46, 73
Marx, K., 26
Maslow, A. H., 138, 148, 300, 301
Mason, J. W., 43, 44, 73
Massimo, J. L., 145, 146, 148
Matejcek, Z., 345, 359, 362
Mauldin, W. P., 347, 362
May, J. T., 362
Mazade, N. A., 123, 128
Mechanic, D., 54, 73, 86, 104
Mednick, M., 256
Meichenbaum, D., 47, 73, 97, 104

Mendelsohn, H., 199, 217
Mercer, J., 93, 104
Meyer, A. J., 198, 205, 217
Meyer, E. E., 339, 349, 362
Michael, S. T., 116, 129, 226, 239
Miller, F. J. W., 335, 362
Miller, F. T., 123, 128
Miller, L., 362
Miller, N. E., 31, 71, 202, 218
Miller, W. B., 348, 362
Mitchell, J. C., 337, 362
Milner-Gulland, R., 194
Mindick, B., 348, 362
Minnesota Center for Health
    Statistics, 187, 194
Mohr, J. C., 343, 362
Moody, H. R., 291, 292, 300, 302
Moos, R. H., 58, 73, 146, 149, 339,
    362
Moran, B. K., 330
Morgan, J. N., 294, 302
Morrison, M. H., 294, 295, 302
Mougey, E. H., 43, 73
Mukherjee, B. N., 347, 362
Muller, S., 123, 128
Munander, S. C. U., 347, 362
Munden, K. J., 232, 239
Murray, H., 32
Myers, J. K., 140, 148

Nahemow, L., 113, 114, 128
Nash, J., 198, 217
National Council on Aging, 298,
    302
Naur, M., 349, 362
Neikirk, H. J., 34, 74
Neugarten, B. L., 110, 111, 128,
    297, 302, 309, 310, 331, 342,
    362
Newell, K. W., 338, 339, 362, 363
Newman, S., 360
Nichamen, M., 197, 217
Norton, A. I., 335, 348, 360
Nowak, C. A., 105, 110, 111, 112,
    118, 127, 128
Nuckolls, K. B., 115, 128

Nye, F. I., 362

O'Donnell, M., 347, 363
Offer, D., 96, 104
Olson, D. H., 336, 363
Olweus, D., 132, 148
Omran, A. R., 347, 363
Ondrack, J., 225, 239
O'Neil, B., 199, 218
Opler, M. K., 116, 129, 226, 239
Opton, E. M., Jr., 31, 47, 72, 336,
    361
Oskamp, S., 348, 362
Osler, S. F., 29, 30, 32, 73
Otto, H. A., 336, 363

Park, H. J., 347, 363
Parke, R., Jr., 358
Parker, S., 295, 302
Parsons, J., 331
Parsons, T., 54, 73
Patton, R. E., 88, 103
Paykel, E. S., 309, 311, 314, 331
Pearlin, L. I., 41, 42, 73
Penick, S., 35, 73
Perlow, M. J., 43, 73
Perry, C., 198, 218
Pertejo de Alcami, J., 338, 358
Pervin, L. A., 37, 73
Pettigrew, T., 92, 104
Pfister-Ammende, M., 350, 365
Phillips, V. A., 338, 361
Piaget, J., 16, 23, 24
Pincus, C., 309, 314, 331
Pincus, L., 338, 358
Pinneau, S. T., Jr., 54, 73
Pintner, R., 90, 104
Plantz, M., 105, 117, 129
Plath, S., 234
Plato, 298
Plemons, J. K., 110, 113, 127
Plutchik, R., 73
Poortinga, Y. H., 359
Poppen, P., 146, 148
Porter, L. W., 70
Poser, E. G., 96, 104

Powell, B., 309, 312, 331
Prentis, R. S., 290, 302
President's Commission on
    Mental Health, 346, 356, 363
President's Commission on
    National Goals, 177
Price, C. R., 232, 239
Primary Mental Health Project,
    107
Pruchno, R., 105

Quinn, D., 224, 226, 239
Quinn, R. P., 137, 148
Quinn, R. S., 224, 239

Radding, N., 309, 314, 331
Radloff, L., 246, 257
Radloff, L. S., 136, 148
Rahe, R. H., 110, 127, 128, 231,
    239
Rapoza, R. S., 148
Rappaport, J., 120, 129
Raush, H. L., 35, 74
Raymond, S., 32, 74
Redlich, F. C., 226, 239
Reed, J., 343, 344, 363
Reese, H. W., 71, 74, 126
Rennie, T. A. C., 116, 129, 226
Reyes, F. A., 352, 363
Rhoads, G., 197, 217
Rich, A., 319, 331
Ricks, D. F., 5, 103, 138, 141,
    143, 145, 147, 148, 149
Riegel, K. F., 39, 73, 74, 108,
    109, 128, 129
Riessman, F., 115, 127, 128
Robert, C.-N., 341, 363
Roberts, S. V., 335, 363
Robertson, L. S., 199, 218
Roff, M., 103, 147, 148
Rodgers, W. L., 156, 161, 177,
    224, 239, 246, 247, 256
Rosen, J. C., 128
Rosenberg, M. J., 72
Rosencrantz, P. S., 137, 147
Rosenkrantz, P., 249, 257
Rosenthal, R., 226, 239

Rosenzweig, N. R., 70
Roskies, E., 29, 52, 64, 74
Rosoff, J., 346, 363
Ross, H., 245, 257
Ruben, B. D., 217
Rubin, L., 235, 239, 314, 315
Rubin, L. B., 307
Ruble, D., 331
Rueveni, U., 337, 363
Russ-Eft, D., 156, 177
Russell, B., 78
Russell, S., 202, 218
Rutter, M., 340, 341, 363
Ryan, W., 101, 104, 116, 129
Rychlack, J., 261, 287

Sabshin, M., 96, 104
Sadock, B., 359
Sainsbury, P., 339, 349, 362
Sales, E., 311, 331
Samuels, T. E., 333, 340, 364
Sandburg, C., 288, 303
Sandler, J., 338, 358
Sanger, M., 344
Sarason, E., 8, 9
Sarason, S. B., 3, 7, 9, 11, 24,
    27, 225, 234, 239
Saroyan, W., 191, 194
Sartorius, N., 333, 334, 352, 363
Sartre, J. P., 298
Saul, Z., 19, 27
Sawhill, I. V., 245, 257
Schaefer, C., 30, 31, 35, 47, 52,
    56, 71, 72
Schaller, G. B., 35, 74
Schlesinger, H., 33, 72
Schooler, C., 243, 256
Schopenhauer, A., 298, 303
Schüller, V., 345, 359, 362
Scull, A., 86, 104
Sears, P. S., 243, 257
Seeman, P., 73
Seidman, E., 120, 129
Seligman, M., 97, 104, 137, 141,
    148
Selye, H., 43, 72, 129, 139, 148,
    336, 363

Sevilla, M., 358
Shanas, E., 128, 301, 302, 303
Shapiro, M. I., 333, 340, 364
Shaw, R. P., 351, 363
Sheppard, H., 299
Shore, M. F., 145, 148
Shore, M. R., 341, 363
Shure, M., 135, 149
Sidel, R., 342, 351, 363
Sidel, V. W., 342, 351, 363
Siegel, R., 309, 331, 341
Silver, A., 225, 239
Singaribun, M., 347, 360
Singer, I. B., 234, 239
Skinner, B. F., 45, 74
Skolnick, A., 331
Skolnick, J. H., 331
Smelser, N. J., 40, 74
Smith, J. D., 344, 359
Smith, K. A., 338, 344, 363
Smyer, M. A., 105, 117, 118, 126, 127
Snoek, J., 226, 239
Snoke, A., 123, 129
Socrates, 22
Solano, C., 257
Solley, C. M., 232, 239
Solomon, M., 309, 311, 312, 330
Speer, D. C., 336, 363
Spence, D., 309, 312, 331
Spence, J., 249, 257
Spence, J. A., 30, 74
Spence, K. W., 30, 74
Spielberger, C. C., 126
Spielberger, C. D., 74
Spivack, G., 135, 149
Srole, L., 116, 129, 226, 239
Stahl, S. M., 34, 74
Staines, G. L., 137, 148
Stanley, J., 257
Star, S., 77, 199, 218
Steinbeck, J., 193, 194
Steiner, G., 295, 302
Stern, M., 198, 202, 217, 218
Stewart, S. S., 97, 104
Stierlin, H., 132, 149
Stoddard, S., 337, 363

Stollack, G. E., 119, 127
Stone, A. A., 88, 104
Strachey, J., 239
Stunkard, A. J., 199, 218
Suinn, R. M., 97, 104
Sullivan, E., 345, 364
Sullivan, T. A., 244, 257
Super, D. E., 133, 147
Surgeon General's Report, 196, 216, 218
Syme, S. L., 197, 217
Szasz, T., 124, 129

Taeuber, C., 157, 177
Tallman, I., 357
Tangri, S., 256
Tannenbaum, P., 72
Taylor, R. C., 115, 126
Terman, L. S., 89, 104, 242
Thomas, A., 147, 148
Thompson, V., 360
Thorensen, C. E., 195, 217
Thorndike, E. L., 90
Thurner, M., 310, 311, 330
Tietze, C., 345, 364
Tillotson, J., 197, 217
Timberlake, J., 96, 103
Timeras, P. S., 137, 149
Tinbergen, N., 33, 74
Tolman, E., 32
Toynbee, A., 234, 239
Treiman, D. J., 249, 250, 257
Troll, L. E., 342, 364
Trost, J., 348, 355, 364
Trost, N. A., 126
Truett, J., 196, 202, 211, 218
Tudor, J. F., 247, 256
Turner, R. R., 126
Turow, S., 10, 27
Tyson, A., 239

Ugalde, A., 349, 364
Unger, R. K., 147
UNICEF, 351
U.S. Bureau of the Census, 347, 364
U.S. Civil Service Commission
    Study, 288, 303

U.S. Department of Health, Education and Welfare, 177
U.S. Department of Commerce, 177

Vaillant, G. E., 133, 149, 286, 287
Vallance, T. R., 119
Vance, E. T., 136, 149
Van der Tak, J., 358
Van Lawick-Goodall, J., 35, 74
Vaughn, W. T., Jr., 333, 340, 364
Veroff, S., 156, 177
Vogel, S., 249, 257
Vogel, S. R., 137, 147
Vogel, W., 32, 74

Wandersman, A., 146, 148, 149
Warburton, D. M., 71
Warren, D. I., 116, 129
Warren, R. B., 244, 257
Washburn, S. L., 35, 74
Waterhouse, I. K., 30, 70
Wechsler, H., 71
Weiner, B., 70
Weiner, H., 54, 72
Weiner, I. B., 136, 149
Weisman, A. D., 61, 62, 71, 74
Weiss, L., 311, 331
Weiss, S. M., 339, 364
Weissman, M. M., 309, 311, 314, 331
Wessman, A. E., 138
Westoff, C. F., 358

White, R. W., 31, 74
Whiting, B. B., 241, 257
Widdowson, G. M., 202, 217
Wilenski, P., 339, 364
Willems, E. P., 35, 74
Williamson, N. E., 347, 364
Winkelstein, W., 197, 217
Wishik, S., 364
Withey, S. B., 156, 161, 177
Wixon, C., 199, 218
Wohlwill, J. F., 72
Wolfe, D., 226, 239
Wolfe, H., 182, 185, 194
Wolfson, M., 339, 342, 364
Wolman, B., 148
World Health Organization, 334, 335, 337, 338, 339, 340, 341, 351, 364, 365
Wood, P., 198, 203, 217
Wood, V., 309, 331
Wortis, R. P., 319, 331
Wu, T. S., 347, 357
Wundt, W., 60

Yerkes, R. M., 30, 74, 89, 90
Yevtushenko, Y., 192, 194
Young, C. E., 117, 119, 129
Young, R., 144, 146

Zaleznik, A., 225, 239
Zeidenstein, G., 346, 348, 349, 365
Zeiss, A. M., 136, 137, 148
Zellman, G., 331
Zwingman, C., 350, 365

Subject Index

Ability tests, 258

Abortion: in Europe, 345, self-induced, 34; services in the U.S., 345-346

Active Clevelanders Together, 299

Adaptation theory, 63

Adolescent development: concept of, 178-179; healthy normal, 96; identity crisis, 5; identity formation, 62, 134; physical changes, 132; physical immaturity, 5; rapid change in, 130; reevaluation of values in, 180-181; sexual maturity in, 179-180

Adolescents: alcohol consumption, 187; career goals, 133-134; change, 131-134; college age, 133; communication, 188-189; coping, 187-188, 189-193; coping with institutions, 190-191; creative response, 189-190, 192; depressive reaction, 141-142; disillusionment, 5; drug usage, 187; employment, 185; estimates of boys' performance, 131; estimates of girls' performance, 131; exploration, 133; family relationships, 182-183; identity in, 132; interventions, 5; life force and, 181; parent relationships, 132; participation in society, 181; peer groups, 132, 185-186; poetry, 178, 179, 182-183, 186, 190-191, 193; protest, 143; psychopathology, 137-144; religion, 189; schizophrenia, 135, 141, 142-143; school, 183-184; self-consciousness, 180; separa-tion, 142, 180; socialization, 137; stress, 136-137; stressful life events, 136; suicide, 130; vocational adjustment, 143; work, 185

Adrenal corticosteroids, 43

Adult development, 3, 18; understanding, 16, 22

Adult Development Incomplete Sentence Test (ADIST), 264

Adults: competency, 25; compromises, 18; inability to understand social organization, 23; individual psychology, 25; interviews with, 17; midlife transition, 5; problems, 17, 23, 25; young, 23

Aging: dissatisfaction, 235; self-image and, 234; women, 254

Agism, 76, 296. *See also* Old people

Aggressive behavior: Bell system managers, 266-267; self-directed, 226

Alcoholics Anonymous, 55, 237

Alcoholism, 95; in retired people, 289

Alienation, 143

American Academy of Political and Social Science, 157

American Journal of Insanity, 82, 83

American Psychological Association, 89, 90; presidents, 90

American Telephone and Telegraph Company (AT&T), 222, 262

Amphetamines, 87

Analogues, universalist machine, 31

Animal studies, 35

Anticipatory coping, 118, 119

Antidiscrimination in Employment Act, 293

Anxiety, 29, 143
Apathy, 140, 142, 146
Army: Alpha Test, 91; testing program, 90
Art careers, 11
Ascendancy Scale (A scale), 278
Atherosclerosis, 196
Atomic scientists, 24
Attitude measures, 249
Authoritarianism, 262
Avoidance behavior, 61, 62

Bantus, 79
Battered wife, 242
Behavior: models and theories, 31; self-management, 195–196
Bell Advanced Management Program (BAMP), 265, 266, 267, 269, 271, 272
Bell System, 222, 258, 259, 262, 272, 281, 282; Value Orientation, 281– 82, 283
Bell System managers, 258; career success, 283–284; determinants of adjustment and happiness, 277–283; differential development, 272–275; life satisfactions, 275–277; successful, 268–274
Bereavement. See Grief
Blacks, 78, 81, 82, 83, 161–162; adolescents, 184; children, 93; farmers, 97; intelligence, 90–91; women, 244
"Blaming the victim," 4, 80, 81, 101
Blood pressure, 202, 211; disorders, 34
Boredom, 99, 138, 295
Boston mental health services, 116
Breast feeding vs. bottle feeding, 98
Business Incomplete Sentences Test, 263
Byrnes Repression-Sensitization Scale, 38

California F-Scale, 263
Cancer: breast, 216; colon, 216; lung, 196, 216; search for cures, 76

Cardiovascular disease, 196; community study, 196; cross-cultural studies, 197; dietary factors, 197; prevention, 215–216; risk reduction education, 197–198, 203–204; risk reduction research design, 200
Cardiovascular events, risk factors, 196–197
Cardiovascular risk: medical examinations, 202; surveys, 202
Career choices, 9, 10; administrative sciences, 11, 12; art, 11; theater, 11
Career counseling, 238
Census: U.S., 82; U.S. of 1840, 82, 83; years, 156
Center for Youth Development and Research, 181, 182
CETA jobs, 185
Chicanos, 82; children, 93
Childhood development: normal, 340; relationship with mothers, 326
Child-rearing: high cost of, 348; in unhappy homes, 341
Children: black, 93; Chicano, 93; coping skills, 130; and divorce, 40–41; educable mentally retarded, 93; high risk, 93; hospitalization of, 140; inner city, 93; realization of potential, 22
China, 342
Chinese, 81
Chlorapromazine, 86
Cholesterol: changes in diet, 209–210; concentration, 202; high, 196, 197
Cigarette smoking, 196, 202, 235; behavior changes, 208; community influence, 198; education against, 203, 205, 206, 213, 214; and lung cancer, 216; peer models, 198; recidivism, 199
Clearinghouses, 353
Clinical: practice, 65; psychology, transitions in, 30; treatment model, 119
Cognition, 31; and emotion, 32, 47
Cognitive: appraisal, 47–52; behavior therapists, 53; copers, 137; orienta-

Cognitive (*continued*)
tion in psychology, 47; processes, 31, 47, 57; revolution, 31, 47; theory, 33
College students: first year, 17, 18; graduate, 12, 13, 17, 23; seniors, 9, 10, 11, 17
Collegiality, 7
Commitment procedures, 293
Communities, role in prevention, 5
Community: centers, 122; Helpers Project, 119–120; involvement risk-reduction programs, 215
Competence: adult, 4, 14, 25; athletic, 131; compared to coping, 131; criteria for judging, 11, 12, 25; defining standards, 131; failure, 137–144; as model, 4; in schools, 135; self-perceived, 131
Competency model: adult, 3, 4; bases for, 78; implications of, 79
Conflict, 6, 9
Conformity, 21
Consumption, 79
Contraception, 333, 343, 345, 347
Coopersmith Self-Esteem Scale, 248
Coping behavior: adolescent, 187–188, 189–193; anticipatory, 57, 118; with breast cancer, 51, 54; classification of, 52; as constellation of many acts, 58–60; criteria for judging, 11, 12; with death, 39, 57, 61, 62; difficulties in assessing, 58; direct action, 57; with divorce, 40–41; with doctors, 56–57; by drug-taking, 53; with elderly parents, 7, 12; and emotion, 32; evaluating, 54, 58, 63, 68; failure, 137–144; information-seeking, 56–58; inhibition of action, 57–58; with institutions, 190–191; intrapsychic modes, 57, 58, 66; laboratory research, 34; main functions, 52–55; methods of assessment, 60–68; overview, 52–55; palliative modes, 53; prob-
lems of definition, 29, 32, 60–63; real/unreal beliefs, 53; research strategies, 63, 67; school, 134; self-deception, 53, 56–57; strategies, 4, 53; and stress, 32–47, 52, 186–187; in surgical patients, 38–39, 53–54; as survival, 130; systematizing, 59; at work, 236–239
Coping models, 3, 142, 143–144
Coping patterns, 40–58, 59; appropriateness of, 63, 64; in normal people, 66
Coping skills, increasing, 80, 143
Corporate foot-dragging, 288
Correctional institutions, 14
Counseling, 4; definition of, 289
Counseling Center Group Discussion, 275
Criminal behavior, drug treatment, 88
Crises, as growth opportunities, 109
Crisis, concept of, 108, 109
Critical life events: concept of, 110–112, 119; outcomes, 113–115, 119; social support systems, 114–115, 116
Czechoslovakia, 344

Daycare, 86
Death, coping with our own, 39, 57, 61, 62, 234–235. *See also* Grief
Defect model, 4
Defenses, 62, 63
Deinstitutionalization, 86
Demographic surveys, 116–117
Denial, 61, 62
Depression, 137, 139; profound, clinical, 312; self-blame in, 137
Despair, 141, 143, 145
Detroit, analysis of community helping, 116–117
Development planning, 348
Developmentally disabled, institutions for, 114. *See also* Mental retardation
Diet, recidivism, 199, 213–214
Dietary education, 203–205
Disability, 142; resistance to, 140

Discontinuity, 6–12, 143
Disease, and mental illness, 195
Divorce: coping with, 40–41; family coping, 307; economic problems, 245; rates, 335; and women, 314, 323–326
Drive theory, 31
Drug companies, 98
Drugs, altering behavioral deviance, 88
Drugs, psychotropic, 86, 87; effects of, 87; therapeutic value of, 87

East-West Communication Center, 352
Economic systems, 101
Economics, 83; international, 22
Education: lock-step system, 100; public, 22
Edwards Personal Preference Schedule (EPPS), 263, 266, 269, 275, 279, 280, 284–286
Egalitarianism, 91
Ego: ideal, 226; resilience, 137; self-image related to ego ideal, 226–227, 230–233, 236; synthesis, 63
Elderly. See Old people
Electroconclusive shock, 49
Elitism, 79
Emotion, 31, 47
Emotional life, bases for pathology, 53, 55
Emotional Stability Scale (N Scale), 278
Empathy, 102
Employment: adolescents, 185; and life satisfaction, 162
Employment Retirement Income Security Act (ERISA), 290
Empty-nest syndrome, 246, 254, 309, 310, 329; classical symptoms, 312; denied, 319–320; divorced women, 314, 323–326; fathers, 223–226; or gradual separation, 324–325; investigation, 311–312; language analyzed, 310–311; middle-class/working-class parents, 314–315; mother/child relationships, 315–317; persistence of the myth, 318–320; relief felt by women, 313; women's movement, 316
Endocrine profiles, 43
End-states, 108, 110, 112, 119
England, 83
Enhancement programs, 119
Environmental: poisons, 139; stress, 335, 336
Environments, 3, 146
Epidemiological studies, 83
Epidemiologists, social, 41
Establishment, the, 85
Ethnocentrism, 4, 79
Ethology, 33
Existentialism, 234
Expectations Inventory, 263, 278
External: requirements, 6, 7, 10, 18; structures, 18

Face-to-face instruction, 199, 200, 204, 213
Family: coping, 333; cross-cultural studies, 308, 338; cultural change, 182; death, 337; decline of, 334; functioning, 338; health, 335; interventions, 146; leaving, 132, 142; life cycle, 339, 354; patterns, 135; self-reliance, 342; single-parent, 341; size, 157; slum, 337; strengthening, 338
Family functioning, 307, 336–338; during early years of marriage, 354–355; theory of, 353–354
Family planning, 343–345; India, 347 Indonesia, 377; Thailand, 347
Family relationships: adolescents, 182–183; changing patterns, 351; definition of problems, 336; fathers, 326; traditional, 334
Farm environments, 80
Fathers, 223–226
Federal policies, 20, 86
Feeblemindedness, 84
Fertility-choice behavior, 353
Fortune 500: Corporations, 290;

Fortune 500 (*continued*)
  Retirement Plans and Policies, 290
Foster children, 335
Framingham, Mass., longitudinal
  study, 211, 212
French-Canadians, 79
Freudianism, 352

General Adaptation Syndrome, 43, 44
General Information Test, 263
General Management Attitude Scale,
  281, 283, 286
General Motors, 232
Genetics, 79
Gerontology, 293; and geriatrics, 297
Gestaltists, 16
Gifted children study, 242
Gilroy, Calif., 200, 203, 210
Government, centralized control, 22
Graduate school students, 9, 10,
  13, 14
Grief, 34, 39
Group homes, 86
Guilford-Martin Inventory of Factors
  GAMIN, 263, 277

Harris Poll Survey on old age, 298
Harvard Medical School, 221
Harvard University, 10, 88
Hawaii, 81
Health education, 215
Health habits, cultural effects on,
  199
Heart attack, 195
Helping: community networks, 119;
  skills, 4
Helplessness, 143
Heterosexuality, 279
High Commission for Refugees, 350
Holocaust, 192
Homeostasis, 137-138, 140; in men-
  tal health, 144, 145
Homoclites, 96
Hospital admission rates, 157
Hospitalization, 8, 19, 21, 140
Hospitals, 12, 13. *See also* Psychi-
  atric hospitals

Human development, 124-125; enhancement of, 108-110; theories
  of, 105
Human service agencies, 14; funding,
  106-107
Human services delivery: organizational barriers, 123-124; present
  time, 116; professional barriers,
  122-123; social barriers, 124-125
Hypertension, 196

Idealism, 10
Identity achievement, 133; in ado-
  lescence, 132
Identity formation, 62-63; in ado-
  lescence, 132
Idiocy, 94
Illness model, 80, 83. *See also* Model
Illnessism, 124-125
Immigrants, 81-84, 89
Immigration laws, 90
Income, 13
Individual differences, importance in
  research theory, 30
Individual psychology, 3, 23
Individuality, 10
Industrial jobs, boring and meaning-
  less, 98-99
Industrialization: effects of, 79; evils
  of, 98-100; in underdeveloped
  countries, 350
Industry, 10, 11
Infancy, feeding in, 98
Information centers, 353
Institute for Retirement Studies, 222
Institute of Social Research, Univer-
  sity of Michigan, 224
Institutions, 14, 17, 21
Intelligence measures: cultural bias
  of, 91; male/female differences,
  94; race differences, 89-91; World
  War I soldiers, 90
Intelligence quotient: genetic factors,
  91-92; immigrants, 89, 90; inner
  city children, 93; politics of, 89
Intensive instruction program, 204-
  205, 208, 211, 212, 213

Internal requirements, 6, 7
Interventions, 4; goal of, 108, 109;
    life development, 105; life de-
    velopment model, 116
Interviews, with college seniors, 9
Intrapsychic: modes, 57; supremacy,
    16
Introspection, 60
Ipsative-normative: data analysis, 60;
    methods, in stress and coping
    theories, 33, 44–46; patterns of
    coping, 59
Ireland, 81
Irish, 81, 84
Isolation, 143
Isolationist policy, 18

Japanese, 81
Jews, 79, 89, 90, 91
Job attitude measures, 263
Job performance: appraisal systems,
    229; rating, 261
Job satisfaction: political bias, 225;
    public opinion surveys, 224,
    225–226; women, 253–254
Job situation: dissatisfaction, 227;
    stress precipitating, 227–233
Jobs: ability to hold, 140; ado-
    lescents, 133; boring, 226;
    changes, 228; counseling, 238;
    cultural restrictions, 230; en-
    vironmental factors, 231–232;
    high status, 225; mutual-support
    groups, 237–238; socioeconomic
    forces, 231; as source of self-
    esteem, 233–234; superior/sub-
    ordinate relationships, 231
Joint Commission on Mental Health,
    77

Kenya, 241
Korean War, 29

Labeling, 78, 135, 144
Labor, division of, 319, 327
Laboratory: analogues, 34, 65;
    studies, values and failings, 35

Law students, 9, 10, 11, 12, 13, 17
Leaderless group discussion, 262
Leadership roles, 280
Learned helplessness, 97, 137, 139,
    141
Leisure, use, 295
Leisure-time activities, 296
Levinson Institute, 221
Licensure laws, restrictive, 117
Life Change Units: checklist, 111;
    level of mental health, 138
Life course, perspectives, 39
Life development intervention, 105,
    119; and enhancement, 117–120
Life events, 110, 117; negative, 137–
    138
Life-history oriented model, 96
Life history research, 5
Life satisfaction, 161; predicting,
    160–162
Life skills, 5
Life-span development psychology,
    133
Life stages, studies, 234
Logical positivism, 30
Louisiana, 82
Lunacy, 83, 94

Maine, 82, 83
Male/female: IQ differences, 243;
    roles, 323
Malnutrition, as result of bottle-feed-
    ing, 98
Management Continuity Study (MCS),
    270, 271
Management Progress Study (MPS),
    258, 259, 264, 265, 266, 267, 268,
    270, 271–272; attitudes question-
    naire, 281; managers' family life,
    274
Management Progress Study assess-
    ment centers, 259–262, 263, 268,
    269, 272, 273; adjustment and
    happiness ratings, 277; staff ratings,
    286
Management Questionnaire, 263

Managers, successful, 265–268. *See also* Bell System managers.

Marriage, 115, 118; children leaving, 327; depression in, 246; middle-age and, 235; other options, 335; status in, 41–43

Marxists, 26

Mass media, 5, 83; campaigns, 199–200, 203–206, 211, 213, 214, 215; life style, 24; providing knowledge about life events, 118, 119

Mass teaching model, 119

Massachusetts, 81, 83

Measles, 85

Medical profession: attitudes, 76, 77; profiteering, 87

Medical students, 9, 10, 11, 12, 13, 14, 17

Medicare, 12, 86, 294

Medicine, American, 14; Western model, 349

Mental disorder, 75, 76; concept of, 124; survey on, 77, 78; world figures, 333–334

Mental health: age of, 19; children, 340; continuum, 138–139; "positive," 337; and prevention, 9

Mental health services, 105, 124; inequalities in, 94–95

Mental health workers, 4, 20; in developing countries, 334

Mental hygiene movement, 77

Mental retardation, 95, 114, 134; classification, 92–94; organic model of, 92, 93; world figures, 333

Middle age: coping in, 341–342; crisis, 235, 286

Middlescent Male Picture Test (MMPT), 264

Midlife assessment center, 260

Midlife transition, 132, 238

Midtown Manhattan Study, 116

Migrant farm workers, 80, 95

Migration, 350–351; involuntary, 350; lack of knowledge, 351

Minnesota, 187

Minority groups, 95

Model: attitudes to old people, 291–292, 300; clinical treatment, 119; competency, 3, 45, 78, 95; coping process, 39; defect, 4, 75, 84–86; definition of, 130; human development, 4; human service delivery, 5, 119, 120; illness, 75–78, 80–81; life-history oriented, 96; mass teaching, 119; medical, 109, 119; organic, 80; preventive, 105; psychotherapeutic, 80; public health, 107; remedial, 105

Models of causation, linear, 36

Monadic analysis, 174–177

Monkeys, research on, 43–44

Moody Model, 291–292

Mothers: burden, 322; loss of role, 310; middle-class, 314–315; "unnatural," 320–321; working class, 315

Motivation: and cognition, 31, 47; patterns of, 31

Movies, 19, 20, 24

Multiple levels of analysis, in stress and coping theories, 33, 40–44

Multiple sclerosis, 195

Mutual-support groups, 237–238

Myocardial infarction, 195

Narcissism, 235, 236

National Cancer Institute, 28

National Institute of Education, 161

National Institute of Mental Health, 356

National Longitudinal Survey, 244

Native American Indians, 81

Natural support systems for old people, 293

Naturalistic: emphasis in stress and coping theories, 33–35; focus for research, 46; research, 46

Nazi concentration camps, 192

Need for Succorance Scale, 279–280

Negro. *See* Black

Network intervention, 337

Neurological disorders, 139
Nordics, 79
Normative pattern, 111
Null hypothesis, 92
Nursing homes, 86; calamitous
    conditions of, 293

Occupation, prestigious, 250
Old age: in ancient India, 292; basic
    attitudes to, 291; euphemisisms
    for, 296; hardships of, 297;
    public policy, 291
Old people: drugs and medication,
    298–299; illness criteria, 299–
    300; participation, 292; physi-
    cal abuse of, 293; poverty of,
    292–293; priorities and options,
    292; rejection of, 291; role of
    family, 342; self-actualization,
    292; social services, 291;
    stereotypes, 298. See also Agism
Older Americans Act, 292
Opinion Questionnaire, 263
Organizations: interconnectedness,
    22–23; structure of, 16, 17, 22, 23
Orientals, 79

Palliation, 53, 54, 56, 58
Paradigm, 105; definition of, 28;
    public health, 76
Paranoid schizophrenic, 78
Parent effectiveness training, 110
Parental values, 246
Parenthood: preparation for, 341;
    stereotypic roles, 341
Parents without partners, 237
Patients: dying, 140–141; physician
    relationship, 56–57
Paupers, 81
Peer groups: adolescent, 132, 186;
    and health education, 215
Pennsylvania, patterns in rural
    helping, 117
Pennsylvania State University, 4
Pensions: lack of information, 294;
    niggardly, 298
Perception: gestalt tradition in,

30; New Look movement, 30, 45
Perception theory: classical, 45; con-
    tradictory perspectives in, 30, 31;
    distortions of understanding in, 33
Personal freedom, 7
Personality: questionnaires, 258; re-
    search, 45; theory, 30, 33
Personnel management, 288, 289
Phenothiazines, 87
Phenylketonuria (PKU), 77
Physical stress, 110
Planfulness, 119
Planning for the future, 12
Poliomyelitis, 85
Political philosophy, 4
Population: change, 156; distribu-
    tion, 351; and quality of life, 346
Poverty: children, 340; and coping,
    139; nature of, 83–84; of old
    people, 292–293
Pregnancy, 115
Prejudice, 79
Preschool children, mental retarda-
    tion in, 92
President's Commission on Mental
    Health, 4, 94, 95, 342
Primacy of work, 273
Primary prevention of psychopath-
    ology, 139; absence of rational
    guidelines, 64; concept of, 106; de-
    fining, 332; dual focus of, 3; effec-
    tiveness, 4; establishing a center,
    356; illness model in, 75, 77; model
    for, 80; promotion, 333, 349–350;
    socio-political realities, 351
Primate research, 35, 43
Princeton University, 89, 90
Problem-solving, 56
Process, defined, 38
Project TALENT, 153, 161, 174, 175
Projective tests, 263; new, 264
Pseudo-retardation, 93
Psychiatric hospitals, 19, 20, 21, 82,
    86, 87, 89; admission/age factors,
    130; movies about, 19, 20, 21
Psychiatrists: excessive drug usage, 88;
    unreliable testimony of, 88

Psychiatry: attitude to prevention, 76–77; development of, 82; in the United States, 84

Psychoanalysis, 84

Psychological stress, relationship to psychopathology, 111

Psychologists: information-processing, 31; professional goals, 101–102

Psychology: age of, 9, 19; American, 22, 89; growth of, 19; language of, 145–146; limits of individual, 16, 22, 26; social, 33, 36, 39, 66; traditional, 44; training programs, 78

Psychopathology, 3, 4, 5; environmental causes, 4, 97–98; relationship to prevention, 107; social origins of, 85; and stress, 29, 111

Psychosomatic diseases, 40, 41

Psychotherapy, methods, 146

Puberty, 132. See also Adolescence

Public education, understanding life-work problems, 237

Public health: funding, 76; paradigm, 76

Puerto Ricans, 82

Q-sort, 263

Quality of life, 156; adult Americans, 177; critical incidents, 158–160; defining contributors, 157–160; movement, 232; national surveys, 157; perceived importance, 162–164

Quality of life dimensions: active and participatory recreational activities, 160, 166, 167, 169; activities related to helping/encouraging others, 159, 166, 170; activities related to local and national governments, 159, 164, 168, 170; creativity and personal expression, 160, 166, 169, 170; having and raising children, 159, 163, 164, 165, 166, 167, 170; health and personal safety, 158, 163, 165, 166, 167, 168, 169, 171; intellectual development, 159, 164, 168, 171; material well-being and financial security, 158, 164, 166, 167, 168, 169, 171, 172; occupational role, 160, 163, 164, 165, 166–167, 169, 171; passive and observational recreation, 160, 164, 166, 167, 168, 176; personal understanding and planning, 160, 164, 165, 166, 167, 169–170; relations with friends, 159, 167, 169; relations with parents, siblings or other relatives, 159, 167, 170; relations with spouse, 159, 163, 165–166, 167, 170; socializing, 160, 164, 170, 171

Race: and intelligence, 90, 91; prejudice, 76, 81, 90–91, 233

Reaction formation, 57

Reading, 143

Reappraisal, 49

Religion, in adolescence, 189

Religious persecution, 350

Research: approaches, 28; cross-cultural, 354–355; information-processing, 56, 68; ipsative-normative design for, 46; naturalistic, 4; nomothetic versus idiographic, 45, 68; priorities, 353; on retirement, 299

Research Utilization Projects of the Population Center Foundation (Philippines), 352

Retirement, 118; age, 295; and death, 290–291; early, 289; income reduction, 290; leisure-time activities, 296; linked to psychological disorders, 289; mandatory, 289; research on attitudes to, 299; who fares best, 299

Retirement planning, 222; nomenclature, 285; early, 294; possible goals of, 297; as social services, 293–294

Role-patterns: satisfaction with, 247, 250, 252–253; traditional, 249
Rosenkrantz Sex-Role Questionnaire, 249
Rotter Incomplete Sentences Blank, 263

Salinas and Monterey Community health projects, 214–216
Scandinavia, 82
Schizophrenia, 141; risk in adolescence, 135; vulnerability to, 144
Schizophrenic children, early predictors, 143
Schizophrenics: childhood of, 141; discharge rates, 87
Scholastic Aptitude Test, 90
School, 14; administrators, 12; adolescent response, 183–184; children, 6, 23; learning problems, 134; phobia, 134; services, 337; system, 11, 12
School and College Abilities Test (SCAT), 263, 278
School teachers, 12, 21; and administration, 11; in training, 11
Science, as panacea, 23
Secondary: appraisal, 50–52; prevention, 80
Self-actualization, 22, 300; in old people, 300–301
Self-confidence Scale (I scale), 278
Self-defense, 141
Self-esteem, 80, 134, 226, 227, 233, 242, 244, 246, 312; and child bearing, 250; and competence, 250–251; and femininity, 252; husbands' attitudes, 252; husbands' occupation, 252; sources for married women, 254–255; women, 248
Self-expression, 22
Self-help groups, for job/workplace problems, 237–238
Self-help movement, 4, 115
Self-image, 226, 228, 236
Self-knowledge, 22, 25

Self-realization, 22
Self-reliance, 342
Self-reports, 171
Separation, 140; stages of, 5, 140
Service delivery systems, 122; educational model, 119
Sex education, 345
Sexism, 76, 81
Sex-role: ideology, 249, 252; questionnaire, 249
Shoplifting, 135
Sickness model. See Models
Simulations, 258
Skills: basic, helping, 120–121; crisis intervention, 120; generic, 118, 119; life crisis, 121; life development, 120–121; packages, 120–122; teaching, 121–122
Slavery, 81, 82, 83
Smallpox, 85
Social: dislocation, 350; networks, 337; skills, 135, 143; trends, 157; webs, 18
Social class, and mental illness, 231
Social change, 100–101; necessity for, 101–102
Social indicators: listed, 156; movement, 156
Social Security, 294
Social service agencies, 12
Social science/scientists: relevance, 352; surveys of, 20
Social structure, 3, 12, 14, 19, 23; understanding, 25, 26
Social work/workers: goals, 99–100; training programs, 100
Society: cultural traditions, 14, 17; and the individual, 6, 18, 23; requirements of, 7, 8
Somatic health, 64, 67
Speech therapy, 143
Spence-Helmreich Scale, 249
Stanford University, Heart Disease Prevention Program, 197
Steel Workers Union, vacation plan, 295
Stress, 3; analysis, 48–49, 65; endog-

Stress (*continued*)
  enous/exogenous, 29; theories, 29,
  30, 39; uni-dimensional concepts
  of, 4
Stress, causes of: aging, 228; disease,
  34, 35; economic, 80; environmental, 79, 80; marital status, 41–
  43; marriage, 41–43; organizational, 228; value violation,
  228–230
Stress and coping: concepts, 32;
  husband/wife relationships, 41;
  limitations of laboratory research, 33–35; multiple levels of
  analysis, 40–44; naturalistic emphasis, 33–35, 66; surgical patients, 38–39; theories and
  approaches, 32–46
Stress, reactions to: adaptation, 36;
  approaches, 48; effects on performance, 227; emotional, 36, 48–
  49; endocrine, 43–44; individual
  differences, 30; job performance,
  227; psychopathological, 29
Stress research, 226; designs, 68;
  electric shock, 49; inoculation,
  97; physiological measures, 41,
  44; questions, 29; on surgical
  patients, 38–39
Stressful life events, 4, 110–111, 136;
  coping with, 113–114
Suicide: adolescent, 120; retired
  older males, 289
Sunny/Stormy Exercise, 264
Support networks, 143
Survey of Attitudes Toward Life, 263
Syphilis, 77

Temptation-resistance training, 215
Thematic Apperception Test (TAT),
  258, 263, 264
Therapy, 22; methods, 145; vocation-
  al, 135, 145
Thinking: logical, 24; scientific, 24
Time lines, 264
Tracy, Calif., 200, 203, 208, 209,
  210

Training caregivers in the community,
  120
Trait-centered measurement, 45
Trait determinants, 32
Trait measures, used in stress and
  coping research, 38–39, 58
Transaction: coping with stressful, 57;
  defined, 33; versus interaction,
  36, 37, 38, 66; major elements of,
  38–39; and process, 33, 35–40
Transactional analysis, 59
Transnational Family Research Insti-
  tute, 308
Treiman Scale, 250
Typhoid fever, 85

Unconscious processes, 66
Unemployment, 244
United Nations, 351
United States of America, 18; aca-
  demics, 352; Congress, 82
United States Department of Com-
  merce, 156
United States Department of Health,
  Education and Welfare, 157, 161
University: faculty members, 14; se-
  lection processes, 14–16; structure,
  14–15
University of Vermont, 4
Unreality, 143
Uprooting, 350–351
Urban areas, utilization of profes-
  sionals in, 116
Urbanization, 351

Vacations, 8
Values: hierarchy of, 13; violation of,
  229, 236
Verbalization, 60
Vermont Conference on the Primary
  Prevention of Psychopathology
  (VCPPP), 7, 12, 136
Vermont State Hospital, 87
Vocational guidance, 143
Vulnerability, 143

Wales, 83

Washington, D.C., 21
Watsonville, Calif., 200, 203, 204, 208, 209, 210
Weight Watchers, 237
Welfare policy, 20
Western thought, 78
White males, 94
Whites, 79
Wish fulfillment, 12
Women: black, 244; careers, 309, 311; child-care, 244, 247, 254; children's departure, 309, 311; cross-cultural studies, 241–242; depression, 309, 311; discrimination, 94; divorced, 314, 323–326; economic independence, 240, 242; economic realities, 245, 319; economic status, 348; employment opportunities, 94; equality, 137; exploitation, 81; family life, 244; high-prestige occupations, 243; husbands' attitudes to, 252; identity problems, 317; incarceration, 82; intelligence, life expectancy, 241; loss of hope, 316; married, 240; mid-life transition, 307, 318–319; multiple role involvement study, 247–248, 254; occupational status, 247; old, black and poor, 293; patterns of self-denial, 136–137; psychological well-being, 240; role-pattern satisfaction, 248–255; self-esteem, 248–255; social changes, 240–241; in social science, 310; special problems, 340; stereotypes, 311; traditional roles, 240
Work, 343; volunteer activities, 244; on welfare, 245; working-class/middle-class, 314–315; working mothers, 252–253
Work satisfaction, 221, 343
Working-class men and women, 235, 314–315
Working hours, 335
World Federation for Mental Health, 350
World Fertility Survey, 347
World Health Assembly, 349
World Health Organization, 308, 332, 333, 338, 340, 341
World Plan of Action, 345
World Population Conference, 345
World War I, 90
World War II, 18, 19, 22, 29, 351

Yale University, 3, 13, 14, 15, 16, 17
Young adult, 23
Youth Polls, 181